Administration of
High School Athletics

CHARLES E. FORSYTHE, A.M.

State Director of Athletics
Michigan High School Athletic Association
Michigan Department of Public Instruction

FOURTH EDITION

Prentice-Hall Inc.　　　　　　Englewood Cliffs, N.J.

PRENTICE-HALL PHYSICAL EDUCATION SERIES

LIBRARY OF CONGRESS
CATALOG CARD No.: 62-8577

Third printing .... June, 1964

PRINTED IN THE UNITED STATES OF AMERICA

00568–C

Preface

This book originally was prepared to aid three groups of people: first, those who expect to become teachers, supervisors, or directors of physical education and athletics; second, those already in the field administering high school physical education and athletic programs; and third, those whose primary interest is coaching but who need suggestions and guidance in handling the attendant administrative problems. This fourth edition still embraces the above service objectives.

World War II demonstrated the importance of physically fit personnel for the armed forces. It also showed that civilians at war must be able to "take it" physically. In addition to physical fitness programs in the armed services, considerable emphasis was given to competitive athletics, both from training and morale standpoints. Our high schools and colleges, as well as the armed services, made valuable contributions to these ends during the war, and their experiences should be capitalized upon during the era through which we are now passing. If competitive athletics were good for a man or woman who was defending his country in war time, they are valuable experiences for those who are maintaining it during peace time.

Items discussed deal with national, state, and local policies concerning athletic eligibility, contest management, equipment, awards, finances, budgets, safety, layout and maintenance of facilities, intramurals, girls' athletics, junior high school athletics, and current athletic trends. Figures and tables illustrating and explaining some of the more progressive policies now in effect in schools or state associations have been included.

In this, the fourth edition of *Administration of High School Athletics,* the text of the previous editions has been carefully brought up to date, and the illustrations have been selected from the most recent material available. At the end of each chapter a list of questions has been added for study and discussion designed particularly to help those who are just entering the administrative field.

The author wishes to express his appreciation to those schoolmen, authors, publishers, and executives of state athletic and activity associations and schools who so kindly consented to the inclusion of some of their material.

The effort expended in the preparation of this book will have been justified, as far as the author is concerned, if it serves the single purpose of helping to raise the administrative standards of the athletic programs in American high schools so that they are of greater educational value than they otherwise might have been.

CHARLES E. FORSYTHE

Introduction

The need for a book giving a general treatment of high school athletics was so long felt that the appearance in 1939 of the first edition of the present volume was most timely. It was particularly appropriate, also, that this long-awaited book should have been prepared by a man who had many years of practical experience in this field.

Charles E. Forsythe, the author, was himself a player on athletic teams, both in high school and in college. Later he had experience as an athletic coach and as faculty manager of high school teams. In his present position, that of State Director of High School Athletics in Michigan, he has had the opportunity to gain experience in handling all types of athletic problems. His work in building up high standards of athletic competition in his state has won him the confidence of all individuals concerned with athletics—coaches, players, officials, and school administrators. Moreover, he has a broad viewpoint of athletics in their relation to the general program of education and has striven not only to perfect athletics for the select players but also to broaden the athletic program for the many.

During World War II Charles E. Forsythe (Comdr., USNR) was assistant officer-in-charge of the physical training program of the United States Navy. He was attached to the Training Division, Bureau of Naval Personnel, Washington, D. C., where his work was concerned with the naval recruit, service school, V-12, and rehabilitation physical training programs. He also had general charge of the preparation of the *Physical Fitness Manual for the U. S. Navy,* published in 1943.

As one reads the pages of this book, he is impressed with the importance of athletics as an institution of modern life. One finds that administrative duties and responsibilities are many and varied. The book explains the accepted practices and usages and also many unusual ones as well. In this respect the author has done a tremendous amount of work not readily apparent on the surface. For the reader's convenience, a nation-wide collection of diverse rules has been boiled down into clear and concise form. The volume is characterized, then, not only by authenticity, but by clearness, conciseness, comprehensiveness, and splendid organization. All ideas pertinent to the subject of school athletics will somewhere be found incorporated in it.

Athletics have been called the *one* contribution of the students themselves to American education. The students brought to school life the buoyancy, enthusiasm, and zest for adventure that is characteristic of healthful youth. Nevertheless, under student administration the management of athletic finances and schedules early got out of control. Faculty friends, however, were present to exercise friendly guidance, to supply the necessary restraints, and to develop standards for control of this educational "orphan." The story of athletics in the schools is therefore the story of a long struggle to build up standards—standards under which competition can be carried on with ethical relation and high principles pervading the conduct of players, school officials, and crowds.

The benefits of athletic sports in regard to health, character, citizenship, and recreational enjoyment have been amply treated by the author in this book. It is sufficient here only to note that these educational advantages are attributed to athletics and other forms of physical recreation by progressive schoolmen of the day. This recognition accounts, in large measure, for the present emphasis placed on "Athletics for All." The intramural program, discussed by the author in a practical way, extends the benefits of athletics to larger and larger numbers of participants and attempts to find for each student some athletic interest and some measure of satisfaction in physical prowess and accomplishment.

How this progress has been made and how local, state, and national athletic organizations are vigilantly seeking to promote school athletics throughout the United States is the theme of this work.

Administration of High School Athletics is a practical book needed by the educational coaching profession, and Charles E. Forsythe is ably qualified by experience and broad educational vision to write it.

ELMER D. MITCHELL

Contents

1

History and Objectives of High School Athletics

It was not by accident that high school athletics came into existence. They have closely followed the trends of the times and have emerged in their present form through rather well-defined periods. Likewise, the objectives of high school athletics, both interscholastic and intramural, have changed during their development.

Development of the Control of Athletics

A challenge accepted. Athletic competition in our high schools has come to be an American tradition and institution. In no other country have intercollegiate and interscholastic athletics developed to the same extent as in the United States. Until comparatively recently, our major emphasis has been competition between schools with games played by a selected few. In English schools "the game's the thing," with interschool competition, in its limited way, being the outgrowth of what corresponds to our intramural programs. In some respects the English plan is more logical and defensible than ours has been. However, the higher degree of selectivity of students in English schools makes their athletic problems and policies vastly different from those in the United States, where the high school is a cross section of the community in which it is located.

Like most of the changes in policy, curriculum additions, and emphasis, athletics have come into the schools "from the outside." Communities, generally, have been instrumental in adding such courses as commercial work, mechanical and industrial arts, physical education, music, and the like to the curricula of their schools. Likewise, communities and student interest have added competitive athletics to high school programs. It is significant that, although athletics came into our schools with a decidedly professional and perhaps questionable heritage, today our interschool games have reached unprecedented high amateur and ethical levels. This result is in large measure due to the unceasing efforts of schoolmen to develop and improve standards of athletic competition. In most schools it has been less than half a century since the "good old days," when everyone from the superintendent to the janitor played on the team. Experience showed that efforts should be made to establish an American sport heritage that would keep the games and players at their best. Once our colleges and high schools took over the job, it was not long before interscholastic athletics were established on an educational basis in the schools of the nation. Since then, the problem has been to maintain proper perspectives as they involve player, spectator, school, and community.

The high school athletic pattern. When this new phase of school activity came into being, it was not accepted alike by all. Many schools, in the smugness of their historical backgrounds, had no time for this new and nonacademic orphan. Others seized upon it as a means of bolstering their institutions and attracting interest and attention to them. Naturally, public and private high schools and preparatory institutions developed different ideas as to the functions of their athletic programs and activities. With these differences in aims came differences in methods of control, not only within schools but also in relations between schools.

As a result of these differences, schoolmen themselves throughout the country set up organizations to control as well as to settle their athletic problems. This movement dates from the end of the nineteenth century, but it received its real development in the early 1900's. Naturally, high schools patterned their athletic programs and, to a large extent, their policies in accordance with the universities and colleges.

This emulation was fortunate in some respects but unfortunate in others. It was fortunate in that it enabled high school men to follow patterns that had been generally successful. It was unfortunate because some high schools attempted to take over en masse the athletic programs of institutions of higher learning. The consequent unbalanced growth of competitive athletics in many schools brought about legitimate charges of overemphasis. Schoolmen also soon began to realize that, in the same proportion that there were academic and social differences between high school and college students, so there were corresponding differences in their athletic capacities and possibilities. It was a wholesome sign for high school athletics when these differenes were realized and, as a result, new policies were formulated that had the high school student himself as their major consideration.

Four phases of direct athletic control. From a chronological standpoint it would be ideal to say that local schools first set up standards by which their interschool athletic competition was maintained. Such was not the case. _First,_ schools were influenced by local communities to a large extent in the activities they sponsored as well as in the schedules and policies they adopted. Likewise, policies in effect in a school against which another school competed affected its standards and policies. Thus it would seem logical to assume that the _second_ step was that two or more schools, or larger groups of schools, organized themselves into associations, leagues, or conferences that set up standards, policies, or regulations under which their competition was governed. This was only partially true. It is not to be inferred that no such groups were organized. Many were formed, but records do not reveal that they were especially influential in establishing general athletic eligibility regulations which exist today.

As athletics developed in interest and in scope, it was natural that contests were arranged between schools that did not belong to their local associations of limited membership. With greater range in competition, owing in many instances to improved means of travel, it became apparent that different groups had different standards for their athletic teams. These differences included scholastic regulations, age and previous play requirements, amateur standing, transfer and time of enrollment of students, and other criteria. If schools were to compete under uniform regulations, some form of organization larger than local units was imperative. The result of this need was the formation of state-wide athletic associations, which represent the _third_ phase of control. Most of these were voluntary organizations, but they set up standards to which their members had to adhere in order to retain membership. It is an accepted fact that the development of high school athletics to their present high plane has been largely the result of outstanding pioneer work done by schoolmen who were instrumental in the formation of state-wide organizations for the supervision and control of interscholastic athletic activities.

In the same way in which it was realized that benefit would result from local groups organizing into state groups, it was apparent that a national organization could serve a useful function. Thus, the *fourth* control agency appeared; and in 1920 the National Federation of State High School Athletic Associations was organized. As its name implies, this body is an organization of state athletic associations rather than of individual schools. It has done much to raise athletic standards in certain sections of the country as well as to promote greater uniformity in athletic regulations. Its organization and functions are detailed in Chapter 2.

An undesirable phase of athletic control. From the preceding statements it might be inferred that all the problems of athletics could be settled by tracing them to their conclusions through the four phases of athletic control which have been briefly outlined. Perhaps regrettably, this is not the case. Although educators very properly are promoting and defending athletics on an educational basis, it must be realized that there may be inherent differences between athletics and other school subjects. At least, athletics usually attract the attention of the public to a degree greater than most other school activities. In this connection, school authorities sometimes have become involved in difficulties of a serious nature when public or "downtown" interests have been a part of the policy-forming agency of the athletic program. Specifically, local nonschool groups have, in some instances, become dictatorial because of financial interests. Bond sales for the construction of local stadiums, sponsorship of high school teams by local merchants, organization of "downtown coaches' associations," and so on, all may seem proper at their time of inception, but they may have decidedly improper implications. That school which keeps the administration of its athletics on the same plane as its administration of its other school functions will find itself much further ahead from an educational and scholastic standpoint. As a policy the school should keep the public informed and should invite the public to its contests, but it should keep control of its own athletics, impressing upon the public at all times that the school athletic program is primarily for the participants and student body.

Objectives of Athletics

General objectives. As high school athletics became more firmly established as a part of the educational program, an appraisal of their objectives was inevitable. Although in some instances this appraisal has been a study in introspection, it has been valuable in that it has made possible the placing of emphasis on first things first. With interscholastic athletics as they exist at present in most sections of the country, it is apparent that a study of athletic objectives should include the participant, the school and student body, and the community. By objectives is meant the goal or the end to be realized, and in athletics, especially, it is important that the end be thoroughly understood by the three parties mentioned above. Therefore, the participant, the school and student body, and the community must know in advance what is anticipated during a specific season. This does not mean that the objective of a football, basketball, or baseball season should be to win a definite number of games or to place in a certain position in a league. Neither is it to be assumed that the season is to be considered a success or failure depending upon the number of victories. Rather, the goal might be set up as a series of contests with neighboring schools which have as their chief purposes friendly rivalry, new friendships, development of playing skills, good sportsmanship, and improved community relations. If objectives such as these, together with possible added benefits from each of them, are established, it is difficult to imagine a season in any sport that could not rightly be judged a success. These are general rather than specific objectives, but their generality actually makes them easier to attain than more specific ends would be.

Athletic objectives for the participant. What should be the objectives or ends for participants themselves in any athletic program? One might answer this question by saying that what the participant realizes from the game will depend upon what he puts into it. The purpose here is to consider what we educators have set up as objectives for those who will be participating under our direction, rather than to leave the statement of aims or ends to the students themselves. The following list of participant objectives, while not all-inclusive, points out some possible achievements:

1. Opportunity to learn new games.
2. Improvement in playing skills.
3. Development of physical vigor and of desirable habits in health, sanitation, and safety.
4. Opportunity to make real friendships with squad members.
5. Opportunity to widen a circle of friends by acquaintance with members of opposing teams and to visit and play in other communities.
6. A chance to observe and exemplify good sportsmanship.
7. Realization that athletic competition is a privilege that carries definite responsibilities with it.
8. Association with real gentlemen and true sportsmen in the persons of athletic coaches, contest officials, teammates, and opponents.
9. A chance to enjoy one of the greatest heritages of youth—the right to play.
10. A chance to learn that violation of a rule of the game brings a penalty—and that this same sequence follows in the game of life.

A significant statement of what participation in athletics meant to one student is summed up in an early Oklahoma *Bulletin:*

1. I learned to control my temper.
2. I learned to exercise judgment, to think quickly and act decisively.
3. I learned the meaning of discipline, to take orders and to carry them out to the best of my ability without asking why.
4. Through the training I received I had regular habits knocked into me.
5. I learned to meet, know, and size up men.
6. I learned to smile when I was the most discouraged fellow in the great wide world.
7. I learned the importance of being on time.
8. I learned to better control my nerves and feelings and to demand the respect of my fellow-players.
9. I learned to work out problems for myself, and to apply my energy more intelligently.
10. I secured a wide friendship which money cannot buy.[1]

[1] Oklahoma High School Athletic Association *Bulletin,* March, 1929.

Athletic objectives for the school and student body. As was said earlier in this chapter, athletics were not accepted alike by all schools when they first assumed their control and incorporated them in their programs. Many felt that they were just another burden in an already crowded program. Of course, this was not true in all instances.

Many times the question is asked of school administrators: "Why do you have, and what benefits are derived from, your interscholastic athletic program?" Answers vary with individuals. Some will condemn the program as being of no educational value. Others will express an attitude of toleration. In most cases, however, the school administrator who has the athletic program under proper control is enthusiastic about it. One might well make the inquiry as to what constitutes "proper control" of the athletic program from the standpoint of the school or student body. Following are some of the salient factors:

1. Athletics should occupy a position in the curriculum comparable to that of other subjects or activities.

2. Athletics should be made educational.

3. Athletics should be used to promote a fine school morale.

4. Proper student interest should be created by enlisting student aid at contests.

5. All visiting schools should be treated as guests.

6. A school's program in athletics, and the sports that it sponsors, should be based on the following factors:

a. The number of available students;

b. The financial ability of the school to equip its teams properly and to furnish adequate facilities;

c. Its ability to furnish competent instruction and wise leadership.

7. The athletic program should be an aid to school administration rather than a source of trouble.

8. There should be associated with the interscholastic athletic program a comprehensive plan for intramural activities

9. The athletic program should be broad rather than narrow in its scope. It should include as many activities and different teams as possible in order to interest and be of benefit to more students.

10. In general, there should be no distinction between so-called

major and minor sports. Each sport is of equal importance to the student participating in it.

11. The school policy should be definite so that athletes will not expect special privileges. If none are given, none will be expected.

12. Sportsmanship, fair play, and good school citizenship should be the objectives of all athletic programs. Sometimes these are referred to as spiritual and moral values of athletics.

Athletic objectives for the community. The community in which a school is located should realize that there are at least two parties that should be satisfied in the school athletic program before the interests of the community are to be given any consideration. These are the two that have just been discussed briefly, namely, the participant and the school with its student body. Under no circumstances should community interests be considered if they do not coincide with the well-being of the participant. In all cases his welfare should come first. If the wishes of the community fit in with generally accepted standards for participants, then the former may be reviewed. In other words, if the policies as set up by the school are in accord with community interests in a particular instance, then a happy and fortunate situation indeed exists. During the last few years an increasingly large number of schoolmen have been able to educate their communities to the fact that the athletic program is a phase of the school program. When that end has been realized, it not only has made control of the athletic program easier but also has made possible a much better approach to school patrons on other educational matters. Usually, the community will conduct itself athletically in accordance with the pattern that the school administration has set up for the athletic program educationally. To summarize community athletic objectives, the following might be listed:

1. Communities should realize that control of and responsibility for school athletics rest entirely with school authorities.

2. School athletics should furnish a recreational opportunity for the general public only insofar as a community is willing to see that program conducted with first consideration for student competitors and student spectators.

3. Communities should judge the success of the season on the

number of participants and spectators, new skills acquired, and good citizenship and good sportsmanship taught, rather than on numbers of games won and lost.

4. Communities constantly should keep in mind that, primarily, an athletic contest is a part of a school program because of its educational implications. When it ceases to have educational value, it should cease to be a school function.

Questions for Study and Discussion

1. Discuss the control phases through which interscholastic athletics have passed.

2. What is one distinguishing difference between English and American schoolboy athletics?

3. Distinguish between general and specific objectives of athletics.

4. What are the objectives for the participant in the athletic program?

5. Why are objectives for athletics important for the school and student body? Discuss.

6. The text states that the community should be served by the interscholastic athletic program only after those directly concerned have been benefited? Discuss community athletic objectives.

7. List other objectives of the interscholastic athletic program in addition to those included in the text.

8. What do you consider to be the most important single objective of the interscholastic athletic program in relation to (a) participant; (b) school and student body; (c) community? State reasons why.

9. Support or oppose recent public attacks on or criticisms of interscholastic athletic programs in junior and senior high schools.

2

The National
Federation of State
High School Athletic
Associations

Inception and organization. With the formation of the original
Midwest Federation of State High School Athletic Associations in
1920, there came into being the first cooperative effort of states to
control high school athletics. This original organization of five states
was the forerunner of the present-day National Federation of State
High School Athletic Association. The following background data
are taken from the Federation's *Handbook* for 1960–61.

Origin and Growth. The national organization had its beginning in a
meeting at Chicago on May 14, 1920. L. W. Smith, secretary of the
Illinois High School Athletic Association, issued invitations to neighboring states and state association representatives came from Illinois, Indiana,
Iowa, Michigan and Wisconsin. The primary purpose of the meeting
was to discuss problems which had resulted from high school contests
which were organized by colleges and universities or by other clubs or
promoters. In many cases, little attention was paid to the eligibility rules
of the high school associations or to other high school group regulations
and chaotic conditions had developed. At this first meeting it was decided that the welfare of the high schools required that a more active
part in the control of such athletic activities be exercised by the high
school men through the state associations and that this control necessitated
the formation of a national organization. A constitution and by-laws were
adopted and the group decided on the name "Midwest Federation of
State High School Athletic Associations." Principal George Edward
Marshall, Davenport, Iowa, was elected President and Principal L. W.
Smith of Joliet, Illinois, was elected Secretary-Treasurer.

In 1921, four states, Illinois, Iowa, Michigan and Wisconsin, continued their interest and became charter members through formal ratification of the constitution. Largely due to their efforts, the national organization grew during the early years.

In 1922 the Chicago annual meeting was attended by representatives from 11 states, and the present name of the National Federation was adopted. A number of college and university representatives who attended the meeting expressed sympathy for and interest in the efforts to introduce a high degree of order in the regulation of interscholastic contests.

Since that time the National Federation has had a healthy growth to its present nation-wide membership. By 1940 a national office with a full-time executive staff became necessary and such office was established in September of that year.

The legislative body is the *National Council* made up of one representative from each member state association. Such representative must be an officer or a member of his state board of control. The executive body is the *Executive Committee* of seven state board of control members from the seven territorial sections as outlined in the constitution. Their election is by the National Council at the annual meeting. Such meeting, prior to 1944, was held in February in connection with the National Association of Secondary School Principals of the N.E.A. From 1944 to 1950, the annual meetings were held about January 1. Since that time the meetings have been held near July 1.

From time to time, regional conferences are sponsored.

An annual conference for state executive secretaries has also been held. Prior to 1952, such conferences were held during the summer. Since that time, they have been held early in January, immediately following the meeting of the Football Rules Committee. For such conferences, the host state executive presides and the National Federation Secretary is secretary.

Affiliations. The National Federation cooperates with other athletic organizations in the writing of rules for several of the sports and in acting upon national records in track and swimming.

Cooperative relations are maintained with the United States Office of Education, National Education Association, accrediting bodies such as the North Central, Southern and Inland Empire Associations of Colleges and Secondary Schools, American Association for Health, Physical Education and Recreation, Amateur Athletic Union, National Association of Secondary-School Principals and American Council on Education.

The following states were members of the National Federation during 1960–61 (year of affiliation in parentheses):

Alabama (1924)
Alaska (1960)
Arizona (1925)
Arkansas (1924)
California (1940)
Colorado (1925)
Connecticut (1926)
Delaware (1945)
Florida (1926)
Georgia (1929)
Hawaii (1957)
Idaho (1928)
Illinois * (1920)
Indiana (1924)
Iowa * (1920)
Kansas (1923)
Kentucky (1941)

Louisiana (1925)
Maine (1939)
Maryland (1946)
Massachusetts (1944)
Michigan * (1920)
Minnesota (1923)
Mississippi (1924)
Missouri (1926)
Montana (1934)
Nebraska (1924)
Nevada (1939)
New Hampshire
    (1945)
New Jersey (1942)
New Mexico (1932)
New York (1926)
North Carolina (1949)

North Dakota (1923)
Ohio (1924)
Oklahoma (1924)
Oregon (1931)
Pennsylvania (1925)
Rhode Island (1952)
South Carolina (1947)
South Dakota (1923)
Tennessee (1927)
Utah (1927)
Vermont (1945)
Virginia (1948)
Washington (1936)
West Virginia (1925)
Wisconsin * (1920)
Wyoming (1936)

Allied member: Washington, D. C. Affiliated Canadian members: New Brunswick (1934); Nova Scotia (1925); Ontario (1953); Saskatchewan (1953).

The officers of the National Federation for the school year 1960–61 follow. It will be seen that they represent a wide scope as far as the state association memberships are concerned. The span of years that the members have served or will serve on the Executive Committee is shown after their names.

Executive Committee

Pres. Willard B. Knowles
    (California) 1958–61
Vice-Pres. S. F. Burke
    (Georgia) 1944–61
John V. Bernard (Wyo-
    ming) 1960–63

D. W. McBride (Lou-
    isiana) 1960–62
H. A. Meyer (Ohio) ...1690–63
John J. F. Ruddy (Con-
    necticut) 1960–62
R. R. Watson (Iowa) ..1960–63

* Charter members.

Former Presidents

Fred L. Biester, Illinois—1955–1957 (1954–57)
S. F. Burke, Georgia—1954–1955
Herman F. Keller, Indiana—1959–1960 (1954–60)
R. E. Rawlins, South Dakota—1944–1948 (1929–49)
C. A. Semler, Michigan—1948–1954 (1944–54)
E. R. Stevens, Kansas—1933–1944
Homer Williams, Idaho—1957–58 (1955–58)

Purpose of the National Federation

Protection of athletics. The National Federation has attempted, within proper limits, to effect the national regulation of high school athletics. Its purpose is in general similar to those of the state associations but has been projected nationally. The National Federation was a reflection of the feeling of schoolmen that they should make a nationwide effort to keep athletics in the schools. There was evidence that outside interests, both academic and commercial, had designs for their own advantage. Although local state athletic associations could control matters within their own borders, it was difficult to secure uniformity of action without uniformity and unity in organization. The constitution of the Federation reads:

The object of this Federation shall be to protect and supervise the interstate athletic interests of the high schools belonging to the state associations, to assist in those activities of the state associations which can best be operated on a nationwide scale, to sponsor meetings, publications and activities which will permit each state association to profit by the experience of all other member associations, and to coordinate the work so that waste effort and unnecessary duplication will be avoided.

As indicated in the above statement, the National Federation has concerned itself largely with the protection and regulation of interstate interests of member schools of its organization. This has been a most valuable service, and in it probably lies its greatest contribution. An annual meeting is held, known as the National Council meeting, and one representative from each member state may vote on all legislative matters. At the meeting of the National Council held in 1929, a set of Recommended Minimum Eligibility Requirements was adopted. These recommendations have been important factors in raising athletic standards in many states. The Minimum Eligibility Recommendations include rules dealing with the following: twenty-year age; eight-semester limitation; scholarship and consecutive semester attendance; amateur standing; independent team participation; transfer; recruiting; enrollment; athletic award; grades; physician's certificate; coaches; sanctions; and officials' registration.

Accomplishments of the National Federation

The assertion made by the Federation that it represents the largest closely-knit organized body of amateur athletes in the world bears weight when it is considered that it has grown from a charter membership of four states in 1920 to include forty-nine of the fifty state organizations and the District of Columbia in the United States and the Provinces of New Brunswick, Nova Scotia, Ontario, and Saskatchewan, Canada, as affiliated members. It is significant also that its roster extends from the Atlantic to the Pacific and from the Gulf to the Aleutian Islands. The Federation as a national body has concerned itself with numerous matters. A brief review of some of the accomplishments of this gigantic athletic body will serve best as the basis for discussion of them.

Elimination of outlaw team competition. One of the early accomplishments of the National Federation was the elimination of outlaw teams by means of mutual agreement of state associations not to permit member schools to compete with such teams in other states. This agreement ultimately resulted in their disappearance, and credit must be given the National Federation for this accomplishment. Such a policy also has been of benefit to state organizations because it resulted in emphasizing the importance and value of schools' membership in their local state associations.

Development of greater uniformity in eligibility rules. With the formation of the National Federation, opportunity was presented for exchange of eligibility and administrative procedures in effect in various states. The National Federation recommendations for eligibility rules below, a product of the pooling of many ideas, was prepared and many state associations set up regulations conforming in general to national recommendations. Although there are variations in eligibility rules in different states, the great degree of uniformity that exists today is a result largely of the clearinghouse provided by the National Federation discussions.

RECOMMENDED MINIMUM ELIGIBILITY REQUIREMENTS

It is recommended (not required) that state associations use eligibility rules at least as restrictive as those listed here.

A Student is Ineligible if:

1. 20-YEAR RULE: He has reached his twentieth birthday.
2. 8-SEMESTER RULE: He has attended a four-year high school eight semesters or a senior high school six semesters; or has graduated. (Attendance of 15 days of any semester shall be regarded as a "semester.")
3. SCHOLARSHIP RULE AND CONSECUTIVE SEMESTER ATTENDANCE RULE:
   (a) He has failed to do passing work in at least fifteen periods (three full-credit subjects) per week.
   (b) Or failed to pass at the end of the immediately preceding semester, in fifteen periods (three full-credit subjects). The record at the end of the semester shall be final and scholastic deficiencies may not be made up in any manner.
4. AMATEUR RULE: He has lost his amateur standing, i.e., he has accepted remuneration, gift or donation directly or indirectly for participating in an athletic contest or he has participated under an assumed name or he has competed on a team, some player of which was paid for his participation, or he has entered into a playing contract with a professional club or agent. Reference to 'gift or donation' is not intended to preclude the acceptance of a medal or pin of small intrinsic value which is customarily used for track and similar activities and is presented by the sponsoring organization.
5. INDEPENDENT TEAM PARTICIPATION RULE: He has, after becoming a member of a high school squad, taken part in an independent contest where admission is charged.
6. TRANSFER RULE: He transfers from one school to another without a corresponding change in his parents' residence. (Eligibility may be restored after at least one semester.)
7. RECRUITING RULE: He has transferred from one school to another for athletic purposes because of undue influence by anyone connected with the school.
8. ENROLLMENT RULE: He enrolled later than the beginning of the eleventh school day of the semester.
9. ATHLETIC AWARD RULE: He accepts from any source a sweater, jersey

or any other award exceeding one dollar in value other than those usually given, such as medals, trophies, fobs, letters and other athletic insignia.

10. GRADE RULE: He has not been promoted to the ninth grade.

11. PHYSICIAN'S CERTIFICATE RULE: He has not presented during the year, a physician's certificate that he is physically fit for athletic competition.

12. COACHING SCHOOL RULE: A student is ineligible if, after having been certified as being eligible in football or basketball, he attends any school, camp or clinic organized in such a way that its entire purpose or a part of its purpose is to provide coaching or organized training in such sport. Penalty shall be loss of eligibility in that sport for one year from the last date of such attendance.

A School Shall Not:

1. COACHES RULE: Permit coaching by anyone who is not a certified teacher regularly employed by the Board of Education and whose entire salary is paid by that body; or who has fewer than three regular periods of classes, gymnasium or study-hall duty per day.

2. SANCTION RULE: Enter any meet or tournament involving more than two schools, or any interstate game involving a round trip of more than 600 miles; unless it has been sanctioned by the state high school association and if more than one state is involved, by the National Federation.

3. OFFICIALS' REGISTRATION RULE: Use any paid athletic official who is not registered with his home high school athletic association and is qualified according to the standards of such state association.

4. ALL-STAR CONTEST RULE: No member high school shall permit use of its facilities nor of its employees, directly or indirectly, in the management, coaching, officiating, supervision, promotion or player selection of any all-star team or contest involving high school players or those who, during the previous school year, were members of the high school team, unless such contest is first sanctioned by the State High School Athletic Association or, if interstate, by the National Federation of State High School Athletic Associations.

SUMMARY OF STATE ELIGIBILITY FACTS
(Based on 1960 data)

Age Limits

19TH BIRTHDAY (with modifications such as: right to compete for the school year if birthday is September 1 or later, or, for one state, May 1, or later; or right to compete for remainder of a sports season if birthday occurs during that sports season; or right to compete for the entire school year if his 20th birthday is June 30 or after): Arizona, California, Colorado, Connecticut, Delaware, Florida, Georgia, Illinois, Indiana, Kansas, Louisiana, Maryland, Massachusetts, Michigan, Montana, Nebraska, Nevada, New Jersey, New Mexico, New York, North Carolina, Ohio, Oklahoma, Oregon, Pennsylvania, Texas, Utah, Virginia, West Virginia, Wisconsin, Hawaii, and New Brunswick and Nova Scotia (Canada).

20TH BIRTHDAY: Alabama, Alaska, Arkansas, Saskatchewan (Canada), Idaho, Iowa, Kentucky, Maine, Minnesota, Missouri, New Hampshire, North Dakota, Rhode Island, South Carolina, South Dakota, Vermont, Washington and Wyoming. In Mississippi, Ontario (Canada) and Tennessee, if 20th birthday is after September 1st, competition is allowed through the year.

Semester Attendance Limit

8 semesters for all states.

Award Limits

A. Awards by Schools to Own Athletes:

SCHOOL MAY AWARD ONLY LETTERS: (In most cases, customary medals for meet participation may be accepted) Delaware, Idaho, Iowa, Kansas, Nebraska, Nevada, Ohio, Oregon, Washington and Wisconsin.

Note: In Utah, a school letter may not be awarded.

SCHOOL AWARD VALUE MUST NOT EXCEED STATED LIMIT WHICH VARIES FROM $1.00 TO $5.00: Alabama, Arizona, Colorado, Delaware, Florida, Idaho, Illinois, Kentucky, Maryland, Michigan, Minnesota, Missouri, Montana, Nevada, New Mexico, North Dakota, Ohio, Pennsylvania, South Dakota, Tennessee, Utah, Virginia, West Virginia, Wisconsin and Wyoming.

Elimination of national championships. Among the first problems which came to the attention of the National Federation was the need for a critical appraisal of so-called national championships. A number of considerations led the Federation to action. Some states far from the scene of national tournaments or meets complained that loss in school time, extra competition, and the tremendous expense involved in sending their teams to participate in these games were not consistent with good educational procedure. There was a feeling, too, that possibly high school athletes were being exploited by the institutions or commercial interests sponsoring these events. It was felt also that the determination of state championships provided a sufficient climax to a season. In fact, some states still do not desire that athletic contests be carried even to that conclusion. As a result of these considerations the National Federation has taken action to prohibit schools that are members of state associations affiliated with the Federation from taking part in so-called national championship meets. For the most part, educational institutions and other interests that formerly conducted such meets or tournaments have cooperated in a fine manner, and now national interscholastic championships almost seem to be forgotten.

Sanction of interstate meets and tournaments. In some sections of the country there were interstate or regional meets and tournaments that had all the evils of national championships but were more local in nature. They were "wildcat" affairs in every sense of the word. Usually these events were conducted by some not too scrupulous institutions with little or no attention being paid to welfare of participants or generally accepted state association eligibility rules. Outlaw teams often were allowed to participate, and the state associations concerned were practically powerless to stop their member schools from participating. This undesirable practice has been stopped almost completely by present National Federation regulations. Now a meet or tournament management that desires to invite schools from two or more states must do so in accordance with plans approved by the Executive Committee of the National Federation. This sanction consists of approval by the association of the state in which the event is located as well as sanction by the associations of states from which schools are invited to attend.

The policy of sanctioning meets has resulted in the elimination of numerous undesirable meets and tournaments and has guaranteed to competing schools that only bona fide schools that are members in good standing of their respective state associations will be competing. It also ensures that accepted regulations regarding competition will be followed. In general, a policy has been followed of sanctioning only such meets as are sponsored by educational institutions. States have appreciated this National Federation accomplishment because it has aided them in the administration of their local athletic programs, and they have been strict in insisting that their member schools adhere to this regulation. (See Fig. 2-1.)

Scheduling of interstate contests. With its growth in influence, the

National Federation
of State High School Athletic Associations

Application for Sanction of Multiple Interstate Meet

NOTE: Make application in duplicate and send both copies to the executive officer of the state in which the meet is to be held. He will forward **both** to the National Federation office.

National Federation of State High School   P. O..
Athletic Associations
7 South Dearborn St., Chicago 3, Illinois   Date...19.......

On behalf of..
(School or group conducting the Meet)

I hereby apply for National Federation sanction for the...
(Name and Kind of Meet)

....to be held at ....

on..., 19.......

The meet will be managed by...
(Name of school conducting Meet)

We desire to invite schools from the following states only..

....

The number of schools that will probably compete in this meet is :..

Contest conditions include the following:

1. Each school guarantees its membership and good standing in its own state high school association and also guarantees that participation in this contest will not violate any rule of that association or of the National Federation. The game contract is void if such membership is terminated or if participation is found to be contrary to the state or national rules.
2. Each contestant will be eligible under rules of his home state association.
3. The game will be administered under playing rules and safety requirements approved by the National Federation as meeting the specifications of the various athletic accident benefit associations.
4. Prizes will be limited to such as are permitted by the most restrictive state high school association from which competitors enter.
5. If either party fails to fulfill its contract obligations, that party shall make amends in accordance with terms fixed by the National Federation executive committee after consultation with the executive officers of the states involved.
6. No entry will be accepted for any competitor from any state or section of a state not included in the list of states for which sanction is granted.
7. Only boys will be allowed to compete in this meet.

Signed :..   Official Position :...

RECOMMENDATION OF HOME STATE EXECUTIVE

P. O................................Date.........................., 19......

I recommend that this meet be (SANCTIONED) (NOT SANCTIONED). I have sent endorsement blanks to each state named in the application.

Signature of State Executive...

State..

OFFICIAL ACTION OF NATIONAL FEDERATION

Chicago, Illinois, ..., 19......

This meet is hereby sanctioned for the states of..

....

You should not invite schools from states or sections not included in this list.

By..
(Executive Secretary)

THE EXECUTIVE COMMITTEE
OF THE NATIONAL FEDERATION

(These blanks may be obtained from any state athletic office.)

Fig. 2-1. Application Blank for Sanction of Multiple
Interstate Meet *(National Federation).*

National Federation has made itself a valuable aid to state associations in connection with dual interstate contests. Its regulations simply provide that, in games between schools in different states, local state association regulations apply to each school. No school, however, may compete against a school in another state unless that school is a member of its state association, provided it is eligible for membership. Inquiry may be made to executive officers of state associations concerned regarding eligible schools for interstate games or to the secretary of the National Federation, who will furnish this information. Schools may not compete in interstate tournaments, meets or dual contests which involve round trips exceeding 600 miles unless the events have been approved by all interested state associations through the National Federation. A school under suspension from its local state association, because of violation of state regulations or for other reasons, may not be scheduled for any athletic contest by a school in another state whose state association is a member of the National Federation. (See Fig. 2-2.)

Fig. 2-2. Official Contract Form for Interstate Games or Meets (National Federation).

Writing of playing rules. In 1960, over four-fifths of the member states (44) used rules for football that were formulated by the Football Rules Committee of the Federation. This activity began as an experiment when, for various reasons, it was found impossible to effect the organization of a joint committee to write football rules for National Collegiate Athletic Association colleges and National Federation high schools of this country. Some high schools felt that because of the extent to which football is played in secondary schools, it was only just that there should be active high school members on the above national football rules-making body. This cooperative effort did not materialize, and in 1932 the Executive Committee was authorized to proceed with preparation of playing rules in football for use in such states as desired them. This is the only separate rules-writing project which has been undertaken by the National Federation, inasmuch as joint N.C.A.A. and National Federation committees composed of college and high school men have been set up for basketball, track, swimming, and wrestling. High school football rules now, however, are known as the National Alliance Code since there are representatives on the Rules Committee from the National Association of Intercollegiate Athletics (small colleges) and the National Association of Junior Colleges, as well as from high schools in the 44 states using the rules. By agreement with professional baseball the National Federation publishes its own edition of the official baseball rules. There seems to have been no disposition to seek high school representation or to set up separate rules-writing bodies for high schools in tennis, golf, or hockey, although there is considerable participation in these activities by secondary schools.

While a principle is involved regarding high school membership on football rules-writing bodies, it must be recognized that football traditionally has been a college game and was developed in American colleges in its present form. Most states had little difficulty in making modifications to suit their needs. To some it has seemed unfortunate that differences should develop in the game of football as a result of the writing of different sets of rules by two educational bodies. In fact, it is regrettable that all playing differences, terms, or regulations could not have been arranged cooperatively, so that we might still be playing the same game rather than working toward what appears to be diverging ends. The fact that some of the member states of the National Federation have not adopted its football rules is indicative of a difference of opinion regarding this venture.

However, some feel that the differences are not so great as they were first thought to be and that the high school edition of the rules is serving well in those states in which it is being used. Certainly, the coaches and officials in these states are benefited because in most of them, these individuals themselves are made rules-conscious by having helped to form them. This is one of the greatest values derived from the whole rules-writing project.

Cost and approval of athletic equipment. The National Federation became concerned with the cost of athletic equipment several years before the Second World War, especially in connection with prices paid for such merchandise by high schools of the country. Overtures were made to sporting-goods manufacturers to produce first-grade footballs and basketballs at lower costs to high schools. Some success was achieved in this venture and finally the Federation resorted to placing its approval on one brand of goods priced substantially lower than others. Now this interest has extended to other manufacturers and to some extent to other than inflated goods.

The possibilities of safety equipment in athletics have been studied, and merchandise bearing the label "National Federation Approved" is now on the market. Whether or not this activity by the National Federation has met with general approval of schoolmen and of all member states, it is apparent that the interest given this matter has resulted in the saving of thousands of dollars to the schools of the United States. It directed attention to the possibilities of lower-priced athletic goods on the part of both manufacturers and the schools themselves.

Approval of records. The National Federation has a records committee that passes upon applications for the awarding of national high school records in sports in which they are maintained. Activities in this connection have been chiefly in track, but there also has been cooperation with the collegiate swimming-records committee. It has been possible to set up a recognized list of national interscholastic records that actually have the approval of the high school men themselves. (See Fig. 2-3.)

National policies. During the last few years the National Federation very appropriately has concerned itself with national policies in connection with high school athletics. Because of its broad state membership, its activities in this direction have been powerful and far-reaching. Likewise, its pronouncements have aided local state associations to maintain standards that otherwise would have been difficult for them to establish individually. Among these have been the following: resolution on solicitation; agreement between

National Federation of State High School Athletic Associations

7 South Dearborn Street, Chicago, Illinois

HSAA

INTERSCHOLASTIC RECORD APPLICATION

NOTE: Fill blanks and secure signatures on 3 copies. Send all 3 to your state high school athletic officer. He will sign them and if a state or national record is involved, he will forward them to the National Federation for signatures of the National Committee. In all cases, one copy will be returned to the school for framing or filing.

To The Committee on Interscholastic Records:

Application is hereby made for a Conference, State or National CHAMPIONSHIP RECORD in the (Event)..................

.... The performance was in the

(name of meet) ....

Sanctioned by the....................................State High School Association and (if interstate) by the National Federation..........

Held at (Place)..on (Date)....................................

Full Name of competitor for whom record is claimed (Give all full names if for a team):

....Age in: Yrs..........Mo..........

....Age in: Yrs..........Mo..........

....Age in: Yrs..........Mo..........

....Age in: Yrs..........Mo..........

This competitor is an eligible member of the..High Schoo

of (Place)......................................said high school being a qualified member of the..............State High School Athletic Association under whose rules the school competed.

The claimed record was (time, height or distance)..

Signed:... ....

(Claimant (or captain if for a team)) (Principal of the high school)

††††††††

ENDORSEMENT BY SECRETARY OF STATE HIGH SCHOOL ATHLETIC ASSOCIATION

The foregoing track and field meet was sanctioned by the home State High School Athletic Association and the meet was so conducted as to make the claim worthy of consideration.

Secretary..., ...High School Athletic Association*

STATEMENT OF REFEREE. I am acquainted with the officials who have attached their signatures on the reverse side. I believe they are competent and that they acted conscientiously and in good faith. The conditions were official in every way and there was no tail wind (for sprint, hurdle or broad jump) exceeding 3 miles per hour. I cordially recommend

the claim to the Interscholastic Records Committee for a..................................record. (Note: The referee
(conference, state or national)
should state any exceptions he desires to make to the foregoing statement. He should also describe the condition of the field or track, the force and direction of the wind and any other matters that might in any way have influenced the outcome.)

....

....

....

....

Signed..., Referee Address..

††††††††

Certificate

BY COMMITTEE ON INTERSCHOLASTIC RECORDS

The foregoing application was considered by the..............................Committee on Interscholastic Records on
(Conference, State or National)

(Date)......................................., 19....... and the performance was accepted as a..................................record.
(Conference, State or National)

Signed:...Conference Chairman (For Conference Record)

....State Executive

....National Executive (For State or National Record)

Fig. 2-3. Interscholastic Record Application Form *(National Federation)*.

organized baseball and the National Federation; national and sectional meets; all-star and post-season contests; and sanctioned meets and long-distance contests. These statements of policy are printed below as they appear in the National Federation *Handbook*.

RESOLUTION ON COLLEGE SOLICITATION OF HIGH SCHOOL ATHLETES

The evils which result from the bidding by college alumni groups for the services of high school athletes and the adulation which accompanies the ostentatious banqueting and transporting of such athletes is familiar to high school administrators. It took a series of sports scandals to awaken the college administrators and the general public to the need for action.

In an attempt to assist in curing this condition, the Joint Committee adopted Standard #10 [of Joint Committee on Standards in Athletics] and it was approved by the National Federation at the 1950 and 1951 annual meetings.

STANDARD #10: "The solicitation of athletes through try-outs and competitive bidding by higher institutions is unethical, unprofessional, and psychologically harmful to the boy. It destroys the amateur nature of athletics, tends to commercialize the individual and the program, the use of athletic skill for gain, and takes an unfair and unjust advantage of competitors."

Application of Specific Items to Standard 10

NOTE: The items below are suggested interpretations of Standard 10.

1. The functions of guidance and advisement to assist a student in the selection of a higher institution should be performed by the Principal, Director of Guidance, or designated advisers.
2. Interviews between accredited representatives of higher institutions and prospective applicants for admission should be arranged only through the school Guidance Department.
3. Try-outs of high school athletes should not be permitted and the entertainment and transportation of boys to college campuses to display athletic prowess should be prohibited.
4. Transcripts of high school records should be sent only to the Admissions Office.
5. Standards for admission to higher institutions should apply to the athlete and non-athlete alike.
6. Only bona fide students who are satisfying recognized educational standards in high school or in college should be permitted to compete in athletics.
7. All financial aid to students should be based on demonstrated ability in high school subjects and activities.
   a. No athletic "scholarships" as such should be awarded.

   b. All scholarship aid must be administered by the institution itself and not by alumni, civic groups, or other individuals.

   c. Each institution should publish qualifications for all scholarships offered.

   d. Scholarships should be limited to actual expenses for tuition, fees, room, board.

   e. Payment for employment should be made only when services are rendered.

   f. No grant should be withdrawn because of failure to participate in athletics.

Agreement Between Professional Baseball and the National Federation

AN AGREEMENT between Professional Baseball and the National Federation has been in effect since 1944. This followed a conference on September 15, 1943 of President George M. Trautman and the Federation Executive Secretary who were representing their respective organizations on the National Physical Fitness Committee. A JOINT BASEBALL COMMITTEE made up of Commissioner K. M. Landis, Warren Giles, George M. Trautman, Jack Zellers, Albert Willis, Lyle T. Quinn, R. E. Rawlins and H. V. Porter drew up a statement designed to insure a friendly working relationship between the two groups and to stimulate a healthy interest in high school baseball. This was approved by Commissioner Landis in Chicago on July 18, 1944 and adopted by the Major and Minor Baseball Leagues in December of that year.

The original agreement was slightly revised and expanded at subsequent meetings but the essentials have been retained through the administrations of Commissioner A. B. Chandler and current Commissioner Ford Frick.

At the Professional Baseball meeting in December 1950 it was voted to rescind the agreement but with the knowledge that the rescinding action would not shorten the term of the agreement which did not expire until January 1, 1952. The matter received nationwide attention and many sports writers and national organizations joined forces with the high schools in an attempt to secure a satisfactory agreement to go into effect when the old one expired. In states such as New York and Washington, bills were introduced in the state legislature to prevent the signing of high school boys to a professional contract. The bill in Washington became a law. The bill in New York was vetoed by Governor Dewey with the understanding that the high schools and professional baseball would probably agree on a new regulation before the old one expired.

At the Baseball meeting in December 1951, a new regulation was adopted for the year 1952, and has been in effect since that time. Item 4 about tryouts was revised in 1953, and Item 2 in 1955.

Major-Minor League Rule 3 (h)
(For the year 1960)

(H) HIGH SCHOOL PLAYERS.
1. No student of a high school shall be signed to a contract by a Major or Minor League club during the period the student is eligible for participation in high school athletics. In any instance where such eligibility has expired prior to the student's graduation from high school (a) because of the student's age; or (b) because he has completed the maximum number of semesters of attendance, he may thereafter be signed to a contract which does not obligate him to report for service prior to graduation of the class with which he originally entered high school, i.e., until eight semesters after his original entry into the ninth grade.
2. A student who drops out of high school prior to expiration of his athletic eligibility and continues to remain out for at least one year may thereafter be signed to a contract for immediate service provided his withdrawal from high school was not suggested, procured or otherwise influenced by the club contracting with him, or by any official or employee of such club or of any of its affiliates.
3. Nothing herein shall be construed as prohibiting any Major or Minor League club, its officers, agents, or employees from talking to any high school student at any time concerning a career in professional baseball and discussing the merits of his contracting, when eligible therefor, with any particular club.
4. "Tryouts" to which students may be invited may be conducted during the school year, provided that (1) no student shall be permitted to participate in any such tryout unless the Principal of his high school, if not employed by a Major or Minor League club, shall have approved such participation in writing, and (2) provided further that any such tryout must be limited to not more than five high school students.
5. Any contract made in violation of this rule shall be declared null and void and the offending club (and any club owned by or affiliated with such club) shall be prohibited from signing such player for a period of three years from date of declaration of voidance of such contract. In addition, such club shall be fined $500, by the Commissioner in the case of a Major League club, or by

the President of the National Association in the case of Minor League club, and the official, scout or employee of the offending club who participated in the violation shall be subject to such penalty as the Commissioner or the President of the National Association, as the case may be, shall impose.

National Championships Cannot Be Sanctioned

At the annual meeting on February 26th, 1934, the National Council unanimously voted that the Executive Committee should *refuse to sanction any meet or tournament which is in the nature of a contest to determine a national high school championship.* The Executive Committee has acted in accordance with this vote and no sanction has been granted. No such contest has been held since that time, although there have been many attempts by promoters to hold such contests. This is especially true in basketball. All of them have been prevented except a few attempts which have appealed to the small percentage of high schools which are not members of member state associations or which inadvertently violated state association rules or policies by entering before investigating the validity of the contest. In all such cases, remedial action has been taken and it is now generally understood that no reputable high school will violate its state association regulations by entering an unsanctioned meet. This action concerning national championship meets was the result of overwhelming sentiment on the part of high school administrators that the high schools are provided with enough competition by their own leagues and state associations. If more competition is desired, it would be an easy matter for such leagues or state associations to prolong the season or to arrange post-season games or to increase the number of tournaments. If such action is not taken, it is because the high school educators believe that the additional competition is not desirable. *Matters such as this must be determined by groups rather than by individual high schools because if one high school is permitted to extend the season indefinitely or to travel an indefinite distance to an interstate event, it practically forces other high schools to do likewise, if they are to compete on equal terms* with the one which follows such practices. In this respect, the fundamental principle upon which the group action is based is exactly the same as that which underlies statewide eligibility rules. If one high school were permitted to decide for itself whether it would play twenty-one-year-old boys, it would automatically force all other high schools with whom that school competes to do likewise. It is obvious that the will of the majority must apply in such situations.

Limit on Basketball Tournaments
and Distant Travel

After national championship high school events were stopped, other related problems grew up. Commercial clubs, recruiting divisions from some of the universities, charity organizations and other promoters attempted to circumvent the rules by sponsoring tournaments for half of the country or for one quarter of the country or for a championship between two or three states. This led to threatened excesses through undue extension of the season and through use of high school teams to promote individual interest at the expense of efficiency in the school program. It was necessary for the high schools to protect themselves against the pressures which are engendered in such promotions and this was done by adopting a specific policy concerning the sanctioning of any interstate meet. Basketball tournaments were most profitable to the promoter and caused most difficulty. After a thorough canvass of sentiment of high school administrators and of high school accrediting bodies, the National Council voted that the Executive Committee should refuse to sanction any new interstate basketball tournament except such as might be purely community in character as in the case where a school is located in a panhandle division of a state or where neighboring schools are in a compact area with topographic conditions such that the area forms a natural conference or community.

At the annual meeting on December 30th 1949, the National Council authorized reasonable extension of sanction privilege for certain interstate basketball tournaments in states in which, because of mountain barriers, a small section of the state is isolated in such a way that competition across state lines is essential to the filling of a suitable schedule. Unless such geographic conditions exist, it is the policy to withhold sanction for any proposed interstate basketball tournament other than the few which were established prior to 1952 and which, because of conference or community group needs, warrant continuance for a limited time.

Sanctions for Meets and Distant Games

Many states have adopted by-laws which prohibit the holding of athletic meets or tournaments unless the event is first sanctioned by the state association. Among such states are New York, Maryland, Ohio, Indiana, Illinois, Michigan, Wisconsin, Iowa and Kansas. States such as New York and Indiana have definite regulations which limit meets and tournaments to those which are directly sponsored by a high school or a group of high schools. Nearly all states have adopted sanction policies which limit travel distance for meets and tournaments. For ordinary games (not a part of a meet or tournament), nearly all states have specific policies as to distance which may be travelled for the playing of interstate games. Any game which requires a team to travel more than 600 miles for the round trip must be sanctioned by both interested state associations through the National Federation. States such as Indiana, Iowa, Kansas, Utah and Illinois have adopted rigid policies which prohibit the sanction of any such long distance trip for an athletic contest. Idaho permits sanction of certain distant contests provided they are in an adjoining state.

The restriction on distant travel and on interstate meets and tournaments is necessary to prevent excesses which would otherwise develop. In the case of a large, widely publicized meet, attention is centered on a few outstanding performers and local pressures are exerted in many communities to force the athletic department to spend time, money and effort on developing a few at the expense of the many. In places where a large meet of this kind has been discontinued, many small meets have been substituted and a greater number of athletes participate. Such meets can be held without any great amount of absence from school and without any undue diverting of coaching-time and money for the gratification of a few who have usually already had enough competition. In the smaller meets, competition is such that even the small schools are able to compete.

It is sometimes claimed the facilities are not always available and that a large meet provides use of facilities at certain large colleges or universities. The answering claim is that the encouragement of local meets tends to provide incentive for high schools to acquire proper facilities and to become active in management when they are made responsible for sponsoring such meets.

At the annual meeting on December 30th, 1949, the National Council unanimously voted that the Executive Committee should refuse to sanction any contest in which two or more schools from outside a given state are brought into the state to participate in a *contest in which no home school may legally participate.* This was adopted as By-law II-3 at the 1951 meeting.

All-Star and Post-Season Contests

The continually growing practice of promoting charity, post-season and all-star contests has resulted in many difficult problems for the schools. In most cases, such contests are promoted by an organization not directly connected with the high school. The contests are an advertising medium to add to the prestige or profit of the promoter, either individual or organization. If additional competition were desirable for the high school team it would be an easy matter for the high school organization to provide such competition. If they do not do it, it is because of the conviction that there has been sufficient competition for the given group without the excess number of contests. It is very exceptional to find a high school whose athletic department could not make good use of additional funds for increasing the efficiency of the given school. If they do not attempt to exploit the high school team for the raising of such funds, it is because of unwillingness to overload the athletic program. In self-protection, the state high school associations have adopted regulations which limit the length of a sports season and which discourage or prohibit the playing of post-season games. In a few cases, the regulations are flexible enough to permit extension of the season to cover certain specified contests which are considered desirable by the high school administrators. The National Federation has encouraged strict regulations and the records show specific action by the National Council at meetings scattered through the past ten years. The following resolution expresses the policy concerning such meets.

RESOLUTION: *Concerning All-Star and Out-of-Season Athletic Contests*
     Through the past ten years, the National Council of the National Federation has encouraged strict regulations to prevent the abuses which would grow up if games of the bowl, all-star or charity type were to be permitted without limitation. The following resolution was unanimously adopted at the 1947 annual meeting at St. Petersburg, Florida. The resolution was drawn by a committee made up of L. V. Phillips, Indiana; J. E. Rohr, Wisconsin; and C. E. Forsythe, Michigan, Chairman. The principles which are incorporated in the resolution had been previously adopted in a joint meeting of the Western Conference athletic directors and representatives of the State High School Associations in the Western Conference area.

1. This group is unalterably opposed to the principle of all-star and out-of-season athletic contests in which high school students or high school graduates of the previous year are participants, because:
    a. Such contests do not harmonize with the generally accepted educational philosophy of high school athletics which emphasizes varied seasonal activities, broad participation, and school direction and supervision.
    b. There are few tangible values apparent either to the individual, or to the selected team as a whole, resulting from such contests.
    c. No practical or satisfactory method has been devised to date for the selection of members of all-star teams to insure that injustices are not perpetrated.
    d. There has been growing evidence of commercialism and exploita-

tion of high school athletes through their participation in such contests. In too many instances such games have been the "market place" in which their "wares" have been displayed before the highest bidder.

e. Further, it is the opinion of this group that the clothing of all-star and out-of-season contests in the garment of "sweet charity" is insufficient justification for their existence. Experience has revealed that often pitifully small proportions of receipts from such games have been realized for their avowed purposes.

f. Such contests are likely to imbue immature and inexperienced high school students selected for them with the false idea that their athletic prowess is something upon which they should capitalize commercially, rather than its being an endowed talent that is theirs to use for the pleasure and satisfaction they may receive from athletic competition.

g. In practically all all-star contests, with which this group has been apprised, there have been insufficient and inadequate practice periods provided prior to the playing of the games. In football, particularly, it is impossible to condone a practice period of five or six days for a group of boys who, previously, have never played together, especially after a lapse of an eight or nine months period since previous football competition. Most high school, college, and professional teams require a minimum pre-game practice period of fifteen days or more.

2. Further, it is recommended that states subscribing to the attitude of this group is indicated in (1), give consideration to the adoption of regulatory measures which will prohibit or discourage their member schools, administrative, coaching or instructor personnel, and registered athletic officials from participation, management, supervision, player selection, coaching, or officiating in any all-star or out-of-season athletic contests in which high school students or graduates of the previous year are participants. Reference is made to such regulatory measures now in force in Illinois, Indiana and Iowa as examples to be followed.

Resolution: Concerning Continuing Eligibility

The following resolution was adopted at the forty first annual meeting of the National Federation of State High School Athletic Associations to eliminate, if possible, all-star athletic contests in which high school students or high school graduates of the previous school year participate, unless the contest is sponsored and conducted by a high school association. The resolution adopted at Glacier Park, Montana, July 6, 1960 requests that educational institutions above the secondary-school level implement the idea.

WHEREAS: The fifty (50) member State High School Athletic Associations and/or the State High School Activities Associations members of the National Federation of State High School Athletic Associations and its four Canadian affiliates, at its forty first (41st) annual meeting at Glacier Park Lodge, East Glacier Park, Montana in convention assembled July 6, 1960, reaffirms and endorses the principles enunciated in the resolution adopted by the said National Federation at its 1947 annual meeting held at St. Petersburg, Florida, and the principles and ideals as expressed in the resolutions and minutes of the National Council of the said National Federation at its subsequent annual meetings at Chicago, Illinois in 1948, the 1950 annual meeting of the National Federation at Mobile, Alabama, the 1951 annual meeting at Belgrade Lakes, Maine, and the 1955 annual Federation meeting at York Harbor, Maine, all of which expressed clearly the opposition of the aforesaid National Federation to the holding and sponsorship by individuals and/or organizations, for charitable purpose or for individual profit, of all-star, championship contests, and out-of-season athletic events whereby high school students or high school graduates of the previous year are participants, and

WHEREAS: The aforesaid National Federation, at its forty first (41st) annual convention recognizes and is cognizant of the increasing interest, desire and enthusiasm of individuals and organizations to promote all-star, post-season and out-of-season athletic contests involving high school students and/or high school graduates of the previous year in athletic contests for charitable purposes and/or individual profit, and

WHEREAS: The National Federation and its fifty (50) member associations and four Canadian affiliate associations recognize their inability to individually or collectively prevent the holding of the above described contests by individual and/or organizations for the reason that said individuals and/or organizations are outside the control and regulation of the National Federation and its member state associations, be it therefore

RESOLVED: That the forty first (41st) annual meeting of the National Federation of State High School Athletic Associations express appreciation and commend the National Collegiate Athletic Association for the adoption by the said National Collegiate Athletic Association, in January of 1956 at its Los Angeles meeting, of a regulation and the subsequent enforcement by the National Collegiate Athletic Association of said regulation whereby "no member institution shall permit any employee to participate directly or indirectly in the management, coaching, officiating, supervision, promotion or player selection of any All-Star team or contest involving interscholastic players or those who during the previous school year were members of high school teams.

Facilities of a member institution may be made available provided the contest is first sanctioned by the appropriate State High School Association or, if interstate, by the National Federation of State High School Athletic Associations."

BE IT FURTHER RESOLVED that the National Federation and its fifty (50) member Associations and four Canadian affiliate associations, in convention assembled July 6, 1960, urgently request and invite all associations comprising educational institutions above the secondary school level to adopt, at the earliest possible moment, a "continuing eligibility" rule whereby the participation by a high school student or a high school graduate of the previous year in any all-star athletic contest, unless said contest was promoted, sponsored and operated entirely and completely by a State High School Athletic Association, would render the participant ineligible for varsity intercollegiate athletic competition the first year of his otherwise normal varsity intercollegiate eligibility.

Typical State Association By-Laws About All-Star Contests

CALIFORNIA: Participation by member schools, by their school officials, or by any employee of the school, directly or indirectly, in the furnishing of school facilities or equipment, officiating, management, organization, supervision, player selection, coaching or promotion, of All-Star high school teams, high school championship teams or similar teams in contests or exhibitions in any sport, unless under the supervision, auspices, or approval of the California Interscholastic Federation shall be considered a violation of the spirit and purpose, if not the actual wording, of the California Interscholastic Federation rules. Violation of this rule by any of the aforesaid shall be cause for suspension of the school concerned from membership in the California Interscholastic Federation. Game officials who violate this rule shall be automatically suspended from officiating in C. I. F. contests. Any student taking part in an unsanctioned All-Star contest or similar contest shall be debarred from all C. I. F. athletic contests.

ILLINOIS: No athletic director, coach, principal, teacher or other official of a member school or any athletic official registered with the Illinois High School Association shall assist, either directly or indirectly, with the coaching, management, direction, selection of players, promotion or officiating of any "all-star" or similar contest in which one or more of the competing teams is composed of high school players or players who, during the previous school year, were members of a high school team, unless such contest is sanctioned by this Association.

INDIANA: Participation, directly or indirectly, in the management, supervision, player selection, coaching or promotion of all-star high school teams, high school championship teams or similar teams in contests in any sport, having or not having definite seasons in the I. H. S. A. A., unless under the supervision and auspices of the I. H. S. A. A. by member schools, by their school officials or by their teachers, shall be considered a violation of the spirit and purpose, if not the actual wording of these rules and regulations; and schools violating the spirit, purpose or wording of these rules and regulations as indicated herein shall cause their school to be suspended from the I. H. S. A. A. for such length of time as the I. H. S. A. A. Board of Control deems advisable. Approved officials shall be suspended for promoting such contests.

KANSAS: It shall not be permissible for any member school, its school officials or any employee of the school, or any registered official, to participate directly or indirectly in the furnishing of school facilities or equipment; officiating, management, organization or supervision; player selection; coaching or promotion of any all-star teams composed of high school players or those who during the previous year were members of high school teams, in contests or exhibitions in any sport, unless approved by the Board of Control.

MICHIGAN: No athletic director, coach, teacher, or administrator of a Michigan high school, and no athletic official registered with the Michigan High School Athletic Association, shall at any time assist, either directly or indirectly with the coaching, management, direction, selection of players, promotion, or officiating of any "all-star" or similar contest in football or basketball in which one or more of the competing teams is composed of a player or players, who, during the previous school year, were members of a high school football or basketball team.

Bowl, Charity and All-Star Games
Excerpt from Minutes of 1948 Meeting of the National
Council of the National Federation

"Many problems arise in connection with various promotions in which attempts are made to use the high school athletic program and the high school athlete's prestige in the sponsoring of post-season contests, all-star contests and games or tournaments for the raising of funds for various charities, clubs or other organizations.

"Evils grow up in connection with this type of contest and untenable situations would arise if this type of promotion were permitted without limitation. Such contest divides the allegiance of high school students, tends to undermine respect for the athlete's own high school coach and encourages the type of adulation which gives the high school athlete an exaggerated notion of the importance of his individual athletic prowess as compared with the importance of his entire school activity program. The high schools have consistently refused to be drawn into promotions of the all-star and post-season variety. If the schoolmen thought there were any values in this type of contest, they could easily provide them through the regular school channels. This has not been done on any sectional or nationwide basis because the high school authorities do not believe such contests are desirable. The athletes to whom these appeals are made have already had a sufficient amount of football or basketball for the season. If they have not, the schools could easily provide for additional competition. There is no good reason why any university, club or other organization or individual should attempt to circumvent the school policies or regulations concerning length of season and number of permissible games, by setting up a promotion in which the prestige built up in high school play should be exploited for the purpose of interesting a group of athletes in a given university or for the purpose of raising funds for an organization. If this type of promotion were permitted to develop without limitation, the school program would be disrupted to the point where the entire high school athletic program would be in disrepute with all educational accrediting agencies."

As an example of attempts to take pressures off the individual school, here is one of the State Association by-laws: "No post-season festivals, meets, contests or tournaments shall be permitted during the school year by members of this Association unless special authorization is given by the Board of Control or the Delegate Assembly.

"No member school or official representative of a member school shall participate, either directly or indirectly, in the promotion, management, supervision, player selection, coaching or officiating of an all-star contest or any other contest involving high school students during the school year unless the entire proceeds of said contest shall revert to the schools or association of schools involved."

College All-Star Regulation

At the 1950 meeting of the National Federation at Mobile, Alabama, the National Council urged action in the direction of some type of "continuing eligibility" regulation so that some type of control might be exercised over promotions which involve recent high school graduates but which use the prestige which was built before graduation. At several subsequent meetings and conferences, this subject was further discussed. Partly as a result of these discussions, a number of State Associations adopted regulations which prohibit use of high school facilities or high school manpower in the promotion of all-star bowl contests involving recent high school graduates. In support of a desire to cooperate in this activity, several college conferences, including the Western Conference and the Pacific Coast Conference, adopted a regulation or policy which prohibited use of college facilities or manpower in connection with unsanctioned contests.

During the year of 1955, a conference of representatives of the National Collegiate Athletic Association and of the National Federation drew up a proposed regulation to be presented to the N.C.A.A. for possible adoption in support of similar regulations or policies which are in effect in the State High School Associations. The proposed regulation was outlined to the National Federation at their meeting at York Harbor, Maine, on June 29, 1955. The Federation National Council voted approval of this proposed action by the N.C.A.A. and a desire to have all State High School Associations take appropriate action to assist in implementing the regulation.

At the January 1956 meeting of the N.C.A.A. in Los Angeles, this regulation was adopted. Copy follows:

> "No member institution shall permit any employee to participate directly or indirectly in the management, coaching, officiating, supervision, promotion or player selection of any All-Star team or contest involving interscholastic players or those who during the previous school year were members of high school teams.
>
> "Facilities of a member institution may be made available provided the contest is first sanctioned by the appropriate State High School Athletic Association, or, if inter-state, by the National Federation of State High School Athletic Associations."

At Pittsburgh on January 11, 1961, the following all-star rule was adopted by the N.C.A.A.:

Section 10. PRINCIPLES GOVERNING THE ELIGIBILITY OF STUDENT-ATHLETES: An institution shall not permit a student-athlete to represent it in intercollegiate athletic competition unless he meets the following requirements of eligibility:

He shall be denied his first year of varsity athletic competition if, following his graduation from high school and before his enrollment in college, he was a member of a squad which engaged in any all-star football or basketball contest which was not specifically approved by the appropriate state high school athletic association or, if interstate, by the National Federation of State High School Athletic Associations or all of the state high school athletic associations involved.

Additional National Federation policies. At its annual meeting at St. Petersburg, Florida, Jan. 8–11, 1947, the National Federation was very much concerned with two matters that have been treated to some extent above. A joint committee representing the Federation and the American Association for Health, Physical Education, and Recreation prepared a set of Cardinal Athletic Principles which was adopted unanimously at the meeting. These principles follow:

CARDINAL ATHLETIC PRINCIPLES

NOTE: These principles were drawn up by a joint committee representing the National Federation and the American Association for Health, Physical Education and Recreation. The Joint Committee was made up of: P. F. Neverman, H. R. Peterson, H. V. Porter and A. Willis, representing the National Federation, and V. S. Blanchard, representing the A.A.H.P.E.R. The resolution was unanimously adopted at the Federation annual meeting at St. Petersburg, Florida, 1947 and at the American Association annual meeting at Seattle, Washington, 1948.

Schools provide opportunity for each individual to develop himself to the limit of his capacity in the skills, appreciations and health concepts which engender personal satisfaction and civic usefulness. A good school program includes the means for exploring many fields of activity. One such field is that which involves athletic performance. Participation in and appreciation of the skills in a sports contest is a part of enjoyable living. Ability to recognize degrees of proficiency in these skills is one important attribute of the well balanced individual. The perfectly timed and coordinated activities by which an individual, or a team, strives to achieve a definite objective is an exemplification of cooperation and efficiency. A good school program provides a mixture of benevolent restrictions and freedom; of mental growth and physical development; of liberties and restraints. Developing and maintaining a physically fit nation is one of its important aims.

For developing endurance, strength, alertness and coordination, contests and conditioning exercises have been made a part of the school program. Nature wisely insured a degree of physical development and social adjustment by endowing the individual with a desire to play. Around this desire, as a nucleus, can be built a complete program of beneficial exercises in which healthful and satisfying habits and attitudes are stressed.

To be of maximum effectiveness, the athletic program will:

1. Be closely coordinated with the general instructional program and properly articulated with other departments of the school.

2. Be such that the number of students accommodated and the educational aims achieved justify the use of tax funds for its support and also justify use of other sources of income, provided the time and attention which is given to the collection of such funds is not such as to interfere with the efficiency of the athletic program or of any other department of the school.

3. Be based on the spirit of non-professionalism so that participation is regarded as a privilege to be won by training and proficiency and to be valued highly enough to eliminate any need for excessive use of adulatory demonstrations or of expensive prizes or awards.

4. Confine the school athletic activity to events which are sponsored and supervised by the proper school authorities so that exploitation or improper use of prestige built up by school teams or members of such teams may be avoided.

5. Be planned so as to result in opportunity for many individuals to explore a wide variety of sports and in reasonable season limits for each sport.

6. Be controlled so as to avoid the elements of professionalism and commercialism which tend to grow up in connection with widely publicized "bowl" contests, barnstorming trips and interstate or intersectional contests which require excessive travel expense or loss of school time or which are bracketed with educational travel claims in an attempt to justify privileges for a few at the expense of decreased opportunity for many.

7. Be kept free from the type of contest which involves a gathering of so-called "all-stars" from different schools to participate in contests which may be used as a gathering place for representatives of certain colleges or professional organizations who are interested in soliciting athletic talent.

8. Include training in conduct and game ethics to reach all non-participating students and community followers of the school teams in order to insure a proper understanding and appreciation of the sports skills and of the need for adherence to principles of fair play and right prejudices.

9. Encourage a balanced program of intramural activity in grades below the ninth to make it unnecessary to sponsor contests of a championship nature in these grades.

10. Engender respect for the local, state and national rules and policies under which the school program is conducted.

In view of non-school promotions and commercial schemes which often involve high school athletes and athletic programs, the action indicated below was taken in 1948 concerning such promotions. Recently there has been a limited growth of outside-sponsored all-star and out-of-season contests, especially in football and basketball. There have been differences of opinion regarding the cognizance of state athletic associations over these contests, especially those involving high school graduates of the previous year. As already indicated in general, state associations have been opposed to them because of their unfavorable implications in connection with high school athletic programs. At the 1947 National Federation meeting, unanimous action was taken opposing such all-star and out-of-season contests.

NATIONAL PROMOTIONS INVOLVING HIGH SCHOOL ATHLETES

At the annual meeting in Chicago on December 30th, 1948, there was a thorough discussion of problems which arise in connection with promotions by non-school individuals or groups who attempt to use the high school athletic program and the prestige of the high school athlete as a means of building up an organization which often involves the purchase of literature, emblems, trophies or certificates or which is designed to secure a mailing list of outstanding high school athletes with the purpose of using such a list to assist in solicitation and proselyting.

In many of these cases, the promoter is sincere in his belief that he is rendering a service to the athlete and to the school athletic program. It is apparent that if this type of promotion were carried to the extreme, high school athletes and high school administrative officers would be deluged with requests for use of the school machinery for furthering promotions in which the end result is the sale of products which are given false values. This type of promotion is opposed to the National Federation policy of discouraging the building up of national high school champions and of inflated values connected with national awards and recognitions which are cheapened by combining the athletic achievements with sales promotion.

It was voted to disseminate information to all high school administrators to acquaint them with the dangers which are involved in such promotions and to urge them to refrain from allowing the school machinery to be used in such promotions. Any invitation for a high school athletic group or a high school athlete or a member of the high school athletic staff to join such an organization should be carefully studied and checked with the proper state or national high school organization before such invitation is accepted. Promotions in which membership is solicited in connection with an opportunity to purchase a football or basketball magazine, book or brochure or a membership emblem or medal seldom have values which would warrant approval by the high school organizations. Usually, the alleged service which is being rendered is insufficient to balance the disillusionment which follows the recognition that the claimed honor of membership is, in reality, a device to stimulate sale of a related product.

RECOMMENDATIONS OF THE JOINT COMMITTEE ON STANDARDS IN ATHLETICS

(National Association of Secondary School Principals; American Association for Health, Physical Education, and Recreation; and National Federation of State High School Athletic Associations.)

For the purpose of promoting and stimulating safe and healthful participation among a high percentage of secondary-school boys in a wide variety of wholesome athletic activities and after careful study of the problems which have been created by certain types of interscholastic contests (including meets, tournaments, national championships, contests which require distant travel, contests which are sponsored by individuals or organizations other than a high school or group of high schools, and contests between teams of high school all-stars) the Joint Committee makes the following recommendations. The Joint Committee urges that all of the organizations represented adopt these MAJOR INTERPRETATIONS and place them in the form of policies, standards, or regulations in accordance with the established practice of each organization:

1. The program of athletics should be developed with due regard for health and safety standards as set forth in *Suggested School Health Policies.*

2. Good citizenship must result from all coaching and from all inter-school competition. The education of the youth of the nation fails unless it creates the proper ideals and attitudes both in the game and off the field.

3. The ten "Cardinal Athletic Principles" are accepted as expressing the policies of our organizations, and it is urged that these be displayed in the literature of our organizations.

4. All schools shall use reasonable care in avoiding any participation in a contact sport between participants of normal high-school age and participants who are appreciably above or below normal high-school age.

5. All schools shall fully observe and abide by the spirit and letter of established eligibility requirements which have been democratically developed by each of the state athletic associations.

6. Each state athletic association should attempt to secure the co-

operation which would provide a plan of continuous eligibility from high school to college.

7. For competition in which only one state is involved, no school shall participate in a meet or tournament involving more than two schools unless such contest has been approved by its state high-school association or its delegated constituent or allied divisions.

8. The use of school facilities or members of the school staff shall not be permitted in connection with any post-season or all-star contest unless such contest has been sanctioned by the state athletic association.

9. A school shall not permit any employee or official to encourage or collaborate in any negotiations which may lead a high-school athlete to lose his eligibility through the signing of a professional contract.

10. The solicitation of athletes through try-outs and competitive bidding by higher institutions is unethical and unprofessional. It destroys the amateur nature of athletics, tends to commercialize the individual and the program, promotes the use of athletic skill for gain, and takes an unfair and unjust advantage of competitors.

11. In all interstate athletic contests, each athlete shall compete under eligibility rules which are at least as restrictive as those adopted by the state high school athletic association of his state, except in the case of non-member schools which are not eligible for membership in their state associations.

12. No school shall compete in any of the following contests unless such contest has been sanctioned by each of the interested state high school athletic associations through the National Federation: (a) any interstate tournament or meet in which three or more schools participate; (b) any interstate two-school contest which involves a round trip exceeding 600 miles; (c) any interstate two-school contest (regardless of the distance to be travelled) which is sponsored by an individual or an organization other than a member high school.

13. No basketball tournament which is purported to be for interstate high school championships shall be sanctioned, and no basketball tournament involving schools of more than one state shall be sanctioned unless the tournament is purely community in character.

14. No contest which is purported to be for a national high school championship in any sport shall be sanctioned.

The above recommendations were adopted as representing the policy of the three organizations at the National Federation annual meeting in December 1949; the National Association annual meeting in February 1950; and the American Association annual meeting in April 1950.

Conclusions. In conclusion it should be said that these accomplishments of the National Federation of State High School Athletic Associations discussed here do not by any means represent the entire range of activities of the organization. Regional meetings have been held as aids to state associations in establishing higher athletic standards. Problems concerned with the improvement of eligibility and administrative regulations for interscholastic athletics, ways and means of securing better sportsmanship at athletic contests, the development of wider participation in interscholastic and intramural athletics, as well as the very important problem of keeping athletics educational, all have been matters of concern and consideration at national meetings of the Federation. It may well be said, "We've just begun to fight," as far as the accomplishment of objectives is concerned. No one denies that the National Federation of State High School Athletic Associations, as a body organized for the development and improvement of high school athletics, can accomplish almost anything it may attempt. It has a record of excellent beginnings and accomplishments to date and its future is unlimited.

Questions for Study and Discussion

1. What is the National Federation of State High School Athletic Associations? When was it formed and what were the charter member states?

2. Discuss the purpose of the National Federation. Why is it called a "federation"?

3. Enumerate and discuss briefly the accomplishments of the National Federation.

4. How do the National Federation minimum eligibility requirements compare with those of your home state athletic association?

5. What is the attitude of the National Federation regarding national championships in high school athletics? State arguments for and against this policy.

6. Do you agree with the National Federation policy concerning scheduling of interstate athletic contests? Why should there be objections to a school traveling five hundred or a thousand miles for such a contest?

7. Discuss circumstances that have resulted in football being the only sport in which the playing rules for high schools are written exclusively by high school men. List advantages. Disadvantages?

8. Discuss the National Federation Resolution of Solicitation.

9. Why is the Agreement Between Organized Baseball and the Federation important? What is being accomplished by it?

10. Do you agree with the National Federation policy on all-star and post-season contests? State and discuss its reasons for opposition to them.

11. What are the purposes and value of the Resolution Concerning Continuing Eligibility of the National Federation?

12. What are the Cardinal Athletic Principles of the National Federation? Why are such pronouncements important?

13. Probably the Recommendations of the Joint Committee on Standards in Athletics will be more far-reaching than anything of this type to date. What three agencies were involved? Summarize the fourteen points included in the Recommendations.

3

State High School Athletic and Activity Associations

As indicated in Chapter 1, state high school athletic associations have been important factors in the improvement and maintenance of high standards for the administrative control of interscholastic athletics. In a typically American fashion, schools organized themselves into state associations because it was apparent that "in unity there is strength." It was also evident to schoolmen concerned with the growing importance of the interschool athletic program that better administrative regulations, tempered with greater uniformity and equity, would be the outgrowth of organizations larger than local or sectional groups.

Early state organizations. There is some question as to which was the first state-wide organization for the control of interscholastic athletics. Certainly Wisconsin was early in the list, since a committee was appointed in 1895 in that state to formulate rules to govern interschool athletic contests. Also in 1895 a state field day was held in Michigan in which schools competed under what were considered more or less uniform rules, and a committee of the state teachers' association was appointed at that time to further the organization of the Michigan Interscholastic Athletic Association. Illinois apparently formed its state association that same year, and Indiana set up its organization in 1903. It is apparent, therefore, that the beginnings of state-wide athletic associations were made in most states either in the years immediately preceeding 1900 or within the next few years thereafter. Some of the organizations were not very strong for a number of years, but with the growth in high school enrollments and the increase in amount and scope of athletic competition there were associations in all but six states (Delaware, Idaho, Maryland, Missouri, Nevada, New Hampshire and Rhode Island) by 1926.

Athletic and activity associations. There are athletic or activity associations in all the states at the present time. Not all state organizations are called athletic associations. Some of them embrace activities other than those pertaining to athletics. During the 1940's and early 1950's there has been quite a tendency, in several Middle Western states especially, to form activities associations which include music, forensic, dramatic, commercial, academic, and other activities as well as athletics. The names of state associations other than those strictly athletic in nature follow:

Alaska High School Activities Association; Arkansas Athletic and Contest Association; Arizona Interscholastic Association; Colorado High School Activities Association; Florida High School Activities Association; Georgia High School Association; Idaho High School Interscholastic Activities Association; Illinois High School Association; Kansas State High School Activities Association, Inc.; Maine Association of Principals of Secondary Schools; Massachusetts Secondary School Principals' Association; Minnesota State High School League, Inc.; Mississippi High School Activities Association; Missouri State High School Activities Association; Montana High School Association; Nebraska School Activities Association; Nevada Interscholastic League; New Mexico High School Activities Association; North Dakota State High School League; Oregon School Activities Association; South Carolina High School League; Texas University Interscholastic League; Utah High School Activities Association; Vermont Headmasters' Association; Virginia High School League; Washington Interscholastic Activities Association; West Virginia Secondary Schools Activities Commission.[1]

The remainder of the state associations, including those in New Brunswick, Nova Scotia, Ontario, and Saskatchewan Canada, are strictly athletic in nature and are called either interscholastic athletic or high school athletic associations, leagues, or conferences.

Purposes of state associations. Interesting and valuable informa-

[1] National Federation of State High School Athletic Associations, 1960–1961 *Handbook*, pages 60–75.

tion as to the purposes prompting the organization of state associations may be found by examining their constitutions. Almost without exception there are provisions in these documents of origin that set forth their reasons for existence. Typical purposes and objectives of state associations follow:

To foster and develop amateur athletics among the Public High Schools and Private Secondary Schools of the State.

To equalize athletic opportunities by standardizing rules of eligibility for individuals, and by classifying for competitive purposes the institutions which are members of the Association.

To supplement the physical education program of the secondary schools of New Jersey by making a practical application of the theories of physical activity, and to promote uniformity in the arrangement and control of the athletic program.

To promote uniformity in the arrangement and control of contests.

To protect the mutual interests of the members of the Association through the cultivation of ideals of clean sport in their relation to the development of character. *(New Jersey State Interscholastic Athletic Association)*

The purpose of this organization is:

(a) To direct and control high school interscholastic athletics (grades 9-12) of the State on a high plane so that boards and faculties will regard them as educational resources to be encouraged and fostered.

(b) To locate the responsibility for their administration with reference to satisfactory supervision.

(c) To simplify and make definite their administration by means of a constitution, by-laws, and efficient organization.

(d) To cultivate more cordial and friendly relations among schools through the observance of good standards of sportsmanship.

(e) To promote the acceptance of the Cardinal Principles and Code of Ethics of the California Interscholastic Federation. *(California Interscholastic Federation)*

The purpose of the Association is to approve, promote, develop and direct all activities among its member schools, that will contribute to, or be a part of a well rounded and meaningful educational experience at the secondary school level. The Association shall strive to develop a unified and coordinated activities plan, without destroying the identity of any specific activity. *(Colorado High School Activities Association)*

The object of the Association shall be to promote the best interests of the secondary schools of Maine; to encourage cooperation, professional efficiency and good fellowship among its members; and to regulate all interscholastic athletics in secondary schools. *(Maine Association of Principals of Secondary Schools)*

The Minnesota State High School League was originally organized in 1916 as a State Athletic Association for the purpose of unifying the high schools of Minnesota in the promotion of pure amateur sports and to strengthen and unify eligibility rules governing participation in inter-school contests.

In March, 1929, The State High School Athletic Association changed its name to the Minnesota State High School League and assumed control over all athletic activities as well as debate and speech activity contests. *(Minnesota State High School League)*

Section 1. The Missouri State High School Activities Association is a voluntary association belonging to its member schools for the purpose of promoting, regulating and supervising all interscholastic activities and contests as may be delegated by the member schools to the jurisdiction of the Association. Stated more specifically, the objectives shall include:

a. The promotion of the educational values inherent in interscholastic activities for boys and girls.

b. The assurance that interscholastic activities shall remain an integral part of the secondary education program for the purpose of the development of worthwhile knowledge, skills, and proper emotional patterns in high school youth.

c. The approval, direction, and development of activities and contests under the jurisdiction of the Association.

d. The fostering of good sportsmanship on the part of school representatives, school patrons, and students.

e. The promotion of a cooperative spirit among member schools.

f. The prevention of exploitation of high school youth and of the programs of member schools by special interest groups.

g. The protection of the best interests of the members of the Association in all contests and activity areas.

h. The provision of means of evaluating and controlling local, state, and national contests affecting secondary schools initiated by firms, organizations, and institutions outside organized educational agencies. *(Missouri State High School Activities Association)*

The object of this association shall be to promote pure, wholesome, amateur athletics in the schools of Ohio. *(Ohio High School Athletic Association)*

The object of this Association shall be for the betterment of athletics in the high schools of the State. *(Oklahoma High School Athletic Association)*

HEALTH.

To organize, develop, and direct an interscholastic athletic program which will promote, protect and conserve the health and physical welfare of all participants.

EDUCATION.

To formulate and maintain policies that will safeguard the educational values of interscholastic athletics and cultivate high ideals of good sportsmanship.

COMPETITION.

To promote uniformity of standards in all interscholastic athletic competition. *(Pennsylvania Interscholastic Athletic Association)*

The purpose of this organization of South Dakota Public High Schools is to promote high school athletics, to stimulate fair play and by means of rules and regulations equalize athletic opportunity by standardizing qualifications of contestants, coaching, treatment of visiting teams; and generally to promote the athletic welfare of students in member high schools. *(South Dakota High School Athletic Association)*

The object of this League is to foster among the public schools of Texas inter-school competitions as an aid in the preparation for citizenship (*[Texas] University Interscholastic League)*

To approve, develop and direct interscholastic activities for children of member schools who may participate, and to insure their protection against exploitation by special interest groups.

To stress the cultural values, the appreciations and skills involved in all activities.

To promote well-rounded educational experiences which will satisfy the generally accepted aims of education. *(Washington Interscholastic Activities Association)*

This Association, through the employment of the instrumentalities hereinafter set up, shall (a) supervise and control all of the interscholastic activities in which its member schools may engage, and (b) perform such other educational functions as may from time to time be approved and adopted by the membership.

In the performance of these functions it shall be the aim of the Association (a) to stress the cultural values, the appreciations and skills involved in all interscholastic activities and to promote co-operation and friendship; (b) to limit interscholastic programs as to both character and quantity to such activities and such events as may reasonably be looked upon as promoting the generally accepted objectives of secondary education and as shall not unduly interfere with nor abridge the regular program of teachers and students in the performance of their regular day to day school duties; (c) to encourage economy in the time of the student and teacher personnel devoted to interscholastic activities; (d) to encourage economy in expenses of interscholastic activities; and (e) to discourage long trips for large groups of students. *(Illinois High School Association)*

To provide a central, voluntary, non-profit organization through which the public secondary schools of the state may cooperate for the following ends:

To develop intelligent recognition of the place of athletics and sports in the education of our youth.

To establish and unify policies of administration in interscholastic athletics and sports.

To offer a system that will provide for equitable competition.

To encourage the organization of recreational athletics and play for all students as an integral part of the educational program.

To assist member schools in securing competent officials.

To organize a force of opinion to keep interscholastic athletics within proper bounds, that will expressly encourage all that is honorable, sportsmanlike, and gentlemanly in all branches of athletics and sports. *(Connecticut Interscholastic Athletic Conference)*

The purpose of the Association is to contribute to the education of the high schools boys and girls of Kansas by:

a. Administering a program of interscholastic activities, festivals, clinics and contests among its member schools.

b. Elevating the standards of good sportsmanship and encouraging the growth in good citizenship, not only of high school boys and girls but also of adults and all others who come into contact with school activities.

c. Protecting member schools from exploitation by special interest groups.

d. Encouraging pride in scholastic achievement as a fundamental basis for a well balanced activity program.

e. Serving the best interests of all member schools by influencing the proper type of legislation or any other desirable means. *(Kansas State High School Activities Association)*

To foster and develop amateur athletics among the Public High Schools and Private Secondary Schools of the Province.

To equalize athletic opportunities by standardizing rules of eligibility for individuals, and classifying for competitive purposes, the institutions which are members of the Association.

To promote uniformity in the arrangement and control of contests.

To protect the mutual interests of the members of the Association through the cultivation of ideals of clean sport in their relation to the development of character. *(New Brunswick (Canada) Interscholastic Athletic Association)*

To encourage athletics and to control our interscholastic competition. To develop and direct a wholesome athletic program.

To initiate policies that will safeguard the educational values of school athletics.

To cultivate and stimulate fair play and good sportsmanship. *(Delaware Association of School Administrators—Athletic Commission)*

The object of this organization shall be promotion of education in Georgia from a mental, physical and moral viewpoint; to promote the study of public speaking; to standardize and encourage athletics; and to promote appreciation for music, home making and other cultural arts through District and State Contests. *(Georgia High School Association)*

The purpose of this organization is the encouragement and direction of athletics in the high schools of the state. No effort has been made to suppress or even to repress the athletic spirit that is everywhere in evidence in our schools. On the contrary, this organization gives recognition to athletics as an essential factor in the activities of the pupil and seeks only to direct these activities into proper and legitimate channels. *(Indiana High School Athletic Association—Copied from Introduction to first printing of Constitution in 1904)*

Its object shall be the development, regulation, and purification of athletic activities in the state. *(Kentucky High School Athletic Association)*

The purpose of this organization is to promote the general welfare of the high schools in their relations with each other. This is done through:

Planning, directing, and controlling contests, games, and other interscholastic activities;

Defining and fixing responsibility;

Elevating the standards of sportsmanship by seeking to strengthen the moral fibre of all concerned;

Developing a higher standard of scholarship and encouraging pride in scholastic achievement.

Encouraging the formation and promotion of non-competitive activities which contribute to the molding of moral and spiritual values in character development as part of a well rounded extra-curricular program. *(Mississippi High School Activities Association)*

The object of the Virginia High School League shall be to foster among the public high schools of Virginia a broad program of supervised competitions and desirable school activities as an aid in the total education of pupils. *(Virginia High School League)*

To increase the educational value of interscholastic athletic programs throughout the state.

To assist in the regulation of competition so that there will be ample time both for study and athletics.

To regulate the interscholastic program so as to safeguard the physical welfare of students participating.

To insure a greater degree of physical fitness of high school students by providing opportunities for participation in vigorous competitive athletics, designed to meet the needs and abilities of all. *(Michigan High School Athletic Association)*

From these widely scattered statements of purpose of state associations it is apparent that common objectives are the protection of the athletic and other competive interests of member schools, promotion and regulation of amateur contests, protection of health of contestants, and securing of greater uniformity in contest regulations. It is singular that comparatively few organizations include the educational implications of athletics as reasons for their existence. It may be logical to assume, however, that the educational attributes of athletics and other activities were taken for granted by those associations not mentioning them.

Types of State Associations

State athletic or activity associations fall into three general classifications or types. The great majority are strictly voluntary in nature. The second type are affiliated in some way with state departments of education. The third type consists of those whose control is under the direction of a state institution of higher learning. Each of these plans of organization will be discussed briefly.

Voluntary state associations. State associations in this classification are the most numerous. In them membership is voluntary but is usually dependent upon member schools' meeting specified requirements regarding the financial support of the school, its plan of organization, status of its coaches, and the payment of annual dues. Usually such organizations limit their competition to member schools. There are well-established regulations for the administration of athletic contests and eligibility of contestants. In most states, membership is open to public secondary schools accredited by state departments of education. Some states also allow private and parochial schools to join, provided that they meet the standards for membership. Generally there are elected boards of control, delegate assemblies, or legislative councils whose members are representative of geographical sections and often of schools of different sizes. In most cases there are the usual officers—president, vice-president, secretary, and treasurer. Often the secretary is the executive officer, although in other states he is called commissioner or state director. Typical states with this form of organization, in different sections of the country, are Washington, Colorado, Kansas, Illinois, Wisconsin, Indiana, Connecticut, Florida, Pennsylvania, and Alabama.

There are other states almost identical in form of organization with the type discussed and illustrated above except that a member of their boards of control (usually ex officio and without vote) is the state supervisor or director of physical and health education. There is an increasing tendency to include state physical education directors in the legislative or executive bodies of the state associations. Certainly it seems that nothing but mutual benefit to both agencies could result from such cooperative efforts. Athletics very properly should be considered as a part of the physical education program. California, Ohio, Pennsylvania, Delaware, Maryland, Virginia, and New Jersey are some of the states in which the state physical and health education director is a member ex officio of the state athletic executive or legislative bodies.

State associations affiliated with state departments of education. Michigan and New York are outstanding in this type of organization. The Michigan association has been affiliated with the State Department of Public Instruction since 1924. In 1923 the Michigan legislature passed the following law:

The Superintendent of Public Instruction shall have supervision and may exercise control over the interscholastic athletic activities of all the schools of the state.[2]

Provisions of this law have been carried out by the superintendents of public instruction by effecting a cooperative arrangement with the state athletic association. All junior, senior, private, and parochial high schools of the state are members of the state athletic association. A legislative body (representative council) is elected by schools on a geographical and school enrollment basis. Representatives also are elected by parochial and junior high schools.

[2] Michigan High School Athletic Association 1961–1962 *Handbook*, p. 2.

Two members represent physical education teachers and coaches. Eligibility and administrative regulations are formulated and activities are conducted by the state association with the approval of the state superintendent.

At least two voluntary state associations (Kansas and Minnesota) recently were incorporated under their state laws and also now make annual reports of their activities and financial condition to their respective state superintendents of public instruction.

In the fall of 1938 New York began a new chapter in the general program of administration of interscholastic athletics in that state. Through action of the New York Board of Regents at that time, there were established what are known as Regulations of the Commissioner of Education Governing Health and Physical Education.[3] These regulations made athletics in New York a definite part of the physical education program. The state athletic association actually is a voluntary organization with eleven district divisions. Its general body is a central committee composed of district representatives, with an executive committee of eleven members serving in an executive capacity. The state athletic association has continued to function in furthering its studies of athletic programs, its bulletin publication, its Athletic Protection Fund plan, formation of new rules, and conducting district tournaments and meets. Since the basic athletic code has been given the force of law by action of the Board of Regents, it is the responsibility of that body, through proper state education department officials, to enforce it.

It is not the responsibility of any state or local athletic association or league to enforce the Commissioner's Regulations governing athletics as approved by the Board of Regents. It is, of course, the responsibility of athletic associations and leagues to cooperate in seeing that both the spirit and letter of the Regulations are lived up to by the various school districts throughout the state.[4]

New York's innovation in defining and classifying athletics and the method of control interscholastic contests has been watched with interest.

[3] Hiram A. Jones, "Regulations of the Commissioner of Education Governing Health and Physical Education," New York State Public High School Athletic Association *Bulletin,* October, 1937, p. 2.

[4] *Ibid.,* p. 5

University-directed state associations. Texas presents a unique example of this type of organization. In Texas

. . . any public white school in Texas that is below collegiate rank and that is under the jurisdiction of, and receives apportionment from, the Texas Education Agency is eligible to membership in this League; except schools for defective and correctives.[5]

The league is organized annually by the Extension Division of the University of Texas. It includes elementary, junior high, and senior high schools. The governing body of the league is a state executive committee appointed by the president of the University of Texas. There is an executive committee for each district and region, appointed by the state executive committee. Each county elects a county executive committee, and directors-general and directors of contests are appointed for all twenty-six activities that a unit may sponsor. During the peak years before World War II there were 6,000 member schools. It claims to be the nation's largest and most highly organized school association.[6] Evidently, the Texas plan presents an organization vastly different from that in most other states.

The South Carolina and Virginia state associations also are affiliated with state institutions of higher learning, the Universities of South Carolina and Virginia respectively. While many of the affairs of their associations are administered by the extension divisions of those universities, they are not handled as completely or as extensively as is the case in Texas. Virginia's league activities, however, are administered by an executive committee composed of the chairman of the Legislative Council; the chairman of each of the four Group Boards; the State Director of Secondary Education; the State Supervisor of Health and Physical Education; one division superintendent of schools elected by the Legislative Council from the state at large; three members at large; and the Executive Secretary. In South Carolina the state university has one faculty member on the Executive Committee of seven members and aids in the direc-

[5] Texas University Interscholastic League, *Constitution and Rules*, University of Texas *Bulletin*, August 1, 1960, p. 9.
[6] *Ibid.*, p. 5.

tion of the program, which is not so extensive as in Virginia and Texas.

In concluding the discussion of types of state associations, it is significant to point out examples of different organization plans and to note their scope. Illinois, Ohio, Indiana, Wisconsin, Iowa, and Pennsylvania have voluntary state-wide organizations with strong state executive officers and committees. New York and California actually are associations of district organizations within the states themselves. New York presents an innovation in its definition and control of athletics. Texas is controlled by an institution of higher learning in administering its athletic and other contest programs. Michigan has a state-wide organization of all schools closely connected by state statute with the State Department of Public Instruction. During the years it will be interesting to observe in which of these directions major emphasis will be placed in the administration and control of state-wide athletic and activity programs.

Functions of State Associations

Reasons for the existence of state athletic and activity associations are manifold. As new services have been added there have been increased administrative duties. This has been the case not only in activity associations, which include other than athletic programs, but also in those limiting their jurisdiction to athletics exclusively.

Activities in addition to athletics. Mention has been made previously in this chapter that a number of state associations include more than athletics in their jurisdiction and functional services. No attempt will be made in this discussion to include all these activities, since we are concerned primarily with administration of high school athletics. It will be sufficient to list some of the activities in illustrative state organizations. Texas is the most inclusive in its program, and according to its Constitution [7] it holds contests annually in the following activities:

Baseball
Basketball, Boys'
Basketball, Girls'

Choral Singing
Debate
Declamation

[7] *Ibid.*, p. 12.

Extemporaneous Speech	Picture Memory
Football	Playground Ball
Football, Six-man	Poetry Reading
Golf	Ready Writing
Journalism	Shorthand
Music	Slide Rule
Music Appreciation	Story Telling
Volleyball	Spelling and Plain Writing
Number Sense	Tennis
Original Oration	Track and Field
One-Act Play	Typewriting

As compared with this broad range of activities, many state associations remain strictly athletic in nature. Ohio, Michigan, California, Wisconsin, Connecticut, Pennsylvania, Oklahoma, Indiana, Iowa, and Alabama are examples of this large group. In Minnesota music, dramatics, and speech activities, in addition to athletics, are under the supervision of the state high school league.[8] Nebraska calls its organization an activities association.[9] It embraces declamatory, debating, music contests, and one act plays, as well as athletics in its activities. Kansas also is an activities association;[10] and, in addition to athletics, it directs contests in music, debating, speech, and dramatics. The activities of these three state associations, as well as those of Texas, are examples of a type of service rendered to their schools that seems destined to receive attention from other states during the next few years. The states that have adopted this plan have felt that they had the basic machinery set up in their athletic associations whereby they could efficiently handle these other activities. This assumption seems logical; and, provided sectional or state contests in these activities are desired, such organizations may well provide services broader in scope than athletics.

State athletic associations perform numerous functions other than matters pertaining strictly to eligibility of contestants. Among them are included the following:

[8] Minnesota State High School League, 1960 *Official Handbook,* p. 23.
[9] Nebraska High School Activities Association, *Twenty-Sixth Annual Yearbook* (1960), p. 4.
[10] Kansas State High School Activities Association, 1960–1961 *Handbook,* p. 10.

Regulations for the conduct of contests. These are discussed in Chapter 5.

Interpretations of playing rules. This service has resulted in more uniformity in methods of play and officiating. In many states rules committees have been set up and interpretation meetings are held for coaches, officials, and players. Football, basketball, baseball, track, wrestling, and swimming are the most common sports for which such arrangements are made.

Athletic accident or insurance plans. Wisconsin has more data available and probably has made greater progress in the formation of an athletic accident benefit plan than any other state association. Since a more detailed discussion of such plans appear in Chapter 11, it is necessary here only to mention that the Wisconsin plan is a pattern that has been used in many of the other states that have inaugurated such schemes, which have included Iowa, Kansas, Montana, Michigan, California, Minnesota, Nebraska, Mississippi, Ohio, Oregon, Florida, Oklahoma, North Dakota, South Dakota, Georgia, Pennsylvania, New York, and a group of New England states. Some of the above states and several others now have established contracts with commercial insurance companies because they have felt that they should not, or by local state laws could not, become involved in any form of athletic injury protection or insurance business.

Registration and classification of athletic officials. Michigan was the first state in the Middle West to establish a plan for registration and classification of athletic officials (1927). Similar plans have been set up in several other states. The feeling generally exists that athletic officials should be included as a definite necessary part of the athletic program. The important consideration is the fact that the right to license implies the right to refuse to license, and thus it is possible to dispense with officials who do not meet standards or codes of ethics commonly established.

Registration has brought officials into close contact with state associations. Standards of officiating have been raised through rules-interpretation meetings and officials' knowledge that their license to officiate depends upon their maintaining established standards. In most state associations the fees hardly defray the costs of services rendered. Illinois, Kansas, Wisconsin, Pennsylvania, Minnesota, and Michigan are among the leaders in officials' registration and rating plans. In some states there is affiliation by the state association with state officials' associations or local boards of officials.

Publications. Most state associations publish monthly printed bulletins during the school year. In Texas a newspaper type of publication is issued. These carry activity announcements as well as general items pertaining to intramural and interscholastic athletics. A most important feature of such publications is the accounts of executive and legislative meetings concerning eligibility and administrative matters as they pertain to athletics. Decisions in eligibility cases as they are published often perform a double service in that they establish precedents as well as permanent records and provide schools with information regarding interpretations of state association by-laws. Many states also publish handbooks and yearbooks containing general interpretations, lists of officials, constitutions, committees, and records of activities. Record, report, and general eligibility blanks, contracts, and the like, are materials furnished by virtually all state associations.

Conducting tournaments and meets. In most of the states with well-established athletic associations there are extensive programs of meets and tournaments managed by state associations. This policy already has been illustrated by reference to activities in Texas, Minnesota, Nebraska, and Kansas. Many others have tournament and meet programs limited to athletic events. In many states the income from tournaments and meets represents the chief source of revenue for operating the state association. As a result of this fact, tournaments, especially in basketball, sometimes have been criticized by schoolmen and others. In other states, tournaments have been worked out on a classification basis for schools. Receipts have been prorated among competing schools, entertaining schools, and the state association.

These arrangements generally have resulted in much saner views and administration of the whole program. In 1961 only four of the fifty states did not choose state champions in basketball.[11] These were California, Delaware, Massachusetts, and New York. In California, Massachusetts, and New York sectional champions in basketball are determined. From 1932 to 1947 Michigan held separate Upper and Lower Peninsula final basketball tournaments because

[11] National Federation of State High School Athletic Associations, *1960–1961 Handbook*, p. 44.

of the geographical division of the state into two sections completely separated by Lake Michigan. Beginning with 1948, however, a state-wide final basketball tournament has been held. In thirty-one of the forty-six states holding state championships in basketball, class champions were chosen.[12] This fact is significant in that it shows a trend toward less emphasis on a single champion and results in greater equity in competition. (See Figs. 3–1 and 3–2.)

_____(City—Post Office)_____(Zone)_____(County)_____(School)_____(Street Address)

MICHIGAN HIGH SCHOOL ATHLETIC ASSOCIATION
Classification Information Card 1961-62 School Year

The following is the REPORT ON HIGH SCHOOL MEMBERSHIP on the FOURTH FRIDAY of the 1961-62 school year in the above high school:

(1) Encircle type of regular academic organization used in your school system: 8-2; 6-2-4; 6-3-3; 8-4; 6-6; _____

(2) Encircle the grades included in your High School organization: 9 — 10 — 11 — 12   (Any other)

(3) Indicate membership (number belonging) in grades 9-12, inclusive, on fourth Friday of 1961-62 school year. (See Note in red ink below.) List number boys and girls in each grade below:

	9th Grade		10th Grade		11th Grade		12th Grade	
Total Membership	Boys	Girls	Boys	Girls	Boys	Girls	Boys	Girls

NOTE: ALL HIGH SCHOOLS MUST REPORT AND COUNT their ninth grade enrollments for classification purposes UNLESS the ninth grade is a part of a junior high school in a separate building under separate administration.

(4) Total membership in all grades as reported in No. (3) above _____ on _____, 1961.
                                                                    (Exact date at end of four weeks of school)

(5) If you do NOT have a four-year high school as encircled in No. (2) above, do you draw athletes from the ninth grade?_____
    If so, what is the total ninth grade membership?_____

(6) Students present on_____attended a meeting in this school at which athletic eligibility rules affecting them
    were explained.   (Date)

We certify that the above report is taken from the official enrollment records of this school for the first four weeks of the 1961-62 school year, and is correct.

(Signed)_____and (Signed)_____
       (Superintendent of Schools)   (Principal of High School)
Superintendent's Office Telephone No._____Principal's Office Telephone No._____

PLEASE COMPLETE BOTH SIDES OF CARD AND RETURN TO:
Charles E. Forsythe, State Director of Athletics, Department of Public Instruction, Lansing 2, by
October 2, 1961   61—12C

Fig. 3-1. Classification Information Form (Michigan).

Most of the state associations have tournaments or meets, either sectional or state-wide, in track, tennis, cross country and golf, or in all three. As indicated above virtually all states have a series of basketball tournaments leading to state championships. Wrestling also is a tournament event sponsored by an increasing number of state associations. Several states (19) sponsor championship play-off series in football. Arkansas, Mississippi, Iowa, Texas, Tennessee, and Oklahoma are among the few states reporting state championships in girls' basketball, whereas Arkansas also determines a state junior high school basketball championship.[13] Swimming, likewise, is an

12 *Ibid.*
13 *Ibid.*

activity in which a state championship is declared. Only one state, Mississippi, declares a boxing championship.

______ (City—Post Office) ______ (Zone) ______ (County) ______ (School) ______ (School Telephone No.)

Athletic Roster Information Card — 1961-62 School Year

Please check (√) name of individual to whom correspondence should be addressed concerning schedules, finances, management, etc.: Please print.

PRINT

- ☐ Superintendent______ ☐ Principal______
- ☐ Athletic Director______ ☐ Faculty Manager of Athletics______
- ☐ Boys' Phy. Ed. Director______ ☐ Girls' Phy. Ed. Director______

Please check (√) the interscholastic sports that you are sponsoring this year, 1961-62, and give full name of the coach for each sport. Information relative to State Association Tournaments and Meets for only those sports checked will be sent to you. (If any of the coaches below are not regular members of your faculty, please put an "X" after their names.) Please Print.

PRINT

- ☐ Baseball______ ☐ Gymnastics______
- ☐ Basketball______ ☐ Skiing______
- ☐ Basketball (Girls)______ ☐ Softball______
- ☐ Cross Country______ ☐ Swimming______
- ☐ Football______ ☐ Tennis______
- ☐ Football (Six-man)______ ☐ Track______
- ☐ Golf______ ☐ Wrestling______

Is your school a member of a league or conference?______Name of league______

Name and address of league secretary ______

Please list league member schools alphabetically______

PLEASE COMPLETE BOTH SIDES OF CARD AND RETURN TO:

Charles E. Forsythe, State Director of Athletics, Department of Public Instruction, Lansing 2, by October 2, 1961

Fig. 3-2. (Reverse of Figure 3-1). Athletic Roster Information Form *(Michigan)*.

Some educators feel that such championships have outlived their usefulness and no longer are a necessary stimulus for the development of sports. More than thirty years ago Rogers [14] maintained that, as such, state championships have no educational value. As indicated previously, however, in the many states that have championship series there may be circumstances that justify their existence. Plans whereby schools are classified for competition might be one. The experience of some states where there are no state association-sponsored championships has been that agencies outside the schools have taken over these activities. This result has been reported in at least one state where several leagues or conferences withdrew from participation in the state association series of basketball tournaments. Other agencies set up so-called independent tournaments for their teams.

Another important point should be kept in mind in considering the elimination of tournaments and meets. In each state there is some

[14] Frederick Rand Rogers, *The Future of Interscholastic Athletics*. New York: Bureau of Publications, Teachers College, Columbia University, 1929.

form of organization for the control of athletics. In every instance these organizations are under the jurisdiction either directly or indirectly, of the schoolmen of the state. If these men felt that state association-sponsored meets and tournaments generally were undesirable would they not attempt to do away with them?

It is not the purpose of this discussion either to condone or condemn the activity of state athletic associations in conducting tournaments or meets which may or may not lead to state championships. Rather, an attempt has been made to discuss what is being done, in the belief that existence of an institution of the magnitude of this one justifies some consideration of it. Athletics are in our schools, and with them there is the desire for competition. With competition having been brought relatively close to home through modern methods of transportation, we have seen it seek new and no longer far-off laurels. State-wide contests have been one of the apparent results of increased public interest developed by the press and radio. The National Federation of State High School Athletic Associations has aided states by helping them control the extent of their competition, with the consequent abolition of national championships for high school athletes. If state championships, or variations of them, are to remain, they must be so established and conducted that their purposes, methods, and results are educationally, physically, and financially sound. This is quite an order but it presents a real challenge to schoolmen themselves.

Establishment of athletic standards. In addition to the establishment of eligibility regulations, state athletic associations have performed valuable services to schools of their states by setting standards for the conduct of athletics. Although most state associations are the creations of schoolmen, after they are established they become a somewhat impersonal agency. The point is that the state association, through its secretary, commissioner, or director, may advise with schools as a disinterested party and may, as a result, be of aid to them. Schools frequently ask the advice of the state association on matters of athletic policy.

Opinions from the state association officer may be used to improve conditions and raise local standards. An especially fine opportunity is afforded in this respect if the state association is connected or has a close relation with the state education department or its physical, health, or recreation divisions. It is not to be inferred that state associations which do not have, or do not choose to effect, any of these relations do not possess high ethical and administrative standards. Standards often are established by state associations in schedules, sanitation and safety, school-official relations, sportsmanship, relations between schools, scholarship, respect for and proper treatment of officials, the coach and winning of games, interscholastic-intramural relations, conduct of students, and similar matters.

As examples of recommended standards and codes prepared by state associations, those of New York and Michigan are included. Many other states have equally as good or better ones. Such statements often aid local schools in establishing higher planes for the conduct of interscholastic athletics than otherwise might be possible.

CODE OF ETHICS *(New York)*

It is the duty of all concerned with high school athletics:

1. To emphasize the proper ideals of sportsmanship, ethical conduct, and fair play.

2. To eliminate all possibilities which tend to destroy the best values of the game.

3. To stress the values derived from playing the game fairly.

4. To show cordial courtesy to visiting teams and officials.

5. To establish a happy relationship between visitors and hosts.

6. To respect the integrity and judgment of sports officials.

7. To achieve a thorough understanding and acceptance of the rules of the game and the standards of eligibility.

8. To encourage leadership, use of initiative, and good judgment by the players on the team.

9. To recognize that the purpose of athletics is to promote the physical, mental, moral, social, and emotional well-being of the individual players.

10. To remember that an athletic contest is only a game—not a matter of life or death for player, coach, school, official, fan, community, state or nation.[15]

CODES FOR THE ADMINISTRATION OF ATHLETICS *(Michigan)*

Statement of Relationship

In the final analysis the superintendent is responsible for the athletic

[15] New York State Public High School Athletic Association, 1960–1961, *Handbook,* p. 19.

activities of the school system. His duties will vary according to the size of the school system, ranging from the larger schools, where all duties are delegated, to the smaller schools, where he may be both the administrative and the executive officer. In either case it is his duty to have set up a definite school athletic policy and have a complete understanding of that policy by all concerned.

The principal usually is the official representative of the school and is directly responsible for the general attitude of the student body and the conduct of athletic affairs by the business manager, athletic director, and the coach.

It is the duty of the above named officers to derive from the athletic program a full measure of educational value in developing good sportsmanship on the part of the student body, faculty, parents, and general public. Mutual cooperation is essential in order to carry out properly the work of any or all of these officers.

An Athletic Code for Superintendents and Principals

The Superintendent and Principal are the final authorities responsible for the athletic activities of the school. In realization of this responsibility these guiding principles should prevail:

For the Superintendent

1. I will use all means possible to bring to my community a full realization of the value of athletics as an educational tool in training citizens.

2. I will have a definite understanding with principals and athletic directors concerning the school athletic policy and expect and give mutual support in carrying out that policy.

3. I will judge the success of those in charge of the athletic program by the conduct and attitude of contestants and spectators rather than on the number of games won and lost.

For the Principal

1. I will have a complete understanding of the athletic policy of this school system and of the individual responsibility of all concerned.

2. I will be honest in my certification of contestants and base that certification on complete information concerning the student's athletic and scholastic status. Questionable cases will be referred to the State Director before the privilege of competition is given.

3. I will give my loyal support to the coach in all his efforts to carry out the state and local athletic policies.

4. I will make every effort to instruct the student body in their responsibilities in making the athletic program a valuable one and point out desirable types of conduct at "home" and "away" games.

5. I will endeavor to foresee possible differences and misunderstandings with other schools and, as far as possible, settle them or provide means of settlement before they materialize.

6. I will insist that any misunderstandings that may arise be settled privately between official representatives of the schools concerned.

7. I will require the passing of a medical examination and parental consent before a student is allowed to compete.

8. I will have a definite understanding with the business manager or athletic director about officials, schedules, finances, care of fields and gymnasiums, handling of spectators, etc., and give him every assistance in carrying out his duties.

9. I will consider it unprofessional to withhold any seemingly authentic information from another school which calls in question the eligibility of any of its players.

10. I will attend as many of the athletic contests in which my school participates as school work will allow.

11. I will commend opposing schools for outstanding examples of fine citizenship.

AN ATHLETIC CODE FOR ATHLETIC DIRECTORS AND COACHES

The Athletic Director, or Business Manager, and Coach are the official representatives of the school in interscholastic athletic activities. In this important capacity these standards should be practiced:

By the Athletic Director

The athletic policy of the school should

1. Be definitely understood with director's responsibility clearly defined
2. Include only those schedules which are educationally and physically sound for the athlete
3. Cooperate with the community in making a character building athletic program
4. Refuse admission to athletic contests to persons who have shown a chronic lack of sportsmanship.

The securing of officials should include

1. Mutual confidence and agreement by both teams
2. Complete support of officials in cases of adverse rulings
3. Definite contractual agreements naming fee, expenses, and time and place of game.

Game preparation involves

1. Provision of programs giving rules changes, names of players and officials, and emphasizing good sportsmanship

2. Proper handling of crowds so there is no encroachment on playing space

3. Maintaining side lines for exclusive use of players, coaches and officials.

By the Coach

The school may expect

1. Work of the coach to be an integral part of the school system with its educational contribution

2. Mastery of the principles of pedagogy and consequent improvement in teaching as well as coaching

3. Loyalty to superiors in making athletics fit into the general school program

4. Insistence upon high scholarship and enforcement of all rules of eligibility.

The athletes may expect

1. A genuine and up-to-date knowledge of that which the coach proposes to teach

2. Fair, unprejudiced relationship with the boys

3. Careful attention to the physical condition of players at the time of each contest

4. Competent and trustworthy officials whose decisions will always be supported.

Sportsmanship includes

1. Teaching athletes to win by use of legitimate means only

2. Counteracting unfounded rumors of questionable practices by opponents.

The influence of the coach necessitates

1. His being the sort of man he wants boys under him to become

2. Discouragement of gambling, profanity, and obscene language at all times.

An Athletic Code for Officials and Athletes

Competent, impartial Officials and clean, hard-playing Athletes have made a place for interscholastic athletics in the educational program. Sportsmanship and fair play demand these practices:

By the Official

The contest demands

1. A professional relationship calling for the highest type of service
2. Thorough preparation
3. A rested body and an alert mind
4. Reporting for duty at least thirty minutes before time for the game
5. A neat, distinct uniform.

The rules demand

1. Rectifying mistakes in judgment without "evening up"
2. Adherence to right decisions despite disapproval of spectators
3. Control of temper at all times in warning crowds or inflicting penalties for unsportsmanlike conduct
4. Respect for and aid to fellow officials in making decisions
5. That interpretations and announcements be made clear to both teams
6. That plays or players of other teams not be discussed in the presence of prospective opponents.

The financial consideration demands

1. Fees and services should be a matter of explicit agreement
2. Charges should consider the ability of the school to pay and the type of service rendered
3. Willing consent of both original parties to a release before acceptance of a game paying a higher fee.

By the Athlete

The contest demands

1. Fair play at all times
2. A square deal to opponents by players and spectators
3. Playing for the joy of playing and for the success of the team
4. Playing hard to the end
5. Keeping one's head and PLAYING the game, not TALKING it
6. Respect for officials and the expectation that they will enforce the rules
7. That an athlete should not quit, cheat, bet, "grandstand," or abuse his body.

The school demands

1. Out-of-school and out-of-town conduct of the highest type
2. Faithful completion of school work as practical evidence of loyalty to school and team
3. Complete observance of training rules as a duty to school, team, and self.

Sportsmanship demands

1. Treatment of visiting team and officials as guests and the extension of every courtesy to them
2. Giving opponents full credit when they win and learning to correct one's own faults through his failures
3. Modesty and consideration when one's team wins
4. An athlete will not "crow" when his team wins or blame the officials when it loses.

The judicial function. As has been indicated in the discussion of publications in this chapter, state associations perform a judicial service to member schools. It is necessary that there be a final authority to whom questions may be addressed, controversies presented, and appeals made. The state association is invaluable in this connection. In fact, the ability to render such services has been both the cause of origin of most state-wide organizations and the reason for their continued existence. As a result of delegated powers by schools, they have made rules and regulations under which interscholastic athletic programs have been conducted. In most cases, also, they have been faced with the necessity for acting as the administrative body in connection with the enforcement of these judicial regulations.

Probably it is fortunate that associations have acted in this dual capacity because, knowing the background of the rules and regulations, they have been able to enforce them with the original intent in mind. In acting in a judicial capacity, state associations sometimes are faced with the unpleasant task of deciding disputes between schools. Again, a valuable service is performed in this way because an unprejudiced body can decide the case in question on its merits and by application of state association regulations, Hence, the exercise of the so-called judicial function of state associations may be one of their most valuable services.[16]

[16] Michigan High School Athletic Association, 1961–1962 *Handbook,* pp. 9–12.

Questions for Study and Discussion

1. What are some of the values claimed for state high school athletic associations? Do you agree with them? Why?

2. Several purposes for the existence of state high school athletic and activity associations are listed in this chapter. Indicate those which are similar in two or more states and those that are peculiar to one state alone.

3. What is the difference between an athletic and an activity association? Name states which are examples of each.

4. What are the three general classifications of state athletic or activity associations? Give main characteristics and examples of each.

5. Eight functions of state associations are listed in this chapter. Briefly discuss five which you consider to be the most important.

6. What is the status of registration and classification of athletic officials in your state? Discuss.

7. There is considerable difference of opinion regarding state-wide championship tournaments and meets for high schools. List arguments favoring and in opposition. What is your position on the matter? Why?

8. In what ways have state athletic associations established standards for the conduct of interscholastic athletics? Do you think these have been of value? Why?

9. Prepare a list of objectives or standards for the various individuals or organizations connected with the interscholastic athletic program.

10. What is meant by the judicial function of state high school athletic or activity associations?

4

Athletic Eligibility
Regulations

In the conduct of any well-organized program of activities there must be generally accepted rules or regulations. Eligibility rules for contestants in high school athletics fall into this category. Not all authorities are in agreement as to the type and extent of state association eligibility regulations, and in this discussion opposed opinions will be presented.

Purpose of Eligibility Regulations

Varying opinions. Sometimes there seems to be a paradox in the claims made for athletics and the manner in which the program is administered. Frequently it is said that if athletics are defensible from an educational standpoint, especially for the participant, then all students should be allowed to take part in them. Why have we built up sets of eligibility rules for contestants? Why have definite methods of procedure for the conduct of athletic contests, meets, and tournaments been established by state associations all over the country? The fact they are here is evidence that there must have been some need for them. Still, there are varying opinions concerning eligibility rules for participants. As early as 1929, Rogers was definite in his denunciation of eligibility rules in general:

The single eligibility rule which scholastic athletic associations may properly enforce is the presentation of a medical certificate of physical competence by each player before he may engage in games scheduled by the association. The wisdom of this requirement is so obvious that it should not have to be classified as a rule. Any local administrators who, in the past, have omitted this precautionary measure should immediately take steps to protect their pupils from avoidable strains, and themselves from blame by establishing this requirement.

Other eligibility rules ought to be abolished by interscholastic athletic associations. . . . Most of them are defended because they are supposed to prevent gross inequalities between teams; actually they do not accomplish this objective satisfactorily, but do seem to blind association officials to the need of active measures which will eliminate all but minor and insignificant inequalities between competitors. Moreover, many eligibility rules are unwarranted and cramping infringements upon prerogatives which local school authorities should guard most jealously. Finally, the administration of eligibility rules causes much social friction of a decidedly undesirable and unproductive nature.

Scholastic athletic associations cannot "leave well enough alone" in any event. They must either continue to add more interpretations, and a longer list of requirements, or simplify, or abandon those now in use. Improvement of social relationships in scholastic athletics can be accomplished only by taking the latter road. Along this same road also lie the greatest opportunities for protecting players' health and giving to local authorities the necessary freedom to determine eligibility requirements and "make exceptions" more in accordance with their own broader educational policies and programs.[1]

If the above thesis were to be accepted in its entirety, it would result in no regulations or commonly accepted understandings for the conduct of athletics. Possibly such an ideal situation could exist in an ideal state. Likewise, it might be conceivable that, in such a state, no general laws for the conduct and protection of the lives and property of its people would be necessary. To pursue the point made by Rogers a little further, might it not be logical to ask why regulations were adopted and established by state associations? Local schools could, and did, establish their own rules long before state organizations were formed. The answer seems rather obvious in that individual conceptions of standards varied too greatly, and it seemed necessary and logical to have state-wide codes. Although state association codes may sometimes seem arbitrary, provisions

[1] Frederick Rand Rogers, *The Future of Interscholastic Athletics* (New York: Bureau of Publications, Teachers College, Columbia University, 1929), pp. 100–101.

usually exist for necessary flexibility in their interpretation and administration. Also, state associations are administered by, and are responsible to, the schools themselves, and changes can be made as desired.

In contrast to this view just presented, it is significant to note the opinions held by others. Wagenhorst early discussed this subject as follows:

If high school athletic teams are to contest on a basis of equality, it is necessary above all other considerations to hold the players of the contesting teams to the same standards in regard to their amateur standing, enrollment requirements, scholarship, age, duration of eligibility, residence, and character. While the playing field or gymnasium, the sportsmanship and courtesy of the home team, and the justice of the officials are also very important factors, yet in the final analysis it was, almost without exception, the lack of uniformity in eligibility standards that impelled high school principals to attempt a remedy which resulted in state-wide organizations for setting up uniform standards and the machinery to enforce them. As it is, there is still great disparity in eligibility standards between states.[2]

The opinion expressed by Wagenhorst nearly forty years ago appears to be that generally held today by the vast majority of schoolmen throughout the nation, as is evidenced by the presence of general eligibility standards established by state associations.

Summary. Thus, it will be seen that these three eminent authorities in the field of physical and health education early were of the opinion that interscholastic athletic eligibility standards serve a purpose in the administration of the athletic program. To summarize this discussion, the following are suggested as purposes of athletic association eligibility regulations:

1. They provide like standards for all schools belonging to the state association.

2. They set up definite regulations which may be made known both to students and patrons of the school.

3. They relieve individual schools of possible criticism that the

[2] L. H. Wagenhorst, *Administration and Cost of High School Interscholastic Athletics* (New York: Bureau of Publications, Teachers College, Columbia University, 1926), pp. 43–44.

standards of eligibility in their institutions are lower than, or vary from, those in other schools.

4. Individual school administrators are not called upon to settle doubtful cases when there are established regulations and state agencies to whom appeal may be made.

5. They often serve as minimum scholastic standards, which students must meet and sometimes surpass.

6. They aid in improvement of relations between schools because both sides know that certification of contestants has been made in accordance with common standards.

7. They present possibilities for better public relations as well as for better interschool relations.

8. While generally specific in their statements, eligibility regulations usually are elastic enough, especially from a scholastic standpoint, to allow local schools to adjust their standards to them. In most states allowance is made for individual differences, with the result that scholastic requirements can be met accordingly.

It seems reasonable to assume that there are inherent values in interscholastic athletic eligibility regulations. Some educators would open wide the door to athletic competition, justifying this action in the belief that what is good for one is good for all. Others believe that no scholastic requirement (credit hours during preceding or current semester) should be demanded of athletes. It also is maintained that all should be allowed to take part in athletics, not just those who come within the realm of state association eligibility rules.

These assertions all deserve consideration and usually are made in all sincerity. Athletics are provided for all in some manner in most schools in the form of intramural activities. These take care of the great mass of students from a competition standpoint. Properly, the interschool athletic program should be the apex of the intramural program. And with the ascendancy in selection should go an ascendancy in responsibility and standards. Two separate organizations— two schools—compete with each other. It is a privilege to engage in such competition, and there should be corresponding responsibilities. Good school citizenship is a requisite for membership on school teams. Scholastic attainment, in accordance with the standards of the school, is another responsibility of the contestant. There should be compliance with sound and tried regulations that have been found necessary to keep interscholastic athletics on their present high level. All in all, then, it does not seem unnecessary, unwise, or unsound educationally to have well-established eligibility regulations for the guidance and protection of the competitor, the school, and the spectator. These regulations have done a pretty good job and merit continued consideration until something that is better appears.

Common Eligibility Regulations

Two types of regulations pertaining to athletics will be considered in this and the succeeding chapter. This chapter will deal with those which are quite common and pertain to the athlete himself as far as his eligibility for interscholastic competition is concerned. Chapter 5 concerns itself with those regulations which pertain to the administration of the athletic program and naturally consider schools rather than contestants.

Age. The trend in the upper age limit for contestants is downward. Whereas several years ago the upper age limit was twenty in a majority of the states, now it is nineteen years in thirty-one of them. Undoubtedly the number of states with the nineteen-year limit will be increased in the near future. New York, one of the first states to do so, established this limit in 1938. New Jersey's rules provide that a student is ineligible upon reaching his nineteenth birthday, except that he may finish the season in a sport concerned. Texas had an eighteen-year limit for some time, but now has a nineteen-year age rule. In some states a student becomes ineligible on his birthday; in others he may finish the season or semester after having reached his nineteenth or twentieth birthday, respectively, as the state rule provides. It would seem that allowing a student to finish a season in a sport is fair, both to him and to the other members on the team. In 1961 there were thirty-one states with nineteen-year age limits for competition and nineteen with twenty-year age rules.

Studies made in Michigan and Ohio a few years ago indicated that, proportionately, a small number (between 3 and 5 per cent) of those eligible to compete, and who take part in athletics, are over nineteen. With students finishing high schools younger than formerly, it is logical to assume that upper age limits for athletic competition should be lowered to ensure greater equality. Several states are giving consideration to lower limits for competition in various activities. In New York a boy must be fourteen years old before he may compete in any interschool athletic competition. In Michigan a boy must be fifteen before he may compete in cross country or in any track event of 400 yards or more. Emphasis in some states has been placed on minimum age restrictions that will protect contestants, as well as on regulations that should result in greater equality in competition.

Time of enrollment. Usually the time of enrollment during a current semester is within the first three weeks of the term. If a student enrolls during that period he is eligible for athletic competition that semester. New York provides that a participant must have been in regular attendance at least 80 per cent of the time. Pennsylvania and Oklahoma require a student to attend a school for a period of 60 days after he has been absent for 20 days or more during a semester. In general, enrollment in schools for a period of from 2 to 3 weeks constitutes a semester of attendance in most states. In Illinois a student must be enrolled by the eleventh day of the semester unless late enrollment results from illness or quarantine, in which cases this regulation may be waived under prescribed conditions. Texas requires that a student must be in attendance for 30 days prior to a contest or have been enrolled by the first day of the second week of a semester. New Jersey has a similar rule, except that enrollment may be as late as the first Monday in October. Michigan requires that a student must be enrolled in a secondary school by Monday of the fourth week of the semester in order to be eligible during that semester. The general provision in most states is that failure to be enrolled in a secondary school by a prescribed time (6 days to 3 weeks) results in ineligibility during that semester.

Seasons of competition and undergraduate standing. Practically all state associations have regulations which allow participation by students in sports for four seasons in grades nine to twelve, inclusive. In virtually all states, postgraduate students are barred from membership on regular high school teams. In many states, however, students who have completed the graduation requirements in less than the allowed number of semesters may compete during the full number of semesters for which their regulations provide. Usually they must not have been voted their diplomas by the board of education nor have accepted them.

Number of semesters of attendance. This regulation now generally is uniform in all states with a maximum of eight semesters of enrollment allowed. Four years, in grades nine to twelve, inclusive, represent the normal period of high school attendance. This is the equivalent of eight semesters of enrollment and, in most cases, takes care of the legitimate time during which a student should be allowed to compete in athletics. It is quite common to require that the last two semesters of attendance be consecutive. In most states a semester of attendance is not charged to a student if he withdraws from school within the period during which he must enroll in order to compete during that semester.

Indiana allows a student to compete in basketball during his ninth semester in case he entered school at the start of a mid-year term and did not compete in the sport during his first semester of attendance. New York makes no reference to the number of semesters of enrollment of a student, provided he does not compete in a sport for more than four seasons. Some states report no limit in number of semesters of enrollment allowed, but it is evident that virtually all of them have the eight-semester limit for interscholastic athletic competition. This is as it ought to be, because four years of high school attendance, with two semesters in each year, is regular. If the "thirteenth and fourteenth grades" are added to our school systems to any great extent, it will, of course, be necessary to revamp general athletic regulations relative to semesters of attendance as well as other matters.

Limited team membership. It is an almost universal rule among states that a high school student may not play on another team in the same sport during the same season after he has represented his school in the sport concerned. There are a few exceptions to this regulation. Some states provide that there may be outside participation if the high school student has the written consent of the principal of the high school prior to the contest. Minnesota and Michigan allow dual participation in softball and baseball but in no other sport. Virtually all states rule a student ineligible if he has ever been enrolled in a college, or in an institution offering work above that usually pursued in high schools. Again, high school students are ineligible if they have competed on college athletic teams. In practically all states participation by high school students is allowed on independent teams during the summer vacations, provided, generally, that such teams are amateur. Exceptions are discussed under Amateurism in this chapter.

In some states permission must be obtained from the principal of the high school before a boy may play on an independent team during the summer. This requirement has merit as a safeguard to the boy because it protects him from possible violation of his state association amateur rule.

Parental consent and physical examinations. These regulations are not universal. Undoubtedly, one reason is the difference in court rulings on the liability of schools or school officials in case of accidents. A great many state associations, however, prepare regular Parent's Consent Cards and Physical Examination Forms, which are filed either in the school or the state association office. In a few states, Indiana, for example, and in those having athletic accident insurance or benefit plans, either a statement of receipt of parental consent must be sent to the state association office, or the actual parental approval and physician's examination card must be filed there.

There is no doubt that the securing of parental approval is a good public-relations gesture, if only because it acquaints the school patron with the athletic policy of the school regarding injuries. Not too much emphasis, however, should be placed on the legal value of such permissions in view of some court decisions involving schools or coaches in cases in which students have been injured in athletic competition. In very few states can local boards of education be held responsible for costs of injuries incurred by students while engaging in any school activity, athletic or otherwise. This does not mean, however, that local school athletic associations, having funds, may not be sued with quite a possibility of obtaining judgments. Also, if negligence on the part of agents of the board of education—superintendents, principals, coaches, or assistants—can be proved, action is very likely against any or all concerned. This has happened in California and New York. The theory held by the court is that no one has the authority to sign away the rights of a minor as far as his opportunity to recover for personal injuries is concerned. In most cases parental consent obviates any misunderstanding and means that the parent is assuming the obligation in case of injury, rather than the school or local athletic association.

Figures 4-1, 4-2, and 4-3 show the Physician's and Parent's Cer-

KANSAS STATE HIGH SCHOOL ACTIVITIES ASSOCIATION
Physician's and Parent's Certificate for Athletics—(For Both Boys and Girls)

I hereby certify that_____was examined

Name

by me and found physically fit to engage in all high school athletics.

_____   _____
Date of Examination   Signature of Physician

PARENT OR GUARDIAN'S PERMIT

I hereby give my consent for_____whose date of birth

Name

is_____to compete for_____

Month   Day   Year   Name of School

High School in K.S.H.S.A.A. approved sports, and go with the coach or other representative of the
school on any trips.

It is understood that neither the K.S.H.S.A.A. nor the high school assumes any responsibility in case an
accident occurs. The undersigned agrees to be responsible for the safe return of all athletic equipment issued
by the school to the above named pupil.

Date_____   _____
                                                      Signature of Parent or Guardian

Note:—The K.S.H.S.A.A. rules require the above permit for competition be filed with the principal before a pupil may take part in high school athletics.

Return This Copy to the Commissioner of the K. S. H. S. A. A.

Fig 4-1. Physician's and Parent's Certificate Form
(Kansas).

MINNESOTA STATE HIGH SCHOOL LEAGUE
ATHLETIC ACCIDENT BENEFIT PLAN
EXAMINATION AND PERMIT CARD

Name of School_____

Name of Pupil_____

PARENT'S OR GUARDIAN'S PERMIT

I hereby give my consent for the above named pupil to compete in Minnesota State High
School League approved sports, **except those crossed out below,** and to go with the coach on
school sponsored trips.

Football	Track	Softball	Hockey	Swimming	Wrestling	Golf
Basketball	Baseball ·	Volleyball	Skiing	Phy. Educ.	Skating	Tennis

A pupil will not be covered until his Examination and Permit Card and registration fee have been
received in the office of the Executive Secretary of the Minnesota State High School League.

Neither the Minnesota State High School League nor the high school assumes any responsibility in case
an accident occurs. The League's allowance will be based upon published schedules; any charges in excess
thereof are a responsibility of the parent.

The Plan is a mutual benefit plan, and is not insurance.

Report of any injury must be received in the Executive Secretary's office within 15 days from date of
injury. A claim must be completed within three months from date of injury, or a request for extension of
time be made by the school within said period.

Date _____   _____
                                                      Signature of Parent or Guardian

UPON COMPLETION OF THIS FORM RETURN TO YOUR HIGH SCHOOL
ATHLETIC DIRECTOR WITH PROPER FEE.
(OVER)

Fig. 4-2. Parents or Guardians Form (Minnesota).

77

tificate for Athletics forms used by Kansas and Minnesota. It will be observed that both of these states require parent's consent as well as physician's approval. Indiana has a form similar to that in Minnesota, with the Parent's Certificate on one side of the card and the Physician's Certificate on the other. Indiana requires the high school principal to certify to the state association office that the Parent's and Physician's Certificate is properly filed in his office before a student is allowed to participate.

Wisconsin and Minnesota have athletic accident benefit plans in effect. In connection with their plans, cards similar to Figures 4-2 and 4-3 are filled out and signed by the parent or guardian of the

---

**MINNESOTA STATE HIGH SCHOOL LEAGUE
PHYSICIAN'S CERTIFICATE**

I certify that I have examined........................

representing.....................High School with results
noted as follows:

Heart	
Blood Pressure	
Lungs	
Hernia	
Orthopedic Defects (a) Feet (b) Spine	
Urine (a) Spec. Grav. (b) Albumen (c) Sugar (d) Casts	
Height	
Weight	
Age	

As indicated by the above record of examination, I do recommend this student physically fit to participate in Inter-school Athletics.

Signed.......................... } M.D.
             Examining Physician   } O.D.

Date of Examination........................

Remarks:

Fig. 4-3. (Reverse of Fig. 4-2). Physicians Certificate Form (Minnesota).

student and by the examining physician. One copy is forwarded to the state association office, one filed in the local school office in Minnesota. In Wisconsin the card is filed in the local school office until an injury occurs, at which time it is forwarded to the benefit

---

SOUTH DAKOTA HIGH SCHOOL ATHLETIC ASSOCIATION

....
Name of high school
———

STUDENT'S STATEMENT

I, ..., hereby certify that I was born on the.....................day of

..................., 19......., at (city).. (state)..........................;

that I have not graduated from or met the graduation requirements of any four year high school or its equivalent; that I have not represented any high school or high schools in any athletic competition during four school years; that I have never accepted any remuneration or any award exceeding one dollar in value, for any athletic participation, except as provided for in the rules of the South Dakota High School Athletic Association; and that I shall willingly comply with all requirements of the South Dakota High School Athletic Association and regulations of the local high school and of the faculty representative in charge of athletic teams both while at home and away.

Date......................................, 19........   Student's Signature ....

PARENT'S STATEMENT

I, ..., hereby certify that I am the parent or legal guardian of

....; that the date of birth given in the above statement is correct; and that I give my consent for him or her to take part in high school athletic competition.

Date......................................, 19........   Parent's Signature ....

THESE STATEMENTS MUST BE FILED WITH THE SUPERINTENDENT OR PRINCIPAL OF THE HIGH SCHOOL BEFORE THE STUDENT IS ELIGIBLE FOR ANY ATHLETIC COMPETITION.

(Additional blanks may be secured from the Secretary)

Fig. 4-4. Student's and Parent's Statement Form *(South Dakota)*.

R. 55

JOHN R. ROGERS HIGH SCHOOL
Department of Physical Education

———

....:... has my permission to participate in competitive school athletics in the John R. Rogers High School. I hereby

certify that he was born at ....:. in the year ....

Month .... Day ....

While I expect school authorities to exercise reasonable precaution to avoid injury, I understand that they assume no financial or moral obligation for any injury that may occur.

I am advised that students are held responsible for all players' equipment owned and issued by the school.

Date .... 19..........

....
Signature of Parent or Guardian

Fig. 4-5. Parent's Permission Form *(John R. Rogers High School, Spokane, Washington)*.

plan office. On the reverse side of the Wisconsin cards is a dental examination chart which must be completed and certified by a qualified dentist.

South Dakota's form concerns only the student and his parent

PLEASE PRINT: (Last Name)   (First Name)   (Initial)   (School)

Date................................19...... Date of Birth.. Place of Birth................................
                                            (Month—Day—Year)

MICHIGAN HIGH SCHOOL ATHLETIC ASSOCIATION
STUDENT PARTICIPATION AND PARENTAL APPROVAL FORM
PHYSICAL EXAMINATION SUMMARY (Form 4)

This application to participate in athletics at the above high school is voluntary on my part and is made with the understanding that I have never received money or merchandise in any amount, or any emblematic award worth more than three dollars ($3.00), for participating in athletic events, and that I have never competed under an assumed name. After I have represented my high school in any sport, I promise not to compete in any outside athletic contest in this sport until after the high school season has been completed.

KEEP IN HIGH SCHOOL OFFICE   (Signature of Student)..

Parent's or Guardian's Permission

I hereby give my consent for the above high school student to engage in physical education, intramurals, and interscholastic athletics at the above high school in M.H.S.A.A. approved sports EXCEPT THOSE CROSSED OUT ON OTHER SIDE OF THIS CARD, and to accompany the team as a member on its out-of-town trips.

We also carry accident or health insurance with..
                                                              (Name of Company)

(Signature of Parent or Guardian)..

(Address)......................................   ....
                        (Street)   (City or Town)
NOTE: This form should be detached and filed in the office of the high school principal or the office of the superintendent.

Fig. 4-6. Student Participation and Parental Approval Form (Michigan).

PLEASE PRINT: (Name of Student)   (City and School)

PHYSICAL EXAMINATION SUMMARY (Form 4)

(For use in compliance with provisions of Regulations I and III, Section 3)   **KEEP IN HIGH SCHOOL OFFICE**
To be filled out and signed by examining physician.

1. Heart condition: SATISFACTORY-UNSATISFACTORY (Cross out one)

2. Lungs: SATISFACTORY-UNSATISFACTORY (Cross out one)

3. Is there evidence of hernia?....................Would athletic competition be likely to be injurious?................................

4. Is the general condition of feet, ears, eyes, and nose satisfactory?................................

5. Are there apparent cavities in any teeth?....................Is there a bridge or false teeth?................................

I certify that I have on this date examined the above student and recommend him (or her) as being physically able to compete in supervised athletic activities NOT CROSSED OUT BELOW:

BASEBALL	FOOTBALL	ROWING	SPEEDBALL	TENNIS
BASKETBALL	GOLF	SKATING	SWIMMING	WRESTLING
CROSS COUNTRY	GYMNASTICS	SOCCER	SKIING	VOLLEY BALL
FIELD HOCKEY	ICE HOCKEY	SOFTBALL	TRACK	

....................................19. ....
(Date)   (Signature of Examining Physician)

NOTE: This form should be completely filled out and filed in the office of the high school principal or superintendent or schools prior to student's participation.

Form A—60—120M

Fig. 4-7. (Reverse of Figure 4-6). Physical Examination Summary Form (Michigan).

(Fig. 4-4). It calls the attention of students to general eligibility rules of the South Dakota High School Athletic Association before they sign the blank. This information also is made known to the parent or guardian because he signs the same blank.

The parental consent card in use at the John R. Rogers High School, Spokane, Washington (Fig. 4–5), is an excellent example of a local form of this type. It acquaints the parent or guardian with

---

Virginia High School League

Box 3697 University Station, Charlottesville, Virginia

Athletic Participation — Parental Consent — Physician's Certificate Form

(Separate form required for each school year. File in Office of Principal)

Regulation: "To be eligible to represent his school in any interschool athletic contest, a student shall have submitted to the principal of his school, prior to becoming a member of any school athletic squad, League Form No. 2 (Athletic Participation-Parental Concent-Physician's Certificate Form), completely filled in and properly signed, attesting that he has been examined and found to be physically fit for athletic competition, and that his parents consent to his participation."

PART I—ATHLETIC PARTICIPATION
(To be filled in and signed by the candidate)

Name: _____ School Year: _____

Home address: _____ Home address of Parents: _____

Date of birth: _____ Place of birth: _____

This is my _____ semester in _____ High School, and my _____ semester since entering the lowest of the last four years of any high or prep school. I attended _____ school last semester. I passed· in _____ subjects last semester, and am carrying _____ subjects this semester.
I am familiar with the eligibility rules of the Virginia High School League (SEE REVERSE SIDE OF THIS SHEET) and believe that I am eligible to represent my present high school in this sport. If accepted as a squad member, I agree to make every effort to keep up my school work, and to abide by the rules and regulations of the school authorities and of the Virginia High School League.

Date: _____ Signed: _____
                                                    (Student)

PART II—PARENTAL CONSENT
(To be filled in and signed by the parent or guardian)

In accordance with the rules of the Virginia High School League, I give my consent and approval to the participation of the student named above for the following sports:

_____
(List all for current year in which student is expected to participate)
                      not
I will ⌃hold the school authorities responsible in case of accident or injury as a result of this participation.

Date: _____ Signed: _____
                                                    (Parent or Guardian)

PART III—PHYSICIAN'S CERTIFICATE
(To be filled in and signed by the examining physician)

In accordance with the rules of the Virginia High School League, I certify that I have on this date examined the general
                                                                         IS
physical condition of _____ In my opinion he IS NOT physically fit to participate
                              (full name of student)
in _____ as a member of the high school squad in that sport during the current season.

I noted the following conditions:

Heart: _____ Hernia: _____

Respiratory: _____ Weight: _____

Feet: _____ Teeth: _____ Ears: _____

Eyes: _____ Nose and Throat: _____

Bones: _____ Ligaments: _____ Muscles: _____

The following recommendations are made for the correction of abnormal conditions found: _____

_____

Date: _____ Signed: _____, M.D.
                                                    (Examining physician)

Fig. 4-8. Athletic Participation Form *(Virginia).*

the local policy of the school in regard to responsibility for both injuries and care of athletic equipment used by the student.

Michigan has a combination Student Participation–Parental Approval–Physical Examination Form, which the state athletic association supplies to all schools in the state (Figs. 4–6 and 4–7). Evidence of a physical examination of a participant during the current school year must be on file in the school office prior to competition by the student.

The Virginia High School League has a Form for Athletic Participation (Fig. 4–8) which appears to be very satisfactory. It gives the student more responsibility in making statements and furnishing information relative to his athletic eligibility.

Too much attention can hardly be paid to the importance of adequate physical examination of athletes or, in fact, of all high school students. Many schools are stressing this matter with excellent results. In some instances tuberculosis tests are required of all athletes as well as complete venereal disease examinations. These are important, and certainly heart and lungs should receive first consideration. Adequate physical examinations do at least three things: (1) they protect the participant; (2) they protect school authorities in case of any unusual occurrence; and (3) they maintain higher and safer standards for athletic competition. Certainly rules requiring physical examinations, which are found in practically all states, stand in the first rank of importance.

Current and previous semester scholarship. The problem of relation of scholastic standing to athletic competition is one of our oldest. We came through the period of early development in the control of interschool athletics, when there were no scholastic requirements for athletes, to the present time when, in virtually all states, to be eligible for athletics a student must be doing work of a passing grade in the prescribed amount of work. At present all fifty states require that a student be doing passing work for the current semester in at least three subjects (15 hours). California requires twenty.

As stated above the general and almost universal trend in thought and practice is that participation in athletics and scholarship are complementary to each other. New York, however, broke away from this tradition some time ago. With the application of the Regulations of the Commissioner of Education,[3] which became effective in September, 1938, there is no direct requirement regarding the previous or current semester's scholastic work of a contestant in interschool games. New York felt that the time had come when interscholastic athletics should become a definite and integral part of the physical education program of a school and made this a reality by the Board of Regents' action. Commenting on the omission of the scholastic requirement in the Regulations, Dr. Jesse Feiring Williams had this to say in its favor at that time:

> The regulations of the Commissioner of Education are a distinct advance in administrative procedure and I highly commend this forward move in education. I am particularly pleased that the requirement that boys must pass three subjects in order to participate was omitted. If athletics are desirable experiences for boys in schools, they should be allowed to gain the advantages of sport, precisely the same way they are allowed to engage in other parts of the school program.[4]

The New York departure from traditional scholastic requirements for interschool competition has points in its favor as previously indicated. It assumes that school standards in that state generally will be uniform. Undoubtedly, New York is one of the best states in which to inaugurate such a plan because of its central educational control program as administered by the Board of Regents. Although there is some difference of opinion regarding the merits of this plan, the New York experiment has been watched with interest, especially in regard to the elimination of sholastic requirements for athletes. No one questions the logic that athletics may properly be classed as part of the physical education program. It is difficult, however, to reach the conclusion that scholastic requirements alone should be eliminated because they might interfere with the possibility of a student's competing in athletics, while the commonly accepted rules regarding duration of competition, time of enrollment, transfer, and limitations of competition are retained. The

[3] "Regulations of the Commissioner of Education Governing Health and Physical Education," New York State Public High School Athletic Association, *Bulletin*, October, 1937.

[4] J. F. Williams, New York State Public High School Athletic Association, *Bulletin*, October, 1937, p. 11.

question might logically be asked why these restrictive regulations were not discarded.

In contrast to New York's departure from the traditional pattern for academic requirement, Wisconsin has the common type regulations regarding scholarship:

> In order to be eligible for interscholastic competition, a contestant must
> a. Have completed all of the required work below the 9th grade or the equivalent of two of the six units of a 6-6, 8-4 or 6-3-3 organization.
> b. Have a program calling for not less than fifteen hours of work per week.
> c. Be doing passing work in at least fifteen hours.
> d. Have at least fifteen hours of credit for the last regular semester in attendance. In case of incomplete work, the work must be made up within two weeks after the beginning of the subsequent semester under the direction and the supervision and with issuance of credits by the same school in which the work was taken.[5]

The provisions in California regarding academic standing also are quite generally those followed in other states except that the student must be doing satisfactory work in four rather than three subjects in order to be eligible for interscholastic athletic competition.

No boys shall compete in a game with another school who are not making a passing grade in twenty semester periods of new work. By new work is meant subjects which boys have not already taken or in which they have not previously made a passing grade. (*Note:* For crediting purposes the semester closes with the last day of school in the given semester. For playing contests one semester does not end until the next one begins.) [6]

Michigan's previous and current semester record rules indicate the period of enrollment involved in determining academic standing and also are illustrative of provisions in several other states whereby students may make up work for which they were absent at the end of a term.

[5] Wisconsin Interscholastic Athletic Association *Thirty-Seventh Annual Year Book* (1960), p. 20.
[6] California Interscholastic Federation, *Constitution and By-Laws,* 1959, pp. 2–3.

Previous Semester Record

No student shall compete in any athletic contest during any semester who does not have to his credit on the books of the school he represents at least fifteen (15) credit hours of work for the last semester during which he shall have been enrolled in grades nine to twelve, inclusive, for a period of three weeks or more, or during which he shall have taken part in any interscholastic athletic contests.

In determining the number of hours of credit received during a semester under this Rule, the usual credit allowed by the school shall be given. However, reviews and extra-curricular work, and work for which credit previously has been received, shall not be credited. Deficiencies, including incompletes, conditions, and failures from a previous semester may not be made up during a subsequent semester, summer session, night school, or by tutoring, for qualification purposes that semester.

The record at the end of the semester shall be final for athletic purposes, except that conditions or incompletes, resulting from inability to finish the work of the semester on account of disabling illness during the last two weeks of the semester, or for other reasons equally valid during the same period, may be removed after the close of the semester, provided application is made to the State Director by the superintendent or principal. In such cases it is to be certified that the student was in attendance and carried his work successfully and continuously up to within two weeks of the end of the semester.

Interpretations

The word "semester" as used in this Rule is defined as one of the two terms of the usual school year, exclusive of summer sessions.

The mark recorded in the usual manner is regarded as final for the semester for athletic purposes. In some instances it may be a card marking, teacher's class book, teacher's report, or a permanent school record. The record for athletic purposes is the mark given at the end of the semester.

Any change in the status of eligibility of a student under this Rule occurs at the beginning of the first full day of the new semester rather than on the last day of the previous semester.

This Rule is interpreted to mean that a regularly enrolled undergraduate high school student may take courses in advance of the high school level during the first or second semester of a current school year. These courses may be included for high school graduation credit and for athletic eligibility purposes when arrangements for previous and current semester eligibility reports are made.

CURRENT SEMESTER RECORD

No student shall compete in any athletic contest who does not have a passing grade, from the beginning of the semester to the date seven (7) calendar days prior to the contest, in studies aggregating at least fifteen (15) credit hours of recitation per week. In determining the number of credit hours of recitation per week under this Rule, reviews and extracurricular work, and work for which credit previously has been received, shall not be counted.

Interpretations

"Credit hours of recitation" is defined as the number of hours of credit given for the course at the end of the semester.

Courses taken in a school other than the one in which a student is enrolled, which are not available to him in his own school, may be counted toward athletic eligibility, provided arrangements for current eligibility reports are made in accordance with the provisions of this Rule.

This Rule is interpreted to mean that a regularly enrolled undergraduate high school student may take courses in advance of the high school level during the first or second semester of a current school year. These courses may be included for high school graduation credit and for athletic eligibility purposes when arrangements for current semester eligibility reports are made in accordance with provisions of this Section.

Only that work is to be counted for credit which is given in regular classes. Work taken by a student from a tutor or special instructor, exclusively, may not be counted for athletic eligibility purposes during a current semester.

Note: Attention is directed to the fact that a student's eligibility depends upon a "passing grade from the beginning of the semester to the date seven (7) days prior to the contest." [7]

As indicated previously, it seems as though there is a defense for the scholastic, as well as other eligibility, requirements which such a large majority of the state associations of the country have seen fit to establish. True, athletics are activities in which all high school students should have the right to participate. With this right to participate, however, it should be recognized that certain responsibilities obtain. The situation in an athletic contest between schools is somewhat different from that in an activity within the school or

[7] Michigan High School Athletic Association, 1961–1962. *Handbook*, pp. 33–35.

class itself. Competition should not be considered as *against* another school but *with* that school. Since the interschool competition should be between teams that are the apex of broad intraschool programs, membership on those teams inevitably will be selective. Therefore schoolmen have felt that team members should meet minimum established standards, including character, school citizenship, and scholarship as well as athletic prowess. Also, it is apparent that the establishment of a state-wide minimum scholastic requirement has enabled local schools to use this standard to advantage in their own institutions.

Most schoolmen also have felt that, with a general regulation requiring successful work in at least three subjects, their schools have been relieved to some extent of possible question on the part of others regarding eligibility of some of their team members. In a great many schools the members of athletic teams must be doing passing work in all their subjects. Experience seems to indicate that scholastic requirements for athletes have done considerable to improve school citizenship and maintain proper morale and attitude toward school subjects. Usually school standards within a local system are sufficiently flexible that no injustices are done. If this is the case, undoubtedly minimum scholastic standards have done a great amount of good in setting up achievement goals that athletes have had to meet in order to play.

Transfer and undue influence rules. In all states students are as eligible in a school to which they transfer as they were in the school they left, provided their parents or legal guardians have moved into the new school district, unless the exercise of undue influence can be proved. Undue influence is a phase of athletic transfers that has come to the attention of state associations comparatively recently, judging by the adoption of new by-laws dealing with this matter. Iowa has such a rule:

No student shall be eligible to participate in the contests of this Association if it shall be known that he, or any member of his family, is receiving any remuneration, either directly or indirectly, to influence him or his family to reside in a given school district in order to establish eligibility on the team of said school.[8]

[8] Iowa High School Athletic Association, 1960–1961 *Record Book,* p. 19.

The Illinois High School Association on page 17 of its 1960–1961 *Handbook* states the following rule:

The use of undue influence by any person connected or not connected with the school to secure or retain the attendance of a student whose parents do not reside in the district where the student attends school, or to secure or retain the residence of the parents of a student in the district shall cause the student to be ineligible for a period to be determined by the Board of Directors, but in no case shall the period of ineligibility be less than one year.

In the interpretation of this rule the Board shall, unless vital and impressive reasons to the contrary be submitted, accept as prima facie evidence of undue influence: The award of free tuition, free textbooks, allowance for transportation, priority in assignment of jobs or any other privileges or considerations not accorded to other students similarly conditioned whether athletes or non athletes. However, since, in general, affiliated member schools or schools conducted by colleges or universities for purposes of educational experimentation, research and practice teaching have no "districts," the solicitation of beginning freshmen by representatives of those schools shall not be regarded as "undue influence."

Indiana also has a definite provision relative to undue influence:

The use of undue influence by any person or persons to secure or retain a student or to secure or retain one or both of the parents or guardians of a student as residents, may cause the student to be ineligible for High School athletics for a period subject to the determination of the Board of Control and shall jeopardize the standing of the High School in the I.H.S.A.A. By action of the Athletic Council and Board of Control this rule is interpreted to include any undue influence that may be exerted by anyone on a student who has not yet entered the ninth grade, to enroll in a high school other than his home high school or the one he ordinarily would be expected to attend or any school where he and/or his parents previously had filed a choice of subject matter card or other written evidence of preliminary enrollment or registration.[9]

Ohio has a rule which is almost identical in wording with the Indiana rule. Oklahoma refers to this problem as "recruiting of athletes."

[9] Indiana High School Athletic Association, *Fifty-Seventh Annual Handbook*, 1960, p. 43.

There shall be no recruiting of athletes. Recruiting shall include the influencing of a pupil or his parents or guardian, to move from one school district to another in order that the pupil might engage in athletics. If this rule is violated the pupil becomes ineligible.[10]

At least these five states have had sufficient difficulty with this problem to adopt by-laws concerning it. It is very probable that other states may have been faced with cases of solicitation, recruiting, or exercise of undue influence and have handled such situations without the enactment of special by-laws.

When transfers are made between school systems, between schools in the same system, from public to private schools, and vice versa, not accompanied by change in residence of parents, regulations in various states are about equally divided as to whether there shall be a semester or full year of ineligibility. Transfer and undue influence rules have been designed to prevent the prevalence of "tramp athletes" and proselyting, and to make student athletic competition incidental to change in parental residence rather than an occasion for such change. Most states have found that the strict interpretation of these rules has been instrumental in the improvement of relations between schools. It has practically eliminated the student who "shops around" for his athletic competition and reserves the opportunity for team membership to those legitimately entitled to it.

Awards. Theoretically, all sports participation should be for the love of the game and for the enjoyment of playing. Children play this way, and older people do not expect awards or rewards for participation in activities that, to them, are sport. It is almost an indictment of adults that they have been responsible for the establishment of award policies in schools and colleges and in independent and club competition. Of course, this practice has come about as a result of the desire of well-meaning groups to honor those to whom they felt honor was due. In some instances this practice has outstepped all realms of propriety and has given false importance to interschool athletic competition. The result has been that state athletic associations have set the limits for awards which may be presented to athletes, either by local schools or by outside

[10] Oklahoma High School Athletic Association, 1960–1961, *Constitution and Rules,* p. 10.

individuals or organizations. Twenty-five states limit the value of an award to from $1 to $5, and the trend is to make them of little or no intrinsic value. Michigan limits specified awards to $3, as do Montana and Wyoming. In Pennsylvania a student may accept a sweater awarded by the high school. The unattached school letter is most commonly given and is all that may be accepted by a student in ten states. Several states have no limit on what may be accepted by an athlete.[11] In Utah a school letter only may be awarded. Medals and certificates also are presented. A more complete discussion of awards and award policies followed in schools of various sizes will be found in Chapter 9.

Rather than enumerate all the states having different award regulations, the procedure to be followed here will be that of listing typical award rules with a few examples. These should not be confused with amateur rules which are discussed in a separate section of this chapter. Alabama's award rule is common in most of the states with a $1–$5 limit:

No reward of any kind having a utilitarian value of more than two dollars, other than medals, shall be made to players. Violations of this rule on the part of school officials shall subject that school to suspension for one year. Acceptance of these rewards by a player from any source whatsoever shall disqualify him.

No individual club, or organization of any kind shall present or give to players any awards of the above mentioned nature.

Group action in the raising of funds by such means as dances, shows, entertainments, sale of refreshments, pictures, etc., is regarded as a violation of this rule.

Purchase by pupils when any part of the purchase price is donated or raised through methods similar to those mentioned above is regarded as a violation.

Presentation of sweaters or similar athletic awards or trophies at graduation is regarded as an evasion of this rule and calls for disciplinary action.

Medals won in open competition such as track meets, swimming meets, etc., or in scholastic contests for athletes is not a violation.[12]

In line with these definite statements, other states indicate that

[11] National Federation, 1960–1961 *Handbook* p. 13.
[12] Alabama High School Athletic Association, 1960–1961 *Handbook,* pp. 100–101.

outside organizations may not make such awards; students may not raise funds by shows, dances, and the like, for purchase of them; and the school may not present sweaters, other athletic awards, or trophies at graduation time. Medals and trophies won at state association-approved meets and tournaments are excepted in the administration of this rule. Iowa does not allow a student to accept anything for his competition "except the unattached letter, monogram, or other insignia of the school." [13]

Oregon has a similar award rule with the summer exception:

Any student who has received any article, or compensation for athletic skill, other than the school's official athletic letter, or awards given by the Oregon High School Activities Association shall be declared ineligible. This rule shall not apply to summer activities sponsored by amateur groups or organizations provided the Amateur Athletic Union (A. A. U.) Code is observed.[14]

Indiana is a little more lenient regarding awards, and its rule represents a policy followed by several other states:

Rule 1. The giving and receiving of awards and medals shall: (a) be kept within reasonable bounds; (b) have symbolic value only, and (c) be done by and with the consent and under the supervision of the high school principals concerned.

Note—The giving and receiving of awards by and with the consent and under the supervision of the high school principals concerned shall mean that the high school principal in each school shall have real control and supervision without pressure of any kind from outside persons or groups of persons.

Rule 2. Only one sweater, jersey, jacket, blanket or similar article may be given in each sport to a high school student for participation in athletics in high school.

Rule 3. Awards such as a trophy, metal football, metal basketball, metal track shoe or similar article of symbolic value only may be given in addition to the one award permitted in Rule 2, provided the cost of the award shall not be more than the cost of the award in Rule 2.

Note—The word "symbolic" shall be understood to refer to a symbol, an emblem, or a token rather than to an article having intrinsic value. A diamond ring, a gold watch, an automobile or similar awards

[13] Iowa High School Athletic Association, 1960–1961 *Record Book*, p. 19.
[14] Oregon High School Activities Association, 1959, *Constitution*, p. 18.

do not fall under the term "symbolic" even if the award is duly inscribed. An inscription cannot validate such awards in the I. H. S. A. A.

Rule 4. Schools belonging to athletic conferences, or participating in tourneys and meets under the rules of the I. H. S. A. A., except in the championship series conducted by the I. H. S. A. A., may make awards to the winning school or winning participants, provided such awards are made within the bounds of Rules 1, 2 and 3.

Rule 5. Suitable awards may be given by such organizations as: service clubs, patriotic organizations, civic groups, Dads' and Mothers' clubs, and the sports department of a newspaper or radio station. No awards should be accepted which, in any way, advertise any firm or individual so far as commercial or business interests are concerned.

Rule 6. The Board of Control shall have the authority to designate, give and control the medals and trophies to be awarded to the schools and to the individuals on state championship teams in any sport, with the understanding that these be kept within the bounds of Rules 1, 2 and 3.

Rule 7. Awards, medals, recognitions, gifts, trips and honors shall not be accepted by players or schools from colleges, universities and higher institutions of learning or their alumni. High school athletes should be permitted to complete their high school careers without being molested by outside sources. The acceptance of travel expenses either directly or indirectly from a college as a prospective student-athlete shall be considered a violation of this rule.

Rule 8. Athletic equipment is considered as merchandise. Any student who attempts to evade the rule by "purchasing" a merchandise prize for a nominal or token sum will be considered as having forfeited his amateur standing in the I. H. S. A. A.

Rule 9. Penalties for violations of the above rules shall be determined by the Board of Control after all the evidence and circumstances have been considered.[15]

Pennsylvania's regulation is more varied in its scope:

It is permissible for a school to purchase a sweater, jacket, medal or similar trophy for an athlete who has earned the official school letter or award and to present the same at the time the official school award is made.[16]

[15] Indiana High School Athletic Association, *Fifty-Seventh Annual Handbook*, 1960, pp. 44–45.
[16] Pennsylvania Interscholastic Athletic Association, 1957 *Constitution and By-Laws*, p. 25.

Oklahoma's rule [17] on this matter is similar to that in Pennsylvania, except that the award limit for all but one article is $1. Most states also provide that the acceptance of medals or trophies by outstanding students among athletes is not considered a violation. Some state associations make no mention of award regulations in their by-laws. In such cases, undoubtedly, they are handled through interpretations of their amateur rules.

In concluding this discussion on awards it may be significant to quote the recommendation relative to them from the Recommended Minimum Eligibility Requirements of the National Federation of State High School Athletic Associations. It provides that

A student is ineligible if he accepts from any source a sweater, jersey, or any other award exceeding one dollar in value other than those given, such as medals, trophies, fobs, letters, and other athletic insignia.[18]

This recommendation apparently is indicative of the trend relative to awards, even with the $1 limit; otherwise it would not have received favorable consideration as a recommendation by this national organization.

Amateurism. When one begins to investigate the meaning of amateurism he is confronted with the ambiguity of the term. There seem to be almost as many definitions of it as there are types of organizations that seek to restrict their competition to what they term amateurs. International sports committees have set up standards that receive most attention during, or immediately preceding, Olympic years. In turn, there are national and sectional organizations that maintain affiliations with international groups; and although their interpretations may vary for their local competition, they are definitely bound to these internationally established precedents. In the United States we are concerned chiefly with rulings on this subject as made by four bodies or groups of bodies: (1) National Amateur Athletic Federation; (2) Amateur Athletic Union of the United States; (3) National Collegiate Athletic Association, and its constituent bodies; (4) National Federation of State High School Athletic Associations, and its member state associations. The

---

[17] Oklahoma High School Athletic Association, 1960–1961 *Constitution and Rules,* p. 8.
[18] National Federation, 1960–1961 *Handbook,* p. 12.

United States Golf Association and the United States Lawn Tennis Association also are organizations with which high school athletic associations sometimes come in contact in connection with awards and amateurism.

The long-standing definition of an amateur as formulated by the Amateur Athletic Union and the National Collegiate Athletic Association is one of the most general and universally accepted:

An amateur sportsman is one who engages in sport solely for the pleasure and physical, mental or moral benefits to be derived therefrom and to whom sport is nothing more than an avocation.

This rule probably has been the basis for most of those concerning amateurism which have been formulated throughout the country. It also is the identical definition of an amateur as stated by the Intercollegiate Association of Amateur Athletes of America.[19] Because of violations and evasions of the spirit of this rule, organizations with local or sectional competition to control became more specific in their terminology. As an example, the Western Conference (Big 10), in essence, declares a college student a professional if he participates in an outside game or contest for which admission is charged at the gate or if he receives pay for playing after his matriculation in the member institution. In most collegiate organizations as well as in the A.A.U. a boy may not compete with or against a professional in a match, game, or race. A professional, in such instances, is defined as one who is, or has been, paid for his athletic services. The United States Golf Association considers a boy a professional if he caddies for pay after having reached the age of eighteen years, but allows winners of its so-called amateur tournaments to accept prizes of considerable intrinsic or commercial value. The Michigan Amateur Athletic Union, a few years ago, awarded winners of its amateur boxing matches merchandise orders for food and clothing and still felt that it was not violating its amateur code. Athletes have often competed for "expenses," which sometimes have been far in excess of actual expenditures.

From these examples it will be seen that variations in general rules pertaining to amateurism are natural and probably inevitable.

[19] Intercollegiate Association of Amateur Athletes of America, *Constitution, By-Laws, and Athletic Rules* (1924), Art. XIX, Sec. 1, p. 13.

Even among high school athletic associations there are differences. There are also a great many similarities, however. High schools are pretty much our most cosmopolitan organizations, especially in those states with compulsory attendance laws. Schoolmen have wanted their interschool athletics to be open to all who had average ability to play. They have tried to keep this principle inviolate by ruling out the boy who, because of his special athletic prowess, could improve himself by professional competition and at the same time receive pay for his services. Such boys, in most cases, are asked to make the choice of remaining amateurs, in accordance with the school or state athletic association definitions, or to participate in what would be nonamateur competition. If they choose the former, their participation would be more nearly on a par with those with whom and against whom they are likely to compete. If they choose the latter, they are merely stepping out of the high school competition and making room for other boys.

An attempt will be made here to list typical definitions of amateurism, together with some interpretations, as they have been set up by representative state high school athletic associations throughout the country. The recommended amateur rule of the National Federation of State High School Athletic Associations may be considered typical of the present trend.

A student is ineligible if he has lost his amateur standing, i.e., he has accepted remuneration, gift or donation directly or indirectly for participating in an athletic contest or he has participated under an assumed name or he has competed on a team, some player of which was paid for his participation, or he has entered into a playing contract with a professional club or agent. Reference to "gift or donation" is not intended to preclude the acceptance of a medal or pin of small intrinsic value which is customarily used for track and similar activities and is presented by the sponsoring organization.[20]

It should be kept in mind that this is a recommended rule made by the National Federation and that the regulations of this body do not require its member states to have rules that conform to it. However, the rule undoubtedly can be considered as indicative of the thought on this matter. The amateur rule as formulated by the Ohio

[20] National Federation, 1960–1961 *Handbook*, p. 12.

High School Athletic Association illustrates the detailed manner in which many state associations have attempted to define amateurism:

Only amateurs are eligible. Amateur standing must be determined in accordance with the following:

INTERPRETATIONS

A. A pupil is ineligible if he receives or is promised money or other valuable consideration for competing in a sport recognized by the O.H.S.A.A. Sports recognized by the Association are football, basketball, baseball, track, tennis, swimming, wrestling, cross-country and golf (May, 1959). This applies whether school is in session or not (summer vacation.) (November 13, 1959).

B. Acceptance of money or other valuable considerations as expenses renders a pupil ineligible. No money is to be given to a contestant however, his expenses may be paid by others.

C. A pupil is ineligible if he competes under an assumed name.

D. Participation in donkey baseball or basketball, skating demonstrations, stock car racing, skeet shooting, bowling or as a life guard, caddy or caddy master, or officiating, is not to be regarded as a violation of the High School Amateur Rule. (May, 1959).

E. A professional in one sport is a professional in all.

F. A pupil who has lost his amateur standing may be reinstated after the lapse of one complete high school season in the sport, provided he has not persisted in breaking the amateur rule.

G. A pupil may play on summer baseball teams where one or more of his teammates may be paid and still be an amateur provided he accepts no compensation or money for expenses.

H. The signing of any contract by a pupil whereby he agrees to compete in any athletic competition for profit or the promise of profit, makes said pupil immediately ineligible for further interscholastic athletic competition.

I. A high school team may play against a team composed wholly or in part of professionals without its boys losing their amateur standing.

J. Professional baseball and college try-outs which in any way interfere with a high school student's school work or which involve a game in violation of Ohio High School Athletic Association rules may result immediately in that student's ineligibility for further interscholastic athletic competition.

K. Golf, one of the sports recognized by the Association has increased to such an extent that it is necessary to emphasize that Rule 9 applies to all golf tournaments whether school is in session or not and no exceptions can be made for high school boys playing in summer golf tournaments.

No member of a high school golf team is permitted to participate in a Pro-Amateur Golf Tournament and other tournaments while a member of the high school golf squad. (See Rule 17 Section 1). After a squad has closed its season in golf, a pupil may participate in golf tournaments of any type during the summer or off-season but he must maintain his Amateur standing as stated in Rule 9.

Under the Association rules, accepting an athletic award or prize exceeding $1.00 is a violation of the Amateur Rule and the Awards Rule. Scholarships may be accepted but the amount of the scholarship must be paid directly to the College of choice by the sponsors of the golf tournament. (May 27, 1960).[21]

This rule, with its specific interpretations as part of it, should leave no doubt in the minds of Ohio schoolmen regarding the status of amateurism in that state as far as high school athletics are concerned. Ohio, as will be noted, does not even allow expenses for outside competition. Not many states are quite so specific as Ohio in this regard, but certainly more nearly simon-pure athletics should be the result of such provisions. Many other states have provisions in their amateur rules, or interpretations of them, that are similar to those listed in the Ohio rule. High schools are specific, with the result that they probably have less difficulty than some other organizations. Michigan's rule considers actual competition for money or other valuable consideration, as well as the officiating of interscholastic athletic contests and signing a contract with a professional league baseball team. (See Fig. 4–9.)

No student shall be eligible to represent his high school who: (1) has received money for participating in athletics, sports, or games listed in Section B; (2) has received money or other valuable consideration for officiating in interscholastic athletic contests; or (3) has signed a contract with a professional baseball team.

SECTION 11 (B)—A student will render himself ineligible under this Rule if he violates its amateur provisions only in the following activities: Baseball, Basketball, Boxing, Cross Country, Football (11-man, 8-man, or 6-man), Golf, Ice Hockey, Skiing, Soccer, Softball, Swimming, Tennis, Track, or Wrestling.

[21] Ohio High School Athletic Association, 1960–1961 *Constitution and Rules*, pp. 22–23.

Michigan High School Athletic Association
SUMMARY OF
ELIGIBILITY RULES FOR SENIOR HIGH SCHOOL STUDENTS
FOR THE 1961-62 SCHOOL YEAR

STUDENTS: You might better be "safe than ineligible," therefore—

1. Read these Rules carefully and be sure that you understand them.

2. If you have any questions ask them of your coach, athletic director, principal, or superintendent BEFORE you endanger your high school athletic eligibility rather than AFTER it is too late. Complete Eligibility Rules and Interpretations may be found in the 1961-62 Michigan High School Athletic Association Handbook.

TO BE ELIGIBLE TO REPRESENT YOUR SCHOOL IN INTERSCHOLASTIC ATHLETICS—

REGULATION 1, SECTION 1

ENROLLMENT—You must have been enrolled in a high school not later than Monday of the fourth (4th) week of the present semester.

REGULATION 1, SECTION 2

AGE — You must be under nineteen (19) years of age at time of contest unless your nineteenth (19th) birthday occurs on or after September 1 of a current school year, in which case you are eligible for the balance of that school year.

REGULATION 1, SECTION 3

PHYSICAL EXAMINATION—You must have passed a satisfactory physical examination during the present school year. Record of this examination must be on file in the high school office.

REGULATION 1, SECTION 4

SEASONS OF COMPETITION—You must not have competed for more than four (4) first and four (4) second semester seasons in a sport in a four (4) year high school; or for more than three (3), each, first and second semester seasons, in a three (3) year high school.

REGULATION 1, SECTION 5

SEMESTERS OF ENROLLMENT—You must not have been enrolled in grades nine to twelve (9-12), inclusive, for more than eight (8) semesters. The seventh and eighth (7th and 8th) semesters must be consecutive. Enrollment in a school for a period of three (3) weeks or more counts as a semester. Participation in one (1) or more interscholastic athletic contests also constitutes a semester of enrollment.

REGULATION 1, SECTION 6

UNDERGRADUATE STANDING—You must not be a high school graduate.

REGULATION 1, SECTION 7

PREVIOUS SEMESTER RECORD—You must have received at least fifteen (15) credit hours for work taken during your last regular semester of enrollment.

REGULATION 1, SECTION 8

CURRENT SEMESTER RECORD — You must be carrying successfully at least fifteen (15) credit hours of work during the present semester.

REGULATION 1, SECTION 9

TRANSFERS—Your only parent, parents, guardian, or other persons with whom you have been living during the period of your last high school enrollment, generally, must have moved out of the district or service area of the high school you previously attended and into the district or service area of the high school you are now attending, if you are a transfer student this semester.

REGULATION 1, SECTION 10

AWARDS—You must not accept any award for athletic performance other than a trophy having a value of not more than three dollars ($3.00). A trophy is defined as a medal, ribbon, badge, plaque, cup, banner, picture, or ring.

REGULATION 1, SECTION 11

AMATEUR PRACTICES—You must not accept any money or other valuable consideration (merchandise, etc.) for participating in any form of athletics, sports, or games, for officiating in interscholastic athletic contests, or have signed a contract with a professional baseball team.

REGULATION 1, SECTION 12

LIMITED TEAM MEMBERSHIP—(A) You must not participate in any athletic competition during the season in a sport not under the sponsorship of your high school, after you have represented your school in that sport; (B) If you represented your high school in basketball after February 15, you must not participate in any outside basketball competition after that date (February 15) during the remainder of the present school year; (C) You must not participate in any so-called "all-star" charity or exhibition games in football or basketball.

NOTE TO SCHOOLS: Please post this information on your school bulletin boards. Additional posters, in limited quantities, are available upon request to the State Director of High School Athletics, Department of Public Instruction, Lansing 2, Michigan

61—2M

Fig. 4-9. Athletic Eligibility Poster (Michigan).

SECTION 11 (C)—A student ineligible under this Rule may not apply for reinstatement until the equivalent of one full school year of enrollment has elapsed following the date of his last violation.

INTERPRETATIONS

51.—(A) Under the term "valuable consideration" is included such items as sweaters, athletic equipment, wearing apparel, watches, or any similar articles or merchandise, as well as memberships or privileges in clubs or organizations, or personal services. No such items, memberships, privileges, or services may be accepted by students as prizes or payments without incurring athletic ineligibility.

52.—(A) For the purposes of this Section, a professional league baseball team is defined as a major or minor league team which is a member of the National Association of Professional Baseball Clubs.

53.—(A) Awards for any school bowling are to be in accordance with the Awards Rule limitations. Any bowling activity conducted by a school or by a local, state, or national bowling organization, IN WHICH SCHOOL UNITS OR REPRESENTATIVES OF SCHOOLS COMPETE AS SUCH, also is subject to the Amateur Practices Rule limitations. The Amateur Practices Rule does not apply to non-school bowling.

54.—(A) In general, students may work in school or other local recreation programs, on playgrounds, as golf caddies, at swimming pools, or at beaches and receive pay without incurring athletic ineligibility.

55.—(A) If a student takes part in an athletic try-out he is not to handle tickets or expense funds personally. This must be done by someone who is in charge of the event or trip. No negotiable items (money, tickets, gifts, etc.) are to come into possession of the high school student at any time.[22]

Oklahoma's amateur provisions are similar to the above except that additional restrictions concerning boxing and wrestling are included:

Any student who shall appear on a bout or card for boxing or wrestling if, on the same bout or card a professional appeared, or who participated in any athletic contest where cash or merchandise is offered, given or

[22] Michigan High School Athletic Association, 1961–1962 *Handbook*, pp. 38–39.

paid to his team or individual members of his team, shall be ineligible for interscholastic contests in the sport in which he participated or appeared until such time as it has been proved to the satisfaction of the Board that he did not receive cash or merchandise prizes or gifts, because of such participation. If a student has appeared on a bout or card for boxing or wrestling where a professional appeared or has received a merchandise prize or gift, and refrains from further violations of rules of the Association and forfeits one year's eligibility, he may be reinstated by the Board of Control.[23]

In contrast to Oklahoma, California has set up these regulations:

A professional is one who:
Coached or taught athletics for pay.
Competed in any athletic game or contest in which he received compensation of any kind for his services.
Participated in any tryout for a collegiate or professional team at any time during the school year (September 15th to June 15th).
Solicited employment for gain for his athletic ability. (When an athlete signs a contract for his services as an athlete, he automatically becomes ineligible for amateur competition.)
Interpretation:
A boy is ineligible and deemed to be a professional if he participates in any tryout for a collegiate or professional team at any time during the school year (from September 15th to June 15th). He may participate in tryout from June 16th to September 14th, but can receive no expense money. Requests of professional baseball clubs for boys to participate in tryouts during the school year shall not be approved.
Competed in high school competition while enrolled in high school:
For cash, for merchandise, or for any compensation.
For a personal prize or award of over $10.00 in value.
Under an assumed name.
One who has been declared a professional shall automatically be debarred from competition during the remainder of that season and for one full year thereafter; and further until re-instated as an amateur.[24]

Texas does not allow a boy within the last twelve months, to play "on an athletic team with a paid player or contestants." [25] The

[23] Oklahoma High School Athletic Association, 1960–1961 *Constitution*, pp. 7–8.

[24] California Interscholastic Federation, 1959 *Constitution and By-Laws* p. 3.

[25] Texas University Interscholastic League, 1960 *Constitution and Rules*, p. 19.

amateur rule in Kansas is similar to the Ohio regulation except that

Ineligibility under the provisions of this rule holds for the entire period the student is in school, unless he is reinstated by the Board of Control.[26]

Thus, in Kansas it would be possible for a freshman in high school to have violated the amateur rule and be ineligible for the rest of his high school career unless there is reinstatement by the executive board. In most other states the period is one year, but in Wisconsin:

A boy becomes permanently ineligible in a sport if he
a. Has accepted money for participation.
b. Has signed a contract or entered into an agreement to participate in play for pay.
c. Has agreed to the use of his name for promotion of any item, plan or service.
d. Has accepted the equivalent of pay in awards or expense money.[27]

There are other provisions of the Wisconsin amateur rule, however, that render a boy ineligible for only one year if he violates them, as by playing under an assumed name or by playing in a game with professionals, in one played on an uneven winner-loser basis, or one where money or other articles are offered for prizes. Illinois regulations are similar to those in Wisconsin. New Jersey states: "Athletes must be amateurs as defined by the National Collegiate Athletic Association." [28] Then follows the definition of an amateur as it appears on page 94 and the acts which are considered violations of the amateur code by the National Collegiate Athletic Association. Colorado defines an amateur in a manner somewhat different from that in most other states:

"An amateur is a person who has never knowingly competed in an open competition, or for money, or under a false name, or with a professional where gate money is charged." But nothing in this definition shall be considered to prohibit the competition between amateurs for medals, cups,

26 Kansas State High School Activities Association, 1960–1961 *Handbook*, p. 24.
27 Wisconsin Interscholastic Athletic Association, *Thirty-Seventh Yearbook* (1960), p. 21.
28 New Jersey State Interscholastic Athletic Association, 1960–1961 *Constitution and By-Laws* p. 35.

or prizes other than money. To prevent any misunderstanding in reading the above, the Conference draws attention to the following explanation and adjudications:

An athlete has forfeited the right to compete as an amateur and has thereby become a professional, by—

(a) Ever having knowingly competed in open competition, i.e., a competition the entries to which are open to all, irrespective as to whether the competitors are amateurs or professionals, and whether such competition be for a prize or not, in any athletic exercises.

(b) Ever having competed for money in any athletic exercises.

(c) Ever having competed under a false name in any athletic exercises.

(d) Ever having knowingly competed with a professional for a prize or where gate money is charged in any athletic exercises.

(e) Ever having directly or indirectly accepted or received remuneration for engaging in any athletic exercises.[29]

Nebraska exempts baseball, with certain exceptions, and other sports from the athletic activities in which a boy may engage and use his athletic skill for personal gain as follows:

A high school boy will jeopardize his high school eligibility if he participates on an organized baseball team or in any other organized forms of athletics during the season of that sport in his high school (an organized baseball team meaning any team affiliated with the National Association of Professional Baseball Clubs, not semi-professional or "sandlot" teams).

Any boy who plays on any baseball team belonging to a league affiliated with the National Association of Baseball Clubs (an "organized" baseball team) shall be ineligible for further athletic participation on the teams of schools which are members of the N. S. A. A.

A high school athlete is permitted to use his athletic skill for gain through baseball (other than so-called "organized" baseball), kittenball, basketball or other activities wherein money or material awards might be granted *except during the season of the particular sport in his high school.*[30]

The Nebraska regulation regarding amateurism is a distinct de-

29 Colorado High School Activities Association, *Handbook* (1960), p. 23.
30 Nebraska High School Activities Association, *Twenty-sixth Annual Yearbook* (1960), p. 11.

parture from those most common in other state associations. Such a policy is not generally accepted by schoolmen, but apparently it works in Nebraska, where it has long been in effect. Pennsylvania's regulations are in general conformity with those of the state associations which are strict in their interpretations and do not allow students who might be classed as professionals to compete in high school athletics.[31]

A pupil must be an amateur in order to be eligible to participate in any interscholastic athletic contest. An athlete becomes a professional in a sport:

A. Whenever he enters competition for money.

B. Whenever he sells or pawns his prizes.

C. Whenever he accepts money.

D. Whenever he competes under a false name.

E. Whenever he plays, or has played, on a team any of whose players have received, or are receiving directly or indirectly, compensation for their athletic services. This rule does not apply to a high school athlete who has participated in summer baseball where no player on his team received any form of remuneration for athletic services in that particular game; however, the division of any receipts, whether obtained from admissions, collections, or donations, among the members of the team at any time, shall be construed as a violation of the provisions of this Article.

F. Whenever he receives a consideration for becoming a member of an athletic organization or school.

G. Whenever he accepts money or any valuable consideration for teaching, training, or coaching in the sport other than acting as a summer playground instructor.

Pennsylvania's exemption of playground instruction and supervision is generally accepted. Alabama adds a new thought in the consideration of amateurism when mention is made of wagers on athletic contests:

A pupil is ineligible if he has received money as a prize, or has sold a prize received in a contest, or has bet on a competition in which he is a participant.[32]

[31] Pennsylvania Interscholastic Athletic Association, *Constitution and By-Laws* (1957), p. 17.

[32] Alabama High School Athletic Association, 1960–1961 *Handbook*, pp. 99–100.

Indiana allows students to accept expenses for athletic competition but explains very definitely the manner in which they may be accepted:

All contestants in the I.H.S.A.A. must be amateurs.

Professionalism is defined in the I.H.S.A.A. as accepting remuneration, directly or indirectly, for playing on athletic teams, for officiating in athletic games or for managing athletic teams; or for playing, officiating or managing under assumed names. Reasonable meals, lodging and transportation may be accepted, if accepted in service and not in any other way. Any high school student who directly or indirectly signs a professional contract loses his amateur standing and immediately becomes ineligible for all high school sports.[33]

Georgia defines an amateur in this manner:

An amateur is defined as one who has never violated his or her amateur standing by receiving money, tuition, board or pay of any description as compensation for playing on a professional athletic team or in a professional exhibition, or playing under an assumed name. This rule does not prevent a pupil from playing on a semi-pro ball team during the summer vacation or from participating in summer camp work (*Note:* To violate any of the above will be interpreted as subsidization.) [34]

Evidently there are wide variations in state high school athletic association conceptions of amateurism. Yet, it also is apparent that, in general, schools desire to keep their athletes from using their athletic skill as a means of livelihood or incidental remuneration. Athletics, with their definite place in the educational program, should be kept educational in nature. At the same time there are interschool relations to be fostered, and in all probability they will be better relations if the students who comprise athletic teams are of the rank and file of the schools concerned. For this reason state athletic associations, which in reality are schoolmen themselves, have said that athletes must be amateurs as they have chosen to define the term. The one nearly universal criterion is that pay shall not be given for play.

[33] Indiana High School Athletic Association, *Fifty-Seventh Annual Handbook*, p. 48.

[34] Georgia High School Association, 1960–1961 *Constitution and By-Laws*, p. 35.

Special Eligibility Regulations

Nearly all the regulations that have been discussed in this chapter have been common to most states, or at least have been variations of the central themes found in most state association regulations. In this section it is proposed to list some of the most significant special or unusual rules that certain states have seen fit to establish. It would be interesting to know some of the reasons for these regulations, but it is safe to assume that there were "cases" that prompted most of them. After all, that has been the way most of our laws, as well as athletic regulations, have been established.

Conduct or character rule. Regulations pertaining to this matter appear almost frequently enough in state association regulations to be classed as a regular rule. The Oklahoma rule is typical:

Any student who is under discipline or whose conduct or character is such as to reflect discredit upon the school, is not eligible.[35]

Tobacco and liquor rule. Regulations specifically prohibiting the use of tobacco or alcoholic beverages appear in a few states. In others this matter seems to be left to local schools as a disciplinary problem for their settlement. The North Dakota rule is an example of this type of by-law:

He shall not use tobacco nor intoxicating liquors during the school term of two semesters.[36]

Antifraternity-membership rule. In several states there are statutes prohibiting membership by high school students in fraternities, sororities, or other secret organizations. Some state associations have regulations that rule a student ineligible for high school athletics if membership in organizations of this kind is proved. The California rule is illustrative:

Whenever it is shown that a member of a High School team is a member of a High School Fraternity, as defined by the State Law, all the

---

[35] Oklahoma High School Athletic Association, 1960–1961 *Constitution*, p. 7.
[36] North Dakota High School Activities Association, 1960 *Constitution and By-Laws*, p. 79.

games which that student participated in shall be forfeited, and the school may be debarred from further participation in that sport for one year.[37]

Military service rule. Illinois, like most other states, made specific reference to the fact that a student was not to be ruled ineligible because of absence from school for military service.

He shall not be ineligible through absence on account of military service to state or nation in time of war or in time of any national or state emergency.[38]

Coaching school rule. This rule also is from Illinois and is typical of the few specific references to this subject found in the examination of numerous state association constitutions:

He shall be ineligible for a period of one year immediately after having attended a regular coaching school in this or any other state.

Note: This rule shall not be interpreted to prohibit attendance at baseball schools during the summer vacation months.

Note: This rule shall be interpreted as prohibiting a player from attending any camp organized for the purpose of training or practicing an athletic team of his school and conducted away from the school's regular practice or playing field.[39]

No uniforms on non-eligibles rule. South Dakota's rule on this matter is different from most other states:

No student shall be allowed to wear an athletic uniform for the sport represented in the contest in the vicinity of an athletic contest connected with this Association who is not eligible at the time to participate in the contest.[40]

Ineligibility of teachers rule. Texas, apparently, plans to take no chances of allowing teachers to take part in league contests, because it has a rather unusual rule:

[37] California Interscholastic Federation, 1959 *Constitution and By-Laws*, p. 4.
[38] Illinois High School Athletic Association, 1960–1961 *Handbook*, p. 18.
[39] *Ibid.*, p. 21.
[40] South Dakota High School Athletic Association, 1959 *Rules and Regulations*, p. 18.

A person who is teaching whole or part time is ineligible for any League contest.[41]

Unsportsmanlike conduct rule. A few states have definite rules concerning unsportsmanlike conduct of competitors. The regulation of the Kentucky High School Athletic Association is typical of those which have such provisions:

Any student who is under penalty or discipline or whose character or conduct is such as to reflect discredit upon the school is not eligible.

Any student using insulting language to another player or to an official in any interscholastic contest, or who has been ruled out of such a contest because of foul tactics, shall be disqualified for that game, and the Commissioner shall be notified immediately of such action by the principal of the home team school. When an official disqualifies a player, he shall report the name of the player to this principal. If the Commissioner finds upon investigation that the offense was sufficiently serious, the offender shall be permanently disqualified.[42]

Married students rule. Indiana has a rule that covers this matter, and similar ones are found in several other states:

Married students shall not be eligible for participation in inter-school athletic competition. Students who have been divorced or whose marriages have been annulled are bound by the above rule.[43]

Pupil supension rule. Louisiana's rule in this regard is unique:

A pupil suspended from one school is ineligible to take part in athletics in another school until he presents a clearance card from the school from which he has been suspended.[44]

No letter award rule. Utah has an unusual award rule which allows the acceptance of medals only, the cost of which does not exceed $1. Specifically, the nonacceptance of school letters is provided:

[41] Texas University Interscholastic League, 1960–1961 *Constitution,* p. 22.
[42] Kentucky High School Athletic Association, 1960–1961 *Constitution and By-Laws,* p. 15.
[43] Indiana High School Athletic Association, 1960 *Handbook,* p. 45.
[44] Louisiana High School Athletic Association, 1960–1961 *Handbook* p. 34.

No reward of any kind having value of more than one dollar ($1.00) other than medals shall be made to players participating in interschool activities.

No fabric letter of any kind shall be awarded by a school or by any other organization for activities.

Any member of the Association violating this rule shall be suspended for one year.[45]

Summary

This summary of eligibility rules for contestants is an attempt to show general practices in effect in most states. There may be exceptions in some instances to the general conclusions indicated.

Age. The upper age limit of nineteen years is the most common one, with thirty-one states having this maximum at present. There is some tendency to establish lower age limits in some states for participation in certain sports.

Time of enrollment. In general, students must be enrolled at least by the third or fourth week of the semester to qualify for athletic eligibility during a current semester. In some states attendance from 30 to 60 days is required, after a continuous absence of 20 days or more, before a student regains his athletic eligibility.

Seasons of competition. In practically all states there is a limit of four seasons of competition in a sport in grades nine to twelve, inclusive.

Number of semesters of attendance. Eight semesters of attendance in grades nine to twelve, inclusive, is the common rule. Some states allow a ninth semester for students who first enrolled at the beginning of a midyear term, provided they did not compete in interscholastic athletics during the first semester of attendance.

Limited team membership. It is an almost universal regulation that membership on a team in the same sport, other than that of the high school, is prohibited during the season of the sport concerned.

Parental consent and physical examinations. Virtually all states require that a student must have passed a physical examination before he may compete in athletic activities. Some require a separate examination for each sport, but in most instances one examination

[45] Utah High School Activities Association, 1960–1961 *Handbook,* p. 15.

during the school year is sufficient. In at least one-third of the states, consent cards must be signed by parents or guardians before students may participate.

Current and previous semester scholarship. All states have requirements that students must have received credit in a specified amount of work (usually 15 hours) the preceding semester in order to be eligible. Likewise, virtually all states have regulations requiring a student to do passing work in at least 15 hours during the current semester. New York has removed its previous and current semester scholastic work requirements.

Transfer and undue influence rules. In general, a student is eligible in a new school if his parents or guardians have moved into the new school district. Usually a semester, but sometimes a full year, of ineligibility follows a transfer by a student from one school to another without an accompanying transfer of parental residence. Undue influence rules, with penalties of ineligibility for students and discipline for schools, have made their appearance in several states.

Awards. Twenty-five states limit the value of athletic awards to one to five dollars. In others, one sweater may be awarded during the year, in addition to the letter or medal award of the school. Some states allow the presentation of awards in excess of the stated value to be made to seniors after their competition is concluded. The trend is definitely toward making awards which have little or no intrinsic value for athletic team membership in high schools.

Amateurism. With very few exceptions a high school student may not use his athletic skill or knowledge of athletics for personal gain. Many states do not allow a boy to compete with, or against, a team any of the members of which are paid for their services. Others require only that the student himself shall not accept pay or a valuable award for playing.

Special rules. A few states in each instance have established regulations dealing with the following:

1. Conduct or character
2. Tobacco and liquor
3. Fraternity membership
4. Military service
5. Coaching schools
6. Eligibles only in uniform
7. Ineligibility of teachers
8. Unsportsmanlike conduct
9. Married students
10. Suspended students
11. No letter awards

Questions for Study and Discussion

1. Discuss purposes of athletic eligibility regulations. Do you agree with those who believe they are unnecessary? Why?

2. What is the trend regarding the upper age limit for participation in high school athletics? Do you think this age is too low? Too high? Why?

3. Discuss common trends regarding (a) Time of enrollment; (b) Semesters of attendance; (c) Seasons of competition and undergraduate standing.

4. Why do most state associations have rather similar rules regarding limited team membership?

5. State reasons why parental consent to participate and physical examinations for athletics are important.

6. Discuss reasons for and against the requirements that athletes must be carrying a definite amount of academic work in order to be eligible to represent their school.

7. Why is it said that there are responsibilities as well as privileges connected with representing one's school in interscholastic athletic competition?

8. Discuss the common Transfer Rules in effect in most states. Do you agree with the Undue Influence Rules which exist in some states? Why?

9. Write a brief paragraph giving your philosophy of high school awards and amateur rules. Why is there so much controversy and misunderstanding about these rules in high schools and colleges?

10. Several rather unusual eligibility rules are in effect in various states. Indicate those that you consider to be unnecessary and state why.

5   Athletic Contest Regulations

Chapter 4 was concerned with eligibility regulations pertaining to the student contestant. An attempt was made to show reasons for such regulations and to enumerate and illustrate those which were most common among the states as well as some which were rather special in nature. A similar plan will be followed regarding provisions governing contests as they affect schools.

Purpose of Contest Regulations

Difference between contest and eligibility regulations. There is a definite distinction between eligibility regulations for contestants and contest regulations which apply to a school. The former have as their reason for existence the establishment of rules that not only serve the school but also present a code by which the student himself may determine his own eligibility. They set up regulations with which the contestant should be made familiar and in most instances he should be able to see the reasons for their establishment. Usually, athletic eligibility regulations have been set up as the result of experiences which have come to the state associations themselves. They are not theoretical, untried, or unworkable ideas that someone has attempted to put into practice. Their worth and value have been proved. Local schools are doing themselves and their students a real service when they acquaint their student bodies and school patrons with these regulations. Following such a policy makes the administration of their programs that much easier. (Fig. 4-9 is illustrative of such an attempt.)

The philosophies and reasons behind contest regulations are different from those which resulted in ordinary contestant eligibility rules. Two separate schools, two separate organizations, are involved when an athletic contest takes place. Experience has shown that, for mutual harmony, it is necessary to have common understandings if a contest is to be successful. In the first place there is a common set of rules for playing the game. Competent and impartial officials are selected to officiate the contest. It has been found that numerous details also must receive attention before the contest takes place if it is to be the right kind of educational experience. So with this purpose, athletic contest regulations as they pertain to high school athletic association rules came into existence.

Contest regulations were adopted to ensure, as far as possible, the fulfillment of certain before-game responsibilities. They have become common codes within their states because they have worked well in most cases. They have not been imposed upon schools in order to display the powers of state associations, as sometimes is charged. Rather, they have been adopted by state associations, through schoolmen themselves, as aids to their own schools and to bring order out of chaos. Although the degree of success in this accomplishment may be a matter of opinion, the regulations in effect in most states must be agreeable to the majority of schools concerned; otherwise they could and undoubtedly would be changed.

Common Regulations

In the remainder of this chapter there will be presented common rules pertaining to the conduct of interschool contests. An attempt has been made to make the illustrations typical and representative of various sections of the country.

Contracts for athletic contests. It is an almost universal rule that state associations furnish standard contract forms for use of member schools. Some states require that arrangements for all games be made on such forms. Many state associations refuse to assume jurisdiction in disputes between schools regarding contract violations unless arrangements for games were executed on standard forms which were properly signed by authorized representatives of the schools concerned. In general, the essential provisions of state association contracts for games are similar. West Virginia's easily understood contract (see Fig. 5-1) has provisions for either single or multiple contests. It provides for a forfeiture fee, as most state association contracts do, in case there is failure to fulfill contract provisions. In most states contracts may be cancelled or their pro-

---

WEST VIRGINIA SECONDARY SCHOOL ACTIVITIES COMMISSION
OFFICIAL CONTRACT FOR GAMES

_____ W. Va., _____ 19____

The _____ High School of _____ , _____
    (Name of High School)   (City)   (State)

AND

The _____ High School of _____ , _____
                Hereby Enter into a Contract for

One Game of (or Event in) _____ to be played at
                        (Activity)

_____ , _____ on _____ , 19____
    (City)   (State)   (Date)

OR

Two Games of (or Events in) _____ to be played as follows:
                       (Activity)

One at _____ , _____ On _____ 19____
      (City)   (State)   (Date)

One at _____ , _____ On _____ 19____

All activities are to be conducted under the following stipulations:

1. The suspension or termination of its membership in the commission by either of the parties to this contract shall render this contract null and void during time of suspension or termination.

2. The rules of the West Virginia Secondary School Activities Commission are a part of this contract.

3. Financial agreement: _____

_____

(Both schools agree, also, that the sum named shall cover all claims arising under this contract.)

4. Officials shall be chosen from those registered with the West Virginia Secondary School Activities Commission and shall be mutually agreed upon by the competing schools at least two weeks before the scheduled date of contest. Other arrangements such as hour of contest, price of admissions, etc., should be agreed upon at the same time. It is understood, unless stated otherwise, that the home school will bear the cost of securing the officials.

_____

(Refer to sections in Constitution and By-Laws for topics governing Officials, Contracts and Eligibility Lists.)

5. This contract may be altered only by mutual agreement of the contracting schools.

6. The school failing to carry out the provisions of this contract shall pay the other a forfeit of _____ dollars, unless the principal, or official in charge of visiting school, relieves the home school from penalty of forfeiture on account of weather or other conditions which make playing practically impossible. This amount should be sufficiently large to recompense the school for damage caused by cancellation of the event by the other party.

I certify that I have read the suggestions given on the back of this contract and understand their significance.

Agreed to and signed in duplicate _____ 19____   Agreed to and signed in duplicate _____ 19____
               (Date)   (Date)

THE _____ HIGH SCHOOL   THE _____ HIGH SCHOOL
By _____   By _____

By _____   Principal   By _____   Principal
                       Coach   Coach

☞Important suggestions are listed on the back of this contract.☜
READ THEM

Fig. 5-1. Official Contract for Games (West Virginia).

visions altered only by mutual consent of the contracting schools. Payment of the forfeiture fee by a contracting school when a game is not played is deemed fulfillment of the contract in some states. In others, there must be very good reasons for the cancellation of a contest, even though the forfeiture is paid, unless both schools agree to it. Failure to fulfill contract provisions usually results in suspension. In most states the principal of the high school, or a faculty representative authorized by him, signs contracts. In many states the contract is between the two schools as such, whereas in others it is in reality an agreement between the principals or other administration officials of the schools concerned. The Washington High School Activities Association contract for athletic contests is quite similar to the type used by most state athletic associations (see Fig. 5-2).

Fig. 5-2. Official Agreement Form for Games (Washington).

It is desirable to have definite financial stipulations in contracts. Usually, flat guarantees are made, with the result that the visiting school may do as it sees fit in the entertainment of its team. This seems to be the best procedure, although the contracts of some state associations provide for definite numbers of players for whom expenses are to be paid by the entertaining school. In some states specific amounts are designated for meals, lodging, and transportation. The provision for listing officials for the game appears on many

---

MISSOURI STATE HIGH SCHOOL ACTIVITIES ASSOCIATION

CONTRACT FOR GAMES WITHIN THE STATE
(Ask for special form for interstate games)

This contract, dated _____ 19_____, is made and subscribed to by the authorities of the _____

High School and of the _____ High School for _____ contest(s) in _____ to be played
as follows: _____(Name of Sport)

	PLACE	DATE	HOUR
First team contest at			
First team contest at			
_____ at			
_____ at			

A guarantee of $_____ is made that these contests will be played. In case either school fails to fulfill this contract, the guarantee shall be paid by the offending school to the offended school. A money guarantee is required under By-Law #4. If dissolved by mutual consent or because of reasons beyond the control of either party, this contract shall not be binding upon either party.

Other financial terms are: _____

It is further agreed that the rules of the Missouri State High School Activities Association which are in force on the day of each contest shall be upheld by each school.

1. _____   2. _____
   Superintendent or Principal   Superintendent or Principal

_____   _____
High School   High School

NOTE: List suggested registered officials on the back. The visitors should scratch those not acceptable and number the others in order of preference.
Form 8—70M—1960   (To be made in duplicate)

Fig. 5-3. Contract Form for Athletic Contests *(Missouri)*.

CONTRACT FOR ATHLETIC CONTESTS

OHIO HIGH SCHOOL ATHLETIC ASSOCIATION

MEMBER NATIONAL FEDERATION OF HIGH SCHOOL ATHLETIC ASSOCIATIONS

_____, Ohio, _____, 19____

This Contract is drawn under the supervision of the Ohio High School Athletic Association and must be used in arranging games participated in by schools of this Association.

THIS CONTRACT, Subscribed to by the Principals and Faculty Managers of the _____ High School

and of the _____ High School, is made for_____games of_____to be played as follows:

One game at_____ on_____ at_____P. M.

One game at_____ on_____ at_____P. M.

Do not use term "corresponding dates" — use specific dates.

All games to be played under the following stipulations:

The _____ High School agrees to pay to the _____ High School

the sum of _____ dollars ($_____), and the latter
school agrees that this sum shall cover all its claims arising by virtue of this contract, except as provided in Item 1 herein below set forth.

1. If either party hereto fails to fulfill its obligation of any part of this contract, the defaulting party shall pay to the other party the sum of $_____ as damages, which said sum must be accepted by the injured party as complete compensation for any damages it may have suffered, the remainder of the contract shall not be binding on either party, and the breach of said contract shall be reported to the Ohio High School Athletic Association.
2. Postponement cannot result in annulment except by mutual consent.
3. The constitution and rules of the Ohio High School Athletic Association are a part of this contract.
4. The suspension or termination of its membership in the State Association by either of the parties to this contract shall render this contract null and void.
5. It is urged that a suggested list of state approved officials be made on the back of this contract sheet and its duplicate. The principal of the visiting school should scratch the names of those not acceptable and number those acceptable in the order of preference on both the original and duplicate. All officials used on football and basketball games must be registered.
6. Inter-state games should be scheduled on National Federation State High School Athletic Association contracts which may be obtained free of charge from the Ohio High School Athletic Association.
7. Unless otherwise specified, this contract shall call for a first team game.

Principal	Faculty Manager or Athletic Director	School	State
Principal	Faculty Manager or Athletic Director	School	State

25M—5-60

Fig. 5-4. Contract Form for Athletic Contests *(Ohio)*.

contracts. This usually is done by the entertaining school, and the visiting school is allowed to cross out the names of listed officials who are not acceptable to it. See Figures 5-3 (Missouri) and 5-4 (Ohio) for briefer types of Athletic Contest Contracts.

Following are a few typical provisions of state association by-laws regarding contest contracts:

It is the responsibility of the principal—
    To see that all contracts for interscholastic athletic contests in which his school participates, are in writing and bear his signature. (Pennsylvania)[1]
    All contracts for high school games shall be made by the principals of the high schools, on official contract forms, and shall bear their signatures. These forms may be secured from the Commissioner's office.
    NOTE: All contracts should specify a particular date for each game rather than the words "corresponding date." Contract forms show numbered playing dates.
    In case of a breach of contract for athletic games, without mutual consent, the school that cancels without the consent of the other may be penalized by the Executive Committee up to one year's suspension from the Association, as provided on the contract form.
    Note: Acceptance in writing for an athletic contest shall constitute a contract in sports other than football for the purpose of this rule. (Louisiana)[2]
    Official contracts furnished by the Board of Control must be used for all contests between schools. Any school violating the contract may be suspended from membership for one year. No school suspended shall be reinstated until the superintendent shall make personal application to the Board of Control. (Iowa)[3]
    The final management of all interscholastic athletics shall be in the hands of some member or members of the faculty, who shall sign all contracts. (Michigan)[4]

Eligibility list procedures. All state associations have some procedure whereby lists of players are exchanged between schools prior to athletic contests. Upon these lists are the names of eligible stu-

[1] Pennsylvania Interscholastic Athletic Association, 1958 *Constitution and By-Laws*, p. 14.
[2] Louisiana High School Athletic Association, 1960–1961 *Handbook*, p. 46.
[3] Iowa High School Athletic Association, 1960–1961 *Record Book*, p. 20.
[4] Michigan High School Athletic Association, 1961–1962 *Handbook*, p. 44.

dent contestants and varying amounts of data regarding their scholastic and athletic histories. The time for exchange of eligibility lists, or eligibility certificates, as they are called in some states, varies from the filing of one blank at the start or close of the season to an exchange at the time of the contest. In most instances eligibility lists are exchanged between competing schools from within three days to a week prior to the contest. There are three general plans followed relative to eligibility list procedures which are typical of those in effect in most states.

KANSAS STATE HIGH SCHOOL ACTIVITIES ASSOCIATION
ATHLETIC ELIGIBILITY CERTIFICATE
THIS APPLIES TO BOTH BOYS AND GIRLS

1. Each competing athlete must be a bonafide undergraduate pupil and in attendance in high school not later than Monday of the fourth week of school.
2. He must be under 20 years of age the day of the contest. Age limit for junior high school pupils is 17 in 3-yr schools and 16 in 2-yr junior high schools.
3. He must not have attended high school eight semesters and his seventh and eighth semesters must be consecutive. In 3-yr senior and junior high schools he must not have attended six semesters. In 2-yr schools the limit is four semesters.
4. He must not have competed more than four seasons in one sport, beginning with the ninth grade, and not more than eight semesters altogether.

5. He must not engage in outside competition in any sport.
6. He must be an amateur. (Read the Amateur Rule.)
7. He must be passing in at least three subjects of unit weight. Junior high school pupils must be passing in at least three-fourths of their work and in not less than three subjects of unit weight.
8. He must have passed in at least three subjects of unit weight his last previous semester in attendance.
9. He may not transfer from one school to another and be eligible until after eighteen weeks' attendance, unless his parents move.
10. He must not be a member of a high school fraternity.
11. He must pass an adequate physical examination given by a physician.
12. He must have the written consent of his parents.

HE MUST MEET ALL ELIGIBILITY REQUIREMENTS AS GIVEN IN RULE 1 OR RULE 2. READ THEM.

I hereby certify that each of the pupils whose names appear below is eligible under each of the provisions of the eligibility rules and may, therefore, compete for_____High School in the_____contest with_____
_____High School, on_____, 19____. It is agreed the contest will be played at_____
on_____ at_____o'clock and that the following registered officials shall officiate:_____
Date

Color of Jerseys_____   Signed_____
H. S. Principal or Superintendent must sign.

NAME OF CONTESTANTS (Listed Alphabetically)	Jersey Number	BIRTH Month Day Year	Date of Enrollment for present Semester	No. of full and regular studies carried successfully Last Semester	No. of full and regular studies carried successfully to date This Semester	No. years in this sport previous to this year	Total Semesters in High School including Present Semester	Has he passed Physical Examination by Physician?

(OVER)

Fig. 5-5. Athletic Eligibility Certificate Form *(Kansas)*.

The most common procedure is that of exchange of a form before each game which gives the complete history of all contestants. Such data usually include birth records; dates of enrollment during the current semester; indication that contestants have passed the required physical examinations; number of semesters enrolled in grades nine to twelve, inclusive; number of subjects carried successfully during the preceding and current semesters; and number of seasons of participation in the sport concerned. In some instances space is provided on such blanks to indicate whether contestants are transfer students from other schools; and, if so, the names of the schools usually are stated. The Athletic Eligibility Certificate of the Kansas State High School Activities Association is used to illustrate this type of blank (see Fig. 5-5).

Several points of this blank are especially desirable, and the forms used by the large majority of states are similar. Attention is called to the brief résumé of the eligibility rules for contestants that appears at the top. The next section of the blank provides for listing of pertinent information relative to the contest concerned. The location, date, hour, and officials for the contest may be listed by the entertaining school. Such information is essential, and although much of it may have appeared on the contract blank or in previous correspondence, it is an excellent administrative procedure to call it to the attention of all those concerned immediately preceding the contest.

The use of forms similar to the one in Kansas has the advantage of furnishing all data on contestants immediately preceding each contest. There has been some objection, however, to the amount of clerical work involved in the preparation of such detailed information on each contestant for each contest. In some instances, also, there has been the feeling that eligibility data would be more valuable if it were in the hands of all schools at the beginning of the season rather than just before a game, with the result that it does not reach some schools until the end of the season.

A second type of plan is used in Michigan. Virginia uses a variation. These two states have what are called Master Eligibility Lists. They are similar in form to the Kansas blank but are prepared by schools only once during the current season. In Michigan, copies are sent to all schools on the schedule at the beginning of the season and to the state association office; only the latter is done in Virginia. In that state it is understood that all students whose names are on the first list remain eligible during the entire season unless a competing school is notified to the contrary by letter.

For each contest during the season in Michigan, a Current Eligibility List (see Fig. 5-6) is sent to each school. This form contains only the names of those students who are eligible for the contest concerned. There is the stipulation that their names with complete athletic and scholastic data must have appeared on a Master Eligibility List previously sent to the school. This procedure has the advantage

MICHIGAN HIGH SCHOOL ATHLETIC ASSOCIATION
Current Eligibility List (Form-2)

Names of Contestants Eligible to Represent...

(Name of School)

High School in a .... Contest on.................... with.................................... High School
　　　　　　　　　　(Sport)　　　　　　　　　　　　(Date)　　　　　(Name of School)

(This Section MUST be filled out IN FULL by the host school.)

Contest will be held at..
　　　　　　　　　　　　　　　(Name and location of field or gymnasium)

Contest will begin at................o'clock. Color of jerseys of our team:.................... Color of football....................
The *officials for the contest will be: (After name, please indicate whether referee, umpire, headlinesman, etc.)

....whose address is....................................
　　　　　　　　　　(Capacity)

....whose address is....................................
　　　　　　　　　　(Capacity)

....whose address is....................................
　　　　　　　　　　(Capacity)

HOST SCHOOL SHOULD REMIND OFFICIALS OF DATE AND PLACE AT LEAST FIVE (5) DAYS PRIOR TO THE GAME.
(*Football, basketball, and baseball officials and track and swimming referees and/or starters must be registered with the State Association for the current school year.)

NOTE:—The names and complete eligibility records of all contestants listed below must have appeared on a Master Eligibility List (Form-1) previously sent to all competing schools and to the office of the State Director of Interscholastic Athletics, Department of Public Instruction, Lansing 2. Contestants whose names appear hereon also must be eligible scholastically in accordance with the provisions of Regulation I, Sections 7 and 8, (Senior High Schools) or Regulation III, Sections 7 and 8, (Junior High Schools).

NAME OF CONTESTANT (Please type full given names alphabetically. Do NOT use initials or nicknames.)	NAME OF CONTESTANT (Please type full given names alphabetically. Do NOT use initials or nicknames.)	NAME OF CONTESTANT (Please type full given names alphabetically. Do NOT use initials or nicknames.)

Fig. 5-6. Current Eligibility List Form (Michigan).

of furnishing all schools concerned with data on all contestants of a school at the beginning of a season. In Michigan this plan has resulted in better relations between schools. Questions concerning eligibility of contestants are brought up before the contests in many instances, with the effect of decreasing the number of protests after games have been played. Another advantage in using the Michigan type of blank for each contest is its ease of preparation. Only the names of students who are eligible for the contest are listed. These may be taken from the master list after scholastic standings of students for the current contest have been determined.

Uniform Eligibility List Form

From...High School   To...High School
...., Connecticut   ...., Connecticut
The following boys are eligible under the rules of the Connecticut Interscholastic Athletic Conference, printed on the reverse of this sheet and above, to represent this school in the...game to be played at...on...19.......

....19.......   ....
                                                                                      Principal

It is recommended that this be signed in duplicate—one copy going out by mail, and the second copy being exchanged at game time by the team manager or coach.

Fig. 5-7. Uniform Eligibility List Form (Connecticut).

A third procedure in the exchange of eligibility information is illustrated by forms used by the Connecticut, Oregon, and Indiana state associations. Plans used in these typical states are the easiest of all from an administrative standpoint (see Figs. 5-7, 5-8, and 5-9). Procedure in these states simply provides that the competing schools shall exchange lists with only the names of eligible contestants on them. It will be seen that the plan is similar to that followed in Michigan as far as use of the current list is concerned. But in these states no blank with complete data on contestants has been exchanged previously between the competing schools. The chief advantage claimed for this plan is its simplicity. In Maine no prepared forms are exchanged; the principals of competing schools

[ORIGINAL]

Certificate to Competing School

OREGON SCHOOL ACTIVITIES ASSOCIATION OFFICIAL ELIGIBILITY LIST

The following pupils of the..................................High School are eligible, under the Rules of the Association, to represent above named High School in the..............................Game to be played at....................................on ...., 19........, between the..H. S. and the....................................H. S.

LAST NAME	GIVEN NAME	LAST NAME	GIVEN NAME	LAST NAME	GIVEN NAME
1		11		21	
2		12		22	
3		13		23	
4		14		24	
5		15		25	
6		16		26	
7		17		27	
8		18		28	
9		19		29	
10		20		30	

This...........day of......................, 19........ ...., Principal. ...., High School

Use This Form and Avoid Misunderstanding with Competing Schools

FORM 2

Fig. 5-8. Athletic Eligibility Certificate Form (Oregon).

send names of eligible students on school stationery, which they sign.

It is felt by some that responsibility for eligibility rests with each individual school and that no advantage is gained by compiling a great amount of data on contestants, much of which is never used. The other plans discussed here are defended by states and schools using them because they feel there is a distinct advantage gained by all concerned when all data on eligibility of contestants are common knowledge. Local schoolmen often feel that such a plan is good for them in that it is a constant check on their own procedures and information and obviates many difficulties that otherwise might arise later.

It should be kept in mind that some type of eligibility information must be sent to most state association offices either seasonally or annually. This requirement is fulfilled by the preparation, either at

---

Indiana High School Athletic Association
OFFICIAL ELIGIBILITY LIST

Principal.., 19......

...., Indiana

I hereby certify that the following named students of the..High School

are eligible to play under IHSAA rules with the..High School

in the ....game(s) to be played in..

on.., 19......

The students listed below have been checked for th e following IHSAA eligibility requirements: Scholarship, Enrollment, Independent Participation, Parent's and Physician's Certificates, Birth Record, Amateur Standing, Residence and Athletic Transfer Blank. I find them in good standing.

....Principal

Name of Student		Name of Student		Name of Student	
Last	First	Last	First	Last	First

☞ NOTE—This blank properly filled out and signed must be given or mailed to the Principal of the opposing school prior to each contest.

Form C—6-1-60—50M

Fig. 5-9. Official Eligibility Form (Indiana).

the beginning or the end of the season, of special blanks giving this information or by having copies of eligibility blanks forwarded. For example, Kansas, Oregon, Louisiana, Minnesota, and Oklahoma require that athletes' or participants' summaries for all sports be filed in the state association office by specified dates. Alabama and

LOUISIANA HIGH SCHOOL ATHLETIC ASSOCIATION
Annual Report to the Executive Board
Due June 1st
SEE ARTICLE II, SECTION 4, BY-LAWS

_____, 19____

I hereby certify that the following pupils and no others have represented the_____High School of_____, in Parish of_____, in Interscholastic Athletics between September 1, 19_____, and June 1, 19_____, that this list is complete, and that the data set opposite the names are correct:

| Enter Alphabetically, Last Name First | Date of Birth Year, Mo., Day | Number Semesters in High School at End of this Year | Number of Years of Participation Including Present Year | | | | | | | | | Remarks |
			Football	Basketball	Baseball	Track	Boxing	Tennis	Six Man Football	Soft ball	

If any of the above players participated, while in the grades, as a member of a High School team, so state or the year will be counted as one of the four years allotted a high school player.

NOTE—Copies of this blank may be obtained from the Commissioner.

Blank 2   Principal of_____High School

Fig. 5-10. Form for Annual Report to Executive Board (Louisiana).

Iowa follow such a plan and also require that a Permanent Book of Record for the School Year be kept on file by the school itself. This contains all eligibility information as well as results of all athletic contests and financial records. Such a procedure provides complete information for preceding years and should be valuable, especially when changes in the administration of schools take place. Missouri requires that an Athletic Participation Report for each school year be sent to the state association office. This includes not only all eligibility and participation data for all contestants, but also all schedules and scores of all contests in which the athletic teams of the schools competed during the year. The Annual Report to the Executive Board blank used by the Louisiana High School Athletic Association is an example of a participation survey as used in a number of states (see Fig. 5-10).

Typical state association by-laws relative to the exchange of eligibility lists, as they apply to each of the three plans discussed, follow:

The principal shall certify to the eligibility of all contestants in accordance with the Constitution and By-Laws of this Association. Such statements, including date of birth, place of birth, date of enrollment for current school year, number of seasons of competition beyond the eighth grade including the present season, number of semesters of attendance in the ninth grade including the present semester, and number of seasons of competition in the ninth grade, shall be presented in writing to the principal of the opponent school or schools at least four days prior to the contest. (Pennsylvania) [5]

This regulation illustrates a detailed by-law which establishes the data to be tabulated concerning each contestant for each contest (see Fig. 5-5). Blanks such as are used in Michigan are governed by the Michigan regulation concerned (see Figs. 5-2 and 5-6).

Five (5) days prior to the first game in each season each high school shall submit to all scheduled opponents and to the office of the State Director, a Master Eligibility List (Form-1) of all students eligible for that sport under the provisions of the By-Laws, including current semester record. Additions to the squad will be certified at once to competing schools in a similar manner on an additional Master Eligibility List. Also,

[5] Pennsylvania Interscholastic Athletic Association, 1958 *Constitution and By-Laws*, pp. 32–33.

in those sports which carry over into two semesters, an additional Master List is to be submitted at the opening of the second semester to each remaining school on the schedule and to the office of the State Director.

Subsequently for each succeeding game, a Current Eligibility List (Form-2) carrying names of eligible students only will be submitted to schools concerned five (5) days prior to the contest.

These Lists shall be certified by the superintendent of schools or the principal of the competing high school. Certification shall be based on complete information concerning the student's age, athletic, and scholastic status. Questionable cases shall be referred to the State Director before the privilege of competition is given. (Michigan) [6]

The Indiana Rule on exchange of eligibility lists is similar to the Connecticut and Oregon rules (see Fig. 5-9):

The eligibility of all contestants shall be certified to by the Principal of the school in accordance with the rules hereby adopted. Such statements shall be exchanged by the Principals, in writing, prior to the beginning of any contest. (Indiana) [7]

The regulation which the Missouri State High School Activities Association has in effect concerning a permanent record for the state secretary is typical of those which many other states have. Such a by-law illustrates the type of permanent record blank used by Louisiana (see Fig. 5-10).

At the close of each school year each member school shall report to the Executive Secretary on a standard form a list of all the students who have represented that school in athletics the year immediately preceding, file on standard form reports requested by the Board of Control of athletic contests with the names of the officials that officiated the contests, and a rating of the officials. Membership for the next following year shall not be continued after July 1 unless these reports have been filed with the Secretary. (Missouri) [8]

Records of transfer students. The discussion on pages 87–89 indicated that state associations have definite regulations on transfer

---

[6] Michigan High School Athletic Association, 1961–1962 *Handbook*, p. 45.

[7] Indiana High School Athletic Association, *Fifty-seventh Annual Handbook* (1960), p. 38.

[8] Missouri State High School Activities Association, 1960 *Official Handbook*, p. 14.

and undue influence. Several states have prepared blanks that must be executed when a student who transfers from one school to another wishes to compete in athletics at the second school. These forms usually are in addition to the regular scholastic and child-accounting blanks which accompany a transfer student. The object of such forms has been to simplify the recording of athletic and scholastic information and to ensure the inclusion of all pertinent and necessary data.

The Student Transfer Record Form (Fig. 5-11) used in Maine is an excellent example of a combination scholastic and athletic activities record blank. The blank itself indicates that it is "Approved by the Maine Association of Principals of Secondary Schools for official record of participation in athletics and eligibility status of pupil on date of transfer." The blank accompanies a transfer student to his new school and at once gives both his scholastic and athletic record. This seems to be a desirable feature in that the execution of two similar blanks is unnecessary.

The Transfer Blank in use by the Michigan High School Athletic Association illustrates a strictly athletic transfer form (Fig. 5-12). Such a blank is necessitated in this and many other states because of the existence of standard academic record forms. It has served its purpose well in this state and, as indicated in the first section of the blank, it is executed by the school to which a student has transferred. The Michigan regulation also provides that a transfer student cannot safely be certified for athletics in the school to which he transfers until his transfer blank, completely filled out, is on file there. The result is to expedite the forwarding of information concerning transfer students.

Certification of athletic coaches. It is an almost universal rule among the state associations that only regularly certificated and full-time faculty members of schools may be coaches of athletic teams. Several reasons are behind this policy. Most state associations are voluntary organizations; that is, they control their memberships by the validity of the regulations which they establish. Thus, it is possible to set up regulations that coaches must be full-time faculty members who receive their pay solely from public funds, and that only schools having such coaches may join the association. In Michigan, one of the very few states in which this general plan is not followed, all public, private, and parochial high schools in the state

STUDENT TRANSFER RECORD
FOR HIGH SCHOOLS AND ACADEMIES

Pupil's Name _____ Age _____ Parent or Guardian _____ Date _____

Transfer From _____   Transfer To _____

School _____   School _____
Town _____   Town _____
Principal _____   Principal _____

SCHOLASTIC RECORD

Studies	No. Wks.	Periods Per Week	Min. utes	Per Cent	Rank A, B, C, D, or E
English					
English					
English					
English					

Check ranks transferred from another school.
Name of such school _____
Month and year that work was completed _____

NOTE.—This form is to be used when a pupil leaves a school and expects to enter another school. It should be made out in details as it becomes the permanent record of the school which the pupil enters.

UNIFORM RANKING SCALE

A — High
B — Above average
C — Average
D — Below average
E — Low or failure

PERSONAL TRAITS

Accuracy _____
Cooperation _____
Industry _____
Leadership _____
Personal Appearance _____
Reliability _____

Rate as A, B, C, D, E

ATHLETIC AND ACTIVITIES RECORD*

	BRANCH	Record - Number of games played, first or second teams, and other activities.	Year
1st Year	Baseball		
	Basketball		
	Football		
	Track		
2nd Year	Baseball		
	Basketball		
	Football		
	Track		
3rd Year	Baseball		
	Basketball		
	Football		
	Track		
4th Year	Baseball		
	Basketball		
	Football		
	Track		

This pupil was not eligible for athletics on date of transfer.
was

*Approved by Maine Association of Principals of Secondary Schools for official record of participation in athletics and eligibility status of pupil on date of transfer.

Check here _____ (if additional data is given on reverse side of this sheet.

Pass mark _____ College Certificate Grade _____
Signed _____
Position _____
Additional forms may be secured at the rate of 50 cents per 100.
Address: Secretary of Maine Association of Principals of Secondary Schools, State House, Augusta, Maine.

Printed by Portland High School Printing Department

Fig. 5-11. Student Transfer Record Form (Maine).

127

MICHIGAN HIGH SCHOOL ATHLETIC ASSOCIATION

TRANSFER BLANK (FORM-5)

(For use in connection with provisions of State Association Regulations I or III, Section 9.)

To the Principal of..High School ...., ...
(Name of school) (City) (State)

....High School needs the following information concerning a former student
(Name of inquiring school)

in your school by the name of..in order to determine his athletic eligibility.
The prompt return of this blank will be appreciated inasmuch as the student concerned cannot be considered for certification by us as being eligible to compete in interscholastic athletics until we have the information requested below on file in our office.

Yours truly,

....
(Superintendent or Principal)

Date..   ...., Michigan
(City)

(To be filled in by superintendent or principal of school to which inquiry is made.)

1. Our record of his date of birth is.., ..., ...
(Month) (Day) (Year)

   Our record of his place of birth is..
   (City) (State)

   Source of this information..
   (School record, birth certificate, etc.)

2. Our record of his number of semesters of enrollment in grades 9-12, inclusive, (if a senior high school student) is..

   Our record of his number of semesters of enrollment in grades 7-9, inclusive, (if a junior high school student) is..
   "Enrollment in a school for a period of three weeks or more, or competing in one or more interscholastic athletic contests, shall be considered as enrollment for a semester under this rule." (State Association Regulations I or III, Section 5.)

3. The number of subjects he carried successfully in our school last semester was..

   This number would be equivalent to..hours of credit.

4. He WAS—WAS NOT enrolled in our school by Monday of the fourth week of the last semester he attended.
   (Cross out one)

5. He DID—DID NOT enter our school from another high school.
   (Cross out one)

   The name of that school was..

6. The date this student first enrolled in our school was..

   The date this student last attended our school was..

7. His parents, guardian, or other persons with whom he has been living during the period of his last high school enrollment HAVE—HAVE NOT moved from our district. According to our best knowledge they HAVE—HAVE NOT
   (Cross out one)   (Cross out one)
   moved to your district.

8. Our school is a THREE—FOUR year high school.
   (Cross out one)

9. The number of seasons of participation for this student in our school in each of the following sports is:

   Football.................., Basketball.................., Baseball.................., Track..................

   Swimming.................., Tennis.................., Golf.................., Cross Country..................

   Other.................., Remarks..................

   (The above student DID—DID NOT play eighth grade baseball under provisions of State Association Regulation I, Section 1.)
   (Cross out one)

10. We WOULD—WOULD NOT have considered above student eligible for participation in athletics during his next semester had he remained in our school.
    (Cross out one)

Date..   ....
(Superintendent or Principal)

NOTE: Use other side of this sheet for explanation of any unusual circumstances which might be helpful in this case.

Fig. 5-12. Student Transfer Record Form (Michigan).

automatically are members of the state association by virtue of its relation with the Department of Public Instruction. Because of the lack of male teachers in some parochial and small public high schools who could act as coaches, Michigan was faced with the necessity of making this special regulation:

The person responsible for the immediate training or coaching of a high school athletic team should be a member of the regular teaching staff of the school. If a non-faculty member is used he must be registered by the school in the office of the State Director on a form provided for that purpose before he begins his duties. Such non-faculty member coaches must be at least twenty-one (21) years of age or have completed two (2) or more years of college work.

All coaches (head and assistants) of interscholastic athletic teams in Class A high schools shall hold teaching certificates which would qualify them as teachers in the high school whose teams they are coaching.

NOTE: The Representative Council urges that all schools work as rapidly as possible toward realization of the standard that only qualified faculty members are to be used as coaches of interscholastic athletic teams.

Coaches of girls' interscholastic athletic teams shall be women.[9]

Michigan prefers that all coaches be regularly certificated faculty members and will work toward this realization. In the meantime the registration of nonfaculty coaches has helped to fix responsibility for athletic coaching with school officials when outsiders are engaged.

As indicated previously, the Michigan situation is the exception rather than the general practice. Most state association by-laws are definite in establishing the status of coaches. From educational as well as administrative standpoints, it is important that the coach be a regular faculty member, because all faculty members should have the school point of view and its educational interests at heart. By and large, there is no question that athletics will be much better administered if the coach is a regular part of the school system. There should be much less possibility of "downtown influence" if all the control and policy making for athletics are administered in the same manner as other phases of the education program in a

[9] Michigan High School Athletic Association, 1961–1962 *Handbook*, p. 45.

school. A few examples of state association by-laws relative to coaches follow. Oklahoma privides that

The coach shall be in charge of the training and participation of contestants. He shall be a certified teacher regularly employed by the Board of Education or a Governmental Agency, and his entire salary shall be paid by that body. He shall have not less than three regular periods of classes, gymnasium, study hall, or administrative duty per day.[10]

Wisconsin's regulation is similar except that it allows for certain emergencies:

No athletic team representing a member school for this Association shall be coached by other than a person holding a State Certificate of grade and rank required by said member school of their instructors. In addition, such qualified person shall be a full time member of the school faculty. However, the Board of Control shall have the power to give emergency relief or to permit a school team to be coached by some one other than a hired teacher for some one reason provided that a written agreement between the school and individual requested has been submitted to and approved by the Board of Control.[11]

Louisiana definitely rules that coaches must teach at least three classes per day:

The coach of any athletic team shall be a member of the faculty of that school and teach at least three classes each day unless such coach be either Principal or Assistant Principal.[12]

The California rule on coaches is definite:

All teams must be coached by a certified teacher. A certified teacher is designated as a person holding a valid California State Teaching Credential or, in case of a non-public school, a person engaged by that school on a yearly contract basis as a regular member of the school teaching staff and certified by the administrator of that school as competent for the position held. Such a person may not be reimbursed for his services

[10] Oklahoma High School Athletic Association, 1960–1961 *Constitution and Rules,* p. 12.

[11] Wisconsin Interscholastic Athletic Association, 1960 *Yearbook,* p. 17.

[12] Louisiana High School Athletic Association, 1960–1961 *Handbook,* p. 46.

from any source other than school funds, nor be subject to any bonus arrangement dependent upon the success of his teams. Teams of affiliated C.I.F. member schools must be coached by teachers certified in their own State (for certain schools outside California).

Participation of cadet teachers is approved in coaching activities when they are regularly assigned to a school for practice teaching and under the supervision of a regular certified coach.[13]

The Pennsylvania regulation concerning coaches brings the discussion of this subject to a close:

Only full time teaches certificated by the Pennsylvania Department of Public Instruction, who are employed in a full time teaching capacity by the school district in which they are employed shall coach, direct, or assist in coaching athletic teams in the school district where employed.

Full-time teachers who are employed by two or more school districts may coach in any of the school districts by which they are employed.

Student-teachers may assist in coaching provided they do not replace any coach, head or assistant, and provided they assist only during the time they are assigned to a school as a student-teacher.

Coaching shall be interpreted to mean instruction or direction of members of interscholastic athletic teams, individually or as a group, for the purpose of developing ability or skill to perform in athletic contests. It includes such voluntary instruction as that which in some cases has been given, in the past, by high school alumni, professional athletes, and citizens of the community who are interested in developing winning teams. Such instruction shall be given only by full time teachers employed by the school district.[14]

Registration of athletic officials. With the exception of a few states, among them being Pennsylvania and Connecticut in the East, Alabama and Louisiana in the South, and Oregon in the West, the policy of registration and classification of athletic officials by state associations is pretty much a Middle-Western development. The following states in this section have such plans in effect: South Dakota, Kansas, Nebraska, Minnesota, Iowa, Wisconsin, Indiana, Illinois, Missouri, Ohio, Oklahoma, and Michigan. The registration of athletic officials has had as its chief purpose that of improvement

[13] California Interscholastic Federation, 1959 *Constitution and By-Laws,* p. 3.
[14] Pennsylvania Interscholastic Athletic Association, *1958 Constitution and By-Laws,* p. 29.

in officiating and effecting a closer and better relationship between officials and schools. State associations have sought to aid schools in effecting this improved relationship through registration requirements. This policy has given state organizations the opportunity to have control over officiating as well as to establish general rules interpretations in various sports.

Requirements that only registered officials be used by schools usually apply to football and basketball but often also to baseball, track, swimming, and wrestling. Some states require registration in all sports. Registration usually is an annual matter. Fees range from $1 a year in one or all sports to $5 for registration for the first year and $3 to $4 a year thereafter. Officials usually receive sports rules books and state association publications, and often they are required

---

KANSAS STATE HIGH SCHOOL ACTIVITIES ASSOCIATION

C. H. KOPELK, Executive Secretary, Topeka, Kansas_____, 19____

I hereby apply for certification as an approved Kansas State High School Activities Association Official and enclose fee of $_____ (Fee for one sport, $4.00; For both sports, $7.00)

Name _____ Present Occupation _____
(Please Print)

Street _____ City _____ Phone _____
(Mailing Address)

Last year's address_____

Were you registered last year?_____ Did you take the required rules examination last year?_____
(Yes or No)   (Yes or No)

Certification desired (check one or both) Football_____ Basketball _____
I agree to all registration requirements, including attendance at official rules interpretation clinics at least once each season.

Signed_____ Official.

For all who were registered last season there is a penalty of $1.00 per month for late registration, beginning August 1 in football and October 1 in basketball.

Fig. 5-13. Application Form for Registration of Official (Kansas).

to attend rules interpretation meetings. In some states they must take written examinations in various sports in order to reregister or be promoted to higher classifications. Frequently there are two or three classifications of officials, membership in which is dependent upon the number of games they have officiated, examination grades, rules-meeting attendance, and ratings of schools for which they officiate. Schools send in ratings on officials to the state association office after games or at the end of the season, and the average or individual ratings by schools are then generally available to officials. Lists of classified registered officials are published in state association bulletins or handbooks, which are sent to schools.

The Kansas rules relative to registration of athletic officials, and the procedure to be followed, are typical of those in many states (see Fig. 5–13).

Only officials who are registered with the K.S.H.S.A.A. may be used by member schools to officiate in first team and second team football or basketball games. In order for an official to become properly registered the following requirements must be met:

a. There must be on file in the office of the K.S.H.S.A.A. an application requesting registration as an official in the sport or sports in which the official desires to officiate. He must agree to meet all requirements established by the Executive Board.

b. Each official must pay a registration fee as determined by the Executive Board.

A penalty of at least one dollar ($1.00) per month for late registration shall be charged each football official who fails to renew his registration by August 1. A like penalty will be charged each basketball official who fails to renew his registration by October 1.[15]

In contrast to the simplified form used in Kansas for the registration of athletic officials, several other states require additional data. The Illinois form used for this purpose is illustrative (see Fig. 5–14).

As indicated in the Kansas rule, officials in that state must have registration cards for the current year in their possession to be eligible to officiate. This regulation is common in most states (see sample registration cards, Officials' Registration Form [Illinois]. Figs. 5–15, 5–16, 5–17, and 5–18). In addition to the use of cards as evidence that an official is properly registered with the state association for a current year, some states furnish officials' emblems that are worn on the shirt or sleeve. Iowa and Michigan have followed such a practice (see Fig. 5–19). The general instructions to officials regarding wearing of the Michigan emblem which appear on the envelope containing it are as follows:

[15] Kansas State High School Activities Association, 1960–1961 *Handbook*, p. 33.

ILLINOIS HIGH SCHOOL ASSOCIATION
11 SOUTH LA SALLE STREET, CHICAGO 3, ILLINOIS

REGISTRATION FOR MEMBERSHIP IN OFFICIALS' DEPARTMENT
(To be accompanied by $5.00 Registration Fee)

Name_____ _____, 19____
                                                                              (Date)

Mailing Address_____
                    (Street, Etc.)   (Town)   (State)

Occupation:_____ Age:_____ Height:_____Weight:_____ Race:_____
                                                                              (White or Colored)

Check the sports in which you are prepared to officiate: Basketball_____ Football_____ Track ____

Baseball_____ Swimming_____ Wrestling_____

ACADEMIC TRAINING

Names of High Schools Attended	Location	No. Years	Dates in Years	Major

Name of College or University Attended				

ATHLETIC TRAINING   PLAYING

Name of High School	(Number Years You Played in)					
	FOOTBALL	BASKETBALL	TRACK	BASEBALL	SWIMMING	WRESTLING
College or University						

Please star (*) sports in which school letter was earned.

COACHING

Name of School	No. Years	Dates in Years	Sports

OFFICIATING

Number of years of officiating: high school_____ college_____ other_____

Number of contests officiated during last 3 years in FB_____ BB_____ SWIM_____

BASE._____ TRACK_____ WREST._____

REFERENCES: Give names and addresses of three references who know of your character and qualifications as an official.

	Name	Street	Town or City	State
1.				
2.				
3.				

Mail this with application blank to the Illinois High School Association, 11 South LaSalle St., Chicago 3

Fig. 5-14. Official's Registration Form (Illinois).

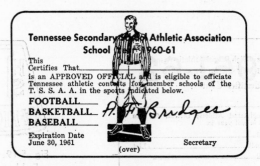

Fig. 5-15. Official's Registration Card (Minnesota).

Minnesota State High School League
REGISTERED OFFICIAL 1960-61 No. 1548
EXPIRES MAY 31, 1961

SPORT	CLASSIFICATION			RECIPROCITY	IN	FROM
	R	A	C			
Baseball				Michigan		
Basketball				Wisconsin		
Football				Iowa		
Hockey				South Dakota		
Wrestling				North Dakota		

Amount Paid $_____ Date_____

_____Asst. Executive Secretary

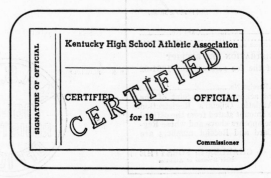

Tennessee Secondary School Athletic Association
School 1960-61

This
Certifies That_____
is an APPROVED OFFICIAL and is eligible to officiate
Tennessee athletic contests for member schools of the
T. S. S. A. A. in the sports indicated below.

FOOTBALL_____
BASKETBALL_____ A. F. Bridges
BASEBALL_____

Expiration Date
June 30, 1961
(over)   Secretary

Fig. 5-16. Official's Registration Card (Tennessee).

Kentucky High School Athletic Association

SIGNATURE OF OFFICIAL

CERTIFIED

CERTIFIED _____ OFFICIAL

for 19____

Commissioner

Fig. 5-17. Official's Registration Card (Kentucky).

To Registered Official:
This envelope contains official's emblem TO BE WORN BY EACH OF-
FICIAL REGISTERED with the Michigan High School Athletic Association during the current school year in football, basketball, baseball,
track, and swimming.

GENERAL INSTRUCTIONS

Football and Basketball Officials—Emblem should be SEWED ON and
WORN ON LEFT POCKET AREA of the official black and white striped
shirt.
*Baseball Umpires, Track and Swimming Starters or Referees, Wrestling
and Women Basketball Officials*—An elastic band should be attached to
emblem (unless sewed on) and it is to be WORN ON LEFT SHIRT
SLEEVE.

Michigan High School Athletic Association
OFFICIAL REGISTRATION CARD
1961-62
This Certifies That

_____
is a registered Athletic Official for the
1961-62 school year in
Football_____List
Basketball_____List
Baseball_____
Track_____
Swimming_____
Wrestling_____

Charles E. Forsythe
State Director of Athletics

Dated_____ Card No._____

- - - - - - - - - - (Detach and retain above card) - - - - - - - - - -
REGISTRATION FEE RECEIPT
Amount of the fee received for 1961-62

$_____Receipt No._____
This card acknowledges receipt of the
1961-62 Athletic Official's Registration
Fee for the amount stated from the official
whose name appears above and whose Registration Card and Receipt numbers are
identical.
CHARLES E. FORSYTHE
State Director of Athletics
61   47C

Fig. 5-18. Official's Registration Card
(Michigan).

Fig. 5-19. Official's
Emblem *(Iowa).*

Fig. 5-20. Official's
Emblem *(Michigan).*

Extra emblems (in addition to those furnished by the State Association) may be purchased by officials at a cost of 25¢ each, and orders may be placed through the State Association Office.

Emblems should be worn as directed, giving evidence that your registration has been completed for the current school year. It also indicates to school officials, players, and spectators that, as an official in the performance of your duties, you are affiliated with, and have the support of, the Michigan High School Athletic Association with its seven hundred member high schools and annual registration list of over two thousand athletic officials.

The Illinois plan for registration and classification of athletic officials is an outstanding one. Its by-law follows:

In all baseball, basketball and football games and in all swimming, track and wrestling meets in which member schools are responsible for the selection of officials, each major official employed must be registered with this Association in the sport he is to officiate. This requirement, however, shall not apply to officials who work without compensation.[16]

There are five classifications of officials in Illinois. An elaborate promotional system exists, which includes examinations, ratings in major and minor games, attendance at rules meetings, and number of years of registration (see the Illinois Form for Rating Officials, Fig. 5–21).

In contrast to the one form procedure for rating all athletic officials used during a season in Illinois, some states have an individual card for each official. This plan has the advantage that each card is easily filed, but unless careful record is kept in the state association office of all schools from which cards are received, it is difficult to determine from which schools ratings have been forwarded. On its form for rating athletic officials, Alabama asks schools to list the strong and weak points of the men who work their games (see Fig. 5–22).

It is common practice for state associations to provide contract blanks for use of schools and athletic officials. The use of these is good administrative procedure and obviates many misunderstandings. A typical blank of this nature is one prepared by the Nebraska High School Activities Association (see Fig. 5–23). It may be used

[16] Illinois High School Athletic Association, 1960–1961 *Handbook*, p. 25.

SHEET FOR RATING ATHLETIC OFFICIALS

MAIL TO

ILLINOIS HIGH SCHOOL ASSOCIATION

11 S. LA SALLE ST., CHICAGO 3

NOTE: List officials for only ONE SPORT on a given Sheet. This is for ....
(Sport)

Please rate all major officials who have been used in your games either at home or away this season. These ratings will be transferred to cards in the state office and will have a bearing on the classification of the official.

SUGGESTED RATING SCALE: SUPERIOR:—Good enough for State Basketball Tournament or a Conference Championship Football game. ABOVE AVERAGE:—Qualified for a Lower Tournament or an important Conference Football Game. AVERAGE:—Acceptable for a game of average importance. BELOW AVERAGE:—Acceptable for a game of minor importance only. VERY POOR:—Not acceptable for any game.

CONDUCT OF THE GAME

1. Knowledge of the rules.
2. Care in supervising and signaling minor officials.
3. Quickness and sureness of decision.
4. Impartiality and fairness.
5. Extent to which his decisions are affected by comments of spectators, players or coaches.
6. Agility in following the ball or the play.
7. Extent to which he maintains complete control of game.
8. Strictness and consistency in his decisions and interpretations.
9. Extent to which his officiating promotes good sportsmanship, a clean, fast game and a festive feeling.
10. Self control and poise on the floor or field.

PERSONAL

a. Neatness of appearance at contests.
b. Degree in which his ideals are such as you would require in a high school teacher.
c. Promptness and business-like attitude in matters pertaining to his contract.
d. Tactfulness and modesty (as opposed to being overbearing and boastful).

NAME	ADDRESS	Month Used	Number of Games	YOUR ESTIMATE AS TO ABILITY					Needs Improvement in Items Number
				Superior	Above Average	Average	Below Average	Very Poor	
Sample—John Doe	Oquawka	Dec.	3		x				6-10-a

.... 19...... Signed:.. Principal or Ath. Director

(List Tournament Officials on Back) ....H. S.,..........Ill.

Fig. 5-21. Form for Rating Officials (*Illinois*).

138

Alabama High School Athletic Association

FORM FOR RATING ATHLETIC OFFICIALS

Suggested Rating Scale: 1. Superior—Good enough for State Basketball Tournament or the best football game. 2. Above Average—Qualified for District Basketball Tournament or important football game. 3. Average—Acceptable for a game of average importance. 4. Below Average—Acceptable for a game of minor importance only. 5. Very poor—Not acceptable for any game. **Give Your Honest Opinion Of The Official's Ability For The Sport Named.** Mark in rating column a 1, 2, 3, 4, or 5 according to above Suggested Rating Scale.

Official's Name (Last) (First or Initials)	Address	Site of Game	RATING	Sport	Date of Game	*Strong Points	*Weak Points

SIGNED:

................................School ....Coach

................................Alabama ....Prin-

*ITEMS to help in rating and for suggested improvement of officials (a) Knowledge of rules. (b) Care in supervising and signaling minor officials. (c) Quickness and sureness of dicision. (d) Impartiality and fairness. (e) Extent to which his decisions are affected by comments of spectators, players or coaches. (f) Agility in following the ball or play. (g. Good control of game situations. (h) Strictness and consistency in decision and interpretations. (i) Officiating promotes sportsmanship, etc. (j) Self-Control and poise. (k) Neatness. (l) Promptness, etc. (m) Tactfulness.

Mail complete report for each sport to—State Secretary, 418 Monroe St., Montgomery, Ala.

Fig. 5-22. Form for Rating Officials (Alabama).

Form D

Nebraska School Activities Association
CONTRACT FOR REGISTERED OFFICIALS

_____, 19____

The_____High School and_____

of_____, an official registered with the Nebraska School Activities Association, hereby enter into the following agreement: The said official agrees to be present and officiate_____ games or meets to be played at_____, Nebraska, on the following dates during the school year 19____-19____.

	Date	Teams Playing	Day	Hour	Total Payment
1					
2					
3					
4					

The said school agrees to pay the said official the amount stated above for his services.

This contract shall be null and void if either the school or the official becomes suspended from the NSAA. Signed in duplicate this_____day of_____, 19____

Superintendent or Principal_____High School_____

Official_____Address_____

Fig. 5-23. Contract Form for Registered Officials (Nebraska).

as an agreement for a single game or for more than one. Attention is called to the fact that the contract is with a registered official and that the contract is void in case either the school or the official is suspended by the state association. Contracts are made out in duplicate, with the school and the official each keeping a copy. Some state association contracts for officials provide forfeiture fees for failure of either party to carry out the provisions of the agreement. In most instances, however, payment of this fee by one of the parties does not release it from contract responsibility unless there is mutual agreement to that effect.

Pennsylvania has introduced a new element into the requirements for registration of athletic officials. Briefly, it provides that football and basketball officials must submit to the state association office an annual Report of Official's Physical Examination (see Fig. 5–24). The reason for this regulation is indicated on the examination blank itself:

Consideration for the physical welfare of officials, due to deaths which have occurred on playing fields and in dressing rooms in the past, has prompted the Board of Control of the P. I. A. A. to formulate requirements that all football, basketball, baseball and wrestling officials, before entering upon an active season, shall subject themselves to a rigid physical examination. The examination may be conducted by the official's personal physician or other physician of his own selection.

There are many reasons why this examination is desirable. The official owes it to himself as a precautionary measure; to his reputation as an official; to his family; to the schools which employ him; to the boys whose games he administers; and to the public in general.[17]

Faculty managers at contests. It is impossible to place too great importance on adequate faculty management of athletics. Usually this need is realized if the coach is a regular member of the faculty. Under no circumstances should athletic contests be arranged or managed by students without the active direction or supervision of adult faculty managers. Likewise, it should be a definite rule in all schools that a member of the faculty be in attendance at all contests either at home or away. This statement may seem unnecessary,

---

[17] Pennsylvania Interscholastic Athletic Association, *Report of Official's Physical Examination—1960–1961* (see Fig. 5–24).

PENNSYLVANIA INTERSCHOLASTIC ATHLETIC ASSOCIATION
Report of Official's Physical Examination

(Note to official: The continuance of your registration as a P.I.A.A. Official depends upon the receipt of this blank (filled in and signed by your physician, or the reverse side signed by yourself) on or before dates specified. This is a Board of Control requirement.)

Consideration for the physical welfare of officials, due to deaths which have occurred on playing fields and in dressing rooms in the past, has prompted the Board of Control of the P. I. A. A. to formulate requirements that all football and basketball officials, before entering upon an active season, shall subject themselves to a rigid physical examination. The examination may be conducted by the official's personal physician or other physician of his own selection.

There are many reasons why this examination is desirable. The official owes it to himself as a precautionary measure; to his reputation as an official; to his family; to the schools which employ him; to the boys whose games he administers; and to the public in general.

FOOTBALL OFFICIALS are required to return the physical examination blank, properly filled and signed by a physician, BETWEEN THE DATES OF AUGUST 15 AND SEPTEMBER 1 TO THE P.I.A.A., 1613 N. FRONT ST., HARRISBURG, PA.

BASKETBALL OFFICIALS are required to return the physical examination blank, properly filled in and signed by a physician, BETWEEN THE DATES OF NOVEMBER 15 AND DECEMBER 15 TO P.I.A.A., 1613 N. FRONT ST., HARRISBURG, PA.

In case an individual officiates in more than one of the above named sports, it will not be necessary for such an individual to undergo two physical examinations. It is necessary for him to submit his physical examination blank before officiating in any one year in the first of his sports in which he is registered. For example: the physical examination before the football season will be sufficient for both football and basketball seasons.

NAME OF EXAMINEE .... DATE OF BIRTH ....

ADDRESS ....

RECENT ILLNESS ....

Eyes R .... L ....

Ears R .... L ....

Are eye glasses recommended for work as an athletic official? ....

CARDIOVASCULAR SYSTEM:

PULSE: Sitting ....   Blood Pressure S .... D ....

After Exercise, Immediately .... Two minutes ....

Is heart action clear and response to exercise normal? .... Is there any murmur or enlargement? .... Is pulse full, compressible and strong? ....

Is pulse regular? .... What is the rate? .... Is there any atheroma of the arteries? ....

CHEST: Normal .... Inspiration .... Expiration ....

ABDOMEN: Masses? .... Hernia? .... Measurement at umbilicus ....

FIGURE: (Good) (Fair) (Poor) FRAME (Heavy) (Medium) (Light) Height ....

WEIGHT: .... Is this over or underweight for general make up? ....

HEMORRHOIDS .... HERNIA? .... VARICOSITIES? ....

URINALYSIS

Specific Gravity————

Albumin: Presence............ Absence............... Sugar: Presence............... Absence.............

Microscopic examination if there is any history of diseases that produce kidney damage.

....

Does examinee meet all physical requirements for employment as an official in strenuous athletic contests? ....

If not, in what way is he deficient and to what extent? ....

....

Remarks and corrective measures: ....

....

Place .... D. O.

                               Signature   M. D.

Date ....

                              Address

TO THE EXAMINING PHYSICIAN: Other information may be submitted in a separate letter. Such additional information will be treated as confidential.

Fig. 5-24. Report Form for Official's Physical Examination (Pennsylvania).

but its importance is indicated by the fact that numerous state athletic associations make such a requirement a part of their by-laws. Of course student managers and student assistants should be given a place in the program, but administrative duties or responsibility should never be delegated to them. In most states the superintendent or principal is charged with the responsibility of local athletic management. He may delegate it to faculty members who assume his immediate responsibility. In the last analysis, however, final responsibility in all cases goes back to the administration of the school. Ohio stresses the fact in this by-law:

The administrative head of the school shall be held ultimately responsible in all matters in his school which concern interschool contests.

The administrative head of the school or some authorized representative shall accompany the team to all contests.[18]

The same regulation pertaining to local management obtains in Massachusetts:

The Principal of the school, or his authorized representative, who shall be an adult employee of the school, shall accompany any group of students representing his school at an interscholastic contest or meeting.

The Principal of the school, or teachers authorized by him, shall be the manager or managers of the teams or groups representing the school. All student managers shall be under the direction of the Principal or his authorized representative.

No school shall engage in any athletic contests without the sanction of the Principal.[19]

Washington makes this direct statement:

During the sport season the team activity shall be under the supervision of a faculty member. Any team activity not under the supervision of a faculty member shall make such team members ineligible for the remainder of the season.[20]

[18] Ohio High School Athletic Association, 1960–1961 *Constitution and Rules.* p. 12.
[19] Massachusetts Secondary School Principals' Association, 1959 *Constitution and By-Laws,* p. 9.
[20] Washington Interscholastic Activities Association 1960–1961 *Official Handbook,* p. 27.

Protests and forfeitures. Machinery for hearing of protests is provided in virtually all states. In most instances, however, it is recommended that contests be played, even under protest, and then evidence upon which the protest is based must be presented in writing, usually within a specified time and in a prescribed manner. This procedure is not universally followed but is in effect in many states. There is a growing tendency to look with disfavor upon protests which are made after contests have been played and lost and which undoubtedly would not have been made had the game been won. Likewise, most states are definite in their dealings with schools that remove their teams from field or court before the natural conclusion of contests in which they are competing. Such a procedure hardly can be justified educationally.

Most states rule that the use of ineligible players by a school automatically results in forfeiture of the game or games in which such players participate. Usually this action results regardless of the circumstances under which the violation occurred. In Michigan, however, leagues or athletic conferences may act on forfeitures insofar as they affect the standings of teams in their own organizations. Circumstances regarding the violation, of course, are reported to the state athletic association and handled in the regular way. It has been felt in Michigan that leagues could do as they wished regarding standings of schools in games won or lost, even if a school had used ineligible players. If the schools competing in contests are not league members, the games have been declared forfeited by the state association if ineligible players participated. It is interesting to note that, in virtually all cases, leagues have declared all games forfeited in which ineligible players have participated. They have hesitated to establish a precedent of nonforfeiture that might cause later embarrassment. The Michigan rule provides:

Accidental, intentional, or otherwise use of ineligible players may result in forfeiture by a junior or senior high school of all games in which that or those ineligible players participated. Any league or association of schools may, by notification to the State Director, determine the standing of schools within its own league or organization with reference to forfeiture.[21]

[21] Michigan High School Athletic Association, 1961–1962 *Handbook*, p. 77.

In contrast to the Michigan policy, again it is significant to note that in most states, protests based on declaration of ineligibility of participants, usually result in automatic forfeiture. South Carolina has such a typical regulation:

Any school that violates any of the eligibility rules of this League may be suspended by a two-thirds vote of the State Executive Committee. Charges may be brought at any time previous to or subsequent to a contest, and if the player or players are declared ineligible he shall be debarred from other participations and all games participated in by such ineligible player shall be forfeited to the team or teams using only eligible players, provided that if a team is eliminated before an inter-conference game the conference from which the eliminated team comes shall have the right to select another conference champion in the place of the eliminated conference champion. Provided, further that if a team is eliminated after the first inter-conference game the ineligible team will be eliminated and the schedule of eliminations will continue as set up. If the team with the ineligible player won the last elimination game previous to the time they were declared ineligible the game shall not count and the team with the eligible players shall continue in the elimination.[22]

Indiana has had experience with court action in protest of the rulings of its state association:

The Athletic Council deplores the action of any individual or individuals in resorting to court action in seeking redress in high school athletic difficulties in the I.H.S.A.A. and authorizes the Board of Control to secure legal advice and fight such cases through the Supreme Court of Indiana if deemed necessary.[23]

The Montana High School Athletic Association sets up a definite procedure for handling protests, stating that they must be written in six copies and accompanied by a $5 deposit. A protest must be filed within 10 days after a contest unless information which was the basis for it was not obtainable within that time. The school against which the protest is made is given a copy of the charges and allowed a reasonable time to answer them, after which the decision

[22] South Carolina High School League, 1960–1961 *Constitution*, p. A 12.
[23] Indiana High School Athletic Association, *Fifty-seventh Annual Handbook* (1960), p. 29.

of the athletic board is made. Montana will allow protests in accordance with the following procedure:

A protest for violation of the Constitution, By-Laws, or rules of the Association may be made by filing such protest in writing with the Executive Secretary-Treasurer of the Board of Directors and paying a filing fee in the sum of five dollars, ($5.00).[24]

New York also has an established procedure for protests. Its rule on forfeitures is definite:

If a school uses ineligible pupils in any interschool contests, such contests shall be forfeited to the opposing school or schools.

All cases of eligibility and differences between schools should be referred to the league president for decision. The league president should be guided by association rules and by-laws and may request help in their interpretation from the sectional board.

Appeal may be made without penalty from decisions of the league president to the sectional board, which will review arguments or evidence, and which will have power to confirm or reverse the judgment of the league presidents.

Appeals may be taken from the judgment of the sectional boards to the executive committee.

If a case cannot be satisfactorily determined by the Executive Committee, it shall be referred to the Central Committee for a decision which shall be final.[25]

Missouri makes this statement regarding charges or protests which one school may make against another:

Any school shall have the right to file charges against any other school to be taken up at the next regularly scheduled meeting of the Board of Control, unless at a special meeting set by the Board of Control, however, such school shall make them in the form of writing and accompany them with a certified check of $15.00, which will be returned when it appears before the Board to press the charges.[26]

[24] Montana High School Athletic Association, *Official Handbook*, 1960–1961, p. 11.

[25] New York State Public High School Athletic Association, 1960–1961 *Handbook*, p. 33.

[26] Missouri State High School Activities Association, 1960, *Handbook*, p. 16.

Minnesota's regulation regarding automatic forfeiture is typical of those in most states:

The penalty for playing an ineligible player shall be forfeiture of the game and disqualification of the player from interschool athletics for one year from date of offense, except that when a participant has been played through an error of the administration or athletic department, his penalty may be reviewed and determined by the Board of Control.[27]

South Dakota has an interesting by-law that has as its purpose the confining of athletic disputes strictly to school officials:

No member school shall be represented at a hearing concerning its alleged violation of Association rules, and no accusing member school shall be represented, by any but bona fide school officials connected with the schools concerned. Lawyers and other people or delegations of people shall be barred from participating in any such hearing.[28]

Several other states have similar regulations.

Approval of meets and tournaments. Regulations for approval of meets and tournaments not sponsored by state athletic associations are universal. They attempt to ensure that there will be equity in competition and protection to the contestants. In some states the approval procedure undoubtedly is a mere formality, whereas in others definite assurance must be given to state association authorities that certain required standards will be met. Minnesota and Illinois are examples of states that require filing in their state association offices of definite information regarding the type of meet, tournament, or interscholastic activity to be held. Their Applications for Sanction are prepared in duplicate by the entertaining organization. Approval is granted for the event, provided that it complies with state association and National Federation regulations (see Fig. 5-25 and 5-26). In Minnesota approval first must be granted by the District Committee and subsequently acted upon by the State Board of Control.

[27] Minnesota State High School Athletic Association, 1960 *Official Handbook*, p. 50.
[28] South Dakota High School Athletic Association, 1960 *Rules and Regulations*, p. 22.

State association approval has also been a method by which undesirable meets have been eliminated. Sometimes the circumstances under which they have been held, or the sponsors of them, have been objectionable. By refusing to grant approval or by withholding sanction until requirements have been met, state associations

---

APPLICATION FOR SANCTION
OF INTERSCHOLASTIC ATHLETIC MEET

Article VII, Section 3. "No school shall participate in any tournament, athletic meet, or state championship contest which has not been sanctioned by the **Board of Control** except intrastate track, tennis, golf, cross country, gymnastics, swimming, and skiing meets involving teams of a conference or teams within 50 miles radius of the site of the meet. providing that all participants are League Members."

Application must be placed on file at least 30 days previous to opening date of proposed tournament or meet.

Make out in duplicate; mail to District Secretary for approval.

District Secretary should, if approval is given, mail both forms to League Office.

City _____

Date _____, 196____

MINNESOTA STATE HIGH SCHOOL LEAGUE
829 Plymouth Building
Minneapolis 3, Minnesota

Dear Sirs:

On behalf of the_____ High School
I herewith apply for the official sanction from the Board of Control of the Minnesota State High School League for the following meet (or tournament):

1. Nature of Tournament or Meet: _____

2. Proposed: (a) Place of Tournament_____ (b) Date_____

3. Manager of Tournament: _____

4. Participating Schools (list schools which will participate or the schools which you anticipate inviting):

°

----

5. Sponsor of Tournament: _____

In consideration of said application I herewith certify that:

1. The eligibility rules and regulations of the Minnesota State High School League will be required and followed by each participating school.

°2. Schools which are not members of the Minnesota State High School League, or members of the state association of a neighboring state, will not be invited to participate.

3. The National Federation rule governing participation in inter-state meets, i.e. limit of 600 miles round trip, will be observed.

                                    Superintendent

                                    School

(See reverse side for actions of District Committee and League Office)

Fig. 5-25. Application Form for Sanction of Interscholastic Meet *(Minnesota).*

ILLINOIS HIGH SCHOOL ASSOCIATION
11 SO. LA SALLE ST., CHICAGO

APPLICATION FOR SANCTION
OF
NON-ATHLETIC INTERSCHOLASTIC ACTIVITY
(Make in duplicate and submit both copies.)

Conditions of Sanctions

The school or organization applying for sanction agrees:
1. To conduct the meet strictly in accordance with the rules of the ILLINOIS HIGH SCHOOL ASSOCIATION.
2. To supply the data asked for below.

Data to be Supplied by Applicant

Name of Manager in direct charge:..

Kind of Meet for which sanction is asked:..

Is participation in this meet limited to schools belonging to some interstate or national organizations?....

Give name of organization:...

On reverse side, give names and addresses of judges to be used.

Day and Beginning hour of each session:

1st.. 4th..

2nd... 5th..

3rd.. 6th..

AWARDS: Description   Approx. Cost

School: .... $...................

--   ----------------

Individual: .... ----------------

--   ----------------

List of Schools to Participate:

....

....

....

....

Illinois High School Association,
11 South LaSalle Street,
Chicago 3, Illinois

...., 19............

I accept the foregoing conditions of sanction and on behalf of...
                                                          (Institution conducting the meet)

I hereby apply for sanction of the IHSA for the...
                                                          (Name of Meet)

to be held in.......................at...........................on......................, 19........
            (City)   (Building or Field, etc.)

....Principal

....High School

Sanction · GRANTED / WITHHELD . Date acted on.., 19........

By...Exec. Sec.
ILLINOIS HIGH SCHOOL ASSOCIATION

Fig. 5-26. Application Form for Sanction of Non-Athletic Interscholastic Activity
(Illinois).

have been able to provide better types of competition for high school contestants. The Michigan regulation, similar to those in most state associations, provides that:

A junior or senior high school conducting or competing in any meet or tournament not approved by the State Director shall be liable to probation or suspension.[29]

In some states meets or tournaments are defined as events in which three or more schools compete. In California the rule is strict in its intent to keep high school athletes from competing in any event except those directed by the schools themselves:

1. In all tournaments, contests, competition, etc., in which high school boys participate as representatives of their high schools, such tournaments, contests, etc., shall be held under the auspices of a member high school. Boys who are not members of the C.I.F. high schools must not be allowed to participate.

2. If an event is a dual contest and involves competition between schools of two adjacent sections, the event must be approved by the two sections involved.

If an event involves competition among four or more schools from more than one C.I.F. Section, it must be approved by the C.I.F. Sections involved, and receive sanction from the State C.I.F. Federated Council.

Any violation of the above rules will automatically suspend the competing schools from California Interscholastic Federation competition.

3. Schools hosting sanctioned intersectional events shall limit invitations to competing schools within a 300 mile radius of the location of the event.

4. If a C.I.F. high school sponsors a sanctioned C.I.F. invitational meet at the same time and place where an open meet is being held, the high school meet must be administered by a C.I.F. member high school and the high school meet must be limited to entries from C.I.F. member schools whose athletes are eligible under C.I.F. rules.[30]

Limitation in number of contests and duration of seasons. Action in the direction of such limitation by state athletic associations is comparatively recent. The thought has persisted in a great many schools that the number of games they should schedule is their own business. During the last few years there has been a tendency to establish limits in number of games, especially in football and basketball. Likewise, more requests have come to state associations to set up season limits in these two sports than in the others, because

[29] Michigan High School Athletic Association, 1961–1962 *Handbook*, p. 75.
[30] California Interscholastic Federation, *Constitution and By-Laws* (1959), p. 3.

of outside pressure for postseason, interstate championship, so-called "bowl," charity, and all-star games. In order that exploitation and undue emphasis might be lessened, many states have set a maximum for the number of games that a school may play and have limited the time during which its contests may occur. In many states these regulations, as they affect basketball, pertain to the regular season and make allowances for state association-sponsored tournament competition. In football especially, the practice period is often defined in its relation to the season. New York's football rule is as follows:

Interschool competition in football shall be limited to a maximum of eight games a season. A boy shall have at least fifteen organized intraschool practice sessions before his first football game. An interschool practice session may be scheduled at the discretion of school authorities, provided no boy is permitted to participate until after his tenth intraschool practice session. Only one practice session a day and only six days of a calendar week may be counted toward the total practice sessions required. All organized practice and games shall be limited to the fall sports season. Interschool competition in football shall be permitted only in those schools which have an adequate number of boys on the squad who are physically fit, eligible, and prepared for participation in each game as follows:

Eleven man football——20 or more
Eight man football——16 or more
Six man football——12 or more

All football games (6-man and 11-man) shall be played following the rules of the National Federation Code of Interscholastic Football Rules. It is recommended that a physician be present at all football games.[31]

New Jersey has set up a regulation concerning all out-of-season practice:

a. Out of season practice, that is, practice after the close of an official sports season, is forbidden until the opening of the next school year on September 1st.
b. Any school proved guilty of violating the above rule on out of season

---

[31] New York State Public High School Athletic Association, 1960–1961 *Handbook*, pp. 35–36.

practice shall be placed on probation for one year from the time the offense occurs.

INTERPRETATIONS:

Thus, for example, football practice in May, or basketball practice in April are forbidden since they would occur after the close of those seasons; but baseball practice in February, golf practice in October or swimming practice in September would be allowed.

With regard to out of season football practice the following statement is to be noted:

"There shall be no instructor nor any coach in charge of any boys using a football. This eliminates any form of practice under any kind of instruction.

The object of this explanation is to make clear the fact that there shall be no practice in football from the time of the last game in the fall to the first of September. Any subterfuge or sharp practice shall be construed as a violation of the rule.[32]

The Washington Interscholastic Activities Association immediately suspends a school which competes in a postseason game for a period of *two* years. Its rule is as follows:

No post-season games or contests shall be played by any team representing a member of the Association without special permission secured in advance from the Representative Assembly. Such permission will be granted only in special cases and in no event for a date later than two weeks after the official close of the season. Any school violating this rule shall be automatically and immediately suspended from the Association for a period of two years from the date of the offense.[33]

Virtually all states have definite regulations against organized summer football practice or before-season training camps. Indiana limits the number of basketball games to eighteen during the regular season and allows teams to play in two tournaments in addition to the state association tournaments, provided that all the games played in one of the tournaments are counted in the season limitation. New York limits basketball to eighteen games, exclusive of sectional

[32] New Jersey State Interscholastic Athletic Association, 1960–1961 *Constitution and By-Laws,* p. 41.

[33] Washington Interscholastic Activities Association, 1960–1961 *Handbook,* p. 32.

games and those necessary to break league ties. There must have been participation in at least ten intraschool practice sessions by a boy before the first basketball game in which he may play.

Michigan has a combination football-basketball schedule limitation. Its regulation limits the number of football games each team representing a school may play, but additional basketball games may be played up to an established maximum.

A high school may have any number of teams but no football team may play more than nine (9) games. No basketball team may play more than eighteen (18) games. Schools having both football and basketball may play a combined schedule in these two sports of not to exceed twenty-four (24) games for each of its varsity, reserve, or other teams. (The Representative Council recommends a limit of eight (8) games in football.)

A high school which does not sponsor football may have a schedule of not to exceed eighteen (18) basketball games for each of its teams.

Lower Peninsula schools sponsoring football may play their first basketball games on any date during the week in which Thanksgiving Day occurs. Upper Peninsula schools, regardless of their sponsorsihp of football, and Lower Peninsula schools not sponsoring football, may play their first basketball games November 15, or thereafter.[34]

State association basketball tournament games are not included in these limitations. The basketball season ends with the start of tournament play by a school. Wisconsin and Kansas also have requirements that there must be at least three weeks of football practice in the fall prior to the first game.

The Virginia High School League bars spring football and before-season practice. The Virginia rule also specifies where practice should be held:

Any form of post-season, winter, spring, summer, or pre-season football practice, organized under the coach or his representative, is forbidden, regardless of what equipment, if any, is used.[35]

Girls' interscholastic athletics. Regulations relative to athletic

[34] Michigan High School Athletic Association, 1961–1962 *Handbook*, p. 53.
[35] Virginia High School League, *Handbook*, University of Virginia Extension Series, August, 1960, p. 57.

activities for girls vary extensively in the different states of the nation. In recent years there has been a tendency to limit competition for girls, with some states having eliminated interschool play entirely. Illinois has the following rule concerning girls' athletics:

No school that is a member of the Illinois High School Association shall permit its girls to participate in any interscholastic competition except in golf, tennis and archery. All interscholastic contests in golf, tennis and archery in which girls in member schools participate must be conducted in accordance with the rules as stated hereinafter.[36]

In New York [37] regulations are specific and mention boys only in the Eligibility Rules.

From the extremes in these states there is the other limit in Oklahoma, Iowa and Mississippi, where state championships in girls' basketball as well as track in the latter state are held. In Iowa a separate state girls' high school athletic association conducts a series of regionals and a state basketball tournament. Further consideration is given to the subject of interschool athletics for girls in Chapter 14. In most states there are no regulations specifically prohibiting girls' athletics. In many of them, however, there are definite restrictions and recommendations. Apparently these are the result of dissatisfaction with the manner in which some of the competition has been conducted in the past, rather than of disapproval of competition as such for high school girls. A number of states limit schedules in certain sports and recommend that only women coaches be allowed to coach girls' teams. In virtually all states the eligibility regulations of the state association apply equally to interscholastic athletic activities for girls and for boys. In states where the interschool program has been eliminated or curtailed, there have been efforts to substitute something for it. Girls' play days, festivals, and the formation of girls' athletic associations are indicative of such efforts.

All-star Football and Basketball Contests. During the past several years so-called "all-star" football and basketball contests have appeared in various parts of the country. In almost no instances are

[36] Illinois High School Association, 1960–1961 *Handbook*, p. 33.
[37] New York State Public High School Athletic Association, 1960–1961 *Handbook*, p. 28.

they conducted by state associations themselves. Some states have approved them; others have assumed a hands-off attitude. In several states, however, definite action has been taken by state athletic associations to prohibit them, in the belief that such contests are generally not consistent with sound educational high school athletic programs. True, the contestants in games of this kind are high school graduates; but there is a definite connection between such events and high school athletics because of the usual methods of selection of players for the games, the coaching, management, and officiating, and use of school equipment and facilities.

This discussion of all-star out-of-season contests should not be confused with state association provisions that definitely prohibit participation by high school students in all-star games during the school year. Virtually all states have either direct or implied rules to that effect. Here we are concerned only with football and basketball all-star games usually played during the summer.

Texas, Ohio, and Wisconsin are among the states that have had all-star football games conducted under the auspices of state coaches' associations. In Texas such a game has been held for several years and is the concluding event of a coaching school, as it also is in Ohio. In Indiana a summer basketball game between "all-stars" of that state and Kentucky has been conducted under the sponsorship of an Indiana newspaper. In Minnesota a state all-star game formerly was sponsored by two state newspapers, but regulations in that state now prohibit such contests. Illinois also has had a state all-star summer basketball game, sponsored by the state coaches' association. Approval for a limited period was granted for this game by the State Association of Illinois, but this no longer is done. An all-star football game for charity, promoted by the recreation department of a municipality and managed by an individual, was played for a time in the Upper Peninsula of Michigan.

Several state associations have adopted by-laws that discourage this type of contest, which usually assumes the aspects of a commercial venture.

Participation, directly, or indirectly, in the management, supervision, player selection, coaching or promotion, of all-star high school teams, high school championship teams, or similar teams in contests in any sport, having or not having definite seasons in the I.H.S.A.A., unless under the supervision and auspices of the I.H.S.A.A. by member schools, by their school officials or by their teachers, shall be considered a violation of the spirit and purpose, if not the actual wording of these rules and regulations; and schools violating the spirit, purpose or wording of these rules and regulations as indicated herein shall cause their school to be suspended from the I.H.S.A.A. for such length of time as the I.H.S.A.A. Board of Control deems advisable. Approved officials shall be suspended for promoting such contests. (Indiana High School Athletic Association)

*   *   *

Participation by member schools, by their school officials, by their teachers or coaches, directly or indirectly in the officiating, management, organization, supervision, play selection, coaching or promotion, of "all-star" high school teams, high school championship teams or similar teams in contests or exhibitions in any sport, unless under the supervision, auspices, or approval of the I.H.S.A.A. shall be considered a violation of the spirit of the I.H.S.A.A. Violation of the rule by a school official, a teacher or coach shall cause that school where said school official, teacher, or coach is employed to be suspended from membership in the I.H.S.A.A. Approved officials shall be suspended for promoting or officiating such contests. (Iowa High School Athletic Association)

*   *   *

No athletic director, coach, principal, teacher or other official of a member school or any athletic official registered with the Illinois High School Athletic Association shall assist, either directly or indirectly, with the coaching, management, direction, selection of players, promotion or officiating of any "all-star" or similar contest in which one or more of the competing teams is composed of high school players or players who, during the previous year, were members of a high school team, unless such contest is sanctioned by this Association. (Illinois High School Association)

*   *   *

A. No athletic director, coach, teacher, or administrator of a Michigan high school, and no athletic official registered with the Michigan High School Athletic Association shall at any time assist either directly or indirectly with the coaching, management, direction, selection of players, promotion, or officiating of any "all-star" or similar contest in football or basketball in which one or more of the competing teams is composed of a player or players, who, during the previous school year, were members of a high school football or basketball team.

B. Any high school which uses an individual as a coach or manager of an interscholastic athletic team who has violated the provisions of Section A of this Rule shall be subject to probation or suspension.

C. Any individual who violates the provisions of Section A of this Rule shall be ineligible for registration as an athletic official with the Michigan High School Athletic Association for a period of at least one year. (Michigan High School Athletic Association)

From the above it will be seen that these regulations in the various states actually do not prohibit all-star contests. Rather, their disciplinary action involves schools that employ violators of the rules concerned. It is also significant to refer to the Statement Regarding All-Star and Out-of-Season Athletic Contests adopted at the National Federation meeting at St. Petersburg, Fla., in January, 1947, inasmuch as it reflects the attitudes and basis for the state actions indicated (see pages 29-33).

Special Contest and Administrative Regulations

Some selected special regulations that have been adopted by state associations are listed below. They may seem somewhat unusual, especially when the reasons for their enactment are not fully understood.

No football championships. In contrast to the nineteen states that decided championships in football in 1960, a few states have by-laws specifically prohibting them. Most of the state associations, however, make no reference to this matter.

Kansas is opposed to the possibility of schools determining state championship in football and makes this additional restriction:

No football games shall be played except those scheduled by and entirely under the control of the principals of the schools represented by the teams playing, or of the Board of Control. No games may be played upon a neutral field without the sanction of the Board of Control.

Note: The Board of Control disapproves the policy of playing games on neutral fields and is opposed to the sanctioning of games which are sponsored in any way by agencies outside the schools.[38]

Conduct of coaches. A number of states have regulations relative to the conduct of athletes and possible penalties for unsportsmanlike actions. Alabama has such a rule which applies to coaches. It is

[38] Kansas State High School Athletic Association, 1960–1961 *Handbook,* p. 27.

also effective against a school that employs a man affected by the rule:

A coach proved guilty of immoral or unsportsmanlike conduct may be disqualified by the Central Board of Control. Any school using a disqualified coach shall be subject to suspension from the Association.[39]

Conduct of team followers. Several states have rules that make the home school responsible for the conduct of the crowd. Several others insist that a team is responsible for its followers wherever it plays. Minnesota has such a rule:

Visiting teams shall be held responsible for the conduct of visitors from the home town regardless of where the contest is being played.[40]

Tennessee fixes the responsibility in the following manner:

Visiting teams shall be accompanied by the principal or someone designated by him.

All games shall be properly supervised and policed to insure a sportsmanlike contest. The host school shall be responsible for providing a sufficient number of policemen to insure orderly conduct on the part of all spectators. If the game is played on a neutral field and neither team is designated as the host team, the competing schools shall share the responsibility of providing sufficient police protection.

Member schools are responsible for the conduct of their own fans and students at every athletic contest, regardless of where it may be held.[41]

No Decoration Day, Sunday, or Christmas Day games. California lists under the heading "Important Rulings" of the California Interscholastic Federation the following statement on this matter:

No interscholastic games of any kind are to be played on Decoration Day, Christmas, or Sunday.[42]

Midweek contests. Several states recommend that games not be played by high schools during school time or on evenings preceding

[39] Alabama High School Athletic Association, *Handbook* (1960–1961), p. 119.

[40] Minnesota State High School League, 1960 *Handbook*, p. 50.

[41] Tennessee Secondary School Athletic Association, 1960–1961 *Official Handbook*, p. 22.

[42] California Interscholastic Federation, 1959 *Constitution*, p. 3.

a school day. In Ohio a definite rule requires that approval be secured from the Commissioner for all such games:

The consent of the Commissioner must be secured before engaging in an inter-school contest on any day of the week when school is in session except Friday.

A request under this rule must be made or countersigned by the superintendent, principal, or faculty manager, and should reach the Commissioner not later than one week before the date of the proposed contest.[43]

Application of athletic rules to all interscholastic extracurricular activities. The regulation concerning this matter apparently is implied in some states but is specifically stated for each activity in others. Some activities associations have specific eligibility and contest regulations for each activity. Texas makes a single statement on the matter as a preface to its eligibility regulations:

The following eligibility rules shall apply to every contest held under the auspices of this League. School principals and superintendents are charged with the responsibility of seeing that these rules are strictly observed in each and every contest in which their pupils engage.[44]

Fees for athletic officials. Texas has established a scale for the payment of athletic officials which is based on the receipts of contests. Several states have established flat maximum fees and expense allowances. The Texas plan is unique: [45]

Receipts	Fee
If up to $100	$ 7.50
If $100 to $200	10.00
If $200 to $500	15.00
If $500 to $1,000	20.00
If $1,000 to $2,000	25.00
If $2,000 to $3,000	30.00
If $3,000 to $4,000	35.00
If $4,000 to $5,000	40.00
If $5,000 to $10,000	45.00
If $10,000 or above	50.00

[43] Ohio High School Athletic Association, 1960–1961 *Constitution and Rules,* pp. 36–37.

[44] Texas University Interscholastic League, 1960–1961 *Constitution and Rules.* University of Texas *Bulletin,* p. 16.

[45] *Ibid.,* pp. 118–19.

Certain specified mileage is allowed, dependent upon the number of officials traveling together (6¢ to 8¢ per mile) as well as meals and lodging. Failure on the part of a school to adhere to the payment schedule ". . . shall carry the same penalty as the violation of any other eligibility rule; that is, forfeiture of the game." The District Committee, however, may decide that an emergency existed and waive the penalty.

No combination of schools for athletic purposes. This rule is implied in most of the state association regulations. Louisiana states it definitely:

No two high schools will be permitted to unite for athletic purposes.[46]

Elimination of interschool boxing. A Michigan regulation that became effective in 1938 states:

There shall be no interscholastic competition in boxing.[47]

This rule originally was adopted and now is operative in most states because of difficulties that appeared inevitable if such action were not taken. Boxing ceased to be a sport of skill and became one of combat in which punishment of one of the contestants was necessary in order that the other might win. Difficulties also have been encountered in teaching and officiating the activity and at the same time keeping educational objectives in mind. Many communities have had too keen an interest in boxing as an interschool activity. Michigan was the first state association to specifically eliminate boxing from the interscholastic athletic program and was prompted in its action by the resolution adopted by the Society of State Directors of Physical and Health Education at its Twelfth Annual Meeting held at Atlanta, Ga., April 19, 1938, and reaffirmed at its St. Louis meeting, April 6–9, 1946, as follows: (This was the first resolution of its kind.)

WHEREAS, There seems to be an increasing tendency to promote interscholastic boxing in some communities and on the part of some individuals; and

[46] Louisiana High School Athletic Association, 1960–1961 *Handbook,* p. 47.
[47] Michigan High School Athletic Association, 1961–1962 *Handbook,* p. 53.

WHEREAS, The activity on such a highly competitive basis is known to be potentially dangerous to the welfare of boys participating; and

WHEREAS, The Society of State Directors of Health and Physical Education desires to strengthen its resolution regarding interscholastic boxing adapted on April 19, 1938;

BE IT THEREFORE RESOLVED, That the Society of State Directors of Physical and Health Education again disavow all intention to give support to this development and again recommend that school officials in positions to control boxing matches between school teams, eliminate this activity from their athletic programs.

BE IT FURTHER RESOLVED, That this Society again encourage the National Federation of High School Athletic Associations to establish an official policy disapproving boxing as an interscholastic sport.

Summary

This summary presents a few brief statements regarding each of the contest regulations discussed in this chapter. They are not necessarily conclusions but rather are attempts to show some of the actual common practices.

Contracts for athletic contests. Most state athletic associations supply contract forms and will not be concerned with disputes between schools involving contract violations unless standard contract forms were properly executed. Written contracts, properly signed by authorized school officials, should be in existence for all interscholastic athletic contests.

Eligibility-list procedures. Virtually all states have some plan for the exchange of lists of eligible players prior to contests. This varies from a formal letter in one state sent by one school principal to the other listing eligible boys for a game, to plans in other states for the preparation of complete scholastic and athletic data on all contestants, which are exchanged prior to each contest. In some states schools send complete data to each school on its schedule at the start of the season, with a supplementary list being sent later carrying names of eligible players only. In a few states, only the latter lists are sent. In many states data on all contestants are sent to the state association office, either at the start or the end of the season.

Records of transfer students. Such records usually are one of two types: (1) a combination scholastic and athletic blank, or (2) a strictly athletic record blank with only such scholastic information as is necessary to determine athletic eligibility. It is usual for state athletic associations to furnish transfer blanks, thus providing a common procedure for recording and forwarding athletic and scholastic information regarding students who transfer from one school to another.

Certification of athletic coaches. It is an almost universal regulation that only faculty members who receive their pay from public school funds may be engaged as athletic coaches. Usually, they must be regularly certificated teachers with specified teaching loads in addition to coaching duties.

Registration of athletic officials. Nearly one-half of the states require that athletic officials in designated sports must be registered with their state associations for the current year in order to be eligible to officiate in high school games. Usually, there are different classifications of officials, dependent upon a number of factors, including ratings from schools, experience, examination grades, attendance at rules meetings, and the like.

Faculty managers at contests. Regulations providing for faculty managers at contests are desirable. They have been incorporated in the by-laws of a majority of state athletic associations. Responsibility for the athletic program rests with the school administration, although phases of it are delegated to faculty managers. Student management always should be under the supervision of faculty managers.

Protests and forfeitures. Protest procedures are outlined definitely in a number of states. Protests usually must be in writing and be made within a specified time. It should be kept in mind, however, that the state association executive body always has the right to make investigations of alleged violations, even though no formal protest has been filed. In almost all states the use of ineligible players by a school automatically results in forfeiture of all games in which such contestants participated.

Approval of meets and tournaments. When three or more schools compete in an athletic event it is common practice in most states to require that there be state association approval of it. This procedure is to ensure that regulations will be in effect which are comparable to those under which regular state association events are conducted. Thus, competing and entertaining schools, as well as contestants, are protected to an extent greater than otherwise might be the case.

Limitation in number of contests and duration of seasons. There seems to be a tendency on the part of state associations to limit the number of games during regular seasons in certain sports, notably in football and basketball. Likewise, season limits are defined in these two sports as well as in some others. Practice periods, in relation to seasons, also are stipulated in several states.

Girls' interscholastic athletics. Most states have no specific regulations regarding interscholastic athletic activities for girls. There is some tendency to limit the program so that it will conform to standards established by national women's organizations. Commonly the general eligibility regulations of state associations apply alike to girls and boys.

All-star football and basketball contests. Such contests are held in seven states, sponsored by various organizations or individuals, generally not by state associations. To stop these games, an increasing number of states are adopting regulatory measures that usually concern violations of established rules in this regard by school personnel who subsequently will be connected with interscholastic athletic programs.

Special contest and administrative rules. The following matters are the subjects of rather uncommon or unusual rules found in the by-laws of one or more state athletic associations:

1. Elimination of football championships.
2. Conduct of coaches.
3. Conduct of team followers.
4. No Decoration Day or Christmas Day games.
5. Midweek contests.
6. Application of athletic rules to all activities.
7. Fees for athletic officials.
8. No combination of schools for athletic purposes.
9. Elimination of interschool boxing.

Questions for Study and Discussion

1. Why are state contest regulations important? How do they differ from eligibility regulations?

2. Discuss the necessity of contracts for athletic contests. Why is the use of state association contract forms important?

3. Which of the eligibility lists procedure plans do you favor? Why?

4. What is the common requirement concerning the certification of athletic coaches? Why should coaches be regular members of the school faculty?

5. Discuss the importance of plans in effect in various states concerning registration and classification of athletic officials.

6. Why should faculty managers be present at all interscholastic athletic contests? Cite illustrative rules in effect in various states.

7. What are the common procedures for handling protests and forfeitures of athletic contests?

8. Why should state associations approve all meets and tournaments, and limit number of contests and duration of season in various sports? Discuss.

9. Discuss attitudes of several state athletic associations regarding interscholastic athletics for girls.

10. What positions are held by various states as indicated by their "all-star" contest rules?

11. List several (8–10) special contest and administrative regulations indicated in this chapter. Which do you consider the most unusual?

6

Policies and Administration Plans for Local Athletic Programs

Just as state associations must have well-defined policies to guide them in the performance of their administrative responsibilities, so a local high school should be certain that its local administrative policies concerning athletics are well understood. If all members of the staff have a thorough understanding of the procedures they are to follow, many pitfalls, embarrassing situations, and misunderstandings may be avoided.

Importance of the Local School Administrative Policy

Knowledge of problems necessary. Previous chapters have considered phases of administration of the athletic program from national and state viewpoints. In each instance there has been reference to the school itself, the local school athletic association, local boards of education, or the school administration. The reason for such consideration is self-evident. Without the local school and its organization for administering the athletic program, there would be no program. The importance of this seemingly trite statement cannot be overemphasized. The measure of success of athletics in our schools today is dependent upon the plans for handling them and the interest and integrity of the schoolmen responsible for the programs.

Many men and women come out of our teacher-training institutions with little or no intimation of the problems in athletics that they may be called upon to face. This is not an indictment of the colleges and universities. Rather, it is the statement of a condition caused by the seeming impossibility of including at least a cursory review of athletic matters in the busy college schedules of men and women who will assume administrative positions in education. In every instance the prospective superintendent or principal will be the final authority for the administration of the athletic program in his school. He should receive some insight into this responsibility, which he is bound to assume. Even if he comes into a system in which much of his responsibility may be delegated, he still should know the problems in order that he may be familiar and sympathetic with them.

The day has gone when, because a man has played outstanding football, basketball, or baseball in college, he may be considered adequately prepared to administer an efficient educational athletic program. Such a program calls for well-defined organization and public relations, understanding of the relation of the school to the state athletic association, delegation of duties and responsibilities, understanding of eligibility and contest administrative regulations, relations with other schools—all these and many others, as well as the ability to coach one or more sports or to see that faculty members are secured who are able to perform such duties. The realization that all these matters may be in the day's work of the superintendent, principal, athletic director, faculty manager, coach, and assistant coach is reason enough that attention be given them before a person is placed in a situation where they are part of his job. Another most important matter in the establishment of the program is that of determining the place of athletics with relation to physical education. Likewise, the relation of interscholastics to intramurals should be definitely understood.

Internal control principles in athletics. Some time ago Dr. Harlan C. Koch of the University of Michigan asked 88 students in a class in high school administration to list principles which they thought should be included in the internal control of high school athletics. Their answers still are applicable. Thirty-eight specific items were mentioned by five or more students in the order of their frequency by at least one-third of the class:

1. Rules of eligibility for participation in interscholastic competition should be adopted under stipulations of the state athletic association.

2. Athletic competition should be developed by the department of physical education as an integral part of its program.

3. The program of interscholastic athletics should be in harmony with objectives of secondary education.

4. The principal should have appellate jurisdiction in athletic matters.

5. The coach should be a full-time member of the teaching staff.

6. The development of good sportsmanship should be the major aim in competition.

7. Athletics should be financed by the board of education.

8. Physical examinations should be prerequisite to participation.

9. Teachers should not be exposed to pressure from any source with regard to matters of eligibility.

10. The principal should delegate the management of finances to a member of the faculty.

11. Both the school and the community should be educated concerning the basic values of interscholastic athletics.

12. Awards having intrinsic, rather than symbolic, value should be eliminated.[1]

Establishing and Defining the Athletic Policy

If an established and well-defined athletic policy is in existence in a school it can be pointed to constantly as the objective of the athletic program. It should include both the interschool and intramural programs, as well as the attitude of the administration toward such common controversial problems as girls' and junior high school interscholastic athletics, awards, schedules, and finances. General policies known ahead of time may alleviate many difficult situations.

Relation of athletic policies and outside groups. Any school, regardless of its size, can and should define its athletic policy and inform its patrons accordingly. This statement simply means that the administration should decide on the program to be followed throughout the year and adhere to it. Circumstances and local situations often affect and sometimes either seriously inhibit or overstimulate school administrators in determining the number and extent of their schools' athletic activities. There are the "downtown" interests that frequently are more concerned with the athletic record and superiority of the local high school team than with the educa-

[1] Harlan C. Koch, "Proposed Principles of Internal Control of High School Athletics," *The School Review,* September, 1937, pp. 525–28.

tional values of athletics and the welfare of the participants. Also, there are those individuals who have no idea of the problems involved in some of the suggestions made by students themselves or by apparently well-wishing school patrons. The activities of such people present a real problem to the school administrator. They make it all the more important that the school's athletic policy should be understood, and it will not be unless it is discussed and brought out in the open. However, one should not be too intent upon an immediate change in the entrenched athletic policies of a community.

It is easiest for the superintendent or principal in a small community to be the leader—if he actually takes the lead. This statement means that he may discuss with his board of education, social and civic groups, influential townspeople, and school student bodies the athletic program to be sponsored during the year. Policies in other progressive communities should be cited. National trends may be quoted. Advice is available from state or national officials on matters pertaining to athletics. The same procedure holds true for schools in larger communities. In larger cities, however, usually there is not the attempt by the public to dictate policies regarding athletics that is to be found in the small town, because urban students and patrons have more varied interests, with the result that there often is not the keenness of interest in athletic details or management found in smaller schools. In large schools, interest in team members is likely to be less personal.

Athletic policy considerations. Problems in determining a school's athletic policy will vary with its locality. However, there are some common matters to which school administrators may well give consideration in establishing their athletic programs and policies:

1. The relation and division of available facilities and personnel between intramural and interscholastic athletics.

2. The number of sports activities in which the school can offer (a) proper teaching and coaching; (b) adequate equipment; and (c) satisfactory playing facilities.

3. Educationally justifiable athletic schedules—length of them and frequency of games.

4. Methods of financing the athletic program.

5. Determining whether girls' interscholastic athletics should be a part of the program. (See Chapter 14.)

6. The place of junior high school athletics in the general athletic program. (See Chapter 15.)

7. The student and faculty relation in the organization for the control of athletics.

8. Understanding of the relation of the local school to its league and state athletic association.

9. The policy of the school in the care of, and payment for, athletic injuries.

10. Delegation of authority to coaches or faculty managers in matters pertaining to contracts, eligibility, equipment, schedules, officials, and the like.

Division of Responsibility in a Local School

It has been stated previously that the local superintendent of schools in virtually all states is, in the last analysis, responsible for the athletic program of a school. In some instances the principal is charged with this responsibility; but ostensibly his authority is derived from the administrative head of last resort, the superintendent, regardless of the size of the school. If the school is a one-man institution, the superintendent acts in all capacities and there is no division of responsibility. If it is larger the principal assumes control and in turn delegates part of the immediate responsibilities to athletic directors, faculty managers, or coaches. The relation of these officials to each other, their responsibilities, and the place to be filled by student managers and athletes will be discussed here.

The superintendent of schools. In the first place it is the duty of the superintendent to keep before the community the fact that athletics are one of the component parts of the educational program. If the athletic program cannot be justified educationally, as are other phases of the curriculum—both in school and outside of school—then it has no excuse for existence. Athletics should always be so conducted that emphasis may be placed on their value as an educational tool for the training of citizens. The superintendent should be instrumental in the formation of the school's athletic policy. He should have a definite understanding with principals, athletic directors, or coaches concerning it and then expect and give support in carrying out that policy. Also, the superintendent should take the responsibility for seeing that the board of education is kept informed on the athletic program and policy of the school or schools. The success of the program no longer is to be measured in terms of number of games won or lost. Rather, it should be evaluated both on the attitude of contestants and spectators and on the harmony with which it fits into the remainder of the curriculum.

The high school principal. The relation of the high school principal to the athletic program is more definite and detailed than that of the superintendent of schools in most instances. Athletics are a part of the curriculum of the principal's school. Actually, athletics should be considered a subject to be taught and one from which educational experiences are to be derived, both by contestants and student spectators. It is only natural, therefore, that the principal will be charged with many details, part of which he may delegate if the school is of sufficient size. He should thoroughly understand the athletic policy of the entire school system. If his school is one of several in the system, the athletic program in his institution should be conducted in accordance with the general scheme advocated or in effect in the city concerned. Early in the school year, all concerned with the program should understand their individual responsibilities. The principal should make sure that they do and then should give his unqualified support to each individual.

Chief among the details for which the principal is responsible is that of eligibility of contestants. Such certification always should be based on complete information concerning students' athletic and scholastic histories. Also, student bodies should be instructed in their responsibilities for contributing to the value of the athletic program. The principal may do much to bring about better relations between schools by attempting to foresee and forestall any possible differences or misunderstandings. Attempts should be made to settle them before they develop, and for most of them every possible effort should be made to avoid publicity. As evidence of his interest in the athletic program, the principal should attend as many of the contests as possible. Commendations of outstanding examples of good sportsmanship or fine citizenship should be given to visiting schools. There should be a definite understanding with all school athletic officials regarding their responsibilities concerning game officials, finances, schedules, care of playing facilities, control of spectators, care of contestants, and so on. Usually it is the principal's duty to proportion existing facilities of the physical plant of the school between intramural and interscholastic athletics, as well as between boys' and girls' activities. The principal should see that athletics are an integral part of the school's physical education program.

The athletic director or coach. In this discussion these terms will be used synonymously. In some large high schools faculty managers perform many administrative details delegated to them by the principal, but in the vast majority of schools the athletic director is the coach. Responsibilities listed for both might thus be considered as applying to the one concerned. The athletic policy of the school should be understood completely by athletic director or coach. It would be futile for either of them to advocate or conduct a program not in accord with the policy of the administration. Either the director should influence the superintendent and principal to adopt the policies proposed, or he should follow theirs. There is neither room nor justification for two athletic policies in one school system.

The proposed athletic schedules should be considered first from the welfare standpoint of the students who will be competing. Likewise, they should be educationally sound. The coach or athletic director may do much to enlist the aid of the community in establishing a character-building program. There should be agreement that persons guilty of exhibiting unsportsmanlike conduct be refused admission to athletic contests. Minute attention should be given to such matters as securing qualified, neutral game officials and complete preparation of all details for athletic contests. The coach, as such, should bring real educational technique into his coaching of each sport and should remember that at all times he is a pattern for the behavior and sportsmanship of the boys under his direction, as well as for many student and adult spectators. The athletic director or coach may develop a relation with other members of the school faculty that will be most beneficial to the program, keeping them informed of schedules, important rulings, eligibility regulations, state association policies, and interesting anecdotes concerning the sport in season. In short, he should keep the school and all its divisions informed regarding athletics. Here a word of caution may be necessary in this connection. The position of coach, faculty manager, or athletic director should never be used to influence a teacher to declare a student eligible. Students soon will learn of such procedures and will seek aid in obtaining special concessions.

The student manager. Student managers should be not only necessary but valuable aids in administering a local school athletic program. They may be made the connecting link between faculty control of athletics and the student body and athletes themselves. In this capacity a student manager may be invaluable to his coach or faculty manager. He has the students' point of view and may be of real aid in making the program run smoothly. His responsibilities should be delegated ones entirely and should not extend beyond the school. The care of equipment and the attending to specific details in connection with visiting teams, game officials, home-game arrangements, and practice sessions—these and many more should be jobs performed most efficiently by student managers.

Some student managers are elected to their positions; others are appointed by the principal, athletic director, or coach. Sometimes they are boys who, because of being over age or having too many semesters of enrollment, are ineligible for further athletic competition. Evidently, though, the most successful type of student manager is not the ex-athlete who has become ineligible. Too many times he is too likely to concern himself with practice and play instead of performing his duties. The student manager should remember that he has been selected for his job because of his honesty, faithfulness, and dependability. In many cases he will have access to records and to equipment valued in hundreds or thousands of dollars. He should treat such material as his own and attempt to safeguard it accordingly. He also should remember that the coach and faculty manager are busy men. Whenever they assign a task to him, it should be possible for them to consider it as being done.

An efficient organization for carrying on the athletic program is as important as a well-coached and well-banlanced team. The student manager should always remember that his contribution is a vital part in the whole athletic scheme of things even though it may not be very conspicuous. Schoolmen should keep the fact in mind also that we learn to do by doing and that more students will be brought into the program by use of the student manager system. In virtually all instances they are more than glad to be of service.

Usually they need not be paid, but they should be given recognition by being awarded a school letter or some other suitable emblem.

The student athlete. Certainly no athletic policy of a school would be complete without consideration of the individuals for whom the program is planned. Rules, regulations, detailed plans—all these are valueless unless the student himself makes his contribution. If we consider him only as the contestant, the real educational implications of athletics are lost. Life in a democracy is the ability to counterbalance one's privileges with one's responsibilities. So it is in athletics. When a student is granted the privilege of playing on his school team, he must assume some responsibility in connection with it. Fair play and courtesy to opponents are basic fundamentals. Playing for the joy of playing and not quitting always should be foremost. A student athlete should play according to the rules of the game, and he has the right to expect that his opponent will do likewise. Officials of the game must be respected, and it should be known that they will enforce the rules.

Faithfully completing his school work is only one of the ways an athlete may give evidence of his loyalty both to his school and to his team. To be true to them and to himself, an athlete must follow in their entirety all training rules laid down by the coach. At all times the conduct of the athlete should be such that it will bring credit and honor to his school. He is its student ambassador when he plays games out of town. The world has little use for the athlete who offers an alibi for his defeat. Neither does it esteem the victorious braggart. The good student athlete is modest and considerate in victory; and when his team loses, he will attempt to correct his faults. Above all, he should be a good sportsman, learning all the implications of the word.

Organization Plans

The preceding discussion has dealt with responsibility for the athletic program and phases of it that might be delegated to various school and student officials or agencies. Recognition of such responsibility is important in the formulation of plans for organization of the athletic division.

Many educators believe the athletic program should be a definite part of the physical education program. That is the thesis also held in this discussion. Further, it is apparent that the breadth of participation and student interest often make the athletic program an entire school program. That is what the term "interscholastic" means —representatives of one school program in competition with representatives of another school program. It is realized that in many small schools there is no regular physical education program, largely because of lack of funds and facilities. Small high schools rather than larger ones are common throughout the nation. In Michigan, for example, over 450 of the 740 high schools which engage in interscholastic athletics have enrollments of less than 400 students; 200 have fewer than 200 students. Another 180 schools have enrollments of 400 to 900. Only about 120 high schools in Michigan have more than 900 enrolled in them. However, nearly half of the high school students in Michigan attend these 120 larger city schools.[2] It is reasonable to assume that the spread in Michigan is fairly typical. It will vary, of course, in accordance with the degree of urbanization and industrialization.

All the above goes to show that suggested plans of organization for athletics in schools of such varying sizes must, of necessity, be different. Although they all have certain fundamentals in common, it is self-evident that the athletic setup in a school with 100 students will be different from that in a school with 1,500 to 8,000. The chief distinction, however, does not arise so much from the number of students, after a certain minimum is reached, as from the number of coaches in the school. It is obvious, of course, that more teachers are used and more coaches are available in schools with large enrollments. However, after a school has its personnel of athletic director, faculty manager, coaches, and assistant coaches, there is not much difference in the plan of organization for athletics, whether 600 or 6,000 students are enrolled. The plans discussed here will deal with (1) the small school with virtually a one-man organization for coaching and managing athletics; (2) the medium-sized high school with a superintendent, principal, one coach, and possibly another member of the faculty who acts as an assistant coach; and (3) the large high school with a principal, athletic director or faculty man-

---

[2] According to information obtained from Michigan High School Athletic Association Classification Information Cards, Michigan high schools in 1960–1961 which sponsored interscholastic athletic activities had an enrollment of 376,000.

ager, and a corps of coaches and assistant coaches, all of whom usually are members of the physical education department of the school.

Organization plan for athletics in a small high school. In a discussion of an organization plan in a small high school, the assumption is made that it is usually a "one-man" school. By this is meant that the superintendent is the only man on the faculty or, at least, that he has to do the athletic coaching. In such schools there seldom, if ever, is a physical education program as such. Regardless of the smallness of the school it seems desirable to bring as many faculty members and students as possible in close contact with the program. Good school administrators do this with other curriculum activities and school programs. Obviously, the school superintendent will have to take the initiative and act as athletic director and coach. He may well form an athletic council which could meet at least informally from time to time. The problems of the small school athletic program generally are not of sufficient magnitude to require regular meetings of this group. It seems advisable that the council be composed of:

1. The superintendent of schools.
2. The three to six additional members who usually constitute the remainder of the faculty in the average small high school.
3. A member of the local board of education.[3]
4. An elected or appointed representative of the student body.

The value of establishing a permanent organization of this type in the small school lies in the fact that it is ready to function whenever called upon to do so. It can be the policy-making body if desirable. Such items as schedules, equipment, awards, and finances are other matters which may be given consideration by this group. Even though these matters may seem to be routine, the most important point is that an actual permanent athletic organization has been established.

---

[3] There is a difference of opinion on this point. Some school administrators do not favor the presence of board of education members on any school committees. Their feeling is that the board delegates its managerial duties to the superintendent or principal and should have no more to say regarding athletic management than regarding other branches of the high school curriculum.

Some small schools may be faced with the problem of having to seek the coaching services of someone who is not a member of the faculty. Others may find that some individual in the town has in the past offered his time and services to the school as coach or assistant coach and wishes to continue. Arrangements of this kind should be entered into only after considerable thought. Many state athletic associations do not allow their member schools to employ or use coaches who are not regularly certificated and full-time faculty members.[4] Others allow nonfaculty members to work only if they receive no remuneration for their services. In the event a small school finds it necessary to allow a nonfaculty member to coach a team or to assist in its training, his duties should be only those of technical instruction. He should have no voice in the establishment of athletic policies of the school or in the management of its teams other than in matters pertaining strictly to their coaching. The safest and most justifiable policy from an educational standpoint is not to use any individuals in any capacity in the administration of the athletic program, or the coaching of teams, who are not regularly certificated, full-time, school faculty members. Seldom are nonfaculty members used for regular curricular duties by schools, or even for other extracurricula activities. The same policy should be in effect for interschool athletics.

Years may pass without anything unusual coming before the school athletic organization; but when an emergency does arise, the machinery for handling it should run more smoothly than if no organized plan were in existence. In most small schools there will be not more than one sport in operation at one time, and in some schools not more than one during the year. This type of schedule does not call for an elaborate organization, but the formation of a council will give the opportunity to effect a public-relations program as well as to establish a democratic agency for administering school athletics.

Organization plan for athletics in a medium-sized high school. What is meant by a medium-sized high school? For the purposes of this discussion, the medium-sized high school will not, in some respects, be considered to differ greatly from the small school in the previous discussion. In addition, however, the high school of

[4] See pages 126–131.

medium size will be understood to mean one with a faculty of from eight to twelve or fifteen members, in addition to the superintendent. In virtually all cases the principal is a man and there are at least three or four male faculty members. One man usually does most of the athletic coaching, with another member of the faculty possibly acting as his assistant or coaching one or more sports himself in case two activities are sponsored by a school during overlapping seasons. Schools in this classification will be assumed to have enrollments of 150 to 300 to 400 students. In such schools it will be considered the exception rather than the rule if there is a regularly organized physical and health education department with its definite physical activity, health instruction, and health service programs. It is obvious that schools as described in this general grouping will represent the great mass of American high schools engaging in interscholastic athletic competition.

An organization plan for the control of athletics in the medium-sized high school presents unlimited educational possibilities. Chief among them is the opportunity to keep the athletic program in its proper place in the curriculum. Sometimes, in the "nearly big" towns, overemphasis on the importance of athletic teams, winning ones especially, is likely to develop. In the same way that it is valuable in the smaller schools, so an athletic council may function well in schools of this size. Recommendations for the personnel of such a body in the medium-sized high school are as follows:

1. The superintendent of schools.
2. The high school principal (who should act as chairman).
3. The athletic coach and the assistant coach, if any.
4. One or two additional members of the high school faculty. (They should be different individuals each semester or year, so that more members of the faculty may have firsthand information concerning the school's athletic policy and program.)
5. One member of the local board of education.[5]
6. One or two representatives of the student body (preferably elected).

It will be seen that the suggested form of organization for schools in this group is, naturally, more elaborate than that for smaller

[5] See footnote 3 in this chapter regarding difference of opinion on this point.

schools. It should not be assumed, however, that proper administration of the program is more important in one instance than in another. It simply is that the larger school system generally lends itself to more efficient organization for the administration of all educational matters, including athletics. It will be noted that the principal has been designated chairman of the athletic council in place of the superintendent. The principal is in charge of the administration of other high school subjects; hence it is logical that he should have immediate responsibility for the athletics. In schools of this size the relations and contacts between superintendent and principal are very close, and ideally they work as a unit. In most cases, however, superintendents are glad to delegate immediate responsibility for the athletic program to their high school principals. The athletic coach and assistant coaches should be members of the council because of their obviously vital connections with the program. In considering matters of policy or procedure it is recommended that the head coach only should vote. One high school faculty member, and possibly two, should serve on the council in addition to the principal and coaches. As was indicated in the list of recommendations it is desirable to rotate this faculty membership frequently in order that more faculty members may understand the school's athletic program and its objectives.

Council membership need not necessarily be limited to men members of the faculty, regardless of the policy of the school concerning interschool athletics for girls. Again, a member of the local board of education is recommended as a member of the athletic council. In most communities in which schools of this size are found, at least one of the board of education members is anxious and willing to serve. Here is a fine opportunity to acquaint a representative of the lay public with problems involved in school athletics. At the same time, if a member of the board of education is accorded the courtesy of acting as a member of the athletic council, such membership may pave the way for financial or other aid from the board for the athletic program. However, as was indicated in footnote 3, there are two sides to the question whether a board of education member should serve on the athletic council in an active capacity. The inclusion of a student representative, or representatives, to membership on the council has a democratic motive because it brings in the student body of the school, other than participants, as a functioning agency. This is a valuable consideration, and provision should be made for it.

It is desirable that the meetings of the athletic council in schools of this size be more formal than those in smaller schools. Usually, there are more matters of policy to be discussed as well as decisions to be made. Accounts of the meetings should be kept, and it may be advisable to publish them in the local newspaper or school paper, if one is issued. If publication is not feasible it is suggested that reports of council meetings be made to the student body at assembly periods. The purpose of these suggestions is that of keeping students and public informed of the athletic policies and program of the school. It is common knowledge, of course, that school athletics, dramatics, forensics, musical activities, and the like, attract the attention of both students and school patrons to an extent greater than do most other school functions. Keep everyone informed regarding the things for which the school stands in all these activities. Precedents can be established and publicized much easier through regular procedures than when unusual circumstances arise.

As to routine business the council should consider and approve all schedules. Athletic equipment should be authorized and purchased on its order. Recommendations for athletic awards should be received by it from the coach or coaches, and be either accepted or rejected. The coach and school officials often may protect themselves from criticism and embarrassment if all awards are granted by action of the athletic council on the basis of character, school citizenship, and athletic ability.

Complete reports of all finances, both receipts and expenditures, should be made to the council by the treasurer. Generally, this officer should be a faculty member. It is impossible to take too much precaution in the handling of the athletic finances of a school.[6] It is recommended, although it may not seem necessary in all cases, that the approval of engagement of athletic officials for home contests be a matter of council record. Such a procedure has value because, if attention is given this important matter sufficiently in advance of the contest, it is probable that better officials will be secured and mutual satisfaction of competing schools will thus be more nearly assured. Likewise, school action in securing an athletic official makes

6 See pages 255–286 for further discussion of athletic finances.

him the school's guest, an important fact for students and school patrons to understand.

Organization plan for athletics in a large high school. The large high school has much the same setup as the medium-sized high school discussed in the preceding section, except that it has a well-established physical and health education program and usually sponsors a much greater range of athletic activities. Much of the detail work in administering the athletic program is delegated to the athletic director or faculty manager, the title of this official being dependent upon school terminology. Several coaches and assistant coaches make up the athletic coaching staff. School policies vary as to whether these men are members of the physical education department. As indicated previously, the enrollment is not an especially important consideration beyond a recognized minimum; it may vary from a few hundred to several thousand.

As in the suggested plans for athletic organization in the small and medium-sized high school, it also is recommended that an athletic council, board of control, or governing board be established. Its personnel should include:

1. The superintendent of schools. (Undoubtedly his connection with the administration of the athletic program in the high school will be entirely advisory.)

2. The high school principal (who should act as chairman).

3. The athletic director or faculty manager of athletics.

4. The head coach of each sport sponsored by the school. (Assistant coaches should meet with the council, if possible, but only in an advisory capacity and in order to be familiar with all action relative to the school athletic policy.)

5. One or two members of the high school faculty, to be appointed by the principal. (The head of the physical and health education department should be included if he is not the athletic director or a head or assistant coach.)

6. One member of the local board of education.[7] (This courtesy should be extended to the board with the request that it appoint a member.)

7. The supervisor of physical and health education for the local school system.

[7] See footnote 3 in this chapter.

8. A boy and a girl to be elected by the student body as its representatives.

This may seem like quite an extensive membership list for an administrative board to handle a high school athletic program. The scope of activities, however, should justify the inclusion of all these individuals when the factors that they represent are considered.

The *superintendent of schools* should be a member of the council by virtue of his office. If there is more than one school in a system it is doubtful if he will take a very active part in the athletic deliberations of any of them. He should always be consulted in an advisory capacity because of his final responsibility for the entire program. As the nominal head of all the divisions of the school system he should be extended the courtesy of exercising his perogative relative to athletics if he desires to do so. The least that may be done is to see that copies of the accounts of council meetings are forwarded to him for his files.

Many details of responsibility for athletics will, of choice and necessity, be delegated by the *high school principal.* This is as it should be. The faculty usually is large enough in these schools so that responsibilities can be delegated in athletics the same as in dramatics, music, and forensics. It is essential, however, that final authority and responsibility for the high school athletic program be kept under close supervision by the principal. He should be permanent chairman of the council, which usually should meet at least once a month or oftener, subject to his call. Frequently the principal in larger high schools actually will be not much more than the presiding officer at the council meetings, especially if the athletic director or faculty manager, coaches, and treasurer are efficient.

The athletic director or *faculty manager of athletics* should be the representative of the high school principal in all athletic matters involving the school. In some respects he might be classified as the head of the business division of the athletic department. When his work is considered from that angle, the term "faculty manager" is more fitting and is properly descriptive. His job should be that of handling all business details relative to the athletic program except that of coaching the teams. All reports should be made to him by coaches and assistant coaches and in turn forwarded by him to the principal or reported to the athletic council. School stenographic services should be at his disposal in order that he may carry on correspondence regarding schedules, officials, game arrangements, and other details. At council meetings the athletic director should have all information at hand regarding matters to be considered at that particular session. Preparation of agenda for such meetings is recommended.

Some schools may find it feasible to combine the duties of the head coach in one or two sports with those of the athletic director or faculty manager. In this event the individual concerned could quite properly be called the athletic director, because his work would be sufficiently inclusive enough to give the term its proper connotation. General experience seems to indicate that a large school's athletic program may be administered more efficiently when the two jobs are not combined. In the present-day large high school there is considerable athletic clerical work, and the inclusion of a faculty manager as a member of the athletic administration staff seems to be a wise procedure. The faculty manager's duties in seeing that athletic eligibility data on each candidate for teams are compiled is usually a job in itself.

In many large high schools there is no head coach as such but a head coach for each sport. In others one man coaches two or three sports. The tendency seems to be for a coach to handle not more than two sports during the academic year, usually sports that are not in successive seasons. In many cases a man acts as head coach for one sport and assists in another. As stated previously, the *head coach in each sport* should be a member of the athletic council. Assistants should sit in on the meetings, if possible, in an advisory capacity. Many coaches feel that they do not have enough to say regarding the making of athletic policy. If they are a part of the athletic council, they have the right to help in the formulation of the program policies. If their suggestions are not adopted, the complete discussion of them in the council meetings should show them the reasons for their nonacceptance.

The coach may add much of value to matters that will come before the council because he is the person who deals most directly with the students for whom the entire program is drafted. Often the coaches are younger members of the athletic staff, and they may bring with them some of the newer ideas relative to athletics in education. The coach always should be used in every possible capacity because it not only broadens the program but also tends to broaden him. It acquaints him with athletic administrative problems involving the entire school, with which he probably would not become familiar in any other way.

At least *two other faculty members,* in addition to the principal, athletic director or faculty manager, and coaches should be members of the athletic council. Preferably one of them should be the dean of boys or the assistant principal of the high school, to provide for continuity in policy and procedure in the principal's absence. The other faculty member of the athletic council should be the school or athletic association treasurer. He should have information available relative to receipts and expenditures, both factors being important items in any athletic program. It is not recommended that these two members be alternated with other faculty members, as was suggested for the medium-sized high school; such an arrangement would not be feasible, owing to the size of the faculty. Information regarding the athletic program of the school or important regulations concerning it that affect faculty members must be prepared in announcements, presented at faculty meetings, or carried in the school paper. In the unlikely event that the head of the physical education department of the school is not the athletic director, faculty manager, or head coach, he should be a member of the athletic board of control. Every year, the relationship between physical education and athletics becomes closer, and rightly so. Certainly, the man who heads the physical and health education program in a school should be a valuable asset to any administrative or policy-making body in interscholastic athletics.

In spite of varied opinions on the matter it is recommended that the *board of education* be advised of the plan for control of athletics in the high school and invited to appoint a member to attend the council meetings if it desires to do so. This arrangement not only gives the board information to which it is entitled but also may be a very valuable connection for high school athletics in a great many ways. It is just good business to see that a copy of all accounts of the athletic council meetings, as well as periodic financial statements, is sent to the secretary of the board of education.

Where there are two or more high schools in a city, the *supervisor of physical and health education* for the school system should be a member of the athletic council of each of the high schools. He may be a very valuable member. At least he may represent the superintendent of schools and see that the latter is kept informed of matters that should come to his attention. The supervisor also may aid in helping to keep the athletic policies and procedures of all the schools in one system more nearly uniform. Moreover, the supervisor usually is a man of considerable athletic and physical education experience and should be decidedly valuable counsel.

Two students are suggested as athletic council members, a boy and a girl. It is recommended that they be elected in connection with student council or all-school elections. This procedure brings attention to the student body that athletics are a democratic all-school function. Often the girl who is elected to the council may serve as its secretary. This is valuable training for her and at the same time may be assurance that complete records of all council meetings are kept.

Meetings of the athletic council should be conducted in a businesslike manner. An agenda should be prepared for each session. As has just been indicated, complete records of all meetings should be kept. It is obvious that matters which will come before the council for consideration in the large high school will be similar to those of the medium-sized school. Many of these also will be the same basic ones that are important to the smallest high school sponsoring interscholastic athletics. The chief differences will be in their number and extent. The following are among the matters that should receive athletic council consideration and approval:

1. *Policies.* The athletic policy of the school should have formal approval of the council. This should be the guiding principle for the school's annual program.

2. *Schedules.* Schedules in all sports should be submitted to and approved by the council prior to their announcement.

3. *Contracts for games.* All game contract provisions should be presented to the council by the faculty manager for approval.

4. *Budgets.*[8] Estimated budgets of receipts and expenditures should be discussed and the latter approved. Complete financial reports should be made to the council.

[8] See "Athletic Budgets" in Chapter 10 for further discussion regarding athletic budgets.

5. *Equipment.* Purchases of all athletic equipment should be authorized by the council.

6. *Officials.* Final approval of athletic officials for all home games should be a matter of council record.

7. *Awards.* The council should receive recommendations from head coaches and authorize all awards to student athletes and student managers.

8. *Athletic injuries.* A definite statement of the policy of the school regarding the care and expense of athletic injuries should be made and well understood.

9. *Duties of administration.* The athletic director or faculty manager should be instructed as to specfic duties he is to perform, subject to the approval of the principal.

10. *Unusual circumstances.* Any unusual circumstances regarding home- or away-game arrangements, officials, equipment, and the like, should be explicitly understood and approved by the council.

A critical examination of the items listed for consideration by the athletic council of a large high school will show that they are nearly all-inclusive, as was intended. The council should be, as its name implies, the body that counsels on athletic matters. Whether the school is large, medium-sized, or small, emphasis should be placed on the importance of having the program-governing board a well-informed organization that actually knows what is taking place. It should be the "board of directors" of interscholastic athletics of the school. Someone might raise the question why an elaborate organization should be accorded the athletic program if it is to be considered as having only its regular place in the educational scheme of things in a school, since no such arrangements are made for music, social studies, sciences, or other regular school subjects. The answer is that the organization is formed so that the athletic program will be kept in its logical place. The nature of athletics, with their wide student and adult interests, is such that sometimes over-enthusiasm might raise havoc with an otherwise sane program. For this reason the athletic council organization in a school may serve as a governing as well as an administering body. Again, the council very conveniently may be used by the high school principal as an agency for making final decisions on requests regarding which he may not care to make a statement. In summation, the athletic council, board of control, or governing board has a valuable place in the high school athletic program because it can be:

1. A policy-making organization.
2. An administrative body.
3. A counseling group.
4. A contact organization.
5. A body for making the athletic program coherent.

Plans for the Control of Interschool Athletics in Large Cities

In most instances each local high school in a large city will have an organization in effect for handling its athletics which may be similar to one discussed under "Organization plan for athletics in a large high school." In several cities, however, there are central agencies for determining and governing the athletic program for local interschool competition. Many such cities feel that they have sufficient competition among their own schools, so that very few or no outside games are played. A brief presentation of salient facts in connection with four such cities will be presented. Detroit, Chicago, Philadelphia, and Los Angeles have been selected because their organizations represent four rather distinct plans, although the Philadelphia and Chicago plans seem to have greater similarity than the others. Detroit sets up a board of athletic control, or athletic council, by appointment of the superintendent, in which the identity of individual schools in controlling their programs is somewhat overshadowed by the central organization. In Chicago the board of control is made up of a representative of each school, in addition to the director of physical education and his men assistants. Philadelphia has a supervisory committee on athletics appointed annually by the superintendent of schools. The director of physical and health education is general chairman. Los Angeles has an advisory committee on athletics, with the physical education section of the public schools being responsible for the general program. Significant parts of the plans or organizations of these four city systems will be quoted and followed by brief summaries and comments.

Detroit. The Detroit organization is called the Detroit Public Secondary School Athletic League composed of twenty high schools.

in the Detroit system. The following statements explain the administration plan in Detroit: [9]

The Senior High School Principals shall be the governing body. The Assistant Superintendent in charge of secondary schools shall be the chairman.

Duties

a. The governing body shall have general control of interscholastic athletic policies not covered by the rules and regulations of the Michigan High School Athletic Association.
b. It shall establish administrative procedures for the conduct of the interscholastic athletic program.
c. It shall exercise all other functions necessary for carrying out their responsibility.

The High School Principals' Health and Physical Education Committee shall consist of *eight high school principals* to be appointed by the Assistant Superintendent in charge of secondary schools. *The Divisional Director of Health and Physical Education* shall be the Secretary, and the Supervisor of Boys' Health and Physical Education shall be the *Assistant Secretary.*

Duties

a. This committee shall study all matters relative to athletic policies and administrative procedures and make recommendations to the High School Principals.
b. This committee will call upon the Health and Physical Education Department Heads' Committee or the Coaches' Committee for advice whenever it is deemed necessary.

The Divisional Director of Health and Physical Education shall be the executive officer in control of interscholastic athletics, subject to the authority of the High School Principals.

Duties

a. He shall advise the High School Principals and the High School Principals' Health and Physical Education Committee on matters pertaining to athletic policies and administrative procedures.
b. He shall be responsible for seeing that the operation and management of the interscholastic athletic program is in accord with the policies adopted by the Senior High School Principals and that at all times the

[9] Detroit Public Secondary School Athletic League, 1960–1961 *Athletic Manual,* pp. 7–8.

operations are conducted so as to contribute the most possible to the health, good sportsmanship and well-being of the pupils in relation to the total school program.

c. All questions arising between schools that are not fully covered by the rules and regulations of the Michigan High School Athletic Association shall be referred to the *executive officer* for necessary rulings. *Such rulings shall be reported to the High School Principals' Health and Physical Education Committee in writing at least once each month.*

An assistant to the executive officer shall be recommended by the executive officer annually *and approved by vote of the High School Principals' Health and Physical Education Committee.*

Duties

a. He shall aid the executive officer in carying out the latter's duties.

The Health and Physical Education Department Heads' Committee shall consist of the Department Heads of the individual schools and the Supervisor of Boys' Health and Physical Education. *The chairman shall be elected by ballot annually.*

Duties

a. The Committee may make recommendations on matters concerning athletic policies and administrative procedures to the High School Principals' Health and Physical Education Committee.
b. The Committee may make recommendations to and aid the executive officer on matters pertaining to the management and operation of the athletic program.

A Coaches Committee in each sport shall be appointed by the *High School Principals' Health and Physical Education Committee.* The committee in each sport shall consist of *three coaches and the Supervisor of Boys' Health and Physical Education. Membership on the committee shall be rotated annually. The chairman shall be elected annually by ballot.*

Duties

a. The Committee may make recommendations to The Health and Physical Education Department Heads' Committee on matters of athletic policies and administrative procedures pertaining to their sport.
b. The Committee may make recommendations to and aid The Health and Physical Education Department Heads' Committee on matters pertaining to the management and operation of the athletic program as it refers to their particular sport.

The Detroit *Athletic Manual* goes on to explain the handling of finances and purchases of athletic equipment through the board of education. Funds realized from athletic contests are sent to the department of educational expenditures. Supplies are requisitioned to the supervisor and bought on bid through the board of education purchasing department. Game officials are assigned by the assistant director's office on the basis of ratings from the preceding season. The account of the Detroit plan has been stated in detail because it is an outstanding one illustrative of rather highly centralized control. Its success has helped to make the health and physical education department of the Detroit Public Schools known throughout the country.

Chicago. The plan of organization for the control of athletics in Chicago high schools is somewhat different from that in Detroit. Each school maintains its own program, controls its own finances, and purchases its own equipment in much the same manner as single high schools do in larger cities.

The Chicago organization is called the Chicago Public High Schools Athletic Association, Boys' Division. Membership is limited to high schools under the supervision of the Chicago board of education. A board of control is the governing board:

The Board of Control shall consist of the Director of Physical Education and his men assistants and one Board of Control representative from each high school in this Association who shall be appointed by the principal of that school.

The Director of Physical Education shall be the Secretary-Treasurer.

The Board of Control may charge each member an entry fee not to exceed $5.00 for each team in any sport in which the school competes. The fee must be in the hands of the Secretary-Treasurer when entries are submitted.[10]

Financial receipts are divided equally between competing schools in Chicago unless mutually agreed otherwise in the contract. Protests by schools may be made to the secretary-treasurer if accompanied by a $5 deposit (forfeited if protest is allowed). Sports committees are set up for each activity, and complete eligibility lists of competing schools must be sent to the supervisor's office two

[10] Chicago Public High Schools Athletic Association, Boys' Division, 1960–1961 *Constitution and By-Laws*, pp. 1, 2, 4.

weeks before the opening of the league schedule. As is the case with Detroit, the Chicago plan seems to have worked satisfactorily, and the athletic program, with its relation to physical education, is well and favorably known.

Philadelphia. In Philadelphia the school code of the state sets up provisions regarding the conduct, management, and control of interschool athletics in public high schools. The Philadelphia board of public education has adopted the following resolution in this connection:

Resolved, That the Superintendent of School shall appoint annually a supervisory committee on athletics, to serve without compensation, to consist of representatives from various types of public schools, together with such persons engaged in work in physical education in the public schools as the Superintendent may select. And the Superintendent may also appoint others in an advisory capacity. This committee, acting under the direction and control of the Division of Physical and Health Education, shall prepare regulations and schedules governing interschool athletic activities throughout the school system, and otherwise assist in the conduct of school athletics, subject to the aproval of the Superintendent of Schools.[11]

The Philadelphia plan also provides that the director of physical and health education shall be a member of each of the four sections of the supervisory committee, of which he is chairman. The committee sections are as follows: Boys' High and Vocational-Technical Schools, Girls' High and Vocational-Technical Schools, Boys' Junior High and Girls' Junior High, High Schools, Elementary Schools, Special Schools, and Evening Schools. Under general regulations the Philadephia rules make provision as follows:

The Supervisory Committee on athletics shall prepare regulations governing interschool athletic activities throughout the school system including:

(a) The number and nature of the contests arranged for or played under its jurisdiction.

(b) The schedules for such contests or games.

(c) The eligibility of the participating contestants and officials.

(d) The length and character of the games or events.

[11] Board of Education, School District of Philadelphia, 1958 *Rules for the Control and Management of Boys' Interschool Athletics,* p. 3.

(e) The basis and mode of awarding honors to the participants.

No athletic team composed of pupils in any public school or schools of this district, or in any capacity representing such school or schools, shall enter into or play any contest or game of any kind with any team of or from any organization or institution located outside of this School District unless the proposed arrangements for such contest or games shall meet the approval of a majority of the Committee and the Superintendent of Schools.

In order to be eligible to participate as an official or contestant in any interschool game or contest, a pupil in a public school in this district must maintain in school such standards in conduct, scholarship, and physical fitness as may be prescribed by this Committee.

The direct control of interschool athletics in each school shall be vested in an authorized body, which authorized body in the case of any school having an incorporated alumni may be its Committee on Athletics as now constituted, subject in each case to the rules laid down by the Board of Education, the Superintendent of Schools, and the Supervisory Committee on Athletics.[12]

The Philadelphia regulations also set up the approved sports, with special rulings on each of them as to their conduct and participation by contestants. The setup is complete and apparently has proved quite satisfactory.

Los Angeles. The Los Angeles plan for control of athletics represents a six-league organization of the senior high schools in the Los Angeles city school district. The regulations ". . . are the result of the varied experiences encountered in the competitive program over a long period of years. The chief purpose of these rules is to coordinate the athletic programs of the several leagues by standardizing practices and regulating the conduct and procedures of all schools and competitors in their relations with one another." [13] The Policy-Determining Committee, which is the athletic board for the Los Angeles City High School District is charged with the responsibility of administering the athletic program.

Unique among the Los Angeles regulations is the four-class competition provided in sponsored activities. Teams are organized on the basis of an age-height-weight classification for all sports. Another

[12] Board of Education, School District of Philadelphia, 1958 *Rules for the Control and Management of Boys' Interschool Athletics*, p. 6

[13] Los Angeles City Schools, 1960 *Rules and Regulations Governing Interscholastic Athletic Contests*, p. 3.

unusual regulation in Los Angeles is the requirement that there are to be few night contests. Several outstanding regulations indicative of policies in effect are given below:

No individual or school atheltic team may participate in night contests unless prior approval has been granted by the Policy-Determining Committee.

* * *

1. All indoor contests must close by 6:00 p.m. except for events specifically authorized by the Policy-Determining Committee.
2. All outdoor contests shall be terminated by ten minutes after sunset, as determined by the United States Weather Bureau at Los Angeles. The only exceptions shall be for events specifically authorized by the Policy-Determining Committee.

* * *

1. There shall be no directed organized practice, scrimmage, or contest on Saturdays, Sundays, holidays, or during any institute or vacation period, other than contests regularly scheduled and approved by the Policy-Determining Committee.
2. Athletes may not report to the Physical Education Plant (gymnasium or field) before the start of the last school period. Practice must close two hours after the normal closing time of the school concerned.

* * *

A school may not protest a game because of decisions involving an official's judgment.

Any protest must be made in writing and signed by the principal of the school making the protest. Copies shall be filed with the Chairman of the Policy-Determining Committee, the Supervisor of Athletics, and the principal of the other school within forty-eight hours following the close of the contest.

* * *

1. Only persons holding California teachers' credentials shall officiate at contests in which high schools of the Los Angeles City School District are involved, except when the Supervisor of Athletics is unable to obtain qualified credentialed personnel.
2. Teachers, upon approval of the principal, may without loss of salary leave their schools in time to start the game as scheduled.
3. It is desirable that a teacher not leave his school early for an officiating assignment unless at least one of the competing schools is from the Los Angeles City School District. However, a teacher may do other-

wise, provided that, in the opinion of his principal, circumstances justify the early departure.

All communications or questions pertaining to high school athletic contests shall be referred to the Policy-Determining Committee.

Rules governing the conduct of athletics in the Los Angeles High School District may not be changed or suspended except by recommendation of the Policy-Determining Committee.[14]

Los Angeles regulations for interschool competition apply to ten sports, and definite rules for participation in each of them are established. Schools may not play outside the Los Angeles district except in a few specified cases. Net funds realized from athletic contests are divided equally between competing schools. Championships in leagues are determined on a percentage basis in some sports and are city-wide in others. Subject to the general regulations in effect, it is apparent that other matters pertaining to athletic competition are handled by local schools in Los Angeles.

Policies of Some Large Cities in the Administration of Athletics

Several years ago an interesting and informative study concerning important athletic policies in several of the larger cities of the nation was conducted by James E. Rogers who then was with the National Physical Education Service. Four questions were asked of twelve city administrators of physical education. The questions follow, together with the summaries for each of them as formulated by Mr. Rogers:

1. In what major cities of the country does the Board of Education supply adequate playing spaces, fields, halls, courts, etc., their maintenance, repairs, and policing, as part of its curricula?

Conclusion summary—Facilities are becoming better and more adequate and school boards are assuming more responsibility in this direction.

2. To what extent does the trained leadership or coach get roster compensation or financial remuneration over and above his regular teacher roster or salary for such work?

---

[14] Los Angeles City Schools, 1960 *Rules and Regulations Governing Interscholastic Athletic Contests*, pp. 3–7.

Conclusion summary—Trained leadership is in demand but there is no extra compensation for coaching. There is a less curricular load for those who coach.

3. To what extent is personal equipment, football uniforms, helmets, footballs, shoes, bats, balls, track shoes and all personal playing material furnished free to the members of the school squads?

Conclusion summary—The practice is divided. The majority of Boards of Education give supplies and equipment such as balls and bats; the different cities vary in degree—some more, some less. Personal equipment comes from the athletic fund. The funds are raised through gate receipts. The students pay a very small, nominal season fee. However, some schools give money for personal equipment from school funds.

4. To what extent is the student body admitted free to see all contests, both as to "Home" games and those of other schools in the same community?

Conclusion summary—Practically all cities make a small, nominal charge, usually $1.00, for a season ticket.

There is a tendency therefore to make athletics educational in content and in administration. There is a tendency to make provision for it like any other subject as regards facilities and equipment. There is a desire that someday athletics will be free from gate receipts so that it will be placed on the same basis as any other subject in the curriculum. These are wishful tendencies. The practice varies as the various answers show.[15]

The City Administrative Directors Section of the American Association for Health, Physical Education, and Recreation has conducted three national surveys on interscholastic athletic standards. In the one made in 1945, the country was divided into sections and replies were received as follows from 189 cities:

1. Should high school teachers of physical education be paid extra for coaching interscholastic sports? *Yes:* 160. *No:* 29. The trend is strongly toward paying extra for after school coaching and the committee recommends that an equable system be adopted.

2. Should high school teachers of classroom subjects be paid extra for coaching interscholastic sports? *Yes:* 172. *No:* 17. When teachers of

---

[15] James E. Rogers, *Study of Important Policies in the Administration of School Athletics,* National Physical Education Service Pamphlet, 315 Fourth Ave., New York, 1938. Cities included in this study were Baltimore, Chicago, Cleveland, Denver, Hartford, Minneapolis, Pasadena, Philadelphia, Pittsburgh, Providence, St. Louis, and Wichita.

classroom subjects not directly connected with physical education are required to coach a sport, the trend is ten to one in favor of awarding extra pay in addition to the base salary. The committee recommends that either money or reduced class periods should be given.

3. If 1, 2, or both is checked *Yes,* should the pay be in money? *Yes:* 92, or in reduced teaching classroom or gymnasium periods? *Yes:* 52, or both? *Yes:* 69. Although the comment shows that a majority of coaches prefer monetary payment, there is a growing trend to require teachers of education to take some reduction in class periods and the balance in money. Many women who coach prefer reduced class periods rather than monetary remuneration. The committee recommends that if any coaches are paid, all should be. Coaches should be paid either in money when there are not enough teachers to carry the standard gymnasium load or in reduced periods when the staff is large. Periods off during the day are not the equivalent of extra pay.

4. What is actually being done for coaches of athletics in your schools? *Paid in money:* 121. *Paid by reduction in class time:* 23. *Paid by combining both methods:* 27. *No payment of any kind:* 18. The trend is five to one in favor of payment in money varying according to the interest shown by the participation of students and the nervous energy expended by the coach. The committee recommends that special teachers of physical education should coach three hours weekly in addition to the regular class load; beyond that they should receive cash in accordance with their roster pay.

5. What is actually being done for coaches of music or dramatics? *Paid in money:* 71. *Paid by reduction in class time:* 28. *Paid in money and reduction in time:* 10. *No payment of any kind:* 87. The returns show that most schools do not pay teachers who work after school in music or dramatics. The trend, however, is to pay those who conduct entertainments for which an admission charge is made. The committee recommends that coaches in dramatics or those teachers who must work long hours after school with a band, orchestra, or chorus should receive money or reduced periods or both. This method will eliminate a source of ill will in many schools.

6. Do all interschool contests in athletics require a coach? *Yes:* 173. *No:* 16. Sports—Aquatics, Archery, Badminton, Baseball, Basketball, Boxing, Bowling, Cross Country. Fencing, Field Hockey, Football, Football-Six Man, Golf, Gymnastics, Ice Hockey, Lacrosse, Rifle, Soccer, Softball, Tennis, Track, Volleyball, Wrestling. Principals are almost unanimous in requiring at least a faculty adviser for all interschool contests. The committee recommends that a coach be assigned from the faculty

for all contests in team games and that an adult adviser be present at individual contests of less interest.

7. Do all groups of students playing away from their own school require a teacher accompanying? *Yes:* 187. *No:* 2. Practically all schools require a teacher to accompany a representative student group when players leave the school premises. The committee recommends that the principal should assign faculty members to attend every contest because mature judgment is needed for safety. Teachers should see that students have a proper means of returning home after the contest.

8. Do girls compete in athletics with other schools? *Yes:* 28. *No:* 161.

9. List sports used by girls—Archery, Aquatics, Badminton, Basketball, Bowling, Cageball, Croquet, Dodgeball, Fencing, Fieldball, Golf, Field Hockey, Lacrosse, Rifle, Shuffleboard, Skating, Soccer, Softball, Speedball, Table Tennis, Tennis, Track, Volleyball. Although five of every six girls' schools have no interschool contests, there were twenty-three different sports in use by those who do compete. Play days are listed by several cities. The committee recognizes that carefully managed contests in charge of women teachers have been successfully conducted for thirty years in some cities and that the trend is to allow contests without awards or admission fees.

10. Does your Board of Education own any enclosed athletic field? *Yes:* 150. *No:* 39. School authorities in most of the larger cities have found it necessary to own and control athletic fields. When privately owned fields are rented, schedules are often disrupted by better paying attractions. The committee recommends that modern fields should have seats and lights and should be owned or controlled by the Board of Education. Each high school should have its own field adjacent to the building and fenced for protection against unauthorized use. The care of fields, running track, pits, and equipment should be in charge of caretakers responsible directly to the Board of Education.[16]

Athletic Leagues and Conferences as Administrative Agencies

During the past three decades especially, high schools have grouped themselves into leagues and conferences for athletic and other interscholastic competition. These leagues have established principles and policies as far as their interschool athletic relations are concerned. Their chief purposes, however, have been the ar-

[16] Administrative Directors Section of the American Association for Health, Physical Education, and Recreation, St. Louis, *Report of Committee on Interscholastic Standards,* April, 1946.

rangement of schedules, declaring of league championships, maintenance and preservation of records, and assignment of athletic officials. High school conferences have been patterned very much after similar collegiate athletic associations and have performed like functions. The one exception is in the matter of interpretation and enforcement of athletic eligibility and contest regulations. In most instances these come from state athletic associations.

Optimum size. Usually, the league or conference includes a comparatively small geographical section of the state, with its membership composed of schools of comparable size and sponsoring similar or identical activities. Preferably, leagues should be small in size (five to eight or ten schools), because an unwieldy organization is ineffective. All member schools should meet each other in all sports sponsored by the league during the season. If they cannot, it is safe to say that the organization is too large. Schools are then likely to "shop around" for games when league schedules are set up so that they may determine their league standing by playing what they consider to be the weaker schools. Invariably this practice leads to dissension; thus it seems wise to advocate that league membership be kept small.

Services of athletic conferences. The value of the services rendered to member schools by athletic conferences and leagues depends on their local administration. Athletic conferences may serve to:

1. Enable member school officials to become better acquainted with each other through their league meetings.

2. Provide opportunities for schools of comparable size to compete with each other.

3. Allow the determination of league championships through comparatively local competition and without excessive team travel.

4. Provide methods for keeping league records of individual achievements and school standings.

5. Assign contest officials by league officers and establish uniform fees.

6. Develop definite ways for the improvement of sportsmanship at athletic contests through programs, exchange assemblies, school visits, and the like.

7. Ensure full schedules of all member schools in league-sponsored sports.

8. Conduct league meets and tournaments in appropriate sports.

9. Act in an advisory capacity with state athletic association officials on matters of general athletic importance.

10. Establish local league regulations for the conduct of games, including student and spectator control, admission prices, complimentary tickets, program arrangements, and so on.

Questions for Study and Discussion

1. Why is it important that the athletic policy of a school be definitely established and defined?

2. Discuss the division of responsibility for the athletic program among: (a) superintendent of schools; (b) high school principal; (c) athletic director or coach; (d) student manager; and (e) student athlete.

3. What are the essentials of an organizational plan for athletics in a small high school? Medium-sized high school? Large high school?

4. Why is it important that organizational plans be in effect for athletics in all schools, regardless of size? Give definite reasons?

5. List general policies of large-city control plans for athletics in (a) Detroit; (b) Chicago; (c) Philadelphia; (d) Los Angeles.

6. What were the general conclusions of Rogers' study of the administration of athletics in several large cities?

7. Discuss common practice concerning athletics in effect in large-city schools as disclosed by the study of the City Administrative Directors Section of the American Association for Health, Physical Education, and Recreation.

8. What are some of the values of athletic leagues and conferences as administrative agencies in the athletic program?

7 Athletic Contest Management

The management of a school's athletic contests may be the barometer by which the administration of its entire athletic program is indicated. Efficient management demands respect for the event itself. Inefficient management, or lack of attention to seemingly minor or unimportant details, lessens the educational value of a game both to contestants and student spectators. At the present time, in most localities, schools carry on their athletics with the help of public support through gate receipts. Probably we all hope for the time when it will be unnecessary to charge for interschool athletic contests and when boards of education will support athletics in their entirety. That day is not yet here. It therefore behooves schoolmen to establish their athletic programs and conduct them in such a manner that they will command the type of support and respect from the public which the coaches and school officials have the right to expect.

Importance of Efficient Management

Well-managed contests. The well-patronized, successful enterprises in the community usually are those which are well organized and are managed efficiently. Every athletic contest should be handled in such a manner. Of course, the interest and concern of student participants and student spectators should receive first consideration. Following these, however, the public must be kept in mind. To do so should not cause any difficulty in the general scheme of things, especially if the policies of the school concerning inter-school athletics have been definitely established and well publicized. Make the athletic contest businesslike, attractive, and a well-organized sports event. The public will recognize it as such, and its educative and good-sportsmanship implications will be primary achievements almost to be taken for granted. In many instances, the reputation of a school may be measured by the manner in which its athletic contests are conducted. Certainly the importance attached to such events offers an opportunity to establish the good name of the school in a community which should not be overlooked by schoolmen.

Size of school. The size of the school and the extent of its athletic program make absolutely no difference in the importance of management of contests. Small schools have smaller squads, smaller student bodies, and smaller communities from which to draw adult crowds. The necessity for efficient management, however, is just as great as for the largest city schools. Games can start on time in these schools, crowds can be controlled, and squads can be neatly uniformed and competently coached just as well as in large city schools. Both students and adults in small communities will be equally appreciative if educated to an experience of this kind as will those who attend larger school contests.

In the attention given to details of management of athletic contests it will be assumed that schools of different sizes will consider only those items which are applicable to themselves. Some matters to be discussed, naturally, will not be of interest or concern to small schools. For example, publicity is not an important matter in connection with small-school athletic contests. An announcement made in the school assembly will reach virtually all the patrons and followers of teams in a village school. This is not true in larger schools. Thus, a publicity program is important in order that details of a given contest may be known to those who are interested in it.

Responsibility. No attempt will be made here to designate every individual responsible for certain details, which will be assigned according to the organization in the school itself. In some schools the superintendent may serve; in others, the principal or athletic director. Often the coach or a student manager will have particular jobs to perform. These persons should be kept in mind when considering the suggestions offered, because plans for administering athletic programs differ to such an extent in schools of various size.

The specialized function of coaching is not considered in the administrative sense. That the team will be trained and instructed to the best of the coach's ability is taken for granted.

Phases of contest management. The other matters to be discussed are those additional to the actual handling of the team at the time of the game or contest. Contest management for home games will be considered under three headings: (1) before-game preparation; (2) game responsibilities; (3) after-game responsibilities. Management details for out-of-town games are discussed separately. The last part of this section will deal with general management items which must receive attention during the course of the year. No attempt has been made to list topics in chronological order. Their importance will vary in different schools, depending upon the individual or individuals who are assigned definite responsibilities in the athletic program, but they will serve as a check list of reminders. It is recognized, of course, that some management details may have been omitted because, again, of variations in local situations.

Before-Game Preparation (Home Contests)

Well-managed athletic contests are not the result of accident. Attending well in advance to all the details pertaining to a home game is evidence of efficient administration and of good planning. It should be possible, in most instances, to have the following items included in this category ready well ahead of the rush of last-minute details.

Contracts. Complete check should be made of dates and days appearing on contracts. Be sure that a game scheduled for Friday, February 10, actually is Friday, and that it is February 10. Both the date and day should appear on the contract. If contracts are made for two or more years, write in actual days and dates for games each year and not "Return game on corresponding date next year," which is bound to lead to confusion and misunderstanding. Contracts should be typewritten in duplicate and signed in all places indicated. Many state associations require that their standard contracts be used for all games, including league schedules. Discrepancies in a contract should be made known to the other school immediately upon discovery. Have a regular filing place for all athletic contracts, so that they will be available at the time of contests.

Eligibility records. A list of students eligible to participate in the approaching contest should have been received from the visiting school. Check to see that it has arrived. Be certain that the eligibility list of the home school has been sent in accordance with state association regulations. The coach should have a copy of the eligibility list in order that there may be no misunderstanding regarding those who are eligible for a particular game. Eligibility lists of both schools should be at hand for possible reference at the time of a game.

Methods of securing current eligibility data vary in schools. In some cases a list of all candidates for teams is kept in the school office, to which teachers come on a designated day and check students in their classes for eligibility for athletics. In others, teachers are given a list of athletes in their classes. They mark this list and return it to the office or faculty chairman of eligibility. Still another plan is that of having each athlete, on eligibility-marking day, take to all his classes a special eligibility card which the teachers sign, indicating his eligibility or ineligibility in each subject. Absences of athletes on this day are checked by student managers, who take the cards of the absentees to the teachers concerned.

Claims are made for the value of each scheme. Local conditions, size of school, and precedents are undoubtedly the determining factors. Apparently the most generally efficient plan is that which places in the hands of each teacher a list of students in his or her class who are candidates for an athletic team. The teacher then may mark the list and note ineligible students or those whose work is of such low grade that ineligibility at the next marking period is inevitable unless there is a change in attitude or accomplishment. Students should be warned before they are marked ineligible. In most states eligibility grades are considered as running from the beginning of the semester to a date approximately a week prior to the contest.

Physical examinations. Make certain that records of physical examinations of all contestants are on file. It is good practice to require that the physical examination record of a student be received and filed before equipment is issued to him. Report the filing of physical examination records for all contestants to state athletic associations requiring it.

Parents' permission. It is good policy to secure parents' permission for all contestants. Such procedure clarifies athletic injury policies. Permission cards should be on file before a student is allowed to report for practice. Report the filing of parents' permission cards for all contestants to state athletic associations requiring it. Eagle Rock High School, Los Angeles, has developed a form for recording parents' consent for participation in athletics, which also includes the signature of the student. The contents of the card furnish valuable information both to student and parents (see Fig. 7–1).

Athletic Application for____________
Sport

Name__________, ____ ________ Birthday________________
Last First Month Day Year City State

I hereby apply for the privilege of trying out for
________ ____________
Sport Semester Year

I recognize my responsibilities and the regulations governing the above sport. I will so govern myself that my connection with the sport will bring honor to it and the school, and **expect to be asked to withdraw from the team in case I do not.**

I promise on my word of honor to do the above

Signed ____________

PARENT'S CONSENT

Date ____________

I hereby give my consent for my son to participate in the ________ program sponsored by Eagle Rock High School.
Sport

I, furthermore, release the said school from all liability for injuries received by my son during, or resulting from participation in this program, whether it be during practice or in an interschool contest.

In addition, I hereby release the school from all liability for injuries received by the participant while en route to or from contests which are held at other schools.

Name__________ **Phone**__________

Address ________________

Do not Write below this line

CLASSIFICATION

Weight		
Height		
Age		
Total Exponents		

Class____

Number of Semesters ____

Semester Hours Passed ____

This boy was examined __________ and is qualified to participate in interscholastic athletics.
Date

____
Physician

This student is eligible to try out for the above sport.

____
Vice Principal

Fig. 7-1. Athletic Participation Form *(Eagle Rock High School, Los Angeles, California).*

Athletic officials. Contracts should be checked with all officials prior to games. Be certain that the officials are registered for the current year, if registration is a state association requirement. A week or ten days before a contest, the entertaining school should remind the official of the date, time, and place of the game and the capacity in which he is to officiate. It is courteous and helpful to inform him also who the other officials in the game are to be. All officials' contracts should be explicit regarding the amount of the fee and the number of games on a given date. Officials' contracts should be made out in duplicate, signed, and filled out in all places provided, with the school and official each keeping a copy. Schools should keep such contracts filed in a regular place, and those involving officials for a particular game should be accessible at that time. Some schools have found it convenient to place game contracts, eligibility lists, and officials' contracts in a large envelope for each game. They also may be filed in this manner. All this information and other pertinent data concerning a definite contest may thus be kept in one place.

YOUR GAME OFFICIALS [1]
(Test Yourself)

1. Do I carefully check the list of proposed officials to be sure they are registered for the current year?
Yes. . . . . . No. . . . . . .

2. Do I secure men who are well trained in the administration of the interscholastic rules and familiar with the interpretations as prescribed by the I.H.S.A.A.?
Yes. . . . . . No. . . . . .

3. Do I use the contract forms supplied by the state office, secure sanction from the opponent, and take care of the details connected with securing officials in a businesslike manner?
Yes. . . . . . No. . . . . .

4. Do I supply the officials with details relative to exact time and place for the contest?
Yes. . . . . . No. . . . . .

5. Do I provide a suitable dressing room for the official apart from the teams?
Yes. . . . . . No. . . . . .

6. Do I effect measures to prevent players and spectators from attempting to influence the officials' decisions by words or actions?
Yes. . . . . . No. . . . . .

7. Do I arrange business matters so that the official will be able to leave promptly after the game?
Yes. . . . . . No. . . . . .

8. Do our contests start promptly at the time specified?
Yes. . . . . . No. . . . . .

9. Do our coaches attempt to influence the official before the game by calling attention to the faults of the opponent players or by dictating what type of officiating is required if he is to be employed again?
Yes. . . . . . . No. . . . . .

[1] Illinois High School Association Recommendations.

10. Are our officials chosen because of their officiating ability or because they are good prospects for a trade?
Yes. . . . . . No. . . . . .

Equipment. Personal playing equipment usually furnished by the school will be discussed in Chapter 8. In this discussion, equipment includes whatever is necessary, in addition to uniforms, for playing the contest. Each school official charged with the responsibility for having all items on hand for a game should have his own check list.[2] Often a student manager may be delegated to take care of these details. They are most important factors in efficient management.

Field or court. Unusual locations or temporary circumstances may make special arrangements necessary concerning fields or courts where contests are to be held. Confirm all such arrangements in writing in order that misunderstandings may be obviated. Be sure that the visiting school is fully informed regarding any such changes in plans. If a game or meet is to be held at another school, rather than at the host school, be certain that all details are thoroughly understood by the administration of the school concerned. Athletic directors and coaches, especially, should be certain that the complete schedules of athletic events or special athletic functions are in the hands of the principal or superintendent so there will be no conflicts in assignments of gymnasiums, fields, or other facilities on specific dates.

Publicity. The regular and accepted means of publicizing athletic events of a school should be followed. The extent of the advertising will depend on school policy, seating capacity, and interest in the game on the part of student body and adults. The news-releasing agency should be either the coach, athletic director, or principal, as they may agree among themselves. Paid advertisements in newspapers may be advisable in some instances. Radio "spots" and theater notices are other advertising mediums. Since the athletic program should give first consideration to the students themselves, they should be made as familiar as possible with it. Athletic assemblies offer this opportunity. This does not mean that student interest should be fanned to a white heat prior to each game. One or two athletic assemblies during each season will provide a means by

[2] See pp. 212–213 for suggested game equipment lists.

which the student body may be educated and advised regarding different games. By this method not only is their interest aroused or maintained, but they also become more intelligent spectators; and the athletic program becomes an educational experience for them as well as for the participants. Successful athletic assemblies can be held in senior high schools to include the following general pattern:

Analysis of plays and demonstration football games are the basis of a football assembly. The entire student body should be seated in the bleachers. Cheerleaders should be on hand for the game. A public address system should be used.

Two full teams should be dressed and used for demonstration purposes. An off-tackle play, a reverse, a punt and a simple forward pass could be analyzed. After an explanation, each boy should do his part separately in slow motion. Then the whole eleven may execute the play together.

The student body will soon realize that there are other players on the team besides the ball carrier and the forward pass receiver. The value of tackles, guards and blocking backs can be impressed upon them. In the game that follows, common fouls may be explained and then demonstrated by specific individuals.

In such an assembly students are made acquainted with the personnel of their team and the details of executing a few simple plays.

Similar assemblies in track and basketball have been held in high schools, which stress the following points. Assemblies must be thoroughly planned in order to carry out their purpose. They must be simple and they must be explained. They should be short and well executed. Since a great amount of adult interest in high school athletics is stimulated by the interest and enthusiasm of a son or daughter, it is apparent that school athletic assemblies may be good means of publicity as well as good educational devices. Some schools have held public clinics in various sports for students and adults, usually before the first game of the season.

Courtesies to the visiting school. The visiting school should be written to a week or ten days prior to a contest and advised concerning the location, time, date, and officials for the game. A number of state athletic association eligibility blanks carry this information and, of course, this obviates the necessity for an additional letter. It is important to be sure that the visiting school has all the necessary data regarding the game. It should be advised concerning admission prices for students and adults, number of complimentary passes it is to receive, and arrangements for its band if it is to be brought to the game. Exact directions as to the dressing place for the visiting team should be sent. A former Michigan High School Conference [3] devised a form (Fig. 7–2) that was sent each week

---

SOUTHWESTERN MICHIGAN HIGH SCHOOL CONFERENCE

Participants...................... vs.............................
Date of game.................... Place of game..................

Preliminary Game   *Main Game*
Referee......................... Referee.........................
Umpire.......................... Umpire..........................
Head Linesman.................. Head Linesman..................
Time....................E.S.T. Time....................E.S.T.
Color of jerseys................. Color of jerseys................
Ball to be used.................. Ball to be used................
Admission...........cents for students; ....cents for adults

   This sheet to be mailed on Monday along with the Current Eligibility List.

Fig. 7-2. Pre-Game Team and Personnel Information Form (Southwestern Michigan High School Conference).

with the Current Eligibility List used in that state. It not only furnished pertinent data and information for the game but also supplied the host school with names and numbers of contestants, which it may use for program purposes. On the reverse of the form is a request that this team personnel information be listed.

Reserve games. If a reserve game is to precede or follow a varsity-team game, complete arrangements should be made for it. Many schools find it more convenient to play outdoor reserve games on dates other than those on which varsity or first-team games are held, especially if fields are likely to be in poor condition for main games. Where schools are in the same or near-by cities such reserve-team games usually can be played without interference with school time.

---

[3] Included the following Michigan high schools: Benton Harbor, Grand Haven, Holland, Kalamazoo-Central, Muskegon, Muskegon Heights.

Arrangements should be definite for such games, good officials should be secured, and participants should be properly equipped. Precautions against injuries should be just as definite, or even more so, in these games as in any others, because the participants usually are less experienced. If two games are held the same afternoon or evening, they both should be started on time as announced and advertised.

Tickets. If special, season, or complimentary tickets are to be prepared and distributed, do it early. Tickets should be distinctive but not necessarily expensive. Have a definite method of charging them out to student salesmen if that plan is followed. Insist on businesslike methods in handling this and all financial matters pertaining to tickets. This point is of particular importance because, in some instances, state admissions tax reports must be prepared. If agreement has been made accordingly, make sure that the visiting school has an available supply of tickets for advance sale to its student body. Keep duplicate records of all ticket releases and sales. Have a definite policy in effect regarding complimentary tickets. The athletic council or board of control usually can remove considerable pressure for complimentary tickets by adopting a list of persons entitled to them and then adhering strictly to this list. In most cases those who make themselves nuisances in seeking complimentary tickets are not entitled to them, and athletic council action can provide a legitimate reason for not granting them. Adequate provision should be made for the selling and taking of tickets at the contest. Adults usually should serve in these capacities.

Contest programs. In general, an athletic contest is raised to a little higher plane if a simple, informative program can be placed in the hands of spectators. A program composed of nine-tenths advertising does not accomplish this purpose. Names and numbers of contestants, names of officials, and a few major rules interpretations are sufficient. If a small amount of legitimate advertising is necessary there should be no objection to it. Sometimes more ill will is engendered in advertisers, if they are continually asked to contribute to school athletic programs, than the receipts from such advertising are worth. The type of contest and the interest taken in it, as well as the size of the school and community, are determining factors in the furnishing of programs. In most instances they should not be sold. Reliable, trustworthy students should be assigned to distribute them.

Concessions. If concessions are to be handled by the local school athletic association, usually a faculty member should be in charge of them. If city or board of health permits for such concessions are necessary, they should be arranged for in sufficient time prior to the season or contest. Uniformed vendors add to the neatness and appearance of the project. If the concession rights are sold to a club or commercial firm, the high school should know what is to be offered for sale and the methods to be employed. Many schools find that local high school clubs or student organizations are glad to take charge of the concessions. Usually, such organizations are worthy ones, and often they perform services for the athletic department that more than offset what might be realized from concession sales if they were handled by the school itself. Regardless of the method of handling the concessions, the athletic association should insist on sanitation, neatness, and the employment of businesslike methods.

Ushers. Ushers are valuable adjuncts at an athletic contest. They not only assist the paying public to find their places in the stadium, gymnasium, or bleachers, but also actually help to enforce laws and rules. Definite arrangements for ushers should be made for all contests where a stadium or bleachers are used. They need not necessarily be uniformed, but they should have some distinctive apparel, badge or button as an identification. Students may be delegated and trained in ushering, and they can do much to maintain a high level of conduct at athletic contests. Some schools use varsity lettermen in sweaters as ushers. Others use boy scouts, girl reserves, or boys and girls from other uniformed organizations for ushering. Some recognition, other than financial remuneration, should be given to ushers. This may be made in the form of school letter awards, invitation to the athletic banquet for the sport, formation of an ushers' club, or the like.

Police protection and parking. As public servants, city and state police should be used at athletic contests for handling crowds, directing traffic, and parking. Most local police departments are willing to detail special officers for duty at a high school game. Some schools feel that the presence of an officer at their contests is an indictment against them. This is not true. Law-enforcing officers are present at all large gatherings, and their presence may be defended because of any emergency which might arise. In too many instances school officials have not taken advantage of this public service, which is usually theirs for the asking. The presence of a uniformed officer also adds dignity to a contest and provides a method for enforcing local regulations regarding conduct of spectators and sportsmanship at contests. When individuals buy tickets for a high school athletic contest, they should realize that its purchase is with the understanding that they may, under certain circumstances, be asked to leave the stadium, field, or gymnasium. The management reserves the right to refund the purchase price of the ticket and, with the aid of an officer of the law if necessary, to eject an unruly spectator who does not conduct himself in accordance with established standards. An occasional justified ejection has a wholesome effect on the general conduct of the crowd. For this reason, if for no other, the presence of uniformed officers at high school athletic contests is justified.

Reserved areas. If the stadium or bleachers are to have reserved sections, these should be plainly marked and roped off or guarded. When a patron buys a reserved seat, he is entitled to it. Also, he should be free from molesting students. Adults often hesitate to attend high school games because of the rowdyism of younger students which sometimes occurs. Reserved areas for bands, parking, or players' spaces should be provided and plainly designated prior to the game.

Cheer leaders. Well-uniformed and courteous cheer leaders can do a great deal to keep the crowd in the right frame of mind. Considerable attention ought to be given to the selection of cheer leaders, who can be sportsmanship leaders as well. Their big job should be that of securing recognition of outstanding plays and examples of good sportsmanship on the part of both teams, and of aiding the school and game officials as the contest progresses. They may also help much in maintaining proper order, and in assisting ushers and officers. A school letter award should be granted to cheer leaders who do the right kind of job.

Score boards. Score boards are almost essential pieces of equipment in modern high school athletic contests. Some excellent electric types are on the market, but these are not a necessity. Usually it is sufficient to have a device that shows the score of each team and the quarter, inning, or amount of time remaining to be played in the period. Definite arrangements should be made to have one or two students manage the score board regularly.

Condition of stadium, bleachers, or gymnasium. Upkeep of facilities should be a janitorial rather than an administrative duty. In certain cases, however, some member of the athletic staff may have to see that these facilities are in proper order for a contest. The stadium and bleachers should be clean. Out-of-date notices and paper and other debris should be removed. Rest rooms should be fully equipped, sanitary, and available. Temperature controls for indoor games should be inspected and regulated so that they are working properly at the time of the contest. Be sure that temporary bleachers have been properly inspected by authorized officials to ensure their safety.

Bands and half-time arrangements. If bands are to be present at a game, make certain that reserved seats are provided for them in the bleachers or stadium or on the field. Advise each band of the amount of time it will have for maneuvers between halves. If a flag-raising ceremony is to precede the game, make arrangements for all details and advise band directors accordingly. At football games especially, the local school band often can be of service in protecting the playing field from encroachment by spectators, which sometimes occurs near the end of the game if the field is not well roped off. The members should be instructed concerning this service and made to realize that spectators will respect their uniforms.

Decorations. If the field or gymnasium is to be decorated for a contest, include the color schemes of both schools. Be sure that decorations do not interfere with playing facilities. Crossbars of football goal posts or basketball backboards never should be decorated or marked in any manner.

Public-address system. Some schools own their public-address or loud-speaker systems. Often they may be used to advantage at athletic contests, outdoor ones especially. A regular policy relative to their use should be established. If the announcers are high school students, they should be trained in their job before the contests. Public address announcements regarding athletic events generally are most effective when made sparingly. Pertinent information regarding completed plays, substitutions, and explanations of penalties usually are sufficient. Do not attempt to give a running account of a contest for those who are seeing it.

Physician at contests. Arrangements should be made well in advance of a contest to have a physician present. In football, especially, it is recommended that a physician be present, or on call, for all practice sessions as well as at games. In most cities and towns there are physicians who are interested in athletics and like to attend the games. Sometimes it may be necessary to pay for the services of a physician in order to have one present. In either case payment is a desirable policy and protects both the contestants and the school. Often, the physicians in a community are willing to arrange their schedules so that one of them is free to attend one or more home games, and thus little hardship is imposed on any one of them. Complimentary tickets, of course, should be available to cooperating physicians as the least courtesy which could be shown them.

Scorers, timers, judges. Adequate provision should be made to have these officials at any contests that require their services. In football some schools keep track of all substitutions and time played by each contestant. Scorers and timers in basketball are very important officials. Members of the faculty usually are most satisfactory for these assignments. Use the same men regularly if possible. Timers and judges for track and swimming meets are difficult to secure. Plan to ask more than are needed, because some usually fail to be present.

Game Responsibilities (Home Contests)

The items listed and discussed in this section will be those to which attention must be given at the time of the contest. Preparation for some of them will have been made previously, but when the day of the game comes around, time is limited and every detail must have received its proper attention. In some instances the checklist items under Game Responsibilities will be restatements of those appearing under Before-game Preparations. It seems advisable to follow this procedure because in both instances they are matters which necessitate consideration at the time indicated.

Supplies and equipment. These items refer to game supplies and equipment, exclusive of uniforms for players. The following is a suggested list of supplies and playing equipment which should be available at game time for the common sports:

BASEBALL

Balls	Catcher's outfit	Official rules book
Bases	Drinking water	Resin
Batter's helmets	First-aid kit	Score book
Bats	Lime	Towels

BASKETBALL

Balls	First-aid kit	Score book
Bonus throw signals	Gun	Towels
Cartridges	Horn	Watches
Drinking water	Official rules book	Whistles
Electric score-board controls		

CROSS-COUNTRY

Cartridges	Gun	Watches
Drinking water	Official rules book	Whistles
First-aid kit	Towels	Yarn

FOOTBALL

Balls	Head linesman's box	Resin
Cartridges	Head linesman's chain	Score-board equipment
Drinking water	Horns	Towels
First-aid kit	Mouth and tooth protectors	Watches
Goal-line flags		Whistles
Gun	Official rules book	Yard markers
	Participation record book	

GOLF

Balls	Official rules book
Local course rules	Score cards

SWIMMING

Cartridges	Gun	Score sheets
Diving judges' cards	Lane markers	Towels
False start line	Official rules book	Watches
First-aid kit	Rope finish line	Whistles

TENNIS

Balls	Official rules book
First-aid kit	Towels
Nets	

TRACK

Batons	Hurdles	Spade or shovel and
Cartridges	Javelins	rake
Crossbars	Javelin board	Starting blocks
Drinking water	Judges' stands	Tape (measuring)
Discus	Jumping standards	Towels
First-aid kit	Line marking material	Vaulting poles
Gun	(not lime)	Vaulting standards
	Official rules book	Watches
	Score sheets	Whistles
	Shot (12 lb.)	Yarn

WRESTLING

Clock or watch	Official rules book
First-aid kit	Points indicator
Gong or whistle	Towels

Tickets. Tickets should be at booths with sellers and takers stationed as previously assigned.

Ushers. Ushers should be at stations previously assigned.

Contest programs. Supplies of programs should be in the hands of distributors who have previously been instructed as to their stations. Distribution of programs never should be wasteful. It is better to have unused programs turned in after a game than to have the stands littered with them during a contest.

Officials' quarters. Officials should have private dressing rooms apart from either team. A student manager should be assigned to direct officials and be at their service.

Visiting-team quarters and courtesies. At least one student manager should be assigned to the visiting team. He should show the visiting school officials their team dressing quarters and the method of reaching field or gymnasium, inquire if they have all the equipment they need, furnish them a supply of drinking water (individual cups or bottle if a fountain is not available on field or in gymnasium), and remain on constant call for any services the visiting coach or athletic director might desire.

Flag raising. Be sure that the American flag is on hand and that students are instructed as to their functions in the flag-raising ceremony. Bands also should understand their part in the program.

Intermission program. If a program is planned between halves of the game, be certain that all arrangements are completed and that student managers know their duties.

Players' benches. Reserved areas for substitute players and coaches of visiting and home teams should be roped off or protected by student guards. No one else should be allowed on these benches.

Physician. Check to see that the physician expected for this contest is present.

Bands. Reserved seats or benches should be provided for visiting-school and home-school bands. Check to see that they are available. Student managers may be assigned to this detail. Be sure that band leaders know the time allotted them between halves, and also what is expected of them after the game.

Contracts. The principal, athletic director, or coach should have game and officials' contracts in his possession at game time for possible reference.

Contract guarantees and payments. Have school athletic association checks available for the visiting school (if contract calls for a guarantee) and also for officials. These should be given to the persons concerned during the intermission period or immediately after the game. In some instances local school policy will provide for mailing checks after the contest.

Eligibility lists. Have the eligibility lists for both competing schools accessible at the time of the contest.

Score-board arrangements. Student managers should be assigned to score boards. Generally, they should be students who have had experience in this work.

Guards for dressing rooms. It is advisable to have a guard on duty in the visiting and home-team dressing rooms during the progress of the game. Even though valuables should be checked, clothing and other articles sometimes disappear if the locker rooms are left unguarded. An alternative is to assign the visiting team to a room that may be locked and then give the key to the coach or faculty or student manager.

Extra clothing for substitutes. Adequate clothing is especially important in football. Parents legitimately object if their sons are insufficiently protected while sitting on the bench. Have an adequate number of warm coats or blankets for all substitutes, or else have fewer substitutes. Treat them all alike.

Concessions. Check to see that concessions are being handled properly.

Cheer leaders. Cheer leaders should be on their assignments at least a half hour before game time.

Police. Police officers assigned to duty at the game should be available before or soon after gates or doors are opened. An officer stationed near the main gate or stadium entrance has a good psychological effect.

Public address system. Check the public-address system prior to the start of the game to see that it is working properly.

Rest rooms. Make certain that rest rooms are properly equipped and are available when the gymnasium door or field gates are opened.

Guarding extra equipment. Student guards should be assigned to see that extra equipment, such as balls, bats, helmets, jackets, sweaters, blankets, and pads, is not lost during games.

After-Game Responsibilities (Home Contests)

After a game is over, there are still several things to be done. Usually it will be the faculty manager, athletic director, or coach whose responsibility it is to see that they are finished. These items will be indicated in the form of a suggested check list.

Payment of officials. The official or officials should be paid between halves, or immediately or soon after the game. An official should be free to leave the school as soon as he desires after the contest. Do not make it necessary for him to hunt up someone in order to get his fee. It should be ready for him without his having to ask for it, unless it is to be mailed.

Payment of visiting school. Again, if this detail was not attended to during or before the half, it should be done immediately after the conclusion of the game. Be sure that the payment is in accordance with contract guarantee provisions.

Storage of equipment. Student managers should be assigned the responsibility of collecting and storing all field, court, or game equipment after each contest.

Contest receipts. At least within a day or two after a game the athletic director, faculty manager, or coach should check receipts for the contest. Such a report should be received from the individual in charge of ticket sales at the game.

General financial statement. It is only good business to have a complete financial statement, showing receipts and expenditures, ready within a week after each game. The reports should be placed in the hands of the high school principal or superintendent of schools, who may dispose of it as he sees fit.

Concessions report. If the concessions are handled by the high school athletic association, there should be a complete report of receipts, expenditures, and inventory after each game. If concessions are in charge of local school clubs or organizations, a financial report still should be made to the athletic director or high school principal. School officials have the right to know the financial status of this agency in order that they may be in a position to answer inquiries concerning it.

Record of officials. Many state athletic associations ask that schools rate officials either after games or at the end of the season. In the latter case it is desirable to keep a record of all officials until the state blank is received. A simple method is to list the name of the official, the game in which he worked, the date of the game, a rating for him based on the state rating plan, and a few remarks about his work. This record also will be of value when officials for another year are being considered. Such records should be kept for out-of-town as well as for home games.

Participation records. Shortly after each game a record of all participants should be made, usually by the coach. This may be used for award purposes, if that policy is followed in the school, and also for final season reports to the state athletic association in states where such reports are required. Oklahoma supplies an Individual Participation Record Form typical of those used in states desiring such information. A copy of this information also is retained as a permanent record of the school (see Fig. 7–3).

Filing of contest data. Usually it is desirable to have all the information concerning a particular contest available in one place. Such a filing procedure is possible if data regarding a game are compiled shortly after its conclusion, while it still is fresh in mind. Such a plan has been developed at Iron Mountain, Mich., High School. A large envelope is used as the filing unit. In it game and

OKLAHOMA HIGH SCHOOL ATHLETIC ASSOCIATION

INDIVIDUAL PARTICIPATION RECORD

(To be kept as a permanent record of your school)

DIRECTIONS—

After each game put name of school and date of game on vertical line. Mark X following each student's name in the column of the school against which he has participated.

Season's Schedule

Date Played

in

School

Name of Student

I certify that the above is a complete record of all students who have participated in any part of any game during the _____season ending_____19_____

School _____

By _____

Principal or Superintendent

Fig. 7-3. Individual Participation Record Form (Oklahoma).

official contracts are filed, together with all correspondence and school and newspaper clippings concerning the contest. On the outside of a 14½ by 9-inch envelope, reading the short way, the following is printed:

Iron Mountain High School vs. ....

At .... Date ....

Score ....

(I. M.)   (Visitors)

Referee ....

Umpire ....

Head Linesman ....

Gate Receipts ....

Guarantee ....

PRELIMINARY GAME

.... vs. ....

Score ....

Officials ....

Remarks ....

....

....

Obviously, such a system enables data concerning any contest to be found readily. It requires only a minimum of effort, but the information must be filled in soon after the game has been played. Some schools keep record books of all games, with satisfactory results. Whatever system is used, the important thing concerning it is regularity and keeping it up to date. Records become valuable with age and they should be kept faithfully.

Preparation for Out-of-town Games

Definite preparation must be made by visiting-school officials for athletic contests to be played away from home. Coaching of the team is not included in this discussion. Regardless of the size of the school, there are numerous matters regarding the trip, management of the team, and financial considerations to which attention must be given. In the smaller schools the superintendent, principal, or coach will attend to them. In larger schools the athletic director or faculty manager usually will take care of these administrative matters. The items presented here may be considered as a check list of duties from which schools may select, or to which they may add, those pertaining to their local situations.

Transportation. Transportation of an athletic team is the most important item in connection with games away from home. Often, especially among small schools, teams cannot be transported in the most acceptable manner because of lack of funds. If at all possible, school athletic teams should be carried only by bonded, public common carriers. School busses also are highly desirable, but some states have questioned the right to use such vehicles for out-of-school activities as they have defined them. Private cars driven by adults are the most common means but should not be used unless absolutely necessary. Schools and private car owners should be sure they understand the public-utility and public-liability laws of their states where such an arrangement is in effect.

Under no circumstances should student drivers of private cars be allowed to transport athletic teams. Where such a policy is followed, school authorities may be charged with negligence in case of accident, with subsequent court action a possibility. Team members should be required to go to the entertaining school together and return the same way. The one exception to this rule is where parents personally request permission of the school official in charge of the team to take their son or daughter home with them. Have a definite time for starting the trip. Plan a definite range in time for the return trip, and notify parents accordingly. Usually team members, student managers, coaches, and school officials only should make up the party if a bus is chartered for the trip. The same applies if a school bus is used. Discipline problems are lessened to a considerable degree if no students other than team members, student managers, and possibly cheer leaders are allowed.

Parents' permits. Some schools do not think it is desirable or necessary to require permission of parents of students for each out-of-town trip that the school athletic team takes. They feel that the original permission for the student to participate covers scheduled trips as well as actual play. This opinion is reasonable. Other schools have forms that they require the student to take home, have signed by one of the parents, and return to the coach, faculty manager, or principal before he may go on the trip with the team. These forms usually state the location, date, and time of the contest. They also indicate the type of transportation to be used, hour of departure, probable hour of return, and a source where information may be obtained in case the return trip is delayed. In signing such a form the parent usually indicates that the school is released from any liability in case of accident. Just how much this apparent release of liability amounts to is questionable. The chief justification for a procedure of this kind is that it keeps parents informed of the school's efforts to cooperate with them in the care and safety of their son or daughter. Following is the type of information appearing on a form of this kind that has been used by Three Rivers, Mich., High School. This form is mailed to the parent and is not returned unless the student may not accompany the team on the trip.

Parents' Notification of Contest

Your son has been selected to represent Three Rivers High School in
. . . . on . . . . in competition with . . . . High
School.

He will need . . . .

He should be neat in appearance.

He must be at the gymnasium not later than . . . . He will leave at . . . . by . . . . and return at approximately . . . .

Should he not return by this time, information may be obtained by calling . . . . Every care will be taken for his safety.

If for any reason your son will be unable to compete on this date please note the reasons and return the card by him.

Signed . . . .

Coach

Finances for trip. The member of the faculty in charge of the trip should be the custodian of all funds. Sufficient money should be withdrawn from the school treasury to take care of meals, lodging (if necessary), and incidentals. A strict accounting of all expenditures should be made to the principal, superintendent, or athletic director immediately after the return. Bus charges should be paid by the school by check. Contract guarantee checks should not be cashed by schoolmen on trips unless absolutely necessary. It is much better to have them pass through the regular financial channels of the school or athletic association treasury.

Equipment. Each player should be charged with responsibility for his personal playing equipment. Duffle bags, with names or numbers on them, are satisfactory means for carrying it. Game equipment, bats, balls, helmets, first-aid supplies, extra shoes, cleats, jerseys, sweaters, coats, and the like, should be the responsibility of one or two student managers. They should see that they are properly assembled, placed in trunks or bags, and loaded at the start of the trip, assume responsibility for their safekeeping during the game, and check to be sure that they are returned. If additional equipment is issued to a player on a trip, it should be charged to him by the person issuing it.

Game details. Complete information should be available before the start of the trip regarding game details. Know the time of the game, the place where it will be played, the location of dressing rooms, who is to officiate, the price of admission, and the regulations concerning complimentary tickets for the visiting team. Band, manager, and cheer-leader arrangements should be understood. Having this information ahead of time will lessen the confusion upon arrival.

Eligibility records. Be sure that all players making the trip are eligible for the contest to be played. Make certain that their names appear on the eligibility list. Take this list, and the one received from the competing school, on the trip for possible reference.

Game contract. The game contract should be accessible for reference in case any differences of opinion concerning it arise. It should be in the possession of the individual in charge of the trip, together with special correspondence concerning the game, and both eligibility lists.

Trip personnel. Have a definite time when the coach will post a list of team members and student managers who will make the trip. State the time the team will leave and then leave at that time. If players know this hour is the deadline they will be on time.

Participation record books. If it is the policy of the school to keep an accurate record of all participants, the record book should be carried on the trip. Responsibility for compiling data in it may be delegated to a student manager.

General Management Duties and Policies

In the preceding sections of this chapter administrative or management matters have been discussed involving before-game, game, and after-game duties. Likewise, items necessitating attention concerning out-of-town games have been considered. Obviously, they all are administrative or managerial functions. In addition, however, there are matters which are not specifically allied with any one event but which concern the whole program. They are what might be classified as school athletic policy administrative functions. Most of them will be or have been submitted to the athletic council or board of control for its approval. Insofar as it is possible to distinguish them from those matters previously considered, they will be presented here. It is obvious that most of the items discussed under the headings previously mentioned also will have been approved by the athletic board.

Permanent athletic eligibility, participation, and scholastic records. The amount of clerical work necessary in compiling eligibility-list data may be lessened considerably by centralized records. Some local schools and state athletic associations have devised forms to accomplish this end. In some instances copies of the regular eligibility lists are retained and filed by schools for use the following year in compiling athletic data and statistics. This is an excellent procedure if no other plan is in effect. Iowa is one of the state athletic associations which require that a Permanent Book of Record [4] be kept on file in each school. The information requested or contained in it includes eligibility data for all athletes during the year; rules and regulations of the Iowa High School Athletic Association; data concerning athletes representing the school during the year; personnel of various teams; results of games and contests held in each sport; school track records; schedules for the ensuing year; high school athletics cash book; notes on each athletic season during the current year. This record book becomes a permanent school record and must be completed upon penalty of loss of membership by the school. In Oregon, a Report to Secretary is made by designated dates, with a copy being retained by each school. In this way a permanent record of athletics, and considerable scholastic data are centered in one place, thus resulting in easier access to sources of information for the preparation of subsequent eligibility lists. [See Eligibility Report to Secretary (Oregon), Fig. 7–4.]

As an example of a central filing system for data on athletes that was worked out by a local school, the Permanent Record Card formerly in use at Central High School, Lansing, Mich., is cited (see Figure 7-5). This card is most complete; and, if it is kept up to date, the complete athletic and scholastic histories of a student are immediately accessible. Such a form should be of considerable aid to those in charge of the clerical work in making out eligibility lists for each sport.

[4] Iowa High School Athletic Association 1960–1961, *Record Book.*

Regardless of the scheme followed in recording permanent athletic records of students, be consistent and faithful. New administrators and coaches coming into schools should find complete records available. Also, there are many cases when information is desired concerning the athletic participation of former high school

OREGON SCHOOL ACTIVITIES ASSOCIATION

REPORT TO SECRETARY

1530 S. W. TAYLOR STREET, PORTLAND 5, OREGON

A school to be eligible to participate in athletics must file this list in accordance with the provisions of Article IV, Section 4, of the rules and regulations not later than 15 days after the beginning of the activity.

I hereby certify that the following students of the ______________________________

high school are eligible under the rules and regulations of the Oregon School Activities Association to compete in (name of sport)

______________________ contests arranged under the rules of the association for the season of 19____

Name	Date of Birth			Place of Birth		Name and Address of	Name and Address of	Number of Subjects Carried	No. of Semesters in H.S.
	Mo.	Day	Year	Town	State	Parent or Legal Guardian	School last Attended		

Form 1 This______day of______________, 19____ Principal High School

Fig. 7-4. Form for Eligibility Report to Association Secretary (Oregon).

LANSING CENTRAL HIGH SCHOOL ATHLETIC ASSOCIATION							PUBLIC SCHOOLS OF LANSING, MICHIGAN				
			PERMANENT ATHLETIC RECORD								

Fig. 7-5. Permanent Athletic Record Form (Central High School, Lansing, Michigan).

students several years after they have graduated. The school athletic department is the place from which it should be obtainable.

Athletic finances and budgets. These items will be discussed in Chapter 10. They are mentioned here, however, because of their proper inclusion under general administrative duties. It is impossible to overemphasize the importance of sound financial policies and accurate bookkeeping in connection with a high school program of interscholastic athletics. That is one reason why an entire chapter is devoted to the subject.

General reports. In some instances the general report for the athletic year may be the permanent records. In others part of it may be in the school paper or school annual. It is highly desirable, however, that a brief but complete, athletic report be placed in the hands of the superintendent or principal at the close of the school year. It is good information for either or both of them to have and is in line with policies in many schools that teachers shall report their year's work at the end of the final semester. The report should include at least (1) financial statement; (2) results of games and meets; (3) number of participants; (4) outstanding features of the year's activities; and (5) proposed schedules for the ensuing year.

Contracting officials. Athletic officials for home games for the following year should be engaged as soon as possible. There always are many officials, but sometimes there are not enough good ones. It is not to be inferred here that great emphasis should be placed on the official or officials in a game. Ninety-nine per cent of them are honest and eager to do a good job because that is their best method of receiving other assignments. It is a fact, however, that certain officials are better known, handle games in a more satisfactory manner than others, and generally are acceptable to all schools. These are the men whose services have to be contracted for early. Home schools should submit lists of officials to visiting schools. Names of officials mutually agreeable should be submitted to the athletic council for approval. Officials then should be approached concerning their availability and contracts sent them. In some cases it may be desirable to ask officials to hold a date or dates tentatively for later confirmation. This procedure will enable the securing of formal approval of the visiting school.

Keep a file of all correspondence regarding approval of officials. As far as possible, officials should be secured from six months to a year in advance of the games in which they are to work. It should be understood that contracts are binding only in case an official is properly registered with the state association, if state regulations require such a procedure. Do not use the same official in too many games. This is not a good policy either for players or spectators. There is question regarding the "trades" in officiating as practiced by some athletic coaches, in which a coach from one school works in a game for another school with the understanding that the coach of the latter school will work a contest for the coach of the former institution. Sometimes this policy leads to difficulties.

A word to the athletic official may not be amiss in this discussion. He has an important part in the successful conduct of an athletic contest. He should be businesslike in his correspondence, be on time, know the rules, and, above all, be honest and fearless. When he reports to officiate a game between two schools, he might well do so with the following thoughts in mind:

I am your official.

I was selected to officiate in this game upon your mutual consent.

I bring to this game a rested body and alert mind.

I shall endeavor to be fair, always to be honest, and I shall exercise my best judgment.

I have attempted to master the rules of the game to the best of my ability.

I shall make my decisions so they will be clearly understood by players and spectators; and, having made them, I shall expect the support of school authorities.

I shall consider this contest a success if each team plays its best and exemplifies the highest type of sportsmanship.

I shall give my best to the good of this game.

Officials whose reputations are best do not solicit games. School officials know which men they want to officiate in their games. If an official's work and reputation are what they should be, he will receive his share of assignments. He should not make himself a nuisance or cause embarrassment to athletic directors or coaches by asking them for games. His job is that of officiating games, and usually, that is all schoolmen or coaches want of him. The late E. C. Krieger offered some sound advice to officials concerning their conduct after games. Although it was prepared some time ago and is directed to football officials, it is applicable to all postgame officiating.

The Ball—In the majority of instances the winner is entitled to the ball and will lose no time in claiming it; but unless the officials are definitely aware of this fact, it is good policy to grab and hold the ball. Following an incident involving much grumbling and threats to deduct the cost of the ball from my fee, I always make it a point to learn if the ball is at stake.

The Spectators—There may be instances when spectators take exception to a ruling and a nasty situation develops at the end of the game. Men who officiate football must school themselves to entirely ignore the comments of spectators during the game, and this seems the best policy to pursue should an unpleasant situation arise when the game is over.

The Coaches—Never ask a Coach for his opinion of your work; you know whether you worked hard and efficiently or whether your work failed to come up to expectations. . . . On occasion, a Coach will approach the officials before he has regained his normal temperament. In these instances there is nothing to do but be courteous or silent, and if anything is said that is to later be regretted, let it be said by the other fellow, not you.

When a Coach inquires about the ruling of a questionable play the official or officials who were responsible should make such answer as is required without involving or implicating the others. "Passing the buck" is the best way I know of for a man to let himself quickly and quietly out of officiating.

Who of us has not "gone to bat" for another official who was in a tough spot? If you haven't, you have not been long in the game. I have observed instances where these attempts to help have been carried to an extreme which destroyed the entire value of the gesture and resulted in discrediting the "good Samaritan."

Among the officials—The customary "you worked a nice game and I enjoyed working with you" is sometimes far from a sincere statement. . . . If contact during a game does not give sufficient opportunity in which to judge the ability and personality of an official, I know of no other test which will reveal it; and what is said, if anything, can well be based upon the facts.

If You Stay Over—When an official remains in the city in which the game was played, his good sense should dictate that his conduct, even though hours after the game, may be the index by which he will be judged for the entire day.

Talking about the game, the players, formations, or the strategy employed is always to be avoided. In the first place, an official who is working efficiently knows much less about these things than any of the spectators, and to those who are "in the know" a detailed description by an official mark him as better fitted for some capacity other than officiating.[5]

Schedules and practice. As indicated previously, schedule making should receive the approval of the local school athletic council or board of control. Generally, it should not be the final responsibility of any one individual. Of course someone will have the task of making arrangements for schedules, but this always should be done subject to the final approval of the council. Schedules usually should be made at least a year in advance. In some sports in which yearly home-and-home games are played, two years will be involved. In general, games should be arranged as nearly as possible so that home contests alternate each week with those away from home. Likewise, they should be arranged so that they do not interfere with school time. The North Central Association of Secondary

[5] E. C. Krieger, *Football Officiating*, (Athens, Ohio: The Lawhead Press, 1737), Chap. IX.

Schools and Colleges recommends that no high school athletic contest be scheduled for an evening preceding a school day. Leagues, conferences, or local athletic associations can aid schools in establishing regular schedules and deciding on days of the week on which games will or will not be played.

Schools are beginning to get away from the policy of playing "setup" games at the beginning of seasons. Usually, the public is not interested in such contests, there is decided inequity in the competition, and schoolmen, both in the large and small schools concerned, often are opening themselves to severe criticism by scheduling such games. Schools should confine their competition pretty much to their own class in order that there may be greater assurance of safety, equality of teams, and real fun for the players.

When schedules have been approved, they should be mimeographed or printed for student and adult distribution. This is an effective means by which a school's policy regarding its athletic schedules may be publicized. By this method it also is possible for a school to protect itself from pressure for postseason games, especially in those states in which games other than those regularly scheduled are prohibited.

There are differences of opinion as to length of schedules. There is a tendency on the part of some state athletic associations to aid schools in establishing maximum limits in the number of games to be played in some activities.[6] Local schools themselves, or local leagues, frequently set up limits as to the number of games.

There is no question that many schoolmen have not heeded their better judgment in setting up athletic schedules, usually from lack of thought rather than from lack of forethought. This same criticism may be made concerning the frequency and length of practice periods.

The number and length of practice periods will vary with the discretion of coaches, experience of the team, and availability of facilities. Undoubtedly the claim that high school players are "burned out" is a greater indictment against practice policies than against the number of games played. A coach properly trained in the science of physical education should understand the elements of fatigue in growing boys and the degree of strenuousness occasioned by partic-

---

[6] See Chapter 5, "Limitation in number of contests and duration of seasons."

ipation in various sports. His practice periods should be governed accordingly. In general, it will be a safe rule to practice a shorter period than had been planned. The following suggestions as to number of regular season games are based largely on state association recommendations or regulations. They may be of aid to schools in setting up schedules in the more commonly sponsored activities.

Baseball. One or two games per week with at least two or three days between games. (No high school player should pitch more than one game per week.) Recommendation of twelve to fifteen games.

Basketball. Generally one game per week with possibly one or two weeks during which two games are played. Recommendation of fifteen to eighteen games during regular season. (Girls' basketball —one game per week with a season maximum of six to eight games.)

Cross-country. One meet per week. Recommendation of five to seven meets.

Football. One game per week. (At least three weeks of practice prior to first game.) Plan an open date near mid-season if possible. Recommendation of seven- or eight-game maximum.

Golf. Physical nature of the sport not important in determining number of scheduled meets.

Swimming. One meet per week. Recommendation of six to eight meets.

Tennis. One meet per week. (Limit competition of individuals either to singles or doubles, not both.) Recommendation of eight to ten meets.

Track. One meet per week. (Limit number of events for individuals.) Recommendation of five to seven meets.

Wrestling. Not more than one meet per week. Recommendation of six to eight meets.

The matter of sectional or state tournament and meet competition, naturally, is closely associated with schedule making. A number of state association regulations regarding maximum number of games to be played by schools have been established, with tournament or meet competition in mind. Local schools should adopt their own policies relative to such participation. In all states participation in tournaments is voluntary. If the schoolmen of the state feel that the state association-sponsored tournaments and meets fill a need, undoubtedly they are set up and controlled with that end in view.[7]

Athletic alumni and varsity clubs. Schoolmen hold different opinions regarding the advisability of encouraging the activities of varsity, lettermen, or alumni athletic clubs. Some feel that such organizations may attempt to dictate the athletic policy of the school and hence should not be recognized. Others see in them the opportunity for another contact in the proper administration of the athletic program. The latter view seems to be the more prevalent. The varsity and lettermen of a school should have had enough experience in athletics to understand some of the problems connected with them. This observation may not be valid for alumni athletic clubs. It seems best to work more closely with the two former organizations than with the latter. Keep them informed of school athletic policies, send them copies of schedules, aid in the arrangement of details for their meetings, and advise them concerning special athletic functions and banquets. By following such a procedure, generally, it will be possible to use such organizations for the purposes desired by the school rather than vice versa.

Athletic equipment. The purchase and care of athletic equipment represents the largest item of expense, except salaries, in the administration of the athletic program. It is mentioned here under general administrative duties and policies because of its major importance. Discussion of this subject appears in Chapter 8.

Local league or conference obligations. Many schools find it advantageous to join leagues, athletic associations, or athletic conferences. As long as membership is maintained in such an organization, all obligations should be fulfilled. Attend meetings of the league, maintain full league schedules, remit dues promptly, and be loyal to the group of schools in the association. If these responsibilities and courtesies cannot be maintained, ask for release from the organization.[8]

Athletic banquets. Have a definite policy regarding athletic banquets. They should be regarded as regular affairs if a school is going to have them at all. Teams that lose all their games have as much, or more, reason to be banqueted as those whose records constitute what is considered as a "highly successful season." The athletic

[7] See Chapter 3, "Conducting tournaments and meets."
[8] See Chapter 8, "Athletic Leagues and Conferences as Administrative Agencies."

banquet should be a school, or school and community, affair, rather than something to which the athletes are entitled. The school owes the athletes nothing, a fact they should be made to realize early in their athletic careers. Instead of limiting an annual or seasonal banquet to members of an athletic team alone as the honored guests, it seems more justifiable to recognize all the activities of the school during the period. Include music, forensics, dramatics, and scholarship as well as athletics. Such an array of talent really gives a community an opportunity to see the broad scope of the school's program.

Athletic blanks and forms. Each local school uses blanks and forms in the administration of its athletic program. It prepares these forms itself or receives them from the state athletic association. The supply of both these types should be checked frequently. Schools may receive excellent suggestions by exchanging samples of blanks and forms. If forms, reports, or accounts of meeting are to be printed, be sure that the copy is correct before it is sent to the printer. It is much easier and cheaper to make corrections before the type is set than after.

Selection of student managers. Some of the qualifications of student managers have been discussed previously (see page 171). It also was pointed out that they might be elected or appointed but that they should not be members of athletic squads. High school students interested in athletics usually are eager to be of help. Make the selection of them a definite and businesslike procedure. Let it be known that the jobs are open to those interested who meet the qualifications. Usually an apprenticeship period should precede full managership appointment. Student managers should be eligible for school letter awards. Definite requirements for senior, junior, and assistant manager awards should be established and understood, if that many are necessary. Generally, student athletic managers should not be paid by the school for their services. It is a good policy to provide a distinctive shirt, coat, or jersey to be worn by student managers when on duty.

Awards recommendations. Each school should have a definite policy relative to athletic awards. Certainly it is an administrative policy of first rate importance. Recommendations regarding awards, standards, and policies followed in schools are discussed in detail in Chapter 9.

Familiarity with state athletic association regulations. It is the local school's responsibility to know and understand the state athletic association eligibility and contest regulations. This should be done for its own protection. In addition to this, however, state association posters concerning eligibility regulations should be displayed on school bulletin boards. Make copies of the monthly state association bulletin available in school libraries. These devices will increase student and faculty interest in and respect for the school and state association athletic activities, and also will help them to see that local school athletics are a part of a state-wide educational athletic program.

Questions for Study and Discussion

1. Why is efficient management of athletic contests important? State several reasons.

2. List and discuss briefly the matters to be considered in the before-game preparations for home contests.

3. What home game responsibilities must receive attention by the athletic director or faculty manager? Discuss each briefly.

4. There are numerous responsibilities following home contests. List and discuss briefly.

5. What are the important considerations that must receive attention in the preparations for out-of-town contests?

6. There are many general management duties and policies concerned with the interscholastic athletic program. List and discuss them briefly.

7. Are you in agreement with the recommendations made in the chapter concerning schedules and practice for the various sports? Support your position.

8

Athletic Equipment

The purchase and care of equipment for high school athletics represents one of the major problems confronting those in charge of the program. In most schools funds are limited, squads are as large as facilities and equipment will permit, and safety precautions require the purchase of the best quality of merchandise for the money available. Many boards of education purchase general playing equipment (balls, bats, nets, and the like) but are prohibited by law from furnishing personal equipment. In most cases this material must be purchased from other than tax money. Thus, sometimes it is possible to buy, not that which is needed, but only that for which there are sufficient funds. Serious question can be raised as to the justification for sponsoring football, for instance, by a school unless it properly and adequately equips the boys who play on its teams.

The Purchase of Equipment

General policy. Good, substantial, and safety-approved equipment in all sports is a minimum essential. The athletic association's dollar must be spent well in order to get the most it can for its money. There should be a regular time and procedure for this important transaction. Items never should be bought just because they are inexpensive, nor should they be bought from unknown firms. Experience will show that recognized and legitimate sporting-goods dealers are the safest ones from which to purchase materials. They need not necessarily be local merchants; but if athletic supplies can be bought as cheaply from them as from anyone, they should be given the business. Equipment should be bought only after needs are known. Regular inventories should be maintained. Purchase orders should be on regular school forms for that purpose and authorized by the athletic council or board of control. Usually the athletic director, faculty manager, or coach will be given authority by the council to issue such purchase orders.

Some of the suggestions in the preceding paragraph may seem superfluous as far as small schools are concerned. Actually they are not entirely so. Instead of having the responsibilities assumed by the individuals mentioned, they will be retained by the superintendent or principal. There is every reason for the small school to be businesslike in its athletic purchases. Usually there are less funds, proportionately, and equipment has to be used longer. Likewise, the more frequent changes in administration in small schools are even greater reasons why athletic purchases and the handling of funds in connection with them should be entirely clear and justified. Generally it is safe to advise that equipment be purchased with school athletic association money in the same careful way that one's personal funds would be used.

Equipment inventory. At the close of each season an inventory of all equipment on hand should be made. A form of inventory blank is shown in Figure 8–1. By comparing this with the inventory made at the close of the same sport season a year ago, and adding any material bought since then, it should be possible to account for all equipment. Of course, due allowance will have to be made for worn-out items. Such an inventory will show four things:

1. How much equipment is on hand for the next season of this sport.
2. What equipment has to be repaired or replaced.
3. How much new personal or game equipment will have to be purchased prior to the start of the next season in this sport.
4. Whether managers or equipment men are efficient, and indicate whether or not athletic equipment is being lost or stolen.

In large schools especially, it seems desirable to have the coach of each sport responsible for turning in the inventory to the faculty

INVENTORY OF EQUIPMENT

_____HIGH SCHOOL

Close of_____Season Year: 19____

(Sport)

Articles Used For This Sport	Previous Inventory Count	Number Purchased During Year	Total Number To Be Accounted For	Present Inventory (First Class Shape)	Present Inventory (Need Repairs)	Number Articles Not Accounted For	Estimated Number New Articles Needed Next Season

Date of inventory, _____19____ Coach_____

Athletic Director_____

Student Manager_____

Fig. 8-1. Suggested After-season Inventory Form.

manager or principal. In this way the coach can have first-hand information regarding the equipment for the sport he coaches. As a result of this inventory he should be in a better position to present his requisition for equipment when the next annual budget is being prepared.

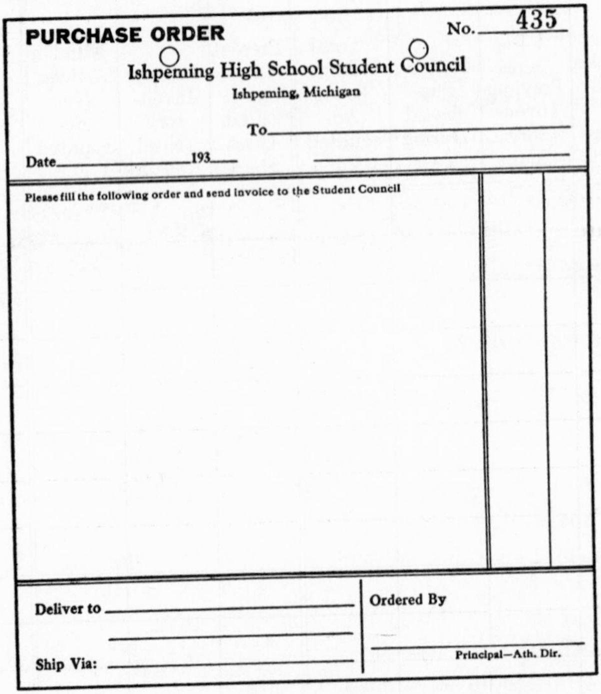
PURCHASE ORDER No. 435

Ishpeming High School Student Council

Ishpeming, Michigan

To__________

Date__________193__

Please fill the following order and send invoice to the Student Council

Deliver to __________

Ship Via: __________

Ordered By

Principal—Ath. Dir.

Fig. 8-2. Equipment Purchase Order Form *(Ishpeming High School, Michigan).*

Purchase orders. After equipment needs are known, samples have been inspected, or bids received, comes the formality of placing the order. When a purchase has been authorized by the athletic council it is much better to have one individual in the school responsible for placing the orders. He should sign the purchase-order form, which should be made out in duplicate at least. In some schools triplicate purchase-order blanks are used so that copies of all orders placed by the faculty manager or coach are accounted for as follows:

Original—Sent to the firm with which the order is placed.

First duplicate—Retained by the individual signing the purchase order.

Second duplicate—Filed in the high school principal's office.

This procedure provides a double check on all school purchases and is especially valuable if the school is large and there are numerous agencies placing purchase orders payable out of general school activity funds. A typical purchase order, from the Ishpeming, Mich., High School is shown in Figure 8–2. This is used for the purchase of all goods authorized by the student council. Special attention should be given to the fact that the orders are numbered serially, so that it is possible to account for all of them. They also are made out in duplicate and punched so they may be filed in a two-post binder for ready reference.

Issuing Equipment

An efficient method for issuing and keeping records of equipment is an essential factor in athletic management, in order that equipment may be preserved and the expenses for such items kept to a minimum. It also is imperative that business methods be employed in this phase of management because of the effect they have on students participating in athletic competition. Respect for, and care of, property should be one of the lessons to be derived from athletics. If students are made to realize that the material furnished them by the school is merely loaned, that the management keeps an accurate check, and that they are held accountable for it, they will learn a valuable lesson. By this method, proper habits may be taught high school students, and every effort should be made to avoid situations in which carelessness, destructiveness, dishonesty, or thievery may develop. Have definite places for all equipment, with someone charged with the responsibility for it. If equipment is issued to a boy with the understanding that it is to be returned by him at the close of the season, insist that it be returned or that restitution be made. It is a worse than idle gesture to go through the motions of charging athletic material to students and then, when only part of it is returned, to disregard the losses. Due allowance in all instances, of course, must be made for natural depreciation of equipment because of normal usage. It will be surprisingly gratifying to observe how careful high school students can be of equipment issued to them if they are made to understand that they are responsible for it. In this connection, however, every effort should be made by the athletic management to aid them in making it easy to take proper care of their equipment.

Marking equipment. Various schools have different systems of marking their game and personal athletic equipment. Marking pencils or pens using permanent ink or waterproof stencil paints are most effective on cotton goods and practice equipment. Care should be taken to be sure that they will show and remain on new plastics and other types of materials. Usually, the name of the school, a number and the size should appear on each garment. Quite often the number is the only identification mark for the equipment issued to a boy. Inexpensive number or school identification labels may be sewed on the inside of woolen or silk jersey seams if no other numbers or marks appear on them. Game jerseys, of course, will be numbered for football and basketball in accordance with rules provisions, but some other identification usually is necessary for baseball, swimming, and track uniforms. Leather goods should be numbered and sized with India ink on white cloth or should have numbers or marks burned in them.

Equipment cards. Every piece of equipment issued to a student should be charged to him on a permanent athletic equipment card, which he should sign. The signature is especially important if he takes the material to his own locker and keeps it there. This plan is not recommended, but of necessity it has to be followed in some schools. Separate equipment cards often are prepared for each sport. In other cases a general card is used that is applicable for all sports. When equipment is issued it is desirable to know that certain other matters have been taken care of by the team candidate. Hence it is advisable to have some place on the card to record that the student is eligible scholastically, has passed his physical examination, and has filed his parents' consent card, if that is a school policy. A general equipment card containing some of the above information is used by the Lansing, Mich., Eastern High School (see Fig. 8-3). It does not have a space for student signature for equipment received. This may be considered an unnecessary formality but the performance of it at least has the psychological effect of a contractual agreement entered into between the student and the school for his athletic equipment.

| Sport_____ | | | Physical Examination ☐ | Parents' Consent ☐ | |
| Locker_____ Lock No._____ | | | Combination_____ | Deposit_____ | |

Article	Issued	Returned	Article	Issued	Returned
Jersey			Track Shirt		
Shoulder Pad			Track Pants		
T-Shirt			Sweat Shirt		
Pants			Sweat Pants		
Hip Pads			Swim Suit		
Stockings					
Socks					
Shoes					
Room	Grade		Name		Date of Birth

Fig. 8-3. Equipment Card (Eastern High School, Lansing, Michigan).

Daily care of equipment. Athletic equipment deteriorates more rapidly because of ill treatment than it does from excessive use or wear. The method of taking care of it between practice sessions and between games is the greatest factor in determining its durability and appearance. Wet and perspiration-soaked cotton and woolen equipment must be thoroughly dried between practice sessions or games. Also, it must be laundered or dry-cleaned frequently. Shoes should be brushed with a stiff brush and oiled. Pads should be dried thoroughly, washed with saddle soap, and painted with shellac. Helmets should be aired and dried thoroughly between practice sessions or games.

```
                                    Space Number_____

    Name_____

    Equipment_____  Number_____

    Shoes_____  Supporter_____

    Helmet_____  Sox_____

   .Shoulder Pads_____  Stockings_____

    Pants_____   Under Jersey_____

    Knee Pads_____  Miscellaneous_____

    Jerseys_____
```

Fig. 8-4. Equipment Card.

Obviously, these duties cannot be performed by team members themselves. Neither does such a plan work well if athletes keep their equipment in lockers. Although some locker rooms have elaborate locker ventilation systems, seldom are they efficient enough to do a drying job such as is required for athletic equipment. The recommended plan is to have a separate equipment room in which a special space is provided for the material issued to each team member. No one is to be allowed in this room except the coach, athletic director, or student manager in charge of equipment. It is suggested that the room have cross ventilation (or be a drying room) if possible. A hook or two should be provided for each athlete. All the material issued to him should be turned in after each practice. The student manager can check it daily by consulting the student's equipment card, which should be above the number of his hook. At the next practice session or game he calls his number at the equipment room window and receives his material. On days of games the game uniforms are substituted for those used in practice.

The equipment card, shown in Figure 8–4, has the items for football. (Other sport items would be listed accordingly.) This appears above the space number.

RECORD CARD												
Space Number	Name	Shoes	Helmet	Shoulder Pads	Pants	Knee Pads	Jersey	Supporter	Socks	Stockings	Under Jersey	Miscellaneous
1												
2												
3												
4												
5												
~~												
42												
43												
44												

Fig. 8-5. Master Equipment Record Card.

A master record card used at many high schools contains a complete check list of all material issued to each team member. It also lists the space on the equipment racks in the drying room that has been assigned to each student. Its general make-up is shown in Figure 8–5.

The advantages of such a system follow:

1. Uniforms that are dry before the next practice result in cleaner equipment. Garments wear longer.

2. Clean clothes are available more often, thus preventing infections.

3. When a boy is dropped from the squad, his equipment is in. Thus, there is no opportunity for loss.

4. When a boy does not use his uniform, it remains on its hanger. When he returns to practice his uniform is just as he left it, whether it is one day or one month later.

5. A boy learns to be careful with his uniform or pay a severe penalty.

6. It does away with the temptation to steal or to use some other boy's property.

7. It relieves the coach of practically all worries caused by loss or mix-up of equipment.

General Care of Athletic Equipment

The value of an efficient system for the purchase and issuing of equipment is lost if proper care is not given to the equipment during and after the sport season. This observation applies to repair of equipment during the season as well as storage of it after the season is concluded. The old adage that a stitch in time saves nine may be literally true with athletic equipment, since repairs sometimes will save a school several times the cost of purchasing new equipment. In some of the larger schools a faculty manager is placed in charge of the purchase, care, and repair of all athletic equipment. Such a plan is in effect at Waite High School, Toledo, Ohio, with most satisfactory results both from the standpoint of efficient management and also from the standpoint of reduction of the athletic equipment budget. Judgment, of course, must be exercised as to what to repair and what method is to be used.

Repairing and cleaning athletic equipment. Check equipment periodically. This should be done frequently to discover tears, breaks in leather, or broken parts. Some schools will have their own cobbler's outfits for minor repairs to shoes and leather goods. Others will have arrangements with local cobblers or leather-goods repairmen. Shoes especially should be checked frequently, because those in poor condition may cause foot injury or infection. Helmets also receive a great amount of abuse. When rips appear in them, have them sewed up at once This also applies to jerseys and pants. Keep them dry, clean, and in repair.

White goods and towels should be laundered frequently. Football pants also can be washed. All laundry service should include mending. By this method clean material in the equipment room will be ready for use. Most woolen goods should be dry-cleaned to prevent shrinkage. It is not advisable to use bleaching materials on white equipment. Generally they do not aid in cleaning the equipment and may be injurious to it. In view of the large number of new materials, both protective and clothing, now on the market it is important that manufacturers' directions for cleaning be followed. This applies to textiles, leather, fibers, plastics, rubber, and metals. Supplying clean, well-fitting athletic equipment to boys on teams is one of the surest means of preventing infection epidemics. Insist on each boy using only his own equipment, keep it clean for him, and repair or replace it if it becomes damaged. Some schools have had considerable success in having their repair work on athletic garments done by home economics (sewing) classes. In such instances the equipment has been thoroughly cleaned before being sent for repairs. In some cases the class members have been paid a small fee for their services, and in others a sewing club has taken over the work as a project for raising funds. Variations of these plans may be worked out for minor repairs at considerable saving to the athletic department.

Storage of athletic equipment. When the season in a sport has been concluded, have the equipment cleaned. Sort out those items which need repairs and which are worth repairing, and send them to repair firms whose workmanship and service are known. All other equipment should be properly conditioned for the off seasons and stored. Airtight bins for trunks for the woolen goods, and special cases or racks for the leather equipment, should be provided. Cotton material may be wrapped and stacked on shelves or in bins. Following are suggestions for conditioning and storage of athletic equipment:

Leather shoes—Clean thoroughly. Brush with neatsfoot oil. Replace laces and cleats. Renumber. Rub track shoes with vaseline. Store in dry place (bins or shelves).

Helmets—Buff or sandpaper and repaint. Follow with a coat of shellac. Place on a wooden form on a rack, or stuff inside of helmet with paper and tie ear flaps together with string. Do not fasten elastic strap, because it will stretch. Clean felt or sponge rubber inside of helmet with soap and water. Tag for size. Renumber. Store in dry place.

Hip, shoulder, and knee pads—Wash leather hip, shoulder, and knee pads with saddle soap. Check with manufacturer for care of plastic or synthetic pads. Renumber. Clean felt or sponge rubber with soap and water. Shellac leather portion of pads. Tag for size. Store in dry place.

Inflated balls—Clean with standard ball cleaners on the market. Deflate to three to five pounds pressure. Store in dry place.

Canvas shoes—Thoroughly dry and brush. Tag for size. Replace laces. Store in dry place (bins or shelves).

Woolen garments—Clean thoroughly (dry cleaning rather than laundering recommended). Check with manufacturer or dealer regarding treatment of synthetic materials. Repair rips and mend holes. Tag for size. Store in airtight bins or trunks. Sprinkle naphthalene, paradichlorobenzene, or camphor crystals throughout woolen garments. Be certain that the container is airtight.

Cotton garments—Launder thoroughly. Inspect for repairs. Renumber and indicate sizes. Store in dry place.

Silk garments—Launder or dry-clean. Tag for size. Pack in boxes or bundles. Store in dry place.

Football pants—Launder thoroughly. Inspect for repairs. Renumber. Tag for size and grade. Save best of worn pants for mending. Store in dry place.

Wrestling mats—Launder cotton ones thoroughly, repair, and fold for storage in dry place. Clean plastic mats in accordance with manufacturer's directions.

Football linesman's markers, box, yard line markers—Repair, repaint, and store in dry place.

Football dummies and charging machines—Clean former and store in dry place. Repair and repaint charging machines and store inside, in dry place.

Baseball bats, balls, bases—Wipe off bats and store in dry place. Save used baseballs for practice. Clean bases and store in dry place.

Hurdles, benches, toeboards, and take-off boards—Repair, repaint, and store in dry place.

Javelins—Hang from a height with point downward to prevent warping. Store in dry place.

Vaulting poles—Lay in straight position to prevent warping. Store in moderately dry place.

Discus and shot—Store in a moderately dry place.

Tennis nets—Fold or roll around wooden pole. Store in dry place.

First-aid kit—Clean kit and bottles. Relabel bottles. Replenish stock as inventory indicates when season opens. Store kit in clean, dry place.

Ticket booths—Clean and repaint. Store in dry place if removable.

Score boards—Clean and repaint. Renumber and paint individual placards if necessary. Check mechanical device and wiring if electrical score board is used. Store removable parts in dry place.

Public-address system—Check transmitters, amplifiers, and wiring. Store in safe place.

Questions for Study and Discussion

1. Why is a school policy concerning purchase of athletic equipment important?

2. Discuss values of a complete equipment inventory. Who should take this inventory? Why?

3. Set up a plan for the issue of athletic equipment, indicating forms and procedures to be used.

4. Why is a central purchase order system desirable for the buying of all athletic equipment?

5. Why is daily care and the checking of all athletic equipment important?

6. Discuss methods of general care of equipment; including repair, cleaning, and storage. Set up an ideal plan or present features of one that has seemed especially good to you.

7. Discuss plans suggested in this chapter for the conditioning and storage of athletic equipment of every kind. Do you agree with all of them?

9 Athletic Awards

General Awards Policies

Since time began it has been customary for victors to receive emblematic or actual evidences of their success. In some instances the reward was wealth, position, or decoration. In others it meant power. These same traditions have been carried on in athletic competition, but in most instances the award is emblematic rather than actual. American high schools have waged determined campaigns through many of their state athletic associations to ensure that awards will be of nonutilitarian value, or practically so.

Sometimes it is difficult for people to understand why awards are presented to athletes. This confusion is only natural because there have been so many policies in effect. The idea used to prevail that awards were given to boys because of services they rendered to their schools. Nothing could be further from the truth if the athletic program is an educational one. Participants should be the greatest recipients of benefits because of having had the chance to play. Anything they may think they have done for the school becomes insignificant in comparison with the opportunities and experiences they have had. When the athletic program is considered part of the general school curriculum, participants in it become regular class students in the sport concerned. From that standpoint there is not much justification for rewarding them for their participation in an activity which benefits them.

The problem of awards from outside sources confronts schoolmen frequently, especially when a high school team has had an outstanding season as measured by the number of games won or lost or championships annexed. Teams often are feted on numerous occasions. Unless the situation is watched, some well-intentioned, community-minded individual, or groups, will want to present team members with awards having intrinsic values greater than school or state association regulations allow. They seem to think that the boys must be given something for what they have done. Recognition of honor brought to their school or to themselves may be all right if kept within reason. Rewards for having done that which was a benefit and pleasure for them to do are not only unnecessary but unjustifiable.

State athletic association regulations relative to awards [1] are helpful limitations to which local school administrators may refer when community interests desire to give excessive gifts to team members. It behooves schoolmen to have their local athletic and other activity award policies well understood by student bodies and public alike. Publicizing them in advance will be an effective means by which the athletic program of a school may be kept in its proper place in relation to the other educational phases of the curriculum. It will help keep athletics on an even keel no matter whether a school team wins or loses all its games or finishes first or last in its city, league, section, or state standings.

School and Sport Awards Policies

The policy of granting school awards for interscholastic athletic or activity participation should not be a haphazard one. Definite policies and participation requirements should be established, tempered in most cases by recommendations of school authorities concerned. These will enhance the significance of the award and make it actually one of school recognition.

General trends. As indicated previously, state athletic associations in a majority of the states have set up limits as to costs of awards. If the value exceeds one or two dollars, usually the number that may be received is fixed. It is obvious, however, that the deter-

[1] See Chapter 4, "Awards."

mination of standards for award qualifications have been left to individual schools themselves in most cases. Policies vary in accordance with state regulations. They also are dependent upon the size of the school. In a survey made by the author in 125 Michigan high schools of all sizes, some interesting information was revealed as to general practices within one state. Following are the conclusions from this survey which are indicative of policies being followed:

1. In the larger schools awards are being limited to one letter in a sport during a student's high school career, with subsequent recognition usually being a certificate.

2. A majority of the schools award letters of the same size for all sports.

3. Most schools do not limit the number of sports in which a student may compete during the year.

4. In many schools awards are not made until the end of the semester and then are dependent upon the recipient's school citizenship and scholastic standing as well as his athletic ability.

5. Awards generally are made on the basis of a combination of factors including recommendation of the coach, faculty committee action, and a required amount of competition, with exceptions for extenuating circumstances.

6. Schools are not distinguishing between major and minor sports as much as they did a few years ago.

7. In general, schools are paying between seventy-five cents and one dollar for athletic awards.

8. Only six of the one hundred twenty-five schools advocated any change in the present provisions of the Award Rule. (The Michigan award limit now is three dollars.)

9. In schools where a point system is used, the points earned in each sport usually are cumulative, that is, they apply in successive seasons toward the award requirement.

10. Schools vary in the policy of making awards for intramural athletics. Some feel that such activities should be for competition only, while others believe that inexpensive, individual awards are beneficial.

11. Some schools which have general organization or student union plans require that members of athletic teams be holders of such school tickets before they may be members of teams, and thus be eligible for athletic awards.

12. A few schools give a senior, or the winner of a second or third letter, the choice of the letter, or a medal, or a key, the cost of which is comparable with the letter.

13. Schools quite generally are making awards to students for other activities as well as athletics. They usually include dramatics, forensics, and music.[2]

With a few exceptions the above practices may be taken as fairly indicative of the general policies now in effect in schools throughout the states. One exception might be the plan in some states that allows a school to award a sweater or a blanket to a boy once during the year or at the completion of his high school athletic career. Other states definitely rule against such a practice. In general, the most desirable policy to follow seems to be that of making awards of little or no intrinsic value. Some schools find that certificates serve this purpose. Certainly, giving a school letter to a boy is a manifestation of trust in him. He should consider the receipt of it in this light and wear it with honor because his school has given him that privilege. In reality, the awarding of the school letter to a student is giving him the second highest recognition of which the school is capable, the highest, of course, being the diploma. More than mere athletic ability should be the basis for awarding a school letter.

Some schools feel that awarding a great many letters defeats the purpose intended and tends to cheapen them. The award limits as to costs in many states make more expensive awards impossible as well as undesirable. Ann Arbor, Mich., High School has developed a combination scheme of letter and certificate awards that seems worthy of consideration:

The first year a boy wins a letter in any sport, he is awarded that letter. The second and third years, if he again earns his letter, he is given a certificate. Certificates are awarded to all second team and reserve players. Varsity team players are the only ones eligible for a letter. This means that a boy can receive only one letter for each sport. In other words he could not receive over three letters in all his high school athletics while he is a member of the school. This has practically the same effect as awarding only one letter a year regardless of the number of sports in which a boy participates. We like this system because it gives a letter to a boy who makes the varsity team for the first time.[3]

[2] "A study of Athletic Award Policies in 125 Michigan High Schools (1935–1936)," Michigan High School Athletic Association *Bulletin,* March, 1936, pp. 167–72.

[3] *Ibid.,* p. 168.

Method of granting awards. In a previous discussion of awards [4] it was suggested that awards (letters) be granted by the athletic council or board of control in a local school. The following procedure is recommended:

1. At an early season practice session the coach should advise all team candidates of the award policy of the school.
2. Records of the amount of competition of each individual should be kept if that is a requisite on which awards are granted.
3. Recommended list of those to receive the school award should be prepared by the coach and submitted to the athletic director and principal.
4. The athletic director and the coach should confer with the principal in order to check on school citizenship, attitude, character, and scholastic standings of those recommended.
5. Combined recommendation should be submitted to the athletic council or board of control for final approval.
6. Letter awards should be made at a school assembly as near the end of the semester as possible.

Basis for granting awards. There are different plans in effect which form the basis for granting athletic awards in various schools. In some instances they are given solely on the recommendation of the coach. In others this recommendation is combined with those of other school officials. Certain schools pay much attention to the amount of participation as the basis for awards. They set up definite requirements that a boy must have played in so many quarters or innings or have won a required number of points. Another plan is that of awarding only a limited number of letters per year and determining the recipients on the basis of a point system which includes all the sports sponsored by the school. Most schools require that, to receive awards, students must be good school citizens, receive passing grades in their work, have been regular in attendance at practice sessions, and have observed training rules as formulated by the coach.

Examples of awards systems. Two examples of awards systems merit discussion. They illustrate (1) an award system based largely

4 See Chapter 6, "Awards."

on participation in individual sports and (2) general recommendation award system. The basis of each of these is discussed below.

1. Participation in individual sports. This is the system followed in the Detroit Public Secondary School Athletic League. The athletic award regulations follow:

TRACK

1. Letters shall be awarded in track as follows:
   a. 1.5 points average for the number of dual meets scheduled, or
   b. seconds in 50 per cent of the meets scheduled, or
   c. two points in league meets, or
   d. a point or fraction thereof in city meets.

2. The "Champion Stripe" 1¼ inches wide, to run from the right shoulder to the left hip, and to be worn only on gym shirts shall be awarded to place winners in city meets.

3. Ribbon awards suitably printed, commemorative of the event, order of place and the date shall be awarded to city meet winners as follows:

1st place—blue	4th place—orange
2nd place—red	5th place—yellow
3rd place—white	6th place—green

FOOTBALL

Letters shall be awarded in football for the following: Play in at least three city-league games with a total of five quarters, two of which must constitute a half in one game; or play in two city games a year for three years, playing at least one full quarter in each of the games.

BASKETBALL

Letters shall be awarded for playing six full quarters against league teams.

BASEBALL

Letters shall be awarded as follows: play in four league games with a minimum of nine innings; pitchers, five innings in two games, and part of one other game.

SWIMMING

All awards the same as for track and field except as to emblem imbedded in the letter and the championship stripe on the swimming suit.

GOLF

1. Letters shall be awarded in golf as follows:
   a. Play in ¾ of the dual matches; or
   b. Finish among the first six in the spring medal tournament.

CROSS COUNTRY

1. All awards the same as for track and field except as to emblem imbedded in the letter.
2. Awards made in accordance with the stipulations as follows:
   a. Place in the first five contestants from his school in the city meet or,
   b. Place in two quadrangular, triangular or dual meets.

TENNIS

1. Letters shall be awarded in tennis as follows:
   a. Play in ¾ of the dual matches; or
   b. Finish in the quarter finals, in the east or west side meet; or
   c. Finish in the quarter finals in the city tournament.[5]

2. General recommendation. This is the basis of the Grosse Pointe, Mich., High School award system. The regulations follow:

1. In order to receive an award in a varsity sport the boy must be recommended by the coach of that sport. In making recommendations for varsity awards, the coach must take into consideration—(a) Conduct; (b) Attendance; (c) Ineligibility periods.

2. All awards will be made at the end of the semester in which the competition took place.

3. In order to receive either a varsity or intramural award, the boy must pass 15 hours of academic work the semester in which the participation took place.

4. Varsity letters or honor sweaters are not to be worn during any period of ineligibility. (Note—Except after school hours.)

5. Varsity letters or honor sweaters are not to be worn by anyone that has not been awarded a varsity letter. The school reserves the right to withdraw any letter award found in the possession of a person other than the one to whom it was awarded.[6]

[5] Detroit Public Secondary School Athletic League, 1960–1961 *Athletic Manual*, pp. 40–41.

[6] "A Study of Athletic Award Policies in 125 Michigan High Schools," Michigan High School Athletic Association *Bulletin*, March, 1936, p. 169.

Student manager awards. Student managers should receive school letter awards that are distinctive of the type of service rendered by them. In many schools there are various ranks of athletic managers, and it is well to have awards indicative of this fact. The student manager award system in effect in the Detroit schools follows:

1. The boy must conform to the eligibility rules the same as the team which he manages, with the exception that he need not pass a physical examination.
2. The boy must serve at least one year as a house manager and as a team manager one season, or as an assistant manager one season and then manager, or serve as a manager of the same sport for two seasons, or manage two sports in the same school year. The coach and athletic director must also agree that his work has been satisfactory.[7]

The long-time plan in effect at Eagle Rock High School, Los Angeles, for making suitable managerial awards has proved satisfactory there and merits consideration:

1. The senior manager, upon the successful completion of his duties, shall be awarded the school monogram with an "M" superimposed. Only one such monogram shall be awarded.
2. The junior managers, upon the successful completion of their duties, shall be awarded the middleweight letter with an "M" superimposed. The number of such letters awarded shall not exceed the number of junior managers specified for that sport.
3. The assistant managers, upon the successful completion of their duties, shall be awarded the lightweight letter with an "M" superimposed. Not more than four such letters shall be awarded.
The physical education department has also added to the distinction of the managerial office by providing the occupants with jerseys of appropriate color.

These two plans relative to student manager awards offer suggestions that may be followed to a certain extent in schools of various sizes. It seems evident that an award for efficient student manager service is highly desirable.

[7] Detroit Public Secondary School Athletic League, 1960–1961 *Athletic Manual*, p. 41.

Questions for Study and Discussion

1. Discuss prevailing differences of opinion regarding awards for participation in athletic activities. Which do you support? Why?

2. What seem to be the general trends in awards for high school athletics?

3. Discuss the six recommendations suggested in this chapter, regarding the granting of athletic awards. Would you add any others? Which ones, and why?

4. Compare awards systems with which you are familiar with those outlined in this chapter.

5. Do you favor granting awards to student managers? If so, on what basis?

10 Athletic Finances and Budgets

Any consideration of the high school athletic program would be incomplete without attention being given to the method of financing it. One of the first things a school should do in the planning of such a program is to ascertain its approximate cost and then determine, as far as possible, the sources of income from which finances may be expected. Various considerations of this problem are presented in this chapter.

Finances and the athletic program. Since athletics first came into our high schools, methods have been sought by which they could be financed. We have gone a long way in raising the status of the program. In at least one state (New York), athletics, by Board of Regents' action, are a definite part of the physical education program of schools. It is the duty of the local boards of education in that state to provide facilities for conducting them. Facilities mean equipment of all kinds. In many other states boards of education buy general game equipment but not that for the personal use of contestants. There is no doubt that in hundreds of other schools, boards of education make up deficits in high school athletics from balances in "emergency, revolving, or contingent" funds, sometimes illegally by strict interpretation of the law.

All this has come from the humble beginning which athletics had when they first were placed among school activities. Of course, gate receipts still furnish the great bulk of revenue for financing the athletic programs in high schools. There has been a tendency during recent years, especially among the larger schools, to form activity associations or general student organizations as a means of financing athletics and other school activities.

There is no doubt that schoolmen in general would prefer to have athletics financed the same as any other school subject. Certainly, from an educational standpoint, athletics can be justified as having as great, or greater, possibilities for teaching citizenship, sportsmanship, character, self-discipline, health, and use of leisure than any other school subject. As was pointed out early by Principal Riley of Oswego (New York) High School:

> There is real educational value in athletics. The guidance possibilities of competitive games are unlimited. The rules of football, the formations, the plays themselves are as challenging to the mind as are the rules of algebra, the formations in geometry or the experiments in science. Football rules, formations and plays, however, have the added educational advantage of immediacy. We learn them readily because we see an immediate use for them. The football guide book is as comprehensive and specific as any text book used in our schools today. The discipline of the athletic field contributes something to the boy that he can get in no other way. Many boys earned a high school diploma because of their interest in athletics. All this would seem to indicate that the athletic program is a very important part of the educational program and should be taken from the exhibition class and placed in the regular curriculum where it belongs.
>
> It is legal for Boards of Education (New York) to purchase athletic equipment for athletic teams. It is legal for them to provide the playing fields and other expenses of the program. It is also the undeniable right of every boy and girl in school to see his team play without paying an admission fee. Therefore, we should work for the subsidization of the athletic program by the local Boards of Education. The program can never be educational as long as it remains commercial.[1]

Riley stated the situation well. The development of interscholastic athletics in New York has been watched with interest as a result of the broad construction applied there.

Since the time has not yet arrived when gate receipts, in general, can be eliminated, it is imperative that schools control them for their own ends. It seems most advisable that student fees and student

[1] Charles E. Riley, "Financing Athletics," New York State Public High School Athletic Association *Bulletin*, April, 1937, pp. 2–3.

admission prices be kept to a minimum or abolished whenever possible. Since gate receipts are still in effect in the schools of most states (including New York), they should be so adjusted that the adult public pays the bulk of them. Student considerations come first. To adults, athletic contests are a means of entertainment, and adults generally expect to pay for their entertainment. The problem, therefore, is that of striking the proper balance between educational service to high school students and the offering of a program of entertainment to the interested adult patrons of the school. The following discussion recognizes the ideal to be attained. Obviously the administration of the athletic program would be greatly simplified if it could be completely subsidized by the board of education. This goal, however, does not appear to be possible at the present time.

The actual situation as it exists today will be considered in this chapter. It will be taken for granted that finances have to be raised for interscholastic athletics, in most cases without a major portion of them being furnished by boards of education. Furthermore, it will be assumed that those responsible for athletic programs are interested in methods followed in other schools for obtaining, handling, and spending finances most judiciously. In short, the reality of financing a successful interschool athletic program will be the main thesis.

Methods of raising athletic funds. The methods of raising athletic funds are almost as numerous as are the schools that use them. No denial of the fact can be made that the easiest method of raising funds, except by board of education grant, is by having a successful team. Usually public and students alike will pay to see a winner. This seems to be an American tradition. In most schools, however, more than chance gate receipts are necessary to assure successful operation of the program for the year. Some of the methods followed in such schools will be presented. A word of qualification, however, is offered concerning them. Not all the plans mentioned here necessarily are recommended; the ones cited are those which apparently have been successful where they have been tried. They are offered only as suggestions.

Many schoolmen legitimately are opposed to consuming too much school time in "selling" campaigns for financing athletics. In considering this matter, a committee of superintendents of schools in

California said: "The reduction to an absolute minimum of ticket selling within the school for athletic contests should be effected." [2] There is no doubt that too often school time is used unnecessarily for ticket selling of all kinds. Such a practice is not necessary. It can be done at other times, expeditiously and in a businesslike manner. The whole scheme of raising, handling, and disbursing athletic funds in a high school should be made the basis of educational experiences for numerous students that would be good, practical business training for them. It should not become too much of a job for a few people, and it should include methods that are acceptable to students and public alike.

Admission prices. Keep admission prices to athletic contests at a minimum as far as high school students are concerned. They should be the first ones to have the opportunity to see their teams in action. Sometimes it is necessary to limit attendance at indoor contests because of limited seating capacity. In this case take care of students first, and make the admission charges as low as possible, consistent with assurance of reasonably sufficient funds to finance the program. Educationally, it is much more justifiable to fill gymnasiums and playing-field accommodations with students than with adults. Such a policy emphasizes to the public the real individuals for whom the program is maintained. In some instances, also, such a policy has been instrumental in awakening school patrons to the need for additional school facilities.

Season tickets. The sale of season athletic tickets to students and adults is a recommended procedure. This accomplishes at least five things:

1. Prices for season tickets to students can be made much lower.
2. The plan assures the school of a definite minimum fund for program operations.
3. It obtains funds early in the season for use in getting the sport under way.
4. Season-ticket sales reduce the weather hazard that occurs when athletic funds depend entirely on game-day admissions.
5. In smaller communities, especially, season tickets are appreciated by interested adults. They offer a tangible way by which they

[2] Adopted by California School Superintendents' Association (*Superintendents' Recommendations on Interscholastic Relations*).

may support the program. Such individuals are usually the more substantial citizens, and their presence at athletic contests lends a wholesome influence.

Two types of season tickets are recommended: the booklet form and that which has a detachable part to be removed when the ticket holder enters the gymnasium or field. The athletic booklet for students is numbered on the cover which has a space for the name of the owner. There is a separate slip with a number for each contest. Usually a space for the owner's signature is provided on each event slip. For identification purposes the signature may be compared with the cover signature, although some schools are not particular in this regard. The event slip must not be detached from the book prior to presentation at the gate or door. The entire book is then handed to the ticket taker, who tears out the appropriate slip and returns the book to the owner. A similar plan works out very well with adult season tickets and ensures that only one admission is obtained for each event on each ticket. This arrangement also is faster than ticket punching, in which a single ticket with designated punch spaces is used.

Student activity or general organization tickets. In schools in which student activity or general organization ticket plans are in effect, it seems as though, generally, there is a better balance between athletics and other school activities. This is as it should be. Of course athletics appeal to many students, either as participants or as spectators. It is natural and proper to capitalize on this interest to aid in support of other school activities. The common practice in schools having general student tickets is to include some or all of the following, either entirely or partially, among the activities represented:

1. Admission to all home athletic contests.
2. Admission to special school assemblies or programs.
3. Admission, or part admission, to school plays, concerts, and operettas.
4. Subscription to school paper.
5. Part payment on the school annual.
6. Admission to debates and other forensic contests.
7. Admission, or part admission, to all-school parties.

This plan definitely centers finances for all the activities of a school; and, as in the case with season ticket sales in athletics, it establishes a working minimum for all school projects. Usually this arrangement is so set up that students buy their activity tickets by paying from ten to twenty-five cents a week until purchased. In other cases a small fee is paid each week during the entire school year. Generally, it has been found more desirable to arrange the payment schedule so that most of the ticket is paid for before the home football or basketball seasons are concluded. Schools have found frequently that payments on tickets lag considerably if they extend over too long a period. It is necessary to devote only a few minutes during a homeroom, record or utility period for collection of payments. Sometimes activity ticket stamps are sold on payment days to be placed in student folders. The bookkeeping system need not be elaborate; it need merely include the name of the ticket purchaser and spaces for payments on collection dates.

The division or proportioning of receipts from activity ticket sales will depend upon a number of different factors. A general board composed of representatives of all activities concerned should review the requests of each prospective recipient from the funds. Probable additional income to be realized by some of them during the year should be taken into consideration when making apportionments. When the total amount to be received has been estimated as nearly as possible and budgets for the activities of the year have been approved, it is a comparatively simple matter to apportion the percentages. Usually, no single activity should be allowed to exceed its apportionment without the approval of the general activities board. Such a policy will insure that all projects will have their allotted funds, and when balances from certain of them accrue, they may be placed in reserve for future use of all activities.

The idea of the "Ten Cents a Week" student activity plan is supposed to have originated in the Omaha Technical High School. The division of the "activities dollar" at this school is shown in Table 1, and the outline of this plan follows:

As used by Omaha Tech. each student has a folder or card on which are as many spaces as there are weeks in the school year. Stamps are printed and the teachers sell them each week, one teacher being responsible for a certain class weekly. When a boy or girl pays ten cents, the teacher then turns the money over to the Activities Association. As long as the card indicates the owner is paid up it will admit the student free to any school activity whether it be an athletic contest, a school play, a debate or the swimming privilege.[3]

TABLE 1

Division of Activities Dollar at
Omaha Technical High School

Recipient	Amount
Senior play and school annual	21.0¢
Artists	10.4
Football	10.2
Baseball	7.5
Track	6.5
Basketball	5.1
School paper	5.0
Operettas	4.9
Bands and orchestras	4.8
Swimming	3.9
Mass athletics	3.1
Spring festival	2.8
Assemblies and movies	2.7
Wrestling	2.7
Debating	2.4
Honor roll	2.1
Stamps and supplies	1.3
Song books	1.2
Miscellaneous	1.2
Greenhouse	1.2

The student activity or general organization ticket plan in high schools seems to offer the following advantages as a method of financing athletics and other activities:

1. Unifies all school activities.

2. Aids in keeping athletics in their relatively proper place in the school activities program.

3. Capitalizes on student interest in athletics to aid in financing other justifiable school activities.

4. Reduces ticket-selling campaigns to a minimum through regular organization plans.

[3] *Successful Financial Plans For School Athletic Departments* (booklet), pp. 3–4. Lowe and Campbell Athletic Goods Company, Kansas City, Mo.

5. Provides an early-season and known working capital for all activities.

6. Provides accessible funds at the beginning of the school year.

7. May be sponsored as a student activity project.

8. Should result in considerable saving to students because prices may be reduced if sufficient tickets are sold.

Student fee plan. This plan apparently has been borrowed from colleges and universities. Many of the latter charge a definite sum for athletics, which is included when tuition payments are made. Some high schools have found it successful, but generally it is not used or recommended. The plan assesses each student in a high school a certain amount for the athletic program and admits him to all home contests. It is defended on the ground that textbooks have to be purchased and laboratory fees must be paid by students; therefore, an athletic fee from all is justifiable. If such a plan is to be workable in any school, it is certain that its inauguration should be preceded by an extensive educational campaign among school patrons and parents of students.

Other athletic finance plans. Schools frequently find it necessary to put on special functions in order to raise funds to finance athletic programs. In fact, some schools use this method entirely as a means of support, with the result that gate receipts have been eliminated. Sometimes this procedure has been forced on them because of inadequate facilities where athletic contests are held. Quite often it is not possible to accommodate spectators or charge admission, and resort to other finance methods has been necessary. Schemes which apparently have been successful are listed here. Again it is not to be inferred that all the procedures necessarily are recommended. However, they may offer helpful suggestions.

1. Tag sales—preceding or at time of games.
2. Athletic carnival—may be held either indoors or outdoors.
3. School dance—with special athletic or other activity features.
4. School circus—an all-school affair, held in gymnasium.
5. School plays, operettas, minstrels, shows.
6. Band and orchestra concerts.
7. Debating and forensic contests.

8. Moving picture benefits—arrangements with local theater for percentage of advance sale of tickets.

9. Candy and soft-drink sales—at school or community functions.

10. Magazine subscription campaigns.

11. School workday—students work at odd jobs and turn in earnings to activities fund.

12. Pie or cake socials or suppers—auction off pies or cakes made by girls of the high school.

13. Sponsoring of professional entertainments—plays, musicals, athletic events.

14. School newspaper sales day—sell special edition of school paper at school and downtown. Make it a good edition.

15. Popularity or sponsor contests—votes with sale of activity tickets.

16. Old-paper day—students bring old papers and magazines from home. Proceeds from sale go to activities fund. Give prize to homeroom or class collecting most paper.

17. Cooperative enterprises with parent-teacher association or other civic organizations—these groups are interested in the school program. Their cooperation usually can be secured.

18. Water carnivals—very effective in school swimming pools or near-by rivers or lakes.

19. Town cookbook—mothers of students furnish proved recipes. Mimeograph or print for sale.

20. Special auditorium programs—each class being responsible for a program for which a small student admission fee is charged.

The handling of athletic funds. The most important rule in handling athletic or any school activity finances is to have a simple, understandable system and then follow it. Nothing can cause more embarrassment or difficulty to a schoolman than inefficiency or carelessness in handling school or athletic funds. In dealings with someone else's money no transaction should be left unrecorded or unexplained. Be definite and brief, but be complete. At all times the entire records showing receipts, disbursements, balances, or deficits should be open to inspection.

Internal accounting records. In some school systems, board of education accounting divisions handle all financial transactions pertaining to high school athletics. Such a procedure relieves school officials entirely from keeping records of this type and centers financial matters in an agency that is expected by the public to have jurisdiction over them. In other schools, however, boards of education do not feel disposed to assume these duties. They think that athletic and other school activity funds should not be handled by them because they are not tax moneys and do not properly come within their scope of duties. Whether or not board of education officials have expressed themselves definitely on this matter, it is significant that in a great majority of large and small schools, high school activity funds are handled by the schools themselves. Most of them have their own internal accounting systems. Separate bank accounts are established, and funds are disbursed only on order of authorized school executives. In connection with such plans it is an excellent procedure to make regular reports of school activity funds to the finance officer or finance division of the board of education. These reports serve as an additional check on the accounting system of the school's athletic or activity program. Likewise, it is highly desirable to ask that board of education auditors annually examine and certify the recorded transactions of the activity fund accounts.

As far as athletic finances are concerned, it seems immaterial whether a school has a separate athletic association treasurer or a central internal accounting system in effect, with a general school treasurer. In order that each activity may be considered as a part of the entire school program, it is recommended that the latter plan be followed. A central accounting system for all high school activities presents the following advantages over the scheme of having separate systems for each activity:

1. Responsibility for disbursement of all school funds may be delegated to one individual.

2. It is in harmony with the plan of having all school activities under the general supervision of an all-school committee.

3. It enables the school administrator to have a composite picture of the general condition, financial and otherwise, of all the school activities.

4. It provides the possibility for a much more accurate audit of school activities funds than otherwise might be the case.

5. The purposes for which expenditures are to be made may be

more easily checked to ascertain if they are in accordance with authorization.

6. Local banking institutions usually will prefer a single school deposit account rather than separate ones for each school activity fund.

7. By its nature, the plan appeals to students and school patrons as being more businesslike.

Schemes in local schools will vary with their plans of general organization and their size. Some of the most successful ones usually have a general faculty treasurer. It is recommended that the treasurer be someone other than the superintendent or principal. He should receive all funds from the proper officer of each activity organization on a regular form prepared for that purpose. (See example of internal account deposit blank used at Mount Clemens, Mich., High School, Figure 10–1.) This blank is made out in duplicate, with the activity officer and general organization treasurer each having a copy. The amount of this deposit is placed to the credit of the appropriate activity. When funds are received in sufficient quantities from several activities, the general organization treasurer may make one deposit in the bank where the school account is kept. When an activity wishes to make a purchase or to pay an account that has been authorized by its officers or the general activities committee, an order for a check is issued. This is presented to the general organization treasurer (see Figure 10–1). Upon receipt of this request for money, the general school organization treasurer issues a school check that has remittance advice information attached explaining the items covered (see Figure 10–1).[4]

Obviously, the general school activities treasurer and his student assistants will do most of the bookkeeping in a centralized system of this type. Funds will be allocated for each of the activity organizations of a school. In turn, within each activity there will be allocations. The extent of these details will depend upon the number of activities within a school as well as the divisions within each activity.

[4] The three forms illustrating accounting procedures at Mount Clemens (Michigan) High School have been used by permission of that school. They are typical of general forms of this nature used in schools in which a central activities accounting fund system is in operation.

HIGH SCHOOL BANK
Mount Clemens, Michigan

Account No. ....

_____ 19____

Deposited by_____ $_____
                (Organization)

Receipts of _____

_____
                                      Student Treasurer

Date _____	Mount Clemens High School	Organization Account No.

Organization Request for Money

Requisition Number_____

To _____

To the Faculty Treasurer: Date_____

For_____

Please issue check to_____

Balance $_____

_____
Name of Firm

Credited $_____

for_____Dollars ($)

Total $_____

to pay these items_____

This order $_____

Name of Organization   Signed_____
                                      Organization Treasurer

Balance forward $_____

_____
                                      Faculty Advisor

No money will be paid for any account without the Principal's signature.

_____
                                      Principal

GENERAL STUDENT FUNDS   Mt. Clemens High School   N⁰ 552
                             Mt. Clemens, Mich.   Date_____
                                TO THE
                    Mount Clemens Savings Bank   74-208
                          Mount Clemens, Michigan

PAY TO THE ORDER OF

_____ $_____

_____DOLLARS

ACCOUNT CHARGEABLE TO   Mount Clemens High School

_____

                    By_____
                                      FACULTY TREASURER

_____

.... DETACH HERE BEFORE DEPOSITING ABOVE CHECK ....

REMITTANCE ADVICE   NO RECEIPT DESIRED

We issue herewith our check No. 552 for $_____in full
settlement of the following items. If not correct please return all papers
with explanation.

DATE INVOICE	DESCRIPTION	AMOUNT	DISC.	AMOUNT

Issued by Mount Clemens High School
Mount Clemens, Michigan .

Fig. 10-1. Organization Deposit Slip, Request for Money, and General Student
Funds Check (Mt. Clemens High School, Michigan).

266

Publication of financial reports. At regular intervals—monthly, seasonal, term, or semester—statements should be prepared for submission to each activity organization and to the officials concerned. To illustrate a maximum policy in this respect, a list of statements which might be included in a seasonal report for football follows. Each of these could be prepared from the fund allocation heading in the bookkeeping procedure. Other sports would be comparable to this example.

1. Seasonal Summary Football Statement of Receipts and Disbursements.
2. Bar Graph Showing Receipts and Disbursements.
3. Detailed Statement of Football Gate Receipts.
4. Detailed Statement of Football Guarantee Income.
5. Detailed Statement of Football Equipment Purchased.
6. Detailed Statement of Food and Lodging Expense for Football Season.
7. Detailed Statement of Laundry, Cleaning, and Reconditioning Expense.
8. Detailed Statement of Medical Expense and Medical Supplies.
9. Detailed Statement of Officials' Expense.
10. Detailed Statement of Office Supplies Expense.
11. Detailed Statement of Opponents' Guarantee Expense.
12. Detailed Statement of Printing Expense.
13. Detailed Statement of Scouting Expense.
14. Detailed Statement of Telephone Expense.
15. Detailed Statement of Towel Service Expense.
16. Detailed Statement of Transportation Expense.
17. Bar Graph Showing Profit or Loss on Each Football Game.

It is advisable to see that records of finances are known to the public, especially if the public is partly responsible for some of the funds by which the athletic program is conducted. In dealing with this subject elsewhere, it was suggested that reports of receipts and disbursements for all athletic contests be placed in the hands of the superintendent or principal shortly after each game. Further, it is recommended that the school policy provide that such reports be placed on the school bulletin board and published frequently in the school or local newspaper. In this connection, however, be sure that reports of expenses for activities from which there is no income also are listed. These will show some of the expenses for activities that have to be supported out of the income from other sources.

Some schools have regular policies of publication of all financial reports on athletics. There is no reason why their status should not be made known. If funds are low, a published report may be a means by which interest can be aroused for their replenishment. An unreasonably large surplus undoubtedly is indicative that more athletic or other school activities should be sponsored or that student

TABLE 2

Summary of Receipts and Disbursements
Iron Mountain High School Athletic Association
Year Ended June 30, 1960

Gate receipts:		
Football	$ 3,257.10	
Basketball	2,506.85	$ 5,763.95
Insurance claims		617.45
Basketball tournament expense allowance		270.00
Tennis tournament entry fees		120.00
Contributions:		
Iron Mountain City School District	$ 1,669.63	
Booster Club	56.37	
Activities Fund	200.00	1,926.00
P. A. System		80.00
Change for games		254.00
Equipment deposits and insurance		294.50
Money returned from advancement for meets ..		43.72
Sale of equipment		83.50
Miscellaneous—refunds, locker fees, etc.		64.85
TOTAL RECEIPTS		$ 9,517.97
Disbursements:		
Football	$ 4,986.82	
Basketball	3,161.22	
Track	568.51	
Skiing	109.75	
Tennis	254.95	
Golf	23.75	
General athletic expense	656.16	9,761.16
EXCESS OF (DISBURSEMENTS) OVER RECEIPTS		($ 243.19)
Cash balance, July 1, 1959		285.91
CASH BALANCE, JUNE, 30, 1960		$ 42.72

The Athletic Fund balance of $42.72 was on deposit at the First National Bank, Iron Mountain, Michigan, at June 30, 1960.

Disbursements:

TABLE 2 (*Continued*)

FOOTBALL

Officiating	$ 275.70
Medical expenses	719.45
Transportation and travel expenses	41.70
Equipment purchases, repairs, and cleaning	2,084.72
Guard and ticket service	140.00
Insurance and insurance claims	349.50
Scouting and mileage	36.02
Meals	216.00
Change	120.00
P. A. Rental	75.00
Refunds—equipment, etc.	75.00
Awards	163.35
Kingsford High School football field rental—Stambaugh game	122.60
One half of Kingsford High School game proceeds	535.88
Miscellaneous—football clinic, etc.	31.90
TOTAL	**$ 4,986.82**

BASKETBALL

Officiating	$ 456.40
Medical expenses	195.50
Transportation and travel expenses	100.60
Equipment purchases, repairs, and cleaning	883.40
Guard and ticket service	154.00
Meals and hotels	582.83
Insurance and insurance claims	14.00
Armory rental	325.98
Change	134.00
Reserve tournament	177.48
Awards	90.83
Scouting and miscellaneous	46.20
TOTAL	**$ 3,161.22**

TRACK

Travel and food	$ 110.00
Equipment and maintenance	285.51
Medical	167.50
Awards, registration fee, etc.	5.50
TOTAL	**$ 568.51**

SKIING—Supplies and expense   **TOTAL** $ 109.75

TENNIS—Supplies and expense   **TOTAL** $ 254.95

GOLF—Supplies and expense   **TOTAL** $ 23.75

GENERAL ATHLETIC EXPENSE

Movie camera	$ 232.50
Camera lense and film	138.67
Telephone	108.85
Officials meetings	77.41
Miscellaneous—soap, locks, supplies, etc.	98.73
TOTAL	**$ 656.16**

admission fees should be lowered. There is no advantage in maintaining an unnecessarily large athletic or activity fund surplus. Reasonable working and emergency reserve funds are all that are necessary.

As illustrative of a type of complete athletic report, the one published by Iron Mountain, Mich., High School for the 1959–1960 school year is shown in Table 2. It appeared in the local daily paper (Iron Mountain *News*) and was included in the financial proceedings and transaction notices of the City of Iron Mountain and the Board of Education of the Iron Mountain School District. It is complete and understandable.

The bar graph is another effective way of showing receipts and disbursements so that the athletic financial picture may be comprehended at a glance. Graphs of this type may be made projects for advanced members of mechanical drawing classes. A composite

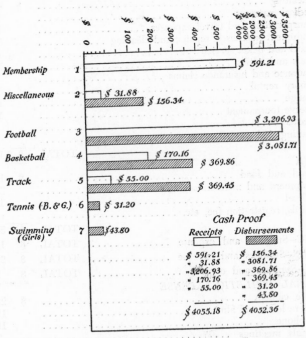

Fig. 10-2. Bar Graph of Athletic Receipts and Disbursements (*Glass Senior High School, Lynchburg, Virginia*).

graph may be made for receipts and disbursements for all activities. Individual sports graphs may be prepared to show income and expenses for each home game. Such a plan has been used effectively at Glass Senior High School, Lynchburg, Va., and is illustrated in Figures 10–2 and 10–3.

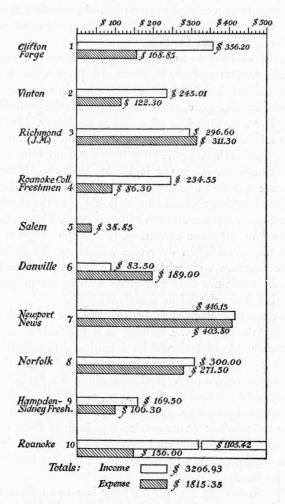

Fig. 10-3. Bar Graph of Football Income and Expenses *(Glass Senior High School)*.

Athletic Budgets

If projects, activities, or programs are to be successful, their approximate costs must be calculated in advance. Within schools, budgets are necessary not only for athletics but also for the operation of the entire school system itself. If several athletic activities are supported from a central source of funds, a budget is especially important because it gives each division reasonable assurance of the amount that will be available to it.

Purpose of an athletic budget. A budget merely is an estimate of probable income and expenditures. Its preparation is of value to those in charge of high school athletic programs because it necessitates that they anticipate, as far as possible, all the probable factors involved. Thus, constructive planning is necessary. Many schoolmen say that their athletic programs are so small that no budget is necessary. Some others assert that they have no time to prepare budgets. Usually these are not legitimate excuses. Although there may be some question about the amount of income to be realized from athletic contests, there can be no doubt as to the absolute minimum necessary to finance an activity or program. This matter should be discussed by all those concerned before the program is established for the year. Then everyone will know the status of the activity or activities with which he is concerned. If funds insufficient for the minimum essentials of an activity are predicted, it is probable that it should not be sponsored.

It is obvious that changes in budget allowances will have to be made in certain instances. Likewise, it is illogical to assume that a budget, once adopted, should be a hard and fast limit to which there must be blind adherence. In general, a budget should not be too specific or detailed. It should allow for flexibility within each activity. In the final analysis, then, an athletic budget simply is an attempt to balance receipts and expenditures, and its adoption should be the result of past experience in both of these matters. If accurate records of income and expenses for one year have been kept, it is a relatively simple matter to establish a budget for the program for the next year.

The athletic budget for one activity has more than the mere sport itself to consider. The budget must be balanced in the sense that it takes all the activities of the athletic program into consideration and sees that funds for their operation are properly proportioned.

Preparation of a budget. No general rule for the preparation of an athletic budget can be formulated that is applicable to schools of all sizes. General estimates of probable receipts from home games may be made from previous records. If there is a student or general organization ticket sales plan in effect, the probable amount forthcoming from that source may be estimated. Any amount to be received for athletics from the local board of education also may be included, and thus a probable total of all income may be determined. A suggested form for a composite report of estimated receipts to be used in preparation of an athletic budget appears in Figure 10–4. It presents a simple method by which this information may be shown.

Estimating details of probable expenditures may involve more time and effort than estimating probable receipts from athletic contests. A school must know what equipment it has on hand, its condition, and the amount of new equipment to be purchased. This information may be obtained from the seasonal inventories.[5] Also to be considered are such items as general administration; game officials; contract guarantees; expenses for games away from home; equipment repairs; new equipment; training, first aid, and medical supplies; awards; and incidentals, including pictures, meet and league fees, and the like. (See Fig. 10–5.) This suggested form will not show all the details necessary under each item; but if it is completely filled out for the sports sponsored by a school, it will disclose the general budget figures for each activity and the totals.

Obviously, one can devise other ways of preparing athletic budgets with possibly more successful application to individual school problems, than the suggestions mentioned in this discussion. The purpose of the forms shown here is to present relatively general ones from which schools may select the parts that pertain to their situations. In some instances, no doubt, schools will add items to those suggested. As stated previously, it will be necessary to set up divisions under each heading. For example, the item "Cost of New Playing and Game Equipment" must be divided into various sports. Each sport then would be subdivided into different equipment

[5] See suggested inventory form on page 235.

BUDGET SUMMARY OF ESTIMATED INCOME

School:_____   School Year: 19____-19____

SPORT	HOME GAMES		AWAY GAMES		TOTAL ESTIMATE
	No.	Receipts	No.	Guarantees	
Baseball.........		$		$	$
Basketball.......					
Football.........					
Hockey.........					
Swimming.......					
Track...........					
Other...........					
(1) Total estimated receipts........		$		$	$

(2) Estimated amount to be realized from student or general organization ticket sale................................ $_____

(3) Total amount, if any, to be received from the board of education for purchase of playing equipment........... $_____

(4) Grand total of estimated receipts for present year (Sum of 1, 2, 3)........ $_____

(5) Grand total of estimated expenditures for present year.................... $_____

(6) Estimated surplus for year (Difference between 4 and 5).................. $_____

or

(7) Estimated deficit for year (Difference between 5 and 4).................. $_____

Fig. 10-4. Suggested Form for Budget Summary of Estimated Income.

Sport	Administration: Cost of Bleachers, Guards, Tickets, Field, Printing, Postage, etc.	Cost of Officials for Home Contests	Home Game Contract Guarantees	Away-Game Expenses	Cost of Equipment, Repairs, and Maintenance	Cost of New Playing and Game Equipment	Cost of Training, First-Aid, and Medical Supplies	Cost of Awards	Incidentals: Team Pictures, Meet or League Fees. etc.	Total Estimate for Sport for Year
Baseball										
Basketball										
Boxing										
Cross-Country										
Football										
Golf										
Hockey										
Swimming										
Tennis										
Track										
Wrestling										
Others										
TOTAL ESTIMATE										

Fig. 10-5. Suggested Form for Budget Summary of Estimated Expenses.

items, with the estimated number of each that are needed and the cost price. In such a manner, total estimates may be obtained that would constitute the total as it appears on the budget summary blanks. Too much emphasis cannot be placed on the importance of correct inventories. Also, it is imperative that prices for sports equipment and material to be purchased be exact. These are items of the budget that can be estimated accurately, and their correctness makes the budget valuable. Budgets from year to year should be preserved for reference and statistical purposes.

A *complete large-school athletic budget.* In order that a complete athletic budget in all its details may be studied, one that was prepared for the consideration of the athletic board of Ann Arbor, Mich., High School for the 1960–1961 school year is included (see Table 3). It is representative of the budgets that are the basis for the management and financing of the athletic programs in larger high schools. (Ann Arbor High School has an enrollment of approximately 2000 students.) Although such a budget may seem too detailed for small schools, it contains suggestions that merit their attention.[6]

TABLE 3

Ann Arbor Senior High School
Tentative Budget Suggested to the Athletic Board
1960–1961

ESTIMATED EXPENSES FOR 1960–1961

Estimated Expenses for Individual Sports:

	Code		Less 5%	
Baseball	7013	$ 1849.73	$ 92.48	$ 1757.25
Basketball	7014	3045.00	152.25	2892.75
Football	7017	9074.84	453.74	8621.10
Golf	7018	553.50	27.67	525.83
Gymnastics	7027	411.00	20.55	390.45
Cross Country	7022	586.40	29.32	557.08
Swimming	7020	1952.55	97.62	1854.93
Tennis	7021	706.60	35.31	671.25
Track	7022	1262.90	63.14	1199.76
Wrestling	7024	2452.60	122.63	2329.97
Emergency Treatment of Athletes	7019	1300.00	65.00	1235.00

[6] The "Ann Arbor Senior High School Tentative Budget Suggested to the Athletic Board" was prepared under the supervision of L. H. Hollway, Director of Physical Education and Interscholastic Athletics. It is reproduced here with his permission.

TABLE 3 (*Continued*)

Athletics Misc. 7011	200.00	10.00	190.00
Omega Pictures ...... ——	75.00	3.75	71.00
6-A League 7025	258.00	12.90	245.10
TOTAL ESTIMATE EXPENSES FOR IND. SPORTS	$23728.12	$1186.36	$22541.72

Estimated Expenses for Meeting Stadium Bond Commitments:

Bond and Interest Redemption . 812	$ 5960.00
Operation and Maintenance Fund 815	1540.00
Bond Reserve Account 813	1000.00
Bond Replacement Fund 816	—————
TOTAL ESTIMATED EXPENSES— STADIUM BONDS	$ 8500.00

Total Estimated Income—1960–61

Estimated Income ...	$31,677.60
Estimated Expense ..	31,041.72
Estimated Balance ..	635.78

Estimated Income from Ticket Sales:

Football

Adult Season Tickets—400 @ $6 ...	$ 2,400.00
Gate Receipts, 4 games—@ $2000 ..	10,785.00
J.V. Games, 3 games—@ $50	150.00
Purple and White Game	100.00
Childrens' Season Tickets—350 @ $2	700.00
Student Activity Ticket ½ (2100 x 2.25) 1st semester	2,362.50
Total Estimated Football Income	$13,712.50

Basketball—8 games @ $175	1,400.00
Swimming—7 meets @ $75	525.00
Wrestling—6 meets @ $30	180.00
Student Activity Ticket—2nd semester	2,362.50
Total Estimated Income from Ticket Sales	$18,180.00

Estimated Income from Other Sources:

Student Fees for Injuries and Medical Exams:

Injury and Medical Exams—125 @ $4.50	$ 562.50
Injury Fees—200 @ $1.50	300.00
Medical Exams—100 @ $1.00	100.00
Estimated Income from Globetrotters	1,000.00
Total Estimated Income from Other Sources:	$ 1,962.50

Total Estimated Income Before Subsidies | $20,142.50 |

TABLE 3 (*Continued*)

Estimated Income from Subsidies:

Bd. of Ed. Subsidy for Injuries	750.00
Bd. of Ed. Subsidy for Athletics	3,000.00
Bd. of Ed. Subsidy—Student Activities	2,000.00
Parking Project	3,000.00

Total Estimated Subsidies	$ 8,750.00
Total Estimated Income—1960–61 + 2,785.00	$28,892.50
	2,785.00
Income	31,677.50
Expenses	31,041.72
	635.78

FOOTBALL

ADMINISTRATION

Officials (1st team) 4 games with 3 officials per game at $25 each and 1 official per game at $10	340.00
Official (2nd team) 3 games with 3 officials per game at $10 each	90.00
Official for scrimmage	90.00
4 ticket sellers at $5 each for 4 games	80.00
6 ticket takers at $5 each for 4 games	120.00
3 ushers at $5 each for 4 games	60.00
8 policemen at $13 each for 4 games	416.00
2. parking lot supervisors at $7.50 each for 4 games	60.00
1 parking lot supervisor at $10 each for 4 games	40.00
student parking lot help—90 hr. @ $1.10	99.00
1 lockerroom attendant at $5 for 7 games	35.00
1 scoreboard man at $5 for 7 games	35.00
1 timer at $5 for 7 games	35.00
1 announcer at $10 for 7 games	70.00
3 guards at $5 for 4 games	60.00
2 men to supervise jr. high section $5 each for 4 games	40.00
1 man to supervise the lobby at $5 each for 7 games	35.00
1 man to supervise over-all program at $10 for 7 games	70.00
1 man for general field responsibilities at $5 for 7 games	35.00
1 man for band supervision at $5 for 4 games	20.00

SUPPLIES AND EQUIPMENT

12	face bars @ 4.00	48.00
20	helmets @ 18.00	360.00
125	chin straps @ .25	32.00
300	cleats @ 9.00 per 100	27.00
48	game pants @ 6.00	288.00
48	white game shirts @ 4.00	192.00
12	shoulder pads @ 16.00	192.00

TABLE 3 *(Continued)*

12		hip pads @ 7.50	90.00
48	pr.	thigh pads @ 4.00	192.00
48	pr.	knee pads @ 3.00..............................	144.00
5	doz.	practice shirts @ 23.00	115.00
2	doz.	scrimmage vests @ 10.00	20.00
12		balls @ 16.00	192.00
12		arm pads @ 3.00	36.00
15	doz.	laces (pad and shoe) @ 1.00 per doz.	15.00
12	doz.	white sweat socks @ 7.00	84.00
8	pr.	game shoes @ 15.00	120.00
1		crowther 2 man charging sled	280.00
1		water can (pressure pump)	25.00
12		helmets (j.v.) @ 18.00	216.00

repair projector 30.00
visual aids 9 games @ 1.00 .... 900.00
scouting 14 games @ 12.00 .... 168.00
office supplies 35.00
awards 170.00
telephone 25.00
cleaning and repair 1000.00
first aid 880.00
miscellaneous 100.00

Printing of single admission tickets, season
tickets, student tickets 400.00

Repair of P. A. System 25.00

Subscription to papers and advertisement 65.00

MEALS AND TRANSPORTATION

	Meals – $1.75		Transportation	
Kalamazoo	38 players–3 coaches = 78.75		51.60 bus	
	2 mgrs., 1 dr., 1 tr.		18.50 truck	
	tip 10%	7.88		
	pregame – 45 @ 1.00	45.00		
		131.63	+ 70.10	201.75
Flint Central	38 players–6 coaches = 84.00		29.65 bus	
	2 mgrs., 1 dr., 1 tr.		12.95 truck	
	tip 10%	8.40	42.60	
		92.40	+ 42.60	135.00
L. Eastern	38 players–3 coaches = 78.75		34.90 bus	
	2 mgrs., 1 dr., 1 tr.		14.80 truck	
	tip 10%	7.88	49.70	
	pregame – 45 @ 1.00	45.00		
		131.63	+ 49.70	181.33

TABLE 3 *(Continued)*

Jackson   38 players–6 coaches = 84.00   23.30 bus
          2 mgrs., 1 dr., 1 tr.   11.10 truck
          tip 10%   8.40
          pregame – 48 @ 1.00   48.00
                                 ─────
                                 140.40   +   34.40 ...... 174.80

Junior Varsity

Transportation – Adrian   24.00 bus
                          11.10 truck   35.10
                          ─────

              Livonia   21.90 bus
                          11.10 truck   33.00
                          ─────

              Ypsilanti   10.40 bus
                           7.40 truck   17.80 ...... 85.90
                          ─────   ─────

        TOTAL ESTIMATED FOOTBALL BUDGET $9074.84

CROSS COUNTRY

SUPPLIES AND EQUIPMENT

3	sweat suits @ 6.00	18.00
20 pr.	shoes @ 2.00	40.00
14	winter underwear (tops and bottoms) @ 1.50	21.00
14 pr.	cotton gloves @ .60	8.40

cleaning 70.00
pictures 5.00
letters, pins, cups 50.00
training room supplies 40.00

MEALS AND TRANSPORTATION

	Meals	Transportation	
Dearborn	28.50	18.00	46.50
Lansing Eastern	28.50	35.00	63.50
Thurston Inv.	16.00	16.00	32.00
Lansing Sexton	28.50	35.00	63.50
6A Meet – Kalamazoo	28.50	40.00	68.50
Albion	16.00	8.00	24.00
Regional (Trenton)	16.00	18.00	34.00
State		2.00	2.00

        TOTAL ESTIMATED BUDGET FOR CROSS COUNTRY $586.40

BASKETBALL

ADMINISTRATION

2 officials at $25 per game – 8 games 400.00
2 officials at $10 per game – 8 games 160.00

TABLE 3 *(Continued)*

1 ticket seller at $5 for 8 games	40.00
2 ticket takers at $5 for 8 games	80.00
1 man for P.A. at $5 for 8 games	40.00
1 man for scoreboard at $5 for 8 games	40.00
1 man for timekeeper at $5 for 8 games	40.00
1 policeman at $9.38 for 8 games	75.00

SUPPLIES AND EQUIPMENT

12 basketballs @ 16.00	192.00
14 pr. basketball shoes @ 8.00	112.00
cleaning and repair	150.00
visual aids	250.00
awards	60.00
printing of tickets	35.00
newspaper	10.00
scouting 14 games @ 12.00	168.00
miscellaneous	25.00
first aid	80.00
basketball cart	25.00

MEALS AND TRANSPORTATION

	Pregame	After game Meals	Transportation	
Arthur Hill	35	66.50	46.00	147.50
Ypsilanti			9.00	9.00
Lansing Sexton	35	66.50	35.00	136.50
Kalamazoo	35	66.50	46.00	147.50
Battle Creek	35	66.50	42.00	143.50
Jackson	35	66.50	21.00	122.50
Lansing Eastern	35	66.50	35.00	136.50

Sophomore Basketball

Officials 2 @ 10.00 for 5 games			100.00
Jackson	Transportation – 21.00	Meals – 29.00	50.00
Adrian	25.00	29.00	50.00
Miscellaneous (score book, etc.)			16.00
			$3045.00

SWIMMING

EQUIPMENT

6 tank suits @ 2.40	14.40
6 pr. sandals @ 1.50	9.00
1 stop watch	30.00
awards	100.00
scorebook	2.50
office equipment and printing	70.00
subscriptions	20.00
phone	10.00

TABLE 3 *(Continued)*

first aid 50.00
outdoor bulletin board 30.00
maintenance and repair 50.00
cleaning 50.00
fee cards and comp. tickets 12.00

MEALS, TRANSPORTATION AND ADMINISTRATION

	Meals	Trans.	Admin.	
Purple and White			15.00	15.00
Grosse Pointe			30.00	30.00
Cereal Bowl Relays	74.00	44.00		118.00
Lincoln Park	50.00	25.00		75.00
Pioneer Championships			60.00	60.00
Birmingham			30.00	30.00
Royal Oak Kimball	50.00	30.00		80.00
Plymouth		15.00		15.00
Kalamazoo	65.00	60.00		125.00
Lansing Eastern			30.00	30.00
Battle Creek	65.00	44.00		109.00
Pontiac Northern	50.00	35.00		85.00
Lansing Sexton			30.00	30.00
Jackson	50.00	27.00		77.00
Ypsilanti		30.00		30.00
6-A Meet Battle Creek				300.00
State Meet Lansing				315.00

TOTAL SWIMMING $1952.55

WRESTLING

ADMINISTRATION

1 official at $15 for 8 meets 120.00
1 official at $10 for 8 meets (j.v.) 80.00
1 ticket seller at $5 for 8 meets 40.00
2 ticket takers at $5 for 8 meets 80.00
1 announcer at $5 for 8 meets 40.00
1 scorer and timer for 8 meets at $5 .... 40.00

SUPPLIES AND EQUIPMENT

2		wrestling rule books @ 1.50	3.00
1	doz.	ear guards @ $78.00	78.00
4	doz.	knee pads @ 24.00	96.00
3	doz.	sweat tights & trunks @ 41.00	123.00
3	doz.	sweat shirts @ 25.00	75.00
24		shoe laces @ .80	2.40
13		game trunks @ 7.00	91.00
13		game shirts @ 7.00	91.00
24		game knee pads @ 2.00	48.00

TABLE 3 (Continued)

6 pr.	game shoes @4.00	24.00
24 pr.	game sox @ 24.00 per doz.	50.00
24	duffel bags @ 39.60	70.20
training room supplies		80.00
cleaning and repairs		100.00
awards		50.00
miscellaneous		15.00
SEMAWA membership fee		15.00

J.V. (3 home meets, 3 away)

Transportation	125.00
Meals	90.00
Equipment	100.00
Adrian	50.00
Bay City Handy and Central	6.00
Flint Northern	3.00
Lansing Inv.	200.00
Ypsilanti	15.00
Garden City	3.00
Ann Arbor St. Thomas	3.00
Kalamazoo	150.00
Lansing Eastern	3.00
Battle Creek	100.00
Lansing Sexton	3.00
Jackson	75.00
Thurston	3.00
Berkeley	3.00
Regionals	50.00
State	50.00
TOTAL WRESTLING	$2452.60

GYMNASTICS

ADMINISTRATION

2 judges @ $5 per judge – 4 meets	40.00

SUPPLIES AND EQUIPMENT

4 pr.	pants @ 18.50	74.00
4	shirts @ 5.00	20.00
magnesium carbonate		10.00
awards		25.00
picture		2.00
entry fees @ .50 per event		25.00
cleaning		15.00
miscellaneous		25.00
first aid		15.00

TABLE 3 *(Continued)*

MEALS AND TRANSPORTATION

	Meals	Transportation	
Jackson	15	10	25.00
Ionia	15	20	35.00
Alpena	15	25	40.00
AAU	15	15	30.00
Kalamazoo Inv.	15	15	30.00
		GYMNASTICS TOTAL	$411.00

TRACK

ADMINISTRATION

Officials 7 home meets 70.00

SUPPLIES AND EQUIPMENT

1½	doz.	sweat suits @ 5.00	90.00
35	pr.	shoes @ 4.00	140.00
½	doz.	track suits @ 9.00	54.00
1		vaulting pole	45.00
2		starting blocks	40.00
4		meet suits @ 25.00	100.00
6		ankle weights @ 5.90	35.40

shells, gun cleaner, yarn 10.00
cleaning and repairs 50.00
awards 50.00
visual aids 15.00
papers 6.00
telephone 3.00
first aid 65.00

MEALS AND TRANSPORTATION

	Meals	Transportation	
E. Michigan Relays			10.00
Cranbrook or Adrian			
Battle Creek	46.00	61.25	107.25
Kalamazoo			
Sexton	39.00	61.25	100.25
Regional			3.00
Jackson			
6A Meet – Lansing	45.00	85.00	130.00
Ypsilanti	9.00		9.00
AAU at U of M			3.00
Ablion or Waters Relays	35.00	50.00	85.00
State Meet – Lansing	22.00	20.00	42.00
		TOTAL TRACK	$1262.90

TABLE 3 (Continued)

BASEBALL

ADMINISTRATION

2 officials at $12 per game for 9 games 216.00

SUPPLIES AND EQUIPMENT

Transportation to West Park		....	75.00
2		score books	2.50
1	doz.	game pants @ 12.00	144.00
1	doz.	sweat shirts @ 2.10	24.20
1	doz.	game socks @ 3.70	44.40
½	doz.	game caps @ 2.75	16.50
6	doz.	game balls @ 25.20	151.20
4	doz.	game bats @ 33.60	134.40
12		sliding pads @ 3.25	39.00
catchers mitt		....	20.00
rosin bags		....	3.50
cleaning and repair		....	125.00
awards		....	75.00
pictures		....	3.00
newspapers		....	7.00
training room supplies		....	15.00

J.V. Expenses 200.00

MEALS AND TRANSPORTATION

	Meals	Transportation	
Ypsilanti		15.00	15.00
Adrian			75.00
Plymouth			25.00
Lansing Sexton	48.13	33.78	81.91
Lansing Eastern	48.13	33.78	81.91
Jackson	48.13	23.40	71.53
Kalamazoo	48.13	55.55	103.68

TOTAL BASEBALL $1849.73

GOLF

SUPPLIES AND EQUIPMENT

9	doz.	balls @ 12.00	108.00
awards		....	25.00
phone		....	5.00
first aid		....	10.00

MEALS AND TRANSPORTATION

	Meals	Transportation	
Sexton	11.50	30.00	43.50
Eastern	11.50	30.00	43.50
Kalamazoo	11.50	40.00	54.50
Battle Creek	11.50	36.00	47.50

TABLE 3 *(Concluded)*

Jackson	11.50	25.00	36.50
Regional	11.50	15.00	26.50
State			110.00
Pending	11.50	30.00	43.50
	TOTAL GOLF		$553.50

TENNIS

SUPPLIES AND EQUIPMENT

2	gross	tennis balls	192.00
1		garage broom	3.50
1		squeeze gee	6.50
picture			2.00
awards			30.00
cleaning			20.00
racket stringing			40.00
first aid			10.00

MEALS AND TRANSPORTATION

	Meals	Transportation	
Lansing Sexton	23.10	30.00	53.10
Kalamazoo	23.10	40.00	63.10
Battle Creek	23.10	38.00	61.10
Lansing Eastern	23.10	28.00	51.10
Jackson	23.10	14.00	37.10
Detroit Austin	23.10	14.00	37.10
Regional			50.00
State			60.00
	TOTAL TENNIS		$706.60

Questions for Study and Discussion

1. Why aren't more interscholastic athletic programs financed in their entirety by boards of education?

2. Discuss methods used in raising funds for interschool athletics. Which do you deem most desirable?

3. What are the values of using student activity or general organization tickets in financing athletic and other school activities?

4. Discuss values of a general school internal accounting plan for handling athletic and all other activity funds.

5. Why is it important that published reports be made at regular intervals of the receipt and disbursement of athletic funds? Illustrate a good procedure in this connection.

6. What are the purposes and values of athletic budgets? By whom should they be prepared?

7. Discuss the budget plan of the Ann Arbor, Michigan, High School. Do you think that a budget as detailed as this one is necessary?

Safety and Sanitation in Athletics — Accident Benefit and Protection Plans

11

Contribution to the health of participants is one of the claims frequently made for athletics. It is pointed out that regularity of habits during training seasons, eating proper foods, and exercise following an adequate training period all are health aids. No denial is intended of these claims. Certainly it is excellent from a physiological standpoint for high school students to eat, sleep, exercise, and play properly and regularly. Moreover, there is a real educational benefit in the opportunity to learn the fundamental skills of a new game. In what other manner may a boy better learn the rules of a game, its lessons in cooperation and sportsmanship, and its disciplinary implications than through the high school athletic program? The possibilities of athletics are unlimited in their opportunities to teach good habits—in health or in other ways.

The Safety Program

School people, however, in their zeal to teach the game itself, must not be guilty of overlooking some of the common things that pertain to the health of participants. Safety in athletics and improved standards in sanitation, as well as health habits, are important. Today as never before there is a health and safety consciousness among school students and adults. The athletic program provides a fine opportunity to emphasize these factors. Safety, probably more than anything else at the present time, catches the attention of the general public. Motivated largely by traffic accidents and fatalities, people are looking for safer ways of doing things. It behooves schoolmen, therefore, to set up safety programs. Many schools, state-wide organizations, and state departments of education have definite safety courses of study that are available for the asking. Athletics in any school may be made a phase of this attention that is being given to better and safer living. Be safe, sanitary, and sane in the conduct of athletics, and the program will be improved immeasurably.

A *safety program check list.* The whole school, rather than isolated parts of it, should be the unit in operation of the safety program. Someone has said that health and safety cannot be taught but that they have to be experienced. Numerous opportunities for such experiences should be provided. A suggested check on the way a safety program in a school works and its accomplishments has been prepared by the Division of Health and Physical Education, Department of Public Instruction of Delaware.

Is your safety program "clicking" or does it "bog down" in spots? Can you show tangible results because of your efforts in the promotion of safety education? These and other similar questions may logically be put to you at any time by school officials, parents, and the public. As a reminder and to enable you to promote an efficient and comprehensive safety program, emphasis, where needed, should be placed on any one or all of the following aspects of safety education:

Type of Safety	*Methods of Promotion*
1. Physical Safety	Safety patrols, leaders' corps, safety councils, student monitors, graded play areas, teach guidance, playground supervision, and equipment inspection.
2. Moral Safety	Instructional courses, i.e., home economics, biology and related sciences, hygiene, physical and health education, guidance by Dean of Girls-Boys, home room teachers, and biographies of famous people.
3. Social Safety	Selection of companions, school socials, dramatics, chaperonage, assemblies, directed interschool contests, teacher-parent-pupil contacts, and modern, attractive sanitary schools.

4. Mental Safety	Tests and measurements, periodic evaluation, decreasing or increasing assignments, supervised study, grouping (slow, medium, fast), committee work and pupil participation in appealing projects.

It will be observed from the Delaware suggestions that safety education is of broad construction in the school program and affects students through numerous agencies. Although this discussion deals primarily with activities in athletics, even within this subject itself there are many teaching and experiencing possibilities. Safety from the athletic standpoint often means only being free from accident or injury. This is only one of the points to be kept in mind. Safe planning, safe doing, safe thinking—these and many more are safety phases of athletics.

Athletics Safety Essentials

Much has been written about the inculcation of safety habits in high school students and adults by various methods. In the discussion of such possibilities in athletics, several contributing factors will be considered and an attempt made to show their importance.

The well-trained coach. There are proper and accepted methods for the teaching of all athletic activities. In order that athletics may be taught properly, the teacher should be one who is well trained and experienced in his field. Frankly, if a school cannot provide a man or woman who is properly trained to teach the sport desired, that sport should not be an activity in its athletic program. It has been stated previously that the best procedure is that of confining the coaching position to men in the physical education field. This seems desirable because, in general, such men will be better trained in fields allied with the physical activity incident to participation in athletics, and hence they should know more about human anatomy, physiology, fatigue, exercise, and body mechanics, and their relation to the sport they are teaching.

In most cases, the coach should be a man who has had actual experience in playing the game himself. This may sound like an unnecessary statement, but quite often members of faculties, in small schools especially, have to coach teams in sports in which they have had no experience. The point of emphasis about the training of the coach is that as a result of it he may be an important safety agent. The better training a coach has had, the greater is the probability that the boys under his care will receive good instruction. Generally speaking, members of better instructed teams receive injuries less frequently than do those who don't understand how to play and how to protect themselves in a sport. Obviously, this is true especially in football and basketball. A school's first contribution to a program of greater safety in athletics is insistence that its teachers in athletics and coaches be well trained in their activities.

Adequate equipment. The second safety essential in an athletic program is adequate playing equipment for the members of a team. This factor is one of first consideration for football especially. Nearly every one of us has seen a frail high school boy on some small-school football team with possibly no headgear, insufficient shoulder, hip, and thigh pads, and improper shoes. After each tackle that he made, we wondered if he would ever get up, and when he did we were impressed with the remarkable recuperative powers of the youthful body and its ability to withstand shock. In our largest colleges and universities we do not ask even the most hardy and robust members of football squads to subject themselves to such dangers as confront some of our high school football players. This is not an indictment against high school football. It is an indictment against the lack of common sense, or safety sense, on the part of some high schools concerning the type of equipment that they furnish their teams. If only improper or insufficient equipment for football is available, for safety's sake, eliminate football from the program.

In other sports commonly sponsored by high schools, the factor of playing equipment is not so important relatively as it is in football. These, theoretically, are not body-contact games; football is. It is essential, however, that proper shoes be furnished by either the school or participant, because many foot, ankle, knee, and leg injuries in all sports are traceable to faulty footwear.

Proper playing facilities. Cross-country running and golf are the only commonly sponsored high school athletic activities that do not require smooth surfaces. In cross-country the path of the course, however, must be smooth for the runners. In golf the fairways should be free from ruts. Football and soccer are supposed to be played on a smooth, grass playing area. The baseball diamond should be smooth and generally level, outfield as well as infield. Tracks and tennis courts, of course, must be smooth. Under no circumstances should football fields have stones, hard surfaces, or ruts. Keep them smooth with a good turf. Obstructions should be well back from boundary lines. Gymnasium floors should be kept clean, not allowed to become slippery, and playing areas should be free for several feet from dangerous obstructions such as posts, stoves, walls, stairways, bleachers, drinking fountains, and tables. Be safety-conscious as far as all playing facilities, both outdoor and indoor, are concerned. It is much easier to prevent an accident in athletics than it is to explain to parents that their son's misfortune was caused by someone's carelessness. All safety and sanitation precautions should be observed just as faithfully during practice sessions as during regular games, because generally there are between four or five times as many opportunities for accidents during practices as during games.

Doctors at Practices and Games—Physical Examinations. If at all possible a doctor should be present during football practice sessions and at games. This is desirable for other sports too, but is especially important for a contact sport such as football. If a doctor's presence is impossible for practice sessions one should be immediately available by being on call. Until a student has had a physical examination he should be issued no playing equipment or be allowed to practice or play in a contest. Evidence of the successful passing of a physical examination should be in the school office.

Adequate training. Strictly speaking, adequate training is a phase of athletic coaching. Good coaches always have insisted on members of their teams being in good physical condition. The necessity for state association regulations requiring minimum training periods in certain sports (see page 148) apparently came about because poor coaches in some schools were not particular about the training periods of their teams. True the normal human body possesses remarkable qualities to withstand unusual demands made of it, and its ability to recuperate from strain is almost unbelievable at times. Athletic competition, however, should not rely or call upon this reserve unnecessarily. Coaches should set up training and conditioning schedules for boys in each sport that will ensure their being in proper condition to compete. After all, training is not difficult;

it is simply getting into condition to play by means of common-sense living and intelligent hard work. The relation between injury and fatigue is more than an assumption. We know we are less able to perform normal functions when we are tired. It is only logical, then, that injuries are more apt to occur when we are fatigued. As a safety measure, therefore, it is essential that boys be in the best possible physical condition and go through an adequate training routine before they are allowed to compete in interscholastic athletic contests.

Sufficient number of reserve players. It is difficult to set definite standards as to the number of reserve players necessary for each activity. Individual capacities and abilities of boys vary, as do also the policies of different coaches in the use of reserve players. As mentioned in the previous section, there is a definite relation between fatigue and the possibility of injury. It is apparent, therefore, that there should be sufficient reserves on a squad to enable substitutes to be used when necessary from a safety standpoint as well as in consideration of the playing ability of the team. It is reasonable to assume that, in general, there should be at least two members on the squad for each position on the team. Coaches know that competition between players for team positions makes a better team. However, that result is not the purpose in making this recommendation. It is made for the good of the boy and to ensure his safety in participation. A great many schools do not attain even this minimum number of players. When this is the case, grave doubt may be raised as to the advisability of conducting the activity, especially in football, basketball, and soccer.

If a boy becomes injured, tired, has been ill, or is not in proper condition to play, he should not be in the game. His physical safety and health are endangered by competition under such circumstances. Be especially careful of boys who, after serious or prolonged illnesses, require approval from doctors before they are allowed to return to practice or competition. Athletic coaches will be raising the standards of the coaching profession and their own reputations, as well as primarily protecting the welfare of the boys entrusted to their care, if they maintain policies of frequent substitutions in athletic contests. It is an old adage that an athletic team is no stronger than its reserves. It is equally true that the best insurance against too much competition, which is likely to result in injuries or harm to a boy, is to have a sufficient number of reserves available—and then not hesitating to make substitutions.

Proper officiating. Great improvement has been made during the last few years in the standards of officiating in high school athletic contests. State athletic associations have had much to do with this through their rules-interpretation meetings and insistence that games be handled with the protection of the participant uppermost in consideration. Opinions of coaches vary as to what constitutes good officiating from a strictly rules-interpretation standpoint. Good coaches, however, usually are in agreement that an official should handle a game in football or basketball so that the physical welfare of contestants has been protected. Officials must know the game rules, be alert physically and mentally, and through their handling of the contest, keep it under control at all times. The day has gone when officials considered that they had properly discharged their duties when they had controlled a game simply by calling technical violations of the rules. While the play is in progress, the boys actually are under their care, especially in high school games. Good officials realize this, and that is an important reason why they are good officials.

Equitable competition. A safety precaution of first importance is the policy of providing as nearly equitable competition as is possible in all athletic contests. Specifically, this means that the scheduling of games between large and small teams generally is undesirable. This observation applies especially in football. Schools invite criticism if those with large squads schedule games with others not comparable in size, and vice versa, especially if injuries occur in such games. Often these contests appeal to large schools as openers. Smaller schools often are interested because of the financial guarantees. Some high schools also play college and independent teams in football, with decidedly unsatisfactory experiences. Although this criticism is not necessarily true in other sports of noncontact nature, in general it is a safe and wise procedure for a school to limit its athletic competition to other schools relatively comparable in size. It is one more safety precaution to which schools are beginning to give more attention than they did a few years ago, and the results will be justified.

Prompt reporting and attention to injuries. As in many activities in which both old and younger people engage, injuries are a part of athletic competition, especially of the body-contact type. Although every possible precaution should be taken to prevent injuries, experience shows that they do happen. When they do, the school should have a definite policy for handling them. Students should be instructed to report injuries to their coaches immediately. This requirement should be as much a part of the training regulations as the playing rules are of the sport concerned. It should be a "must" regardless of membership by a school in an athletic insurance or athletic protection or benefit plan. Participation by a school in any of these usually requires that all injuries must be reported officially within two to twenty days. In reality such a requirement is most beneficial to the student himself because he is the one who receives the necessary treatment. It also is important to him because, in most instances, his rehabilitation is more rapid when there is prompt and proper treatment that enables him to return to competition sooner. The old adage "A stitch in time saves nine" is applicable to athletic injuries.

Summary. In brief, a school may consider that its general athletic safety policy is consistent with good educational procedure if the following are considered:

1. Employment of a well-trained coach or coaches to have charge of the activities in the athletic program. Preferably, coaches should be members of the physical education staff.

2. Adequate, properly fitting equipment should be available for all players. If it cannot be provided, the activity should not be sponsored.

3. Playing facilities should meet common-sense standards. Boys should not be expected to play under conditions and with facilities admittedly unsafe or dangerous. Playing areas should be free from hazards.

4. Adequate training is a requisite for all participants. They should not be allowed to play until they are in proper physical condition. Do not allow a student to practice or participate in a contest until he has had a physical examination by a qualified physician who has approved his participation.

5. Sufficient reserve material is an essential for good teams but it is a greater safety essential. Generally, there should be at least

twice as many members on a squad as there are playing positions on the team.

6. Competent officiating is an added means by which athletic contests may be made safer activities. Engage officials who are known to be strict in their enforcement of rules devised for the protection of participants.

7. Fair and equitable competition in all athletics is a safety essential. In general, schools should limit their athletic competition to schools of comparable size. By so doing there is greater assurance that squads are more nearly equal in size, with the result that competition will be better and safer.

8. There should be insistence that all injuries be reported promptly by members of athletic squads. Frequently, an injury that appears to be inconsequential at the time it occurs later turns out to be serious. If possible, a physician should be present at all contact sport practice sessions and games. At least, one should be on call at such times. Many coaches insist that there be at least a cursory inspection of squad members following each practice session and game in order to check on minor injuries that students might have failed to report. Many serious infections as well as later injury developments may be prevented by this policy.

Safety Suggestions for Various Sports

In many instances safety suggestions are made too late. Great strides in safety education have been made in industry by making workers safety-conscious. This same policy should be followed in athletics as well as in all other phases of the school program. Contestants, as well as those administering athletic programs, have many opportunities to make safety a tangible rather than a theoretical part of athletics.

General safety suggestions. Prior to discussing a few safety suggestions that pertain to the sports more commonly sponsored in American high schools, it is well to consider the individual participant himself. There are many things he may do to further the safety program in any school. In the final analysis much of the success of any safety campaign depends upon his contribution. Schools may well keep their student bodies and athletics safety-conscious by means of safety posters, safety assemblies, and the like. The following list of personal safety habits, suggested by Lloyd, Deaver, and Eastwood some time ago still are effective and should be learned by all individuals—students and adults:

1. Never continue playing a game when fatigued.

2. Do not attempt a hazardous new skill unless under the direction of a qualified person.

3. When jumping see that the landing surface is sufficiently soft for the height of the fall and that there are no obstructions or uneven surfaces.

4. Proper personal equipment should be worn for protection at all times.

5. Refuse to play the game if the equipment is improperly erected, the floor or field is slippery, rough or has obstacles which may lead to injury.

6. When participating in an activity always keep in a position away from flying equipment, such as bats, discus, javelin, shot, etc.

7. Never enter the water unless supervisor is present.

8. See that all injuries are given immediate and adequate attention.

9. Never try any stunts beyond your range of ability.

10. Select activities which are within the range of your physical capabilities, i.e., cross-country running with an organic heart condition is dangerous.

11. Avoid partaking in activities in overcrowded space.

12. Never take advice or instruction from an unqualified person.

13. "Warming-up" before participating in strenuous activities is a wise precaution in preventing strains and sprains.

14. Demand a physical examination before entering physical education activities and a recheck before going out for any arduous sport.

15. It is desirable that those participating in sports be protected against the cost of serious injuries.[1]

In the following enumeration of safety suggestions for high school sports, it will be assumed that methods dealing with safety in each sport, as far as techniques and skill of the game itself are concerned, have been properly covered by the coach. It is part of the coach's job to instruct his players in proper safety methods in sliding, tackling, pivoting, serving, blocking, falling on the ball, and so on. Physical factors pertaining to personal and playing equipment will

---

[1] F. S. Lloyd, G. G. Deaver, and F. R. Eastwood, *Safety in Athletics* (Philadelphia: W. B. Saunders Company, 1936), pp. 215–16.

be the items of chief consideration in the suggestions offered. In all cases it is recommended that a physician be present at contests, and it is assumed that all participants have passed physical examinations.

Baseball safety suggestions. These also apply to other outdoor ball games.

1. Playing areas should be smooth and free from stones and ruts.
2. Spectators should be kept a reasonable distance from playing area.
3. Players' benches and extra equipment should be well away from the base lines.
4. Keep all substitutes seated on benches.
5. Have a first-aid kit on hand and someone who knows how to use it.
6. Be sure that catcher's protective equipment is adequate.
7. Place yard-line markers a safe distance from side lines.
8. Immediate attention by a physician should be given to all injuries and infections.
9. Practice sessions should be well supervised.
10. Be sure of proper conditioning of all players.
11. Insist that all players wear batters' helmets when at bat.

Basketball safety suggestions. Many of these suggestions will apply to volleyball, badminton, indoor tennis, and other gymnasium activities.

1. Be sure of proper conditioning of all players.
2. Practice sessions should be well supervised and of not too great length.
3. Have a smooth, clean, but not slippery, floor.
4. Posts, players' benches, scoring tables, bleachers, and the like should be removed as far as possible from playing areas.
5. Give immediate attention to all injuries and infections. Report them immediately to a physician.
6. Keep all substitutes seated on benches.
7. Have ample space at end of court between end line and bleachers or wall.
8. Have first-aid kit on hand at all games and practice sessions.

9. Allow no injured players to participate in practice or games.

10. Check on proper equipment, especially shoes.

11. Keep players warm prior to participation.

12. Make frequent substitutions and instruct teams to take allowed rest periods.

Cross-country and track safety suggestions. These are also applicable to other running activities.

1. Proper conditioning in cross-country and track is by far the most important safety consideration.

2. Be sure that contestants are thoroughly warmed up before they enter their events.

3. Limit the participation of each individual, as to number and type of events, in accordance with recommendations of best authorities on the subject.

4. Have a first-aid kit on hand at practice sessions and meets.

5. Keep spectators a safe distance away from track and field events, both at practice sessions and at meets. Remember that the discus, javelin, and shot may cause serious injury to spectators. Keep discus and javelin areas roped off and allow no one in them. (Several state high school athletic associations have eliminated the discus or javelin events, or both, from their lists of field activities largely because of danger in conducting them.)

6. Be sure that vaulting and jumping pits are so constructed that they provide a soft landing place for vaulters and jumpers. Keep them spaded constantly.

7. Give immediate attention to all injuries and infections. Report them to a physician.

Football safety suggestions. The majority of these suggestions are also applicable to soccer and touch football.

1. Use only a noninjurious substance for field marking. Lime should not be used.

2. Insist on properly fitting equipment, especially pads, helmets, and shoes.

3. Keep field in good condition—sodded, level, and free from stones.

4. Be sure that substitutes are warmed up before they enter games.

5. Keep substitutes seated on benches.

6. Keep chairs, substitutes' benches, extra equipment, and band instruments a safe distance (5 to 10 yards) from side and end lines.

7. Place yard-line markers a safe distance from side lines.

8. Use flexible-staff goal-line flags.

9. Provide sweaters or jackets for substitutes.

10. Require that helmets be worn during all scrimmages and games.

11. Insist that a fitted, flexible mouth and tooth protector, as well as an approved face guard, be worn during scrimmages and games by each player.

12. Team members should be thoroughly warmed up before the start of each half.

13. Keep spectators off the field during practice sessions.

14. Immediate medical attention should be given to all injuries and infections. Instruct players to report injuries at once.

15. Do not allow a boy who has been injured to return to practice or play until permission is received from the physician in charge of his case.

16. Remove fatigued and injured players from games.

17. Conduct well-organized and well-supervised practice sessions.

18. Check weights of squad members daily if possible.

19. Use tackling dummy instead of "live bait" in tackling practice as much as possible. Be sure that the mechanical release works properly.

Some of the regulations of the Football Committee of the Pittsburgh Public Schools which have been in effect many years are offered herewith as excellent safety guides for the start of football season in the fall:

1. No work of a hazardous nature shall be permitted any individual until he is in *proper condition;* and then only when wearing all the necessary safety equipment.

2. No rolling blocking, or blocking in the open, shall be permitted until *after* the *third* day of practice.

3. No tackling, either live or dummy, shall be permitted until *after* the *fifth* day of practice. If tackling "under punts" is given at all, it shall

be permitted only once a week and then only under the coach's personal direction.

4. No scrimmage shall be permitted until *after* the *sixth* day of practice.

5. No "falling on the ball" shall be permitted until *after* the *second week* of practice.

6. Sufficient "warming-up" exercises shall precede each day's practice, and all boys shall be *kept* "warmed-up" by a continuous and varied program during the entire period. A short, snappy practice is more beneficial and interesting than a long "hit or miss" session.

7. The scrimmaging, tackling and similar fundamentals shall be given before the "tired" or exhaustion point is reached.

8. Strict compliance with the training program (sleep, diet, rest) is absolutely essential.

9. Boys shall be encouraged to keep in good condition all summer, but discouraged from heavy work which will use up the energy they need for normal growth.[2]

Swimming safety suggestions. These apply to class as well as competitive swimming.

1. Have adequate supervision at all times.

2. Proper conditioning for speed and distance swimmers is most essential.

3. Limit entries of contestants to the minimum number of events recommended by the best authorities in the field.

4. Give proper attention to diet.

5. Do not allow swimmers to swim alone.

6. An hour to two hours should elapse between eating and swimming times.

7. Surfaces at sides and ends of pool should not be slippery.

8. Life preservers or "fish poles" should be available at all pools.

9. Bacteria counts in pools should be frequent and accurate.

10. Report all injuries immediately and refer them to a physician for medical attention.

Indiana's safety suggestions. It does not seem feasible to list additional sports activities with possible safety suggestions. Tennis

[2] Dr. Harry B. Burns and C. Lawrence Walsh, "Reducing the Number and Severity of Football Injuries," *Athletic Journal*, October, 1937, pp. 36–37.

and golf, generally, are not considered hazardous games. Comparatively few schools sponsor hockey as an interscholastic activity. In conclusion, there are listed below some general suggestions for the prevention of athletic injuries which have been formulated by the Indiana High School Athletic Association:

1. Thorough examinations of all candidates for athletics by regularly licensed and reputable physicians prior to practice periods in any sport.

2. Periodic examinations of all athletes following sickness, operations, lack of vitality, etc.

3. Elimination of all students from participation in any sport when in doubt regarding the physical fitness of the students for the sport.

4. Parental consent for all students prior to practices and games in any sport.

5. Proper and adequate equipment of the right quality for participants in all practices and games.

6. Proper training of sufficient duration prior to participation in games and strenuous practices.

7. Careful attention to the condition of play fields, tracks gymnasiums, courts and pools, together with their equipment, facilities and accommodations.

8. Good officiating in practices and games. The rules should be observed but if not they should be enforced rigidly at all times. Good officiating is not merely fair, it is efficient.

9. Insistence on fair competition. Schools often go out of their class to compete. Often the matured, the skilled, the trained, the hardened, the experienced, the well-coached boy or team is placed in competition with the boy or team having few if any of these advantages.

10. Removal of players from participation in practices and games when fatigued or injured. Some excellent coaches request the game officials to inform them when their players should be removed from the game on account of injuries or fatigue.

11. First aid service at all times. Minor injuries—cuts, bruises, infections, blisters, abrasions, boils, etc., should be given early and careful attention. Minor injuries can quickly become major ones.

12. Medical attendance at games and scrimmages. Someone has said that a limping football player has no business in the game. The physician should be able to speak with authority and his recommendation should be followed.

13. Coaching of the highest type. This does not mean "goody" or "softy" coaching but it means good coaching, rigid coaching, competent coaching. Mollycoddling is not recommended.

14. Relative sizes of squads. Numbers are not all-important but the football coach who uses 22 players, equal man to man with the 11 players of the opponent team, has a distinct advantage in many ways and in all probability will reach home with fewer injuries. The length of time in a game per player has a bearing on injuries, in all probability.

15. Warm-up periods prior to scrimmage or game entrance. A few bendings are not sufficient along this line.

16. Attention to weather conditions.

17. Proper conditioning of players. This point concerns the mental as well as the physical condition of the player and the morale condition of the whole team.

This list may look long and forbidding but injuries in athletic games are too numerous and too severe. The whole situation can be changed for the better and attention to the points given will effect desirable changes. If we cannot afford to protect—we cannot afford to play.[3]

Safety in Transportation

The subject of transportation has been discussed at length in Chapter 7. It seems advisable to consider it again, however, as an item to receive safety attention. Common carriers or school busses are recommended. In themselves they provide lessons in safety because of the unusual safety precautions of practically all drivers of such vehicles. Members of athletic teams should be cautioned regarding adherence to safety regulations and common courtesies while on the streets of cities or towns in which away-games are played. Definite discipline rules, likewise, should be in effect while en route to and from schools for games.

A problem of considerable importance is that of impressing students with the need for following safety rules in traveling to and from practice sessions. Of course this is not a problem when practice and playing fields are adjacent to the school, but in many instances they are widely separated. If students travel from the school to the practice field in private cars, insist that the number of passengers carried is not in excess of the intended capacity of the car. For violation of this regulation, suspend the offenders from the squad for a definite period. Allow no fast driving or racing from the school

[3] "Athletic Injuries," Indiana High School Athletic Association *Bulletin,* September, 1937.

to the practice field, and for any violation of this rule punish by the same penalty. Emphasize these regulations and enforce them if possible by an honor code. Insist that street parking be in accordance with city traffic regulations. Park cars in the practice field enclosure if possible. The ideal arrangement where a transportation problem of this kind exists is to use a common carrier bus to and from the school and field before and after practice sessions. Many schools follow such a procedure. Insistence on following the best-recognized safety traffic regulations in athletics is just another means of emphasizing safety throughout the entire school safety program.

The Sanitation Program

It was previously stated in this chapter that one of the purposes of interscholastic athletics is to develop health habits in participants. Lessons in sanitation also are important and certainly should become health habits. Ordinarily the athletes of a school are the finest of physical specimens. They come to coaches with almost perfect physiques. We must be sure that, when they have finished their high school athletic competition, they still are physically fine young men. They should have learned how to play; how to cooperate; how to give and take; know what it is to be a goodsportsman; and, above all, know more about how to live and take care of themselves physically. It is folly to think that an athlete will develop habits of health if these habits are not practiced by the athletic-team squad and those in charge of it. When rules of sanitation and safety are disregarded, some of the most valuable "carry-over" lessons of athletics are lost.

Experience in sanitation. Probably all of us have shuddered on seeing at athletic contests things which flaunted all the common-sense rules of health and sanitation. We have seen the single lemon that all the boys used, supposedly to quench their thirst. What about the common towel that all the members of the team used to wipe perspiration from their faces? Surely we remember how the towel went sliding across the floor and then was used to wipe everyone's face and neck. Then there was the common water bucket with its dipper or sponge that everybody used. Often, after the game was over, several boys used the same towel following the shower. Sometimes this towel was not laundered for several weeks. On occasions it was necessary (we thought) to exchange between team members items of personal playing equipment, such as socks, shirts, jerseys, and helmets, without sterilizing them, not to mention washing them.

There were times when cuts, infections, sprains, and bruises were laughed off and not reported because it was thought that an athlete should be able to take it. All these practices and probably many more could be cited. But suffice it to say that we do not want these to remain in the experiences of participants as some of the things they learned in high school athletics. They should remember that at times, the coach, director, or trainer seemed overscrupulous in his enforcement of safety, sanitary, and cleanliness regulations that the physical welfare of the boys on the team meant more to him and to the school than did all of the possible victories during a season.

Of course, no one willfully intends to be negligent in matters of sanitation in athletics. It just happens and sometimes a check-up is needed in order to take stock of one's methods.

A sanitation self-analysis. A self-evaluating check on practical sanitation in high school athletics, part of which is listed herewith, has been prepared by C. O. Jackson of the University of Illinois. How would your school stand?

1. Are medical examinations for varsity athletes required seasonally? .... After illness? ....

2. Do varsity athletes receive some protective, or nutritive food, such as cod-liver oil, orange juice, hot chocolate, or milk after each practice? ....

3. Is a sanitary type of floor finish used in your gymnasium? ....

4. Is it cleaned daily? .... By accepted sanitary standards? ....

5. Are locker and shower rooms cleaned and disinfected daily? ....

6. Are toilets and urinals cleaned and disinfected daily? ....

7. Do you provide sanitary drinking facilities in your gymnasium? ....

8. Do you furnish personal athletic equipment (socks, supporters, jerseys)? .... Are these cleaned adequately each week? ....

9. Do you clean gym mats frequently, using approved sanitary methods? .... Are flannel mat covers cleaned frequently? ....

10. Do you furnish clean towels daily for your athletes? . . . .
Are these laundered by accepted sanitary standards? . . . .

Can you conscientiously and whole-heartedly answer "Yes" to every question? Now, can you give a loud and emphatic "No" to the next two?

1. Do you approve of such practices as:

(*a*) Exchanging personal equipment (sweat clothing, practice jerseys, socks, supporters, or helmets)? . . . .

(*b*) Sharing a common water bottle, sponge, or towel? . . . .

(*c*) Sucking a common lemon or orange? . . . .

(*d*) Spitting on the floor or behind wall pads? . . . .

2. Has any epidemic of boils, colds, sore throat, or athlete's foot occurred among your teams during the past two years? . . . .

If you were able to answer all the questions as suggested, you are to be congratulated for giving the students of your school a real opportunity to participate in sports under clean and healthful conditions. If you have skipped certain items because they worried you, or because you couldn't answer them honestly, perhaps the time has come to study your entire athletic set-up and policies. Certainly any "BILL OF RIGHTS" in athletics should include first of all, definite attention to the health and safety of participants, and secondly, just as close attention to their surroundings, and their equipment.[4]

It is said that "confession is good for the soul." If a school's athletic policy does not require practically all the approved practices advocated in the first set of questions prepared by Jackson, there is something wrong with it. If so, straighten it out, and make the next season the latest time for starting things anew.

Sanitation suggestions. In addition to physical examinations, which it is assumed that all students have had prior to athletic competition, there are numerous other health and sanitation regulations that are imperative. The safety suggestions recommended for various sports [5] in many respects also dealt with health and sanitation. Primarily, however, they were offered as ways of avoiding excessive accident incidents in athletics. Included herewith are several common axioms for health and sanitation as they apply to the average high school athletic program:

[4] C. O. Jackson, "Practical Sanitation in High School Athletics," Illinois High School *Athlete*, December, 1936, pp. 50–51.
[5] See pp. 295–302.

1. Insist on properly fitting equipment. It lessens the chance of infection by irritation from loose or tight apparel.

2. Sterilize personal equipment prior to any interchange between players.

3. Provide sanitary drinking facilities. Use individual half-pint pop or milk bottles or paper cups on the field, and a fountain in the gymnasium.

4. Always have a first-aid kit on hand.

5. Keep personal equipment aired and dry between practice sessions.

6. Be sure players are cooled off and have thoroughly dried themselves before leaving locker rooms.

7. Inspect shoes regularly for nails and breaks that might cause infection.

8. Inspect showers frequently and keep them adjusted so that the possibilities of scalding and hot-water burns are reduced to a minimum.

9. Insist on the use of individual towels.

10. Provide or insist upon clean, dry towels every day.

11. Provide a separate towel for each team member for use at time-outs or between halves of contests. Hand it to him or provide a sanitary receptacle for it. Don't allow it to touch the ground or floor.

12. Permit no exchange between players of personal equipment without coach's permission, penalty to be dismissal from squad.

13. Provide proper facilities in gymnasium for spitting.

14. Insist on a warm shower being followed by a cold one.

15. Keep players off wet ground between halves of football or soccer games.

16. Provide side-line sweaters or jackets for substitutes on rainy, cold days and during outdoor night contests.

17. Inspect players regularly for infections or injuries.

18. Insist that injuries, no matter how slight, be reported immediately after they are received.

19. Clean lockers, showers, and toilets frequently and scientifically.

20. Be sure that taping and bandaging are done correctly.

21. Do not allow ill or injured players to participate in practice or games.

22. Check weights of squad members frequently.

23. Launder uniforms and sweat clothes frequently.

24. Provide foot baths or other accepted treatment for the prevention of athlete's foot.

25. Provide a lemon or orange for each member of the squad.

26. Keep locker and gymnasium floors scientifically clean.

Medical Supervision of Athletics

Schools are treading on dangerous ground indeed if they have not made adequate preparation for medical supervision in connection with their athletic and physical education programs. This statement does not mean, necessarily, that a full-time school physician is required before an athletic program is launched. Rather, it implies that a qualified, licensed physician should be accessible in case of serious injuries. Likewise, he should be available for treatment of the less severe injuries that are incident to athletic competition and physical education.

Methods in effect. Nothing should be construed from any of the suggestions already mentioned that they are to take the place of adequate medical supervision of athletics. There are hazards in virtually everything we do. Participation in athletics, of course, is not an exception. The advantage that athletics offer is the ability to make some preparation for them before they occur. It should be a rule of first importance that arrangements for medical attention be available for all athletic practice and competition; that is, provision should be made for at least first-aid or emergency treatment in case of accident. Policies of schools vary in this particular. Boards of education in some states employ school physicians who are assigned to athletic teams, both for practice sessions and games. In certain instances school nurses also are available. In some schools the athletic association or athletic department of the high school employs a physician who takes care of all physical examinations of athletes and injuries. The school athletic association usually pays the physician a flat fee for his work plus the cost of medical supplies and hospitalization in such an arrangement. Other school systems operate on the theory that the physician of the student's family should take complete care of any injuries he may receive. This does not mean that first-aid and emergency treatment should not be given an injured boy at the direction of the school athletic authorities. Any professional services, however, should be at the expense and direction of the student's family.

Still another arrangement is that whereby the physician is a volunteer as far as his services are concerned. This plan is quite common, especially in small schools. Probably arrangements are not complete in many cases and are not ideal, but they exist because school athletic departments do not have the money to employ physicians at regular fees. Many state courts have decreed that public tax money raised for educational purposes may not be spent to defray cost of athletic or other school activity injuries. In hundreds of high schools throughout the nation public-spirited and interested physicians have given freely of their time and services in order that there might be at least a minimum of medical supervision of athletic programs. Without discounting the well-intentioned and much-appreciated philanthropies of such physicians, it may be pointed out that their services do provide them opportunities for contacts that would be impossible for them to make in any other way. High school students are members of families, all of whom need medical attention. In a few years after their graduation a majority of the boys on athletic teams will marry and have families of their own. Experiences of physicians indicate that many of these boys later employ them as their family physicians. Hence such voluntary service may be considered as a long-range type of professional advertising. On the following pages is a complete discussion of athletic injury benefit and injury insurance plans provided for athletes in many states. Fees received from such plans are used to aid in defraying the cost of care of injuries. Since 1930 the formation of athletic accident benefit and protection plans operated by state associations, or through cooperative arrangements by them with commercial insurance companies, has been a major development in about three-fourths of the states.

Place of coach and trainer. Neither of these individuals should consider themselves doctors. Without exception, diagnosis and medical treatment should be referred to a competent physician. First-aid treatments should be exactly what the name implies and nothing more. The so-called trainer in many high schools often is a student manager or an ex-athlete, and his functions should be those in keeping with his experience. The coach, who should have had training in first-aid work, should direct any bandaging, taping, or emergency treatments administered to team members. The word of the physician in charge of an injured player, not the judgment of the coach as to how badly he thinks he needs the player for a certain game, should shape the absolute and final decision in determining whether a player may compete. The use of faculty trainers is advocated.

Athletic Accident Benefit and Protection Plans

From the beginning in 1930, when the first athletic accident benefit plan was established in Wisconsin, there has been a steady growth of interest by states in such benefit or protection plans. In this chapter there are presented typical data from the operation of benefit plans in three selected states.

General consideration. There are differences of opinion among various state athletic associations as to the advisability of state-wide plans for covering the expense of athletic injuries. Local schools in some states apparently are not interested because of the existence of their own plans for handling injuries, which are satisfactory to them. Some state athletic associations feel that they should not get into the insurance business and that their energies and funds should be directed toward prevention of athletic injuries rather than paying for them after they occur. Schools hesitate to place themselves in the position of appearing to assume responsibility for injuries sustained by high school students who are participating voluntarily in an athletic activity. In many other cases state associations and schools have not been in a financial position to guarantee payment for athletic injuries.

On the other hand, over three-fourths of the states belonging to the National Federation of State High School Athletic Associations now have, or have had, some form of athletic accident benefit or protection plans in effect. Some states, although not having plans of their own, have made data available to their member schools concerning reliable commercial insurance companies that are interested in offering athletic-injury coverage. Other states have waged campaigns for greater protection and safety in conducting the athletic program. State associations that have benefit or protection plans in effect point to the fact that they are for the actual benefit of the injured player and are not theoretical matters. They, too, feel that safety campaigns should be waged, but they also consider that the major interest should be for the boy or girl who has been injured in a game conducted by a school included in their membership.

Athletic-injury data. Regardless of personal or professional opinions regarding athletic insurance plans, their administration has been a valuable method by which data on athletic injuries have been obtained. Prior to 1930, information on the subject was apt to be guesswork. Under the direction of the late Paul F. Neverman, former Executive Secretary, the early data collected by Wisconsin, followed closely by New York and scattered information in other states, has presented valuable statistics for study. Classifications of injuries have been made which have aided materially in the construction of equipment as well as changes in playing rules that have made games safer.

The data also may be a basis for serious consideration as to the advisability of sponsoring some of the present high school athletic activities because of their high incidence of injuries. Football, of course, is the most hazardous interscholastic sport. It is bound to be because of the nature of the game. Statistics concerning the incidence of injuries in various athletic activities have been collected by practically all states operating benefit or protection plans. As an indication of some of the information obtained in this connection that from Wisconsin covers the longest period. For the 1958-1959 school year reports of injuries for which claims were paid in Wisconsin indicate the following percentages: [6]

Football	60.6%
Basketball	18.5%
Physical education	1.5%
Wrestling	6.4%
Track	5.7%
Other sports	7.3%

During the above school year in Wisconsin there were 38,788 students covered for athletics and 6,566 claims were paid for a total $171,377.04. This represents claim payments for approximately 16 per cent of all registered students in athletics during this period.

[6] Wisconsin Interscholastic Athletic Association, *Thirty-Seventh Book* (1960), p. 214.

Minnesota breaks down its injury payments from 1937 to 1960 as follows: [7]

Baseball	4.0%
Basketball	21.0%
Football	59.0%
Hockey	3.1%
Physical education	4.0%
Swimming	0.2%
Track	3.4%
Wrestling	4.2%
Other	0.7%

In the twenty-three year period covered in Minnesota there was a total of 515,649 student registrations and 98,279 claims allowed. Payments amounted to $1,236,140.55. The percentage of allowed injury claims to number of registered students was approximately 19 per cent.

Michigan has compiled the following information from twenty years' experience of benefit plan operation: [8]

Football	68.8%
Basketball	13.2%
Physical education and intramurals	6.2%
Baseball	4.1%
Track and cross country	3.9%
Swimming	0.4%
Wrestling	3.0%
Others	0.4%

During these twenty years' existence of the benefit plan in Michigan, 672,503 students were registered and 60,263 claims were paid for a total of $1,198,294.12 Thus the ratio of injury payments to student registration was approximately 9 per cent.

The experiences in these three states may be taken as fairly typical of those in others. It should be pointed out, however, that variations of percentage ratios in different states are caused by different schedules on which payments are allowed. One state may allow a

[7] Minnesota State High School League, 1960 *Official Handbook*, p. 97.
[8] Michigan High School Athletic Association *Bulletin*, October 1960, p. 124.

claim for a reported injury that might not be paid in another; thus its percentage of injuries would appear considerably higher than that in other states.

As an indication of the spread of types of injuries received during the 1959–1960 school year in athletic competition, the reports of Wisconsin and Michigan are included. They represent different methods of tabulating this information.

The figures included in the Wisconsin and Michigan reports may appear to be staggering, but it must be kept in mind that they represent a relatively small percentage of injuries for the 62,654 boys participating. Thus, strictly from a percentage standpoint, the percentage of claims paid, including negative X-ray reports, in relation to the number of players was not alarmingly large, being approximately 15 per cent.

Purposes of athletic benefit and protection plans. Much has been said about athletic accident benefit and protection plans and the role they are playing in athletic safety. Their development is undoubtedly in keeping with the philosophy of the times, that group provision should be made for the mishaps and eventual infirmities of individuals. Social Security, retirement plans, group hospitalization, and insurance are examples of this trend. Probably the development of benefit and protection plans on the part of state athletic and activity associations during the past thirty years will be remembered as one of their greatest contributions to high school athletics. These plans represent an intelligent approach to, and attempt at solution of, the injury problem that is always present in athletic contests.

As was said previously, practically all of the National Federation states at sometime have operated some form of benefit or protection plans. It is of interest to inquire into the reasons why these state associations have seen fit to take on this added job. California begins its articles of incorporation as follows:

KNOW ALL MEN BY THESE PRESENTS:

Article I

That the name of this corporation shall be "The California Interscholastic Federation Protection Fund."

Table 4

Summary of Athletic Injuries Reported in Wisconsin, 1958–1959 and 1959–1960 [9]

	1958-59 Final Athletic	1959-60 (June 30-60) Athletic
Abrasions	42	57
Concussions	60	57
Dental	566	426
Lacerations	474	470
Medical Attendance	2,454	2,221
Sprains	1,871	1,918
Loss of Life	—	—
Fractures		
Ankle	51	36
Clavicle	73	78
Coccyx	—	
Elbow	13	7
Femur	11	6
Finger	166	136
Foot	46	40
Hand	68	59
Hip	4	1
Humerus	17	21
Jaw	9	9
Knee	7	4
Nose	123	93
Radius/Ulna	76	62
Rib	50	52
Scapula	10	5
Skull	1	2
Spine	—	11
Sternum	—	1
Tibia/Fibula	105	88
Toe	22	19
Transverse Process	—	6
Wrist	29	32
Dislocations		
Ankle	3	1
Arm	—	1
Coccyx	—	—
Elbow	12	10
Finger	40	45
Foot	1	—
Hand	4	
Hip	1	3
Jaw	1	1
Knee	9	10
Nose	2	—
Rib	2	1
Semilunar Cartilage	55	38
Shoulder	66	55
Spine	18	2
Toe	3	2
Wrist	1	3
TOTAL	6,566	6,089

[9] Wisconsin Interscholastic Athletic Association, *Thirty-Seventh Year Book,* p. 218.

Table 5

Summary of Benefit-Plan Injury Aims Allowed in Michigan, 1959–1960 [10]

MEDICAL INJURIES *Total Claims, 3,228	Foot-ball	Basket-ball	Base-ball	Physical Educa-tion and Intra-murals	Track and C oss Country	Wres-tling	*TOTAL ALL SPORTS
ARM—both bones fractured between wrist and elbow	22	2		5(1)	3	1	33(1)
ARM—fractured above elbow	16	1			2	1	20
ARM—either bone fractured between wrist and elbow	49(6)	3	2	5(2)	6	3	*69(8)
ARTERY—operation for ligating							
BONE OPERATION—injured portion removed	(2)	(1)				1	1(3)
CHEEK BONE—fractured	1	2	1				4
COLLAR BONE—fractured	41			4	1		46
CONCUSSION—cerebral	48(12)	7	2	(1)		1(2)	58(15)
COMPLETE DISLOCATIONS (15 day disability) (a) Hip							
(b) Knee	4						4
(c) Shoulder	16(4)	1(1)	1	1			19(5)
(d) Acromio-Clavicular	9(1)	1			(1)	1	11(2)
(e) Ankle		(1)		1(1)			1(2)
(f) Elbow	5(3)	1				1(2)	7(5)
(g) Wrist	2(1)						2(1)
EYE—all injuries	13(1)	4	(1)	2		2	21(2)
FOOT—fractured bone (x-ray plate made)	31(5)	15(2)	2	7(1)	1	2	58(8)
FOOT—fractured bone (no x-ray plate made)	1						1
HAND—fractured bone (x-ray plate made)	119(8)	19	4	18	3	5(1)	*171(9)
HAND—fractured bone (no x-ray plate made)	3			1			4
HOSPITALIZATION	169(389)	23(56)	11(23)	20(27)	12(17)	10(11)	*250(525)
JAW—fractured	3		1(2)				4(2)
KIDNEY—ruptured, positive blood in urine	7						7
KNEE—injured and requiring surgery	59(9)	10(1)	6	4	1(1)	2	82(11)
KNEE CAP—fractured	1						1
KNEE—fracture or injury to semi-lunar cartilage	19(3)		1				20(3)
LACERATION—sutures	207(18)	68(6)	26(5)	22(6)	33(3)	10(2)	*375(43)
LEG—both bones fractured between ankle and knee	13(2)		1				14(2)
LEG—fractured above knee and in cast	13(1)	1					14(1)

[10] Michigan High School Athletic Association *Bulletin*, pp. 137–39. Numbers in parentheses indicate that the major portion of such claims were paid under another schedule.

Table 5 (*continued*)

MEDICAL INJURIES *Total Claims, 3,228	Foot-ball	Basket-ball	Base-ball	Physical Educa-tion and Intra-murals	Track and Cross Country	Wres-tling	*TOTAL ALL SPORTS
LEG—either bone fractured between ankle and knee	67(4)	7(2)	5(2)	8(2)	3		90(10)
NOSE—fractured	66(7)	9(2)	8(1)	3(2)		(1)	86(13)
PELVIS—fractured							
RIBS—fractured							
(a) One	22(1)			1		1	24(1)
(b) Two or more	4			1			5
SCAPULA—fractured	2						2
SKULL—fractured	(1)						(1)
SKULL—fractured, with cerebral hemorrhage							
STERNUM—fractured	1	1					2
TENDON—separated from bone	1(1)			(1)			1(2)
VERTEBRA—fractured	9(1)						9(1)
X-RAY—to determine fracture or dislocation							
(a) Skull, spine, pelvis	130(24)	21(2)	8(1)	13(1)	10(2)	10(1)	192(31)
(b) Hand	165(18)	24(2)	8(2)	15(1)	5	9	226(23)
(c) Others	897(87)	185(7)	50(5)	65(6)	59(3)	34(2)	*1,294(111)
DENTAL INJURIES *Total Claims, 375							
Fracture of enamel not requiring restoration	6(1)	1		3(1)		2	12(2)
Broken facing	5(2)	2		2		1	10(2)
Replacing loosened or displaced restoration	26(3)	9(2)		3		2	40(5)
Loss of one tooth	17	5	3	3	1	2	31
One fractured tooth	113(4)	36(1)	4	12(1)	1	3	*170(6)
Small restoration		2	2				4
Maximum dental injury involving more than 1 tooth	79(3)	16	2	5(1)	1(1)	4	*108(5)

315

Table 5 (*concluded*)

SPECIAL ALLOWANCE ADMINISTRATIVE COMMITTEE	Football	Basketball	Baseball	Physical Education and Intramurals	Track and Cross Country	Wrestling	*TOTAL ALL SPORTS
Non-Scheduled or prolonged treatment injuries allowed by Administrative Committee Total 4 (102)	4(69)	(9)	(8)	(7)	(3)	(6)	4(102)
ARM—fractured (surgery)	(4)	(1)		(1)	(1)	(1)	(8)
BLOOD—poisoning	(1)						(1)
BLOOD VESSEL—surgery	1						1
CHEEKBONE—fractured (surgery)	(1)						(1)
COLLARBONE—fractured (surgery)	(2)						(2)
CONCUSSION—prolonged treatment		(1)					(1)
DISLOCATIONS—surgery	(3)						(3)
ELBOW—bursitis (surgery)	1						1
FINGER—infection (surgery)	1						1
FOOT—fractured (surgery)	(2)						(2)
GROIN—prolonged treatment				(1)			(1)
HAND—fractured (surgery)	(3)					(1)	(4)
HERNIA—surgery				(1)			(1)
JAW—fractured (surgery)	(1)		(2)				(3)
KIDNEY—ruptured (surgery)	(1)						(1)
KNEE—surgery	(35)	(5)	(4)	(3)		(1)	(48)
LACERATIONS—surgery	(4)	(1)	(1)		(1)	(2)	(9)
LEG—fractured (surgery)	(7)	(1)					(8)
NOSE—fractured (surgery)	(2)		(1)	(1)			(4)
SHOULDER—dislocation (surgery)					(1)		(1)
SHOULDER—bursitis (prolonged treatment)						(1)	(1)
SPLEEN—ruptured (surgery)	(3)						(3)
MAXIMUM ALLOWANCE	1						1

INJURY SUMMARY	Football	Basketball	Baseball	Physical Education and Intramurals	Track and Cross Country	Wrestling	*TOTAL ALL SPORTS
Total Number Allowed Claims	2,485(691)	476(95)	148(50)	224(62)	142(31)	108(28)	3,607(963)
Percentage of All Allowed Claims	68.8%	13.2%	4.1%	6.2%	3.9%	3.0%	**100%

*NOTE (1) Totals include 24 paid claims in sports listed below:
Golf.......... 2 allowed claims—Total $ 20.00—Average payment $10.00
Skiing......... 2 allowed claims—Total $ 44.00—Average payment $22.00
Softball....... 2 allowed claims—Total $ 33.50—Average payment $16.75
Swimming..... 13 allowed claims—Total $124.50—Average payment $ 9.57
Tennis........ 5 allowed claims—Total $ 65.40—Average payment $13.08

NOTE (2) Numbers in parentheses ( ) indicate that the major portions of such claims were paid under another schedule.

**NOTE (3) Includes injuries which occurred in Golf, Skiing, Softball, Swimming, Tennis. (.8% of total number of injuries in all sports.)

Article II

This corporation is a relief and benefit association formed by officers of public schools, the privileges of which and application for membership in which are confined to pupils in the public schools.

Article III

This is a corporation which does not contemplate pecuniary gain or profit to the members thereof.

Article IV

The purpose for which this corporation is formed are:

1. To provide for pupils of the public schools who are members of this corporation such benefits and relief, in whole or in part, as may properly be given under the laws of the State of California by a benefit and relief association formed by public schools or officers of public schools, the privileges of which are and applications for membership in which are confined to pupils of the public schools.

2. To possess and exercise all powers now or hereafter conferred by the laws of the State of California upon a non-profit corporation organized under the provisions of Article I, Title XII, Part IV, Division I of the Civil Code of the State of California.[11]

Note that the California Interscholastic Federation Athletic Protection Fund is a corporation engaging in the insurance business in that state. Iowa and New York are organized likewise, the former being called the Iowa High School Insurance Company and the latter the New York State High School Athletic Protection Plan, Inc. In California and New York the schedules of benefits in effect under the state employees' compensation laws obtain for their protection plans. In Iowa schedule of benefits established by the insurance company is operative.

Minnesota states the purpose of its Athletic Accident Benefit Plan as follows:

The Minnesota State High School League—a voluntary organization made up of state high schools—through its Representative Assembly composed of delegates from the thirty-two (32) athletic districts adopted the

[11] California Interscholastic Federation Athletic Protection Fund, *Articles of Incorporation and By-Laws* (1959), p. 6.

following amendment to its Constitution and By-Laws at its annual meeting, March 19, 1937.

"It (the Board of Control) shall establish and maintain a mutual benefit plan for the schools of the Minnesota State High School League; said plan to provide benefit for certain injuries or other contingencies resulting from athletic activities sponsored by the Minnesota State High School League."

"The 1960 Representative Assembly provided that public Junior High Schools in cities of the first class could enroll; providing all eligible high schools, a part of the city school system, are members of the League."

SECTION 2. *Description and Limitation of Plan.* The Athletic Accident Benefit Plan provides *financial assistance* to meet the cost of medical, dental and hospital services rendered as a result of accidental injuries incurred in *supervised high school athletic activities.*

The Plan provides *limited coverage only.*

The allowances will not in many cases provide complete coverage for all services rendered. All charges in excess of the maximums listed in the published schedules are the obligation of the pupil and his parents.

The Plan is not insurance and should not be so construed. It is a benefit plan which provides liberal financial assistance for the fee charged.

Acceptance of membership in the Athletic Plan by any member school does not imply or create any obligation or liability for accidental injuries incurred while pupils are engaged in athletic participation or practice under the direction of the school.

The Board of Control of the Minnesota State High School League is the administrative board for this benefit fund.

The Athletic Accident Benefit Plan covers both boys and girls in all athletic activities sponsored by the Minnesota State High School League.[12]

New York's Protection Plan purpose is stated:

To furnish medical and dental expense indemnity under the supervision of the New York State Public High School Athletic Association to bona fide students in elementary and high schools injured in intramural and interscholastic athletic games and sports activities, or while engaged in preparation for such games, sports, or contests, or in physical education classes, or in any other accidents which in the judgment of the Superintendent of Insurance, should be included; however, the dental expense indemnity applies only in cases of dental expense caused by injury oc-

[12] Minnesota State High School League, 1960 *Handbook,* p. 72.

curring in intramural and interscholastic games and sports activities, while engaged in preparation for such games, sports, or contests, or in physical education classes. The plan shall be open to the participation of every duly licensed physician and dentist in the territory to be served and there shall be free choice by subscribers of physicians and dentists admitted to such plan, subject to the acceptance of patients by the physicians and dentists.

To do all and everything necessary and proper for the accomplishment of any or all of the objects herein enumerated or necessary or incidental thereto or to the protection and benefit of the corporation and in general to carry on any lawful business or understanding necessary to the attainment of the purposes of the corporation, subject, however, to all the provisions of the Insurance Law of the State of New York.[13]

In Wisconsin, as in several other states, the Athletic Accident Benefit Plan is an integral part of the state association itself. Although the purpose of the plan is not specifically stated in the association's regulations, it is included in the constitution of the Wisconsin Interscholastic Athletic Association under its "general welfare" clause.

As indicated previously, Wisconsin has been the "father" of state association-operated benefit and protection plans in atheltics. With the exception of those states using workmen's compensation codes, most benefit schedules today, both in state and in commercial insurance company policies, are based upon or are modifications of the Wisconsin schedules. Data compiled in that state since 1930 have been the basis for a large amount of the information now available concerning high school athletic injuries. The extent to which other states have established benefit and protection plans is indicative of their value and is a tribute to the pioneer work done in this field by the late Secretary Paul F. Neverman.

As a concluding example of a statement of the purposes of benefit or protection plans for those taking part in athletics and physical education, that given by the Michigan High School Athletic Association follows:

The purpose of the Athletic Accident Benefit Plan is to assist member high schools having physical education, intramural, or interscholastic

---

[13] New York State Public High School Association, 1960–1961 *Handbook*, p. 53.

WIAA ACCIDENT BENEFIT PLAN

FOR 1960-1961

ATHLETIC COVERAGE

of the

Scheduled Program

This is an Athletic Accident Plan featuring protection:

1. for any boy of a member school who is physically fit.
2. for every injury occurring while practicing for or participating in interscholastic athletics.
3. enrollment on School Group or Individual basis.
   Individual Rates:

	Grades 9-12	Grades 7-8
a. All sports coverage	$6.00	$5.00
b. All sports excepting football	$2.00	$1.50

4. effective when the Physical Examination and Permit Card is postmarked in the mail with the fee.
5. on a scheduled or limited basis.

SCHEDULED BENEFIT PROGRAM

Objective

The purpose of this Program is to assist in meeting the costs of medical and hospital care necessitated by accidental injuries which result from participation in school sponsored activities. Benefits are on a scheduled indemnity basis and may not meet the full cost of medical and hospital care.

No Health Coverage

This Program does not provide Health Coverage and no payments can be made for treatment which is not the direct result of an accident.

Definitions

For the purpose of this Program, the following definitions will be used:
1. PLAN shall mean the WIAA Accident Benefit Plan.
2. PROGRAM shall mean the Scheduled Program.
3. STUDENT shall mean a pupil who is entitled to benefits under this Program.
4. INTERSCHOLASTIC ATHLETICS shall mean scheduled sports competition between schools. (Even when schools are part of same school system).
   a. Competition within a school is intramural.
   b. No sports activity below the 7th grade shall be considered interscholastic.
5. MEDICAL EXPENSE INSURANCE shall mean coverage by others under which benefits are payable to the student for an injury which is also covered under this Program.
   a. This will include personal accident and health policies, medical payment plans, etc.

Fig. 10-6. W.I.A.A. Accident Benefit Plan—Scheduled Program, 1960-1961, Wisconsin Interscholastic Athletic Association, *Parents Information Folder*, pp. 1-6.

    b. **Third party liability insurance** shall not be considered medical expense insurance for the purpose of this Program.

6. Part II and Part III refer to the Athletic Sections of the Scheduled Benefit Program.

PART II — ALL·SPORTS COVERAGE

Includes Interscholastic Football

Part II will provide coverage on a scheduled basis for accidental injuries sustained by a student in practice for, or participation in, interscholastic athletics.

This coverage is available on a school group or individual basis.

Coverage

Subject to the provisions and limitations of the Program, benefits are provided according to the Schedule of Allowances for covered students for necessary and incurred medical, dental, or hospital service resulting directly from accidental bodily sustained while practicing for, or participating in, interscholastic athletics.

The period of coverage shall be from the date of enrollment and shall terminate on the last day of attendance. In case a season's sport schedule extends beyond the school year, athletic coverage will be extended until the schedule is completed. School sponsored summer activities are not covered.

A student will be covered under Part II of this Plan only when he is participating under the direct control and supervision of his school in the sports that are approved for him on his **Physical Examination and Permit Card.**

    a. Coverage will be effective from the time he reports for practice or contest until dismissed by his coach.

    b. Students may enroll on an individual basis for purposes of physical education and intramurals.

PART III — LIMITED SPORTS COVERAGE

Excludes Interscholastic Football

Subject to the provisions and limitations of this Program, Part III will provide coverage on a scheduled basis for accidental injuries sustained by a student in practice for, or participation in, interscholastic athletics — excepting interscholastic football.

This coverage is available on a school group or individual student basis. For the purpose of Part III the provisions of Part II shall apply except that in no case shall the term "interscholastic athletics" be interpreted to include interscholastic football.

GENERAL PROVISIONS

The following provisions shall apply except where specifically noted.

Benefit Allowances and Limitations of Liability

If a student sustains an accidental injury covered by this Program, the Plan will pay according to the Schedule of Allowances for necessary expenses incurred for treatment by a legally qualified physician or surgeon, dental treatment for natural or restored teeth; and hospital services (excepting that for injury to one or more sound natural or restored teeth the payment shall not exceed $90); and provided that such expense begins within 3 weeks of the date of accident and is incurred within 52 weeks from the date of accident.

The preceding paragraph shall be subject to the following provisions and limitations:

1. If the necessary and incurred **expenses** of a covered student shall exceed **$100,** and if all or part of such expense is covered by valid and collectible medical expense insurance, then the Plan will pay up to the maximum in the Schedule of Allowances, except that in no event shall the combined payments (insurance and Scheduled Allowance under this Program) exceed the actual charges by more than $50;

Fig. 10-6. cont.

321

2. And provided further that if the total expense incurred for necessary medical care shall exceed the combined payments by more than $100 the Plan will pay an additional amount (in excess of said $100) equal to the remaining balance of expenses or a maximum total payment of $500 by the Plan, whichever is the least;

3. And provided further, that should the student by reason of a covered injury sustain one of the following specific total losses within 52-weeks from the date of accident, the Plan will pay in lieu of all other allowances:

Life	$500
Entire sight, one eye	$200
Partial loss of sight, one eye	$100

4. And provided further the maximum aggregate liability of the Plan on account of all injuries and deaths sustained in and arising out of any one accident shall not exceed $5,000.
    a. In case the aggregate loss sustained by covered students shall exceed $5,000, the $5,000 shall be prorated among the several persons entitled to it.
    b. The aggregate loss of covered students shall be the sum of benefits payable under this Plan, including any payments made by the Plan under items 1, 2, or 3 above.

Exclusions

1. Coverage will not apply to injuries sustained while:
    a. Going between home and school.
    b. Participating in any activity which is not under the direct control and supervision of his school, or other properly designated individuals.
    c. Participation in a school sponsored summer sports schedule.

2. The Plan will not provide benefits for:
    a. The following items:

Ambulance services	Orthodontic appliances
Athlete's Foot	Orthopedic appliances
Boils	Prescriptions
Eyeglasses and	Recurrent dislocations
their prescriptions	Skin infections
Hernias	

    b. More than eight (8) Physical Therapy treatments for any one injury. This shall include Manipulative Therapy. (Limitations imposed by Schedule of Allowances applicable.)
    c. Injuries resulting from epilepsy, fits, convulsions, diabetes, or any congenital weakness, constitutional disease and pre-existent conditions, if any of the same contribute to produce such injury.
    d. Loss caused by or as the result of bacterial infection or any other kind of disease, or medical or surgical treatment of it, (except pyogenic infections caused by accidental injury otherwise covered under this Program.)
    e. Injuries resulting from war, insurrection, or riot.

GENERAL REGULATIONS

A. The following regulations must be followed by the school:
    1. Written notice of injury to a student must be received in the Plan's Administrative Office postmarked within 21 days after the date of accidental injury.
    2. Payments for Benefit Requests will be authorized only when the medical and surgical aid is rendered by a licensed physician, that is, a doctor of medicine and surgery or a doctor of osteopathy and surgery.
    3. First treatment must be given within 21 days to qualify a request for benefits.
    4. Upon receiving a notice of injury the Plan will furnish the necessary forms for completing the Benefit Request.
    5. Benefit requests not completed within ninety (90) days of date of injury will be withdrawn and reconsidered only when approved by the Executive Committee. Payment will be authorized only for claims completed and filed in the Plan's Administrative Office within one year from the date of injury.

Fig. 10-6. cont.

6. Benefit payment for the loss of life of a covered student is payable to the parent or parents with whom the child is living or in their absence, to the estate of the student. All other indemnities of the Program are payable to the person or institution rendering the service.

7. A Benefit Request is closed and will not be reopened if the indemnity check for the claim has been presented for payment.

8. Payments for consultation and referral services will be authorized only when requested by the original physician and so indicated in his statement.

B. The following regulations apply:
1. The coverage of a student of a participating school is effective when his completed **Physical and Dental Examination and Permit Card** properly executed is received by the Plan's Administrative Office, effective as of the date of postmark. The Physical examination must be taken on or after August 1.

DENTAL REGULATIONS

1. No benefit payment will be authorized for dental injuries unless the student's completed Dental Examination card properly executed was on file in the Plan's Administrative Office.

2. Benefits will not be authorized for care to injured tooth or teeth recorded on the Dental Examination chart as defective unless the said defects have been repaired within thirty (30) days of the date of this examination and so certified to the Plan within this period by the attending dentist.

3. No benefit payments will be authorized until all dental work has been completed. Requests must be completed and filed within one year from the date of injury.

4. The Plan's Executive Committee reserves the right to ask for evidence beyond that originally submitted if the Association Dental Advisor and the Executive Committee deem such evidence desirable or necessary to establish the validity of a claim.

SCHEDULED ALLOWANCES (DENTAL)

Code		Sili-cate	Plas-tic	Amal-gam	Gold
(71)	Fractures of enamel ....$ (Requiring treatment and polishing only)				3.00
(72)	Replacing broken facing				5.00
(73)	Recementing loosened crown or inlay				2.00
	Recementing loosened bridge				4.00
(74)	Fractured tooth — required fillings				
A.	1 surface restoration	$4.00	$4.00	$3.00	12.00
	2 surface restoration		6.00	6.00	18.00
	3 surface restoration			9.00	25.00
B.	Requiring a ¾ crown gold restoration				25.00
C.	Requiring a gold crown				25.00
D.	Requiring an acrylic or porcelain jacket crown				40.00
E.	Requiring kadon crown or jacket or chrome crown				12.00
F.	Porcelain Davis Crown with Post				15.00
G.	Open Face Crown				15.00
H.	Requiring a crown with veneer window				30.00
(75)	Loss of one or more anterior or posterior teeth requiring bridge work, per tooth				
	Pontic — A Steel Facing				15.00
	B Tru pontic				20.00
	Maximum allowance				90.00
(76)	Injury requiring an upper or lower partial denture acrylic, or acrylic and metal with clasps, $50.00 for 1st tooth, $5.00 for each additional tooth, maximum allowance				80.00
(77)	Injury to tooth requiring pulp removal and root fil'ing				15.00
	Apicoectomy — inc'uding root canal filling				30.00

Fig. 10-6. *cont.*

(78) A. Repairing dentures or partial dentures broken but no teeth involved 10.00
B. Replacing broken teeth on dentures or partial dentures, first tooth 10.00
Each Additional tooth 2.00
C. Adding teeth on denture or partial denture to replace extracted natural teeth, first tooth 15.00
Each additional tooth 2.00
(79) Extraction 3.00
(80) Maximum for chipped teeth for one accident 10.00
(81) Maximum for one dental injury 90.00
(82) Fractures
(Item 7 of Medical Regulations applies to these fractures)
A. Simple fractures of superior or inferior maxilla not requiring wiring or splints, including x-rays and care 37.50
B. Simple fractures of superior or inferior maxilla, reduction, fixation, post operative care and including x-rays 75.00
C. Compound or comminuted fractures of superior or inferior maxilla, reduction, fixation, post operative care and including x-rays 100.00
(83) Where permanent type restoration is not used
A. Palliative treatment — per treatment .. 2.00
Maximum allowance 6.00
B. Temporary crowns, bands or similar appliances, Maximum 10.00
C. Treatment partial 25.00
Each additional tooth 5.00
(84) X-rays — first x-ray $2.00;
each additional $1.00
Maximum x-ray allowance 5.00
No allowances for Orthodontic appliances or treatment.

MEDICAL REGULATIONS

Payments will be provided only for items listed in the Schedule below. In each case the amount shown shall be the maximum allowance; however, in no event shall payment exceed actual charges for a scheduled procedure.

1. The fees for fractures and dislocations include pre- and post-operative care, reduction and fixation, but are exclusive of the hospital allowance and x-ray fees.
   a. JOINT SEPARATION WILL BE CLASSED AS A DISLOCATION.
   b. Epiphyseal separation will be interpreted to be a break.
2. When an accident involves injury to more than one part of a person's body, the indemnity will be that for the major injury plus 50% of the fee for each other injury.
3. The maximum allowances for all x-rays shall not exceed the scheduled x-ray benefit.
4. Indemnities will not be provided for medicines and bandages.
5. Matters of arbitration will be considered by the Plan's Executive Committee and the State Medical Society's Advisory Committee. The attending physician's records and x-ray plates as they pertain to the Benefit Request in question shall be available to the arbitration committee.
6. The Executive Committee reserves the right to ask for evidence beyond that originally submitted when the Medical Advisor and the Executive Committee deem such evidence desirable or necessary to establish the validity of the claim.
7. BENEFIT REQUESTS WILL BE VALID AND COMPENSABLE ONLY WHEN THE ATHLETE REMAINS OUT OF ALL ATHLETIC ACTIVITY INCLUDING PRACTICE AND GAMES FOR AT

Fig. 10-6. cont.

LEAST THE NUMBER OF DAYS INDICATED
IN THE SCHEDULE BELOW.
TREATMENT OF TEETH IS EXCLUDED FROM
THIS REGULATION. ONE NEGATIVE X-RAY
IS COMPENSABLE IF AN ATHLETE DOES
NOT REMAIN OUT THE REQUIRED TIME.

		Requiring Reduction	No Reduction
a.	Cuts, contusions, sprains (minor), etc.		3 days
b.	Aspirations		5 days
c.	Broken or dislocated nose, hand, foot, rib, finger and toe	12 days	6 days
d.	Broken bones (excepting those specified in C)	60 days	30 days
e.	Dislocation or separation of joint	30 days	15 days
f.	Injuries to knee (including cruciate and/or medial or collateral ligaments)		
	Moderate		30 days
	Severe		60 days
g.	Injuries to kidneys — contusion		30 days
h.	Injuries to kidneys — developing hemorrhage, albuminuria or evidence of celular structure in the urine		1 year
			or upon approval of WIAA Medical Advisor
	requiring surgery		1 year
j.	Skull and intracranial injuries (Including all concussions)	30 days	30 days

Treatment expense incurred after an athlete returns to
practice or competition following an injury will not
be compensable unless evidence acceptable to the Plan
is provided which justifies such treatment.

SCHEDULED ALLOWANCES (MEDICAL)

Code
(52) X-ray — an allowance for one x-ray will be
payable whenever deemed necessary by attending physician. A second allowance for an x-ray
will be compensable on injuries involving fracture when such an additional x-ray is deemed
necessary.
(53) Concussion ....$ 20.00
(only if loss of consciousness)
(54) Injury to viscus requiring surgery 150.00
(55) Suture of laceration 5.00
(An additional $1.00 will be allowed
each suture over one)
(56) Lacerations 5.00
(Not requiring sutures)
(57) Tetanus Anti-Toxin 3.00
(58) Sprains — Joints of hands or foot 5.00
Joints of wrist, elbow, shoulder,
ankle, knee, back 10.00
Semi-lunar cartilage — surgery 100.00
(59) Abrasion 5.00
(60) Aspiration 5.00
(Limit 3)
(61) Fluoroscope examination 3.00
(62) MEDICAL ATTENDANCE, Maximum 12.00
If an injury which cannot be classified under the
Schedule of Allowances requires treatment other than
on the field at the time of play or practice, an
allowance not to exceed $12.00 will be made. If the
request for Medical Attendance benefit exceeds by
$25.00 the scheduled allowance of $12.00 for this
service, the Plan will pay the amount in excess of
$25.00 up to a maximum of $100.00.
(63) MEDICAL ATTENDANCE —
SURGERY, Maximum ....$ 25.00
When surgery is required in connection with Medical
Attendance an additional allowance not to exceed
$25.00 will be provided when approved by the Plan's
Medical Advisor.

Fig. 10-6. cont.

(64) HOSPITAL BENEFIT, Maximum $100.00
— plus 50% of miscellaneous charges.
Hospitalization benefits are allowable in connection with valid claims. To be compensable the confinement must be for a period of 12 hours or more in a recognized hospital. The maximum daily allowance is $10.00 for Room-Board not to exceed 10 days for a total maximum allowance of $100.00. In addition, 50 per cent of all miscellaneous charges (not including Room-Board and x-rays) will be compensable.
(65) OUT-PATIENT SERVICES, Maximum ....$ 12.00
When the doctor requests the service, a maximum allowance of $12.00 will be authorized for out-patient services such as use of the operating room, drugs, casts, etc., excluding x-rays.
(66) SERIOUS INJURY PROVISION, Maximum $500.00
If the total expense incurred for necessary medical care shall exceed the combined payments (insurance and Scheduled Allowance under this Program) by more than $100 the Plan will pay an additional amount, in excess of said $100, equal to the remaining balance of expenses or a maximum total payment of $500 by the Plan, whichever is the least. (See Item 2 under Benefit Allowances and Limitations of Liability).

	FRACTURES			DISLOCATIONS			X-RAY ALLOW.
	No Reduction	Closed Reduction	Open Reduction	No Reduction	Closed Reduction	Open Reduction	
1. Ankle Joint (one or all malleoli)	$ 25.00	$ 60.00	$ 90.00	$ 10.00	$ 35.00	$100.00	$ 5.00
2a. Clavicle	15.00	25.00	50.00				5.00
b. Inner Joint				25.00	25.00	75.00	5.00
c. Lateral Joint				15.00	50.00	75.00	5.00
3. Coccyx	15.00	25.00	50.00				10.00
4. Colles — Radius, Ulna	20.00	50.00	75.00				5.00
5a. Elbow — T. Fracture	35.00	50.00	100.00		35.00	75.00	5.00
b. Medial Epicondyle	20.00	35.00	75.00				5.00
c. Lateral Condyle	20.00	35.00	75.00				5.00
d. Radial Head	20.00	35.00	75.00				5.00
6. Femur (shaft)	40.00	100.00	135.00				10.00
7a. Forearm - Radius (shaft only)	20.00	50.00	75.00				5.00
b. Ulna (shaft only)	20.00	50.00	75.00				5.00
c. Radius & Ulna shaft	30.00	60.00	100.00				5.00
8a. Hip — Inter-trochanteric	40.00	100.00	150.00		60.00	75.00	10.00
b. Intracapsular	40.00	100.00	150.00		60.00	75.00	10.00
9. Humerus	35.00	50.00	100.00				5.00
10. Maxilla-inferior, superior or zygomatic	32.50	70.00	95.00		10.00	75.00	5.00
11. Metatarsal — single	10.00	20.00	30.00		25.00	40.00	5.00
Each additional	3.00	5.00	12.50		20.00	30.00	
12. Nose	10.00	25.00	75.00				5.00
13. Patella	20.00		110.00		20.00	75.00	5.00
14. Pelvis	30.00	60.00	100.00		60.00	150.00	10.00
15. Rib (one or more)	15.00	15.00					10.00
16. Scapula	25.00						10.00
Shoulder					25.00	75.00	10.00
17. Skull and/or cerebral hemorrhage		50.00	100.00				10.00
Skull — no cerebral damage	25.00						
18. Spine (vertebral body compression one or more)	30.00	75.00	150.00	25.00	·75.00	150.00	10.00 entire 20.00
19. Sternum	10.00	25.00	50.00				5.00
20. Tarsal os calcis	25.00		75.00				5.00

Fig. 10-6. cont.

21. Tarsal (excluding os calcis) ..	20.00	50.00	75.00	35.00	75.00	5.00
22. Tibia (involving knee joint)	30.00	75.00	110.00			5.00
23. Tibia or Fibula shaft or both ..	25.00	60.00	75.00			5.00
24a. Toe — great	10.00	15.00	15.00			5.00
b. Other toe	5.00	10.00	10.00	5.00	10.00	5.00
c. Each additional	3.00	5.00	5.00	5.00	10.00	5.00
25. Transverse process	10.00					10.00
26a. Wrist and hand — carpal ..	25.00	25.00	75.00	35.00	75.00	5.00
b. Metacarpal (single)	10.00	20.00	25.00	15.00	25.00	5.00
c. (each additional)	3.00	5.00	10.00	10.00	10.00	
d. Finger	5.00	15.00	25.00	5.00	15.00	5.00
e. (each additional)	3.00	5.00	10.00	5.00	10.00	

Fig. 10-6. concluded

athletic programs to meet at least part of the costs of scheduled injuries incurred by registered students, provided the activities involved are conducted in accordance, and that there has been school compliance, with Benefit Plan regulations. The Benefit Plan is not injury insurance. No contract is entered into between the participating individual and the Michigan High School Athletic Association or the Benefit Plan division of it. Neither the State Association nor the Benefit Plan guarantees the payment of costs of all or any injuries. It is expected that claims for scheduled benefits made by member schools will be paid in full, but it must be understood that it is impossible to distribute more money for injury claims than is paid in by schools in membership and registration fees. The experience of twenty years of operation of the Benefit Plan in Michigan, however, and that in other states, indicates that the schedule of membership and registration fees effective for 1960–61 will be adequate to meet the adopted benefit schedules for the activities included.[14]

In Michigan the Athletic Accident Benefit Plan is under the general supervision of the Representative Council of the state athletic association. Actual administration, however, is vested in an Administrative Committee of five members elected for five-year terms, the term of one member expiring each year. A superintendent, two senior high school principals, one junior high school principal, and one director of physical education, coach, or physical education teacher constitute this Committee. The State Director of High School Athletics is secretary-treasurer of the Benefit Plan.

Essentials of the Wisconsin Athletic Accident Benefit Plans. Wis-

[14] Michigan High School Athletic Association Athletic Accident Benefit Plan, 1961–1962, *General Information Bulletin,* pp. 1–2.

consin's 1960–1961 two plans of benefits for athletic injuries are presented in part because Wisconsin was the first in the field and as has been indicated previously, has furnished the general pattern for many other states [15] and for most commercial companies offering this type of coverage. The plan sets up two definite schedules of payments for specified injuries, one its Scheduled Program and the other its Special Program. (See Figs. 10–6 and 10–7.)

In addition to the Scheduled and Special Plans, Wisconsin also has a group coverage plan. It provides for the payments indicated and fixes two types of flat rates for schools; one covering students participating in all interscholastic sports including football, the other covering all sports except football. However, this flat rate can be obtained only by schools participating in a third plan. This is the pupil coverage plan, which costs seventy-five cents for each student enrolled in a school or school system and covers the student for scheduled injuries that may occur at any time he is under the jurisdiction of the school, except in interscholastic athletic practice or competition.

To summarize, Wisconsin has (1) the two regular benefit plans that apply to athletics only; (2) a separate plan for pupil coverage without reference to athletic competition; and (3) a combination of the athletic and pupil coverage plans with flat rates to schools for the former, provided all students in the school are registered under the latter. This pupil coverage plan was an innovation on the part of Wisconsin and has been watched with interest because of the information it has yielded concerning school injuries. After fifteen years' experience in Wisconsin this plan has supplied valuable data from the injury claims that had been completed as of June, 1960.[16]

Essentials of the New York State High School Athletic Protection Plan, Inc. The New York State High School Athletic Protection Plan, Inc. is presented and discussed here for three reasons: (1) It is an example of a non-profit corporation dealing with athletic injuries; (2) its benefit schedule is based on the state workmen's compensation code with both payments and fees for student premiums somewhat higher than those in states which have established their own

---

[15] See pages 320–326, and 329–333.

[16] Wisconsin Interscholastic Athletic Association, *Thirty-Seventh Yearbook* (1960), pp. 233–243.

WIAA ACCIDENT BENEFIT PLAN

FOR 1960-1961

ATHLETIC COVERAGE

of the

Special Program

This is an Athletic Accident Program featuring protection:
1. for any boy of a member school who is physically fit.
2. for every injury occurring while practicing for or participating in interscholastic athletics.
3. effective when the Physical Examination and Permit Card is postmarked in the mail with the fee for desired coverage.
4. paying medical expenses up to $2,000 and dental to $100.
5. with enrollment on School Group or Individual Basis.

Individual Rates —	Grades 9-12	Grades 7-8
All Sports	$8.50	$7.25
All Sports excepting Football	$3.00	$2.50

SPECIAL BENEFIT PROGRAM

Objective

The purpose of this Program is to pay the cost of reasonable and necessary hospital and medical expenses incurred as a result of an accidental injury sustained by students while participating in school sponsored activities.

No Health Coverage

This Program does not propide Health Coverage and no payments can be made for treatment which is not the direct result of an accident.

Definitions

For the purpose of this Program, the following definitions will be used:
1. PLAN shall mean the WIAA Accident Benefit Plan.
2. PROGRAM shall mean the Special Program.
3. STUDENT shall mean a pupil who is entitled to benefits under this Program.
4. INTERSCHOLASTIC ATHLETICS shall mean scheduled sports competition between schools. (Even when schools are part of same school system.)
   a. Competition within a school is intramural.
   b. No sports activity below the 7th grade shall be considered interscholastic.
5. MEDICAL EXPENSE INSURANCE shall mean coverage by others under which benefits are payable to the student for an injury which is also covered under this Program.

Fig. 10-7. W.I.A.A. Accident Benefit Plan — Special Program, 1960-1961 Wisconsin Interscholastic Athletic Association, *Parents Information Folder*, pp. 1-6.

a. This will include personal accident and health policies, medical payment plans, etc.

b. Third party liability insurance shall not be considered medical expense insurance for the purpose of this Program.

6. Part II and III refer to the Athletic section of the Special Benefit Program.

PART II — ALL SPORTS COVERAGE

Includes Interscholastic Football

Part II will provide coverage for accidental injuries sustained by a student in practice for, or participation in, interscholastic athletics.

This coverage is available on a school group or individual student basis.

PART III — LIMITED SPORTS COVERAGE

Excludes Interscholastic Football

Subject to the provisions and limitations of this Program. Part III will provide coverage for accidental injuries sustained by a student in practice for, or participation in, interscholastic athletics — excepting interscholastic football.

This coverage is available on a school group or individual student basis.

COVERAGE

Subject to the provisions and limitations of the Program, benefits are provided for covered students for necessary and incurred medical, dental, or hospital service resulting directly from accidental bodily injury sustained while practicing for, or participating in, interscholastic athletics.

The period of coverage shall be from the date of enrollment and shall terminate on the last day of attendance. In case a season's sport schedule extends beyond the school year, athletics coverage will be extended until the schedule is completed. School sponsored summer activities are not covered.

A student will be covered under this Program only when he is participating under the direct control and supervision of his school in the sports that are approved for him on his Physical Examination and Permit Card.

a. Coverage will be effective from the time he reports for practice or contest until dismissed by his coach.

GENERAL PROVISIONS

The following provisions shall apply except where specifically noted.

Fig. 10-7. cont.

Benefit Allowances and Limitations of Liability

If a student sustains an accidental injury covered by this Program, the Plan will pay an amount not exceeding $2,000 for any one accident for necessary expenses incurred for treatment by a legally qualified physician or surgeon, dental treatment for natural or restored teeth, hospital care or services, or the employment of a registered graduate nurse (excepting that for injury to one or more sound natural or restored teeth the payment shall not exceed $100); and provided that such expense begins within 3 weeks of the date of accident and is incurred within 52 weeks from the date of accident.

The preceding paragraph shall be subject to the following provisions and limitations:

1. If the necessary and incurred expenses covered under this Program shall exceed $100, and if all or part of such incurred expense is covered by valid and collectible medical expense insurance, then the Plan will pay the unpaid balance (up to $2,000) or $100 whichever is the greater.

2. And provided further, that should the student by reason of a covered injury sustain one of the following specific total losses within 52 weeks from the date of accident, the Plan will pay in lieu of all other allowances:

Life	$1,000.00
Both Hands or Both Arms	7,500.00
Both Feet or Both Legs	7,500.00
Both Eyes	7,500.00
One Hand and One Eye	7,500.00
One Foot and One Eye	7,500.00
One Hand and One Foot	7,500.00
One Hand or One Arm	1,000.00
One Foot or One Leg	1,000.00
Either Eye	1,000.00

    a. Only one of the above amounts may be elected for any combination of losses. With regard to hands and feet total loss shall mean actual severance through or above the wrist or ankle joint; with regard to eyes, entire and irrecoverable loss of sight.

3. And provided further the maximum aggregate liability of the Plan, on account of all injuries and deaths sustained in and arising out of any one accident, shall not exceed $20,000.00.

    a. In case the aggregate loss sustained by covered students shall exceed $20,000, the said $20,000 shall be prorated among the several persons entitled to it.

    b. The aggregate loss of covered students shall be the sum of:

        (1) All expenses, otherwise covered under this Program, sustained by students for which there is no collectible medical expense insurance; and

        (2) Any unpaid balance of expenses, otherwise covered under this plan, after collectible medical expense insurance benefits have been paid, or are payable to, on behalf of covered students; and

        (3) Any amounts paid for specified total losses as set out in paragraph 2 above.

Exclusions

1. Coverage will not apply to injuries sustained while:

    a. Going between home and school.

    b. Participating in any activity which is not under the direct control and supervision of his school, or other properly designated individuals.

    c. Participating in a school sponsored summer sports schedule.

Fig. 10-7. cont.

2. The Program will not provide benefits for:

    a. The following items:

Ambulance Services	Hernias
Athlete's Foot	Orthodontic appliances
Boils	Orthopedic appliances
Eyeglasses and	Prescriptions
their prescriptions	Recurrent dislocations
	Skin infections

    b. More than eight (8) Physical Therapy treatments for any one injury. This shall include Manipulative Therapy.

    c. Injuries resulting from epilepsy, fits, convulsions, diabetes, any congenital weakness, constitutional disease or pre-existent conditions if any of the same contribute to produce such an injury.

    d. Loss caused by or as the result of bacterial infection or any other kind of disease, or medical or surgical treatment of it (except pyogenic infections caused by accidental injury otherwise covered under this Program.)

    e. Injuries resulting from war, insurrection, or riot.

GENERAL REGULATIONS

A. The following regulations must be followed by the school:

    1. Written notice of injury to a student must be received in the Plan's Administrative Office within 21 days after the date of accidental injury.

    2. Payments for Benefit Requests will be authorized only when the medical and surgical aid given to the injured person is rendered by a licensed physician, that is, a doctor of medicine and surgery or a doctor of osteopathy and surgery.

    3. First treatment must be given within 21 days to qualify a request for benefits.

    4. Upon receiving a notice of injury, the Plan will furnish the necessary forms for completing the Benefit Request.

    5. Benefit Requests not completed within ninety days of date of injury will be withdrawn and reconsidered only when approved by the Executive Committee. Payment will be authorized only for claims completed and filed in the Plan's Administrative Office within one year from the date of injury.

    6. Benefit payment for the loss of life of a covered student is payable to the parent or parents with whom the child is living or, in their absence, to the estate of the student. All other indemnities of the Program are payable to the person or institution rendering the service.

    7. A Benefit Request is closed and will not be reopened if the indemnity check for the claim has been presented for payment.

    8. Payments for consultation and referral services will be authorized only when requested by the original physician and so indicated in his statement.

B. The following regulations apply:

    1. The coverage of a student of a participating school is effective when his completed **Physical and Dental Examination and Permit Card** properly executed is received in the Plan's Administrative Office, effective as of the date of postmark. The physical examination must be taken on or after August 1.

    NOTE: The above regulation applies to all sports coverages.

Fig. 10-7. cont.

2. Indemnity will not be provided for treatment to injured tooth or teeth recorded on the dental examination chart as defective or missing unless the said defective tooth or teeth have been repaired within thirty (30) days of the date of this examination and so certified to the Plan within this period by the attending dentist.

3. BENEFIT REQUESTS WILL BE VALID AND COMPENSABLE ONLY WHEN THE ATHLETE REMAINS OUT OF ALL ATHLETIC ACTIVITY INCLUDING PRACTICE AND GAMES FOR AT LEAST THE NUMBER OF DAYS INDICATED IN THE SCHEDULE BELOW.

TREATMENT OF TEETH IS EXCLUDED FROM THIS REGULATION.

ONE NEGATIVE X-RAY IS COMPENSABLE IF AN ATHLETE DOES NOT REMAIN OUT THE REQUIRED TIME.

		Requiring Reduction	No Reduction
a.	Cuts, Contusions, Sprains (minor), etc.		3 days
b.	Aspirations		5 days
c.	Broken or dislocated nose, hand, foot, rib, finger and toe	12 days	6 days
d.	Broken Bones (excepting those specified in C)	60 days	30 days
e.	Dislocation or separation of joint	30 days	15 days
f.	Injuries to Knee (Including cruciate and/or medial or lateral collateral ligaments) Moderate Severe		30 days 60 days
g.	Injuries to kidneys — contusion		30 days
h.	Injuries to kidneys — developing hemorrhage, albuminuria or evidence of celular structure in the urine		1 year or upon approval of WIAA Medical Advisor
i.	Rupture of viscus requiring surgery		1 year
j.	Skull and intracranial injuries (including all concussions)	30 days	30 days

Treatment expense incurred after an athlete returns to practice or competition, following an injury will not be compensable unless evidence acceptable to the Plan is provided which justifies such treatment.

Fig. 10-7 *concluded*

schedules; and (3) it offers a "double indemnity" coverage in all sports.

It will be observed that both Wisconsin's and New York's Athletic Accident Benefit Plans, as do those of other states, provide full coverage for the school year for interscholastic sports and physical education activities, with the option of including football or not as the individual student may desire. The rate in such instances is adjusted accordingly. The essentials of the New York plan concerning rates and benefit schedules are presented in detail.[17]

1961–1962 PREMIUM RATES (NEW YORK)

	Per Pupil Per School Year	* For Schools Insuring all pupils for I & PE Coverage	
All Interscholastic Sports and All Intramurals and Physical Education		(I)	(II)
Coverage A	$ 7.50	$ 7.00	
Coverage AA—Double Indemnity	$11.00	$10.50	$10.25
All Interscholastic Sports (except tackle football) and All Intramurals and Physical Education:			
Coverage B	$ 2.00	$ 1.50	
Coverage BB—Double Indemnity	$ 3.75	$ 3.25	$ 3.00
All Intramurals and Physical Education (except tackle football), and Cheerleading:			
Coverage I	$ .50		
Coverage II—Double Indemnity	$ .75		

* Schools that are going to insure all pupils in grades . . . . for Intramurals and Physical Education Coverage should complete and return ONE copy of this form, prior to September 1, 19. . ., in order to have this premium credited toward its interscholastic Coverage.

[17] New York State High School Athletic Protection Plan, 1961–1962, *Rates and Schedules Bulletin.*

MAXIMUM MEDICAL INDEMNITY SCHEDULE (NEW YORK)

The following maximum limits are inclusive of any X-ray charges listed below, in the Maximum X-Ray Indemnity Schedule. The Plan will pay for one additional X-Ray when necessary, subject to the Maximum X-Ray Indemnity Schedule.

Dislocations	*Not to Exceed*
Shoulder	$ 40.00
Elbow—closed	50.00
open	75.00
Wrist—closed	40.00
Finger—closed	15.00
open	50.00
Ankle	40.00
Astragalus	50.00
Toe	15.00

Sprains, Contusions and Lacerations	
Medical Expense	50.00
Excision of complete nail	15.00

Eye, Kidney and Knee Injuries	
Eye injuries—minor	20.00
major	S. C.
Kidney or spleen	50.00
If operative	175.00
Knee—cartilage or internal ligaments	50.00
If operative	150.00

Complete Fractures	
Fractured skull (operative)	S. C.
Concussion of brain	35.00
Maxilla or Mandible	75.00
Nose—simple	25.00
compound or displaced (operative)	75.00
Clavicle or Scapula—closed	40.00
open	100.00
Ribs	20.00
Vertebras—transverse process	25.00
body or lamina	100.00
open	S. C.

Not to
Exceed

Pelvis (one bone) 75.00
Multiple 100.00

Complete Arm Fractures

Humerus—closed $100.00
open 150.00
Radius or Ulna—closed 60.00
open 100.00
Both Radius and Ulna—closed 100.00
open 150.00
Elbow involving joint 75.00
Colles Fracture—closed 60.00
open 125.00
Carpals or Thumb—closed 50.00
open 75.00
Metacarpals—closed 40.00
open 75.00
Finger—one 20.00
Multiple on one hand 35.00

Complete Leg Fractures

Femur—closed 150.00
open 200.00
Patella—closed 50.00
open 100.00
Tibia—closed 75.00
open 125.00
Fibula—closed 50.00
open 75.00
Tibia and Fibula—closed 100.00
open 150.00
Astragalus or OsCalcis—closed 50.00
open 100.00
Tarsals or Metatarsals—closed 40.00
open 75.00
Toes—single 20.00
Multiple on one foot 35.00

Services to Be Determined on the Following Per Visit and Treatment Basis   *Not to Exceed*

Office call	3.00
House call	4.00
Incision and drainage	5.00
Additional—strapping, injection, suture	1.00
Consultation (maximum of one per claim) only when referred by treating physician and upon evidence of proper qualifications	10.00
Application of Cast (maximum of one per claim)	
Elbow to fingers	15.00
Hand and wrist	10.00
Shoulder to hand	20.00
Ankle (foot to mid leg)	15.00
Knee (foot to mid thigh)	25.00
Unna boot	10.00
Cervicle plaster collar	20.00

Special Consideration by Committee of Physicians

COMPOUND FRACTURES—Indemnity limits listed in the provisions captioned "Complete Fractures," "Complete Arm Fractures" and "Complete Leg Fractures" shall be increased 50% in the event of compound fractures.

Fracture With Associated Dislocation:

Contiguous area—Maximum for Fracture—Remote area—Maximum for each.

Anaesthesia and Ambulance service indemnified when inclusive of the scheduled maximum indemnity.

Catastrophe Expense: In addition to the scheduled indemnities, the Plan will pay 80% of the incurred expense (medical, dental, x-ray) in excess of the first $300.00, up to $1,000.00 of the expense.

THE MAXIMUM SCHEDULED INDEMNITY IS NOT TO BE CLAIMED UNLESS *ITEMIZED PROFESSIONAL SERVICES* JUSTIFY THAT AMOUNT.

MAXIMUM X-RAY INDEMNITY SCHEDULE (NEW YORK)

Benefits hereunder for any injury covered under the Maximum Medical Indemnity Schedule above shall be subject to the provisions of such Maximum Medical Indemnity Schedule.

X-ray demonstration by physician with:	XD Qualification ***	SD Qualification ***
Single finger or toe	$ 3.50	$ 5.00
Hand, wrist, forearm, elbow, humerus, ankle, foot, leg, knee, femur.	6.00	8.00
Shoulder, clavicle or scapula	8.00	10.00
Nasal bones, mandible	8.00	10.00
Pelvis, hip joint, skull, chest, spine.	11.00	15.00

Multiple x-rays—contiguous parts—50% of the lesser fee. Remote parts—75% of the lesser fee.

*** See Workmen's Compensation Code.

MAXIMUM DENTAL INDEMNITY SCHEDULE (NEW YORK)

	Not to Exceed
Chipped tooth	$ 3.00
Broken back tooth	10.00
One permanent front tooth knocked out or broken	40.00
More than one permanent front tooth knocked out or broken, per tooth	30.00
Fillings knocked out of front tooth—replaced	4.00
Broken front tooth facings—replaced	4.00
Dental X-ray	2.00
Tooth requiring root canal treatment	20.00

Maximum dental benefits increased 50% for football injury incurred while wearing a flexible mouth and tooth protector fitted under the supervision of a dentist.

The cost of restoring artificial teeth, crowns or peg teeth will be restricted to one-half the scheduled payments. Removable dentures should be removed prior to any participation.

Our present insurance covers medical and dental and x-ray costs. Hospital coverage is NOT obtainable.

Limitations

1. No benefits will be paid for treatment by other than duly licensed physicians and dentists.
2. No benefits will be paid for diathermy treatments.
3. No benefits will be paid for lacerations or abrasions unless prompt medical attention was given. (5 days)
4. No benefits will be paid for any treatment after the treating physician has approved in writing the injured student's return to participation.
5. Unless a student has the physician's written permission to return to participation, he shall not be eligible for benefits in the event of subsequent injury.

GENERAL PROVISIONS (NEW YORK)

I. In the case of injury, a notice signed by the Principal or Athletic Director giving the date, place and type of injury must be mailed to the Executive Secretary of the Corporation within twenty days of the injury. Such notice given by or on behalf of the insured to the corporation with particulars sufficient to identify the injured student, shall be deemed to be notice to the corporation. Failure to give notice within the time provided in this subscription contract shall not invalidate any claim if it shall be shown not to have been reasonably possible to give such notice and that notice was given as soon as reasonably possible. Upon receipt of such notice, final blanks necessary to complete the claim will be furnished which must be filled out by the principal, coach, attending physician or dentist, and the injured student, and returned to the Executive Secretary of the Corporation. Proof of claim shall be filed within 90 days from date of loss. The amount actually allowed will not exceed the physician's or dentist's itemized statement which must accompany every request for benefit.

II. No statement by the applicant in his application for this certificate shall void the certificate or be used in any proceeding thereunder unless such application or an exact copy thereof is included in or attached to such certificate. No agent or representative of the Corporation other than an officer is authorized to change the certificate or waive any of its provisions.

III. A grace period of forty-five days will be allowed for making any premium payment due under this certificate.

After a default in the payment of any premium under this certificate, the subsequent acceptance of a payment by the Corporation or by one of its duly authorized agents shall reinstate the certificate, but only to cover injuries occurring after the date of such acceptance.

IV. No action at law or in equity shall be brought to recover on this policy prior to the expiration of sixty days after proof of loss has been filed in accordance with the requirements of this policy and no such action shall be brought at all unless brought within two years from the expiration of the time within which proof of loss is required by the certificate.

V. Payment of claims shall be made to the parent or guardian of the injured student within sixty days after receipt of due proof of loss.

Michigan's nonscheduled injuries provision. Apparently, Michigan has procedure for handling nonscheduled injuries that is somewhat different from those in other states. This state does not pay benefits for minor injuries such as sprains and bruises. Rather, it has felt that schools whose students receive serious or unusual injuries that often run into high costs should be given assistance. With this principle in mind, Michigan's plan has this provision:

NON-SCHEDULED INJURIES

1. Allowances and payments will be made for scheduled injuries under Medical, Dental, and Transportation Schedules before consideration is given any others by the Administrative Committee.

2. Schools may report non-scheduled injuries in the regular manner, and provided Benefit Plan funds are available, they will be considered by the Administrative Committee after all claims for payments of scheduled injuries for a current year have been settled.

3. Non-scheduled injury benefit requests will not be considered by the Administrative Committee until the end of a current school year or until

it is definitely assured that ample funds will be available to cover them or make prorations possible in accordance with such limitations and regulations as it may establish.[18]

Since the establishment of the Benefit Plan in Michigan in 1940, approximately $75,000 has been paid to member schools for injuries that were not on the scheduled list. Such injury charges have not been paid in full and the percentage of payment has been determined after all scheduled benefits had been paid and the amount of money available from the current year income was known. This policy has been very well received by the schools of the state participating in the plan.

Usual benefit plan injury claim procedures. Although it must be realized that the operation of accident benefit and protection plans involves considerable clerical work, both on the part of the member school and the state association office, every effort is made to reduce this paper work to a minimum. If statistics are to be reliable, however, and the funds of all member schools are to be protected, a certain amount of essential information is required. Usually a preliminary injury report card must be mailed within a specified num-

[18] Michigan High School Athletic Association Athletic Accident Benefit Plan, 1961–1962, *General Information Bulletin,* p. 5.

PRELIMINARY INJURY REPORT CARD—FORM D
ATHLETIC ACCIDENT BENEFIT PLAN OF M.H.S.A.A.

(Leave blank)
No._____
Completion
Date_____

..............................Michigan..............................19......

Charles E. Forsythe, Secretary-Treasurer, Athletic Accident Benefit Plan of the M.H.S.A.A.

Dear Sir: Pursuant to requirements outlined in the Athletic Accident Benefit Plan of the M.H.S.A.A.

I hereby advise you that..., a student in the

..............................High School, WAS INJURED ON..............................., 19......, while:

(Check and fill in appropriate one.)

☐ Participating in an interscholastic contest in (sport)...

☐ Participating in a practice session in (sport)...

☐ Participating in an intramural contest (sport)...

☐ Participating in a physical education class (activity)...

☐ Traveling from...............................to...............................as a

member of our high school squad in (sport)...............................to play a
regularly scheduled interscholastic contest.

The best available information shows that his injury is a...............................

and he is being attended by...............................
Kindly forward required Forms for benefit request.   (Indicate Name of Physician or Dentist)

Yours truly,...............................
                    (Superintendent)—(Principal) (Cross out one)

(NOTE: THIS CARD MUST BE MAILED WITHIN TWENTY (20) DAYS AFTER INJURY OCCURS.)

Form D—(58—20M)

Fig. 11-1. Preliminary Injury Report Form *(Michigan).*

ber of days after an injury occurs (see Fig. 11–1). Proof of injury blanks then are sent to the school by the benefit plan office. These blanks generally are filled out by the injured student and the principal of the high school, as well as by the attending physician or den-

---

Form E—60 — 5M
(Football)

ATHLETIC ACCIDENT BENEFIT PLAN
OF THE
MICHIGAN HIGH SCHOOL ATHLETIC ASSOCIATION

Request For Accident Benefit—Form E (Football)

No.................. Completion Date..................

Registered Student..................

School..................

Claim must be completed by above date.

TAKE NOTICE: This Form is one of a series furnished by the Athletic Accident Benefit Plan of the M.H.S.A.A. to a member school desiring to make a request of said Benefit Plan for an accident benefit involving a registered student, the furnishing whereof, or the request for further proofs, shall neither be an acknowledgment of any liability on the part of the member school, or said Benefit Plan of the M.H.S.A.A., nor a waiver of any of the rights of either, whether said Form is called for by a member or officer of this Benefit Plan, Athletic Association, or otherwise.

(PART I) STATEMENT OF REGISTERED STUDENT

1. I, ...certify that the statements herein made, and the answers to the questions herein propounded, are true and correct.

2. I am .... years of age, in the .... grade, and weigh .... pounds. 3. I was injured on..................while: (Date)

☐ Participating in a practice session in football ☐ Participating in an interscholastic game in football

☐ Traveling from .... to .... as a member of our high school football squad to (City) (City)
play a regularly scheduled interscholastic football game.

4. My parents have accident, health, hospital insurance with ....
(Name of Company)

Date.................... 19...... ....
(Of this Report) (Signature of Registered Student)

(PART II) STATEMENT OF SUPERINTENDENT OR PRINCIPAL

1. I certify that the above named regularly enrolled, registered student was accidentally injured on.................... , 19......
(Date)

2. Nature of injury....................
(Description of Injury)

3. Cause of injury....................
(State How Accident Happened—Type of Play, Etc.)

4. I was notified of said injury on....................by .... (Date) (Name of Informer)

5. This student has been treated professionally for this injury by .... (Name of Physician or Dentist) (City)

6. This student was out of school..................days because of this injury. He returned to practice on.................... (Number) (Date)

7. There is hereby requested of the Athletic Accident Benefit Plan of the M.H.S.A.A. the sum of $.................... as per approved Benefit Plan Schedule No....................for the current school year. (See General Information Bulletin, pages 3-5).
(Schedule No.)

8. I have examined the statement of this Registered Student (Part I) and of the Coach (below), as well as that of the Physician or Dentist (Itemized statement for professional services included thereon) and feel that, as a member school, we are entitled to this benefit according to the Athletic Accident Benefit Plan Schedule as approved for the current school year.

Date.................... 19...... ....
(Of this Report) (Signature of Superintendent or Principal—Cross Out One)

NOTE: Forward this Form to CHARLES E. FORSYTHE, Secretary-Treasurer, Athletic Accident Benefit Plan of the M.H.S.A.A., Department of Public Instruction, Lansing 2. This Form must be accompanied by Form F (Statement of Attending Physician) or Form G (Statement of Dentist). All requests must be completed within 60 days from date of injury. (Completion date indicated in upper right-hand corner).

IMPORTANT—In case this injury occurred in a regularly scheduled football field meet the following information MUST BE SUPPLIED:

(a) I certify that the following men officiated in the football game during which this injury occurred:

Referee....................; Umpire....................;

Head Lineaman....................;

(b) This injury occurred during a football game played at.................... (City)

on.................... (Date)

Date....................19...... ....
(Of this Report) (Signature of Coach)

PLEASE LEAVE BLANK

Amount of Check . . . . $....................

Schedule No. . . . . . , :....................

Description of Injury....................

....

....

....

N.S.D. ....

Fig. 11-2. Request for Accident Benefit Form (Michigan).

tist (see Fig. 11–2 and Figs. 11–3 and 11–4). After proof of the injury has been established, and provided it is a scheduled benefit, payment then is made by check to the school, or to a combination

Form F—60—6M

ATHLETIC ACCIDENT BENEFIT PLAN
OF THE
MICHIGAN HIGH SCHOOL ATHLETIC ASSOCIATION

No. _____ Completion Date _____

Registered Student _____

School _____

Claim must be completed by above date.

Statement of Attending Physician—Form F

NOTE: The following statements must be made by the physician who attended the recipient of the injury for which request by a member school for benefit from the Athletic Accident Benefit Plan of the M.H.S.A.A. is hereby being made. If more than one physician attended the recipient of said injury, additional Forms will be furnished for statements of such other physicians or surgeons as required.

The purpose of these statements is two-fold: First, to establish proof of injury; Second, to give such information concerning the injury, personal history of the recipient of the injury, and other matters of importance as will be valuable in tabulating statistics. The attending physician or surgeon is requested to give under "General Remarks" any information on matters which, in his judgment, caused said accident, and which were not otherwise included in this statement.

TAKE NOTICE: This Form is one of a series furnished by the Athletic Accident Benefit Plan of the M.H.S.A.A. to a member school desiring to make a request of said Benefit Plan for an accident benefit involving a registered student, the furnishing whereof, or the request for further proofs, shall neither be an acknowledgment of any liability on the part of the member school, or said Benefit Plan of the M.H.S.A.A., nor a waiver of any of the rights of either, whether said Form is called for by a member or officer of this Benefit Plan, Athletic Association, or otherwise.

1. I, _____am a legal practitioner of medicine and surgery in the state of

Michigan. My office address is _____ City _____
(Number and Name of Street)

2. I was called on the _____ day of _____, 19 _____ to attend _____

on account of _____
(Here State Nature of Injury to Recipient)

3. Did you render first medical-surgical services to said recipient for said injury? _____

★ 4. If an X-ray plate (not Fluoroscope) was made (1) ATTACH COPY OF THE X-RAY READING to this sheet; OR (2) COMPLETE THE REVERSE SIDE of this Form. Request for X-ray allowance WILL NOT BE CONSIDERED unless there is compliance with EITHER (1) OR (2). (See other side.)

5. Describe your treatment and operation, if any, performed on recipient of the injury by you, on account of said injury _____

6. Is there any evidence of an old injury of a similar character? _____

7. State date or dates of examination or treatment _____

8. Prognosis: _____

Itemized Statement of Physician's Fees	
( ) Office Calls @ _____ $ _____	
( ) Home Calls @ _____ $ _____	
( ) Operation _____ $ _____	
( ) X-ray (See 4 above, and other side.) _____ $ _____	
_____ $ _____	
_____ $ _____	
_____ $ _____	
Total _____ $ _____	

★ If there are hospital charges in connection with this injury an itemized hospital statement must be attached to this Form.

9. To your knowledge when did the recipient of this injury again participate in

athletics _____ Authorized by you? _____
(Date)   (Yes or No)

10. General Remarks: _____

TAKE NOTICE

This is to certify that the above student did not participate in physical education, intramurals, or interscholastic athletic practice or competition for a period of thirty (30) days after receipt of a SERIOUS INTERNAL INJURY OR FRACTURE OF ONE OR MORE OF THE FOLLOWING: ARM, CHEEK BONE, COLLARBONE, JAW, KNEE CAP, LEG, PELVIS, SCAPULA, SKULL, STERNUM, AND VERTEBRA.

(Signature) Attending Physician   (Signature) Superintendent or Principal

★ NOTE TO PHYSICIAN: This report, completely filled out, IS TO BE GIVEN TO THE HIGH SCHOOL PRINCIPAL OR SUPERINTENDENT. The statement of Physician's Fees must be completely filled in as indicated.

Date _____, 19 _____
(Of this Report)   (Signature of Physician)

★ NOTE TO PRINCIPAL OR SUPERINTENDENT: Forward this Form, completely filled out, which contains the itemized statement for services of physician, to CHARLES E. FORSYTHE, Secretary-Treasurer, Athletic Accident Benefit Plan of the M.H.S.A.A., Department of Public Instruction, Lansing 2. This Form must be accompanied by Form E (Request for Accident Benefit). All requests must be completed within 60 days from the date of injury. (Completion date indicated in upper right-hand corner.)

Fig. 11-3. Statement of Attending Physician Form (Michigan).

of payees, usually the school principal and the physician or dentist. Iowa is an exception in this respect in that its plan provides for individual policies for each student and payment is made directly to him. In Iowa there is also part payment of the student's premium to the Iowa High School Insurance Company by the Iowa High School Athletic Association.

WIAA Accident Benefit Plan

The purpose of this statement is to establish proof of the injury, the exact nature of the injury, and the details of the services rendered.
The Benefit Programs of the WIAA Accident Benefit Plan are not insurance. They are mutual Benefit Programs which provide assistance in meeting the cost of medical and dental services for school pupils injured while participating in an activity organized by and under the direction and supervision of their school. Since the Benefit Plan is non-profit and established to serve the schools, a maximum scheduled indemnity is not to be claimed unless itemized professional services justify that amount as scheduled.
BENEFITS WILL BE PAID ONLY IF THE SCHOOL AND STUDENT HAVE COMPLIED WITH THE BENEFIT PLAN REGULATIONS AND REQUIREMENTS.
Copies of the rules and the Schedule of Benefits may be obtained from Executive Secretary John E. Roberts, WIAA Accident Benefit Plan, Stevens Point, Wisconsin

STATEMENT OF THE DENTIST

Pupil's Name .... City ....
School .... Date of Injury ....
Place Injury Occurred ....
Activity engaged in at time of injury ....

1. Describe the injury giving the character, extent and complications. State specifically the exact location of the injury, and mark the chart accordingly.

R   L

2. Nature of the injured teeth at the time of injury:

   Natural.................... Artificial.................... Crowned.................... Defective.................... Sound....................
3. Describe treatment, any operation, and necessary restoration:

   ....

   ....
4. General Remarks: ....

   ....
5. Enclose any x-rays taken.
6. I herewith certify the above report is a true account of the injury and the services rendered to the patient, that the services have been completed, and the patient discharged and that the itemized bill is reasonable and just.
7. Statement:

Date	Services Rendered	Amount	
			....
			(Print Name)
			....
			(Signature and Title)
			....
			(Address)
(Kindly itemize your account)			(City - Zone - State)

DENTIST: RETURN THIS STATEMENT TO SCHOOL WITH STUDENT WITHIN 90 DAYS OR AS SOON AS TREATMENT IS COMPLETED BUT NO LATER THAN ONE YEAR FROM DATE OF INJURY.

Fig. 11-4. Statement of Dentist Form (Wisconsin).

Commercial athletic injury insurance. A few commercial insurance companies have become interested comparatively recently in athletic injury coverage. In most cases their schedules of benefits are similar to that of the Wisconsin, Minnesota, and Michigan plans. Their rates vary but, in general, range from $5.00 to $10.00 for the same schedule of benefits as in effect in most state association-operated plans. Many old-established casualty and liability companies have not been interested in entering the field of athletic injury insurance because of lack of experience and available data. This situation may be changed now that more accurate facts are being accumulated.

Summary. In concluding this discussion on safety and sanitation in athletics and the consideration of accident benefit and protection plans, several significant developments should be noted. Greater protection is being given to students before practice or playing of athletic contests through safety and sanitation precautions. Also, there is a definite trend toward the assumption of greater moral or social responsibility on the part of schools by the establishment of athletic accident benefit and protection plans. These developments should aid in raising the standards of physical education and athletic programs and at the same time provide valuable experiences in health education for high school students in general, as well as for members of athletic teams.

It is interesting to consider the attitude of state directors of health and physical education on this matter some time ago. Considerable time was spent in discussing the development and growth of these plans at the twenty-first annual meeting of the Society of State Directors of Health and Physical Education, held at Seattle on April 19–22, 1947. It will be observed from the resolution adopted by this group that its members were interested not only in athletic accident coverage but also in the extension of such plans to include all school pupils.

WHEREAS, There is need for adequate insurance of all school children as well as athletes against accidents on playgrounds, athletic fields, and in the school building; and,

WHEREAS, Some states already have developed adequate and inexpensive coverage available to large numbers of students in the school; therefore,

BE IT RESOLVED, That the Society of State Directors of Health and Physical Education recommend consideration of such plans by the various states and encourage the state high school athletic associations that already have some coverage for athletes to consider a broader plan to include all children.

Questions for Study and Discussion

(1) Prepare a safety program check list for athletics.

2. This chapter lists several athletic safety essentials. Name and discuss each of them briefly.

(3) Discuss safety suggestions for the following sports: (a) baseball; (b) basketball; (c) cross country and track; (d) football; and (e) swimming.

4. What common practices are advocated for safety in transportation of athletic teams?

5. Discuss the importance of a good sanitation program in athletics and physical education. What additions can be made to the sanitation suggestions included in this chapter?

(6) Why is it important to have medical supervision of athletic programs and contests?

7. Discuss the beginnings and growth of athletic accident benefit and protection plans. State arguments for and against such plans being operated by state athletic associations.

8. What are some of the values of athletic accident or benefit plans in addition to the amounts paid to member schools or their students?

9. Compare the essentials of the Wisconsin and New York Athletic Benefit and Protection Plans.

10. What is meant when it is said that such states as Wisconsin, New York, Minnesota, and California also operate pupil protection plans? What do they include?

12

Athletic Facilities—
Layout and
Maintenance

In considering athletic facilities it will be assumed that the problems confronting those in charge of the athletic program deal chiefly with layout and maintenance rather than with construction. Separate treatment would be needed for the consideration of construction data and plans pertaining to the gymnasium, swimming pool, or stadium. Strictly speaking, these are engineering problems concerning which the physical education and athletic men in a school system should be sought for consultation. Experiences that they have had in teaching classes or in coaching teams, as well as observation of outstanding facilities in schools in which they have worked or visited, are the best sources of information to be passed on to architects or engineers.

General and Indoor Facilities

Questions will be raised in schools with which physical education men are connected concerning the layout and dimensions of playing areas for different games. Also, information should be available regarding the most efficient methods of maintenance and repair of common athletic facilities. The presentation of information of this general type is the purpose of this chapter.

Size of playing areas. The minimum amount of space required for various games is well defined in the official rules books. In most cases, however, certain sports may be played under better conditions if more than minimum requirements in space are available. For example, it is desirable to allow for extra outfield space in baseball and football. Indoor game areas, of course, must accommodate themselves to the gymnasium space available. In constructing gymnasiums, more than minimum rules-book recommendations should

TABLE 6

Comparative Areas Needed for Various Sports

(Ranked in ascending order of space required per player)

Game	Area per Player (Square Feet)	No. of Players	Minimum Size (Feet)	Total Area (Square Feet)
Volleyball	150	12	30 × 60	1,800
Handball (single wall)	170	4	20 × 34	680
Basketball (boys)	210	10	35 × 60	2,100
Badminton	220	4	20 × 44	880
Basketball (girls)	245	10	35 × 70	2,450
Softball (playground)	451	20	95 × 95	9,025
Soccer (girls)	1,309	22	120 × 240	28,800
Tennis	1,500	4	50 × 120	6,000
Field hockey	1,564	22	135 × 255	34,425
Soccer (boys)	2,250	22	165 × 300	49,500
Football	2,618	22	160 × 360	57,600
Baseball (hard)	5,000	18	300 × 300	90,000

be allowed if possible in order that spectators may be accommodated. This extra space also will make play safe because it will allow the playing area to be laid out so that the out-of-bounds areas are at a safe distance from walls or other obstructions.[1] The College Physical Education Association has compiled data concerning the areas needed for different sports as shown in Table 6.

Indoor playing facilities. However, once the gymnasium has been built, it is necessary to use the space as it is provided. Care should be taken to remove all possible hazards. Floors should not

[1] Prepared by The College Physical Education Association.

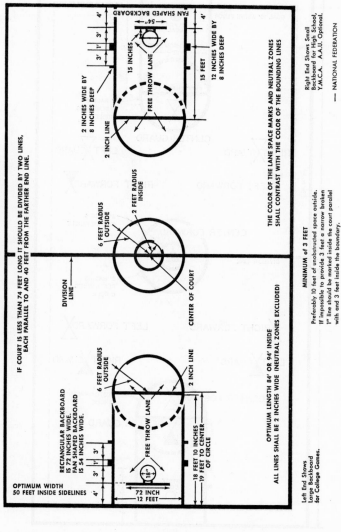

Fig. 12-1. Basketball Court (Boys).

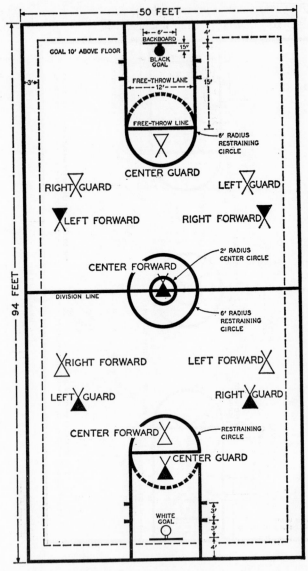

Fig. 12-2. Basketball Court (Girls) (D.G.W.S. *Rules Book).*

be allowed to become unsanitary or slippery. Special finishes for gymnasium floors are popular and some good ones are on the market. The floor should be thoroughly rinsed and dried before another coat of finish is applied. Regardless of the type of finish used on the floor, it should be one that may be washed with soap and water. Caustics should be avoided. Arrange and inspect temporary bleachers so that they are safe for spectators, and keep them as far away as possible from side and end lines. Cover unused bleach-

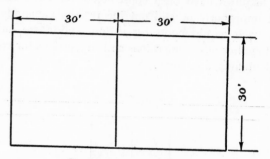

Fig. 12-3. Volleyball Court.

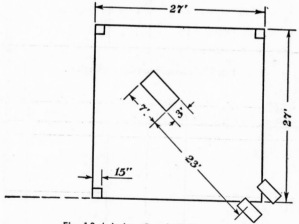

Fig. 12-4. Indoor Baseball Diamond.

ers at the end of basketball courts with gymnasium mats. Keep scoring tables off the playing court. Cover lights with wire guards, paint gymnasium ceilings a light color, and keep the windows clean. Figures 12–1 to 12–8 show diagrams and court dimensions for boys' and girls' basketball, volleyball, indoor baseball, badminton (singles and doubles), handball (four-wall and single-wall), and shuffleboard.

Outdoor Playing Facilities

Many more athletic contests are conducted outdoors than indoors. Often it has been the case that when indoor athletic and physical education facilities have been constructed, outdoor facilities have been built improperly or laid out incorrectly. Generally accepted minimum space requirements for various sports are indicated on page 348, together with dimensions and suggestions for construction of fields, diamonds, and track.

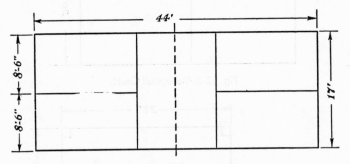

Fig. 12-5. Badminton Court (Singles).

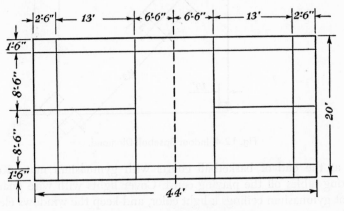

Fig. 12-6. Badminton Court (Doubles).

Football field. Generally it is desirable that a football field extend north and south so that punt and pass receivers do not have to face a late-afternoon sun. The extent to which night games are now played by high schools negates the importance of this suggestion considerably. Since drainage of the field is of most importance, a gravel subsoil is the best base. Drainage tile, 4 or 5 inches in diameter, should be laid diagonally across the field every 15 or 20 feet. Frequently these run into a drainage system encircling the gridiron and emptying into catch basins at each of the four corners of the field. The trenches holding the drain should be nearly filled with

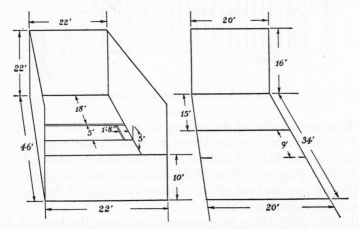

Fig. 12-7. Handball Court (4-wall and Single-wall).

coarse stones so that water may quickly reach the tile. The field should have from 8 to 12 inches of loam topsoil and then should be sodded if possible. It is desirable from the standpoint of drainage facilities to have the field graded so that the center is about a foot higher than the side lines.

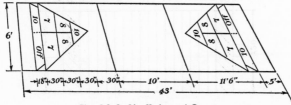

Fig. 12-8. Shuffleboard Court.

If a track encircles the gridiron, the curb should be low enough so that it is not a hazard for football players who are thrown out of bounds. It is obvious, of course, that six-man football, soccer, field hockey, lacrosse, and speedball may be played on ordinary football gridirons with minimum changes in markings. Football fields should

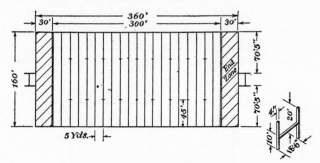

Fig. 12-9. Football Field (High School).

be kept mowed during the season, watered if necessary and cut turf replaced. Practice should not be held on game gridirons if avoidable. (See Table of Maintenance Directions for Athletic Fields, page 365.) Figures 12–9 to 12–14 show diagrams and dimensions of playing areas for football (eleven-man and six-man), field hockey, lacrosse, speedball, and soccer.

Baseball field. Often it is necessary to locate the baseball diamond on part of the football gridiron because of lack of space for separate layouts. This practice is not recommended where it may be avoided, for the reason that a track often is built around the football field, and a conflict arises because baseball and track both are spring sports. Also, the recommended grading of the baseball

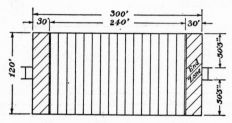

Fig. 12-10. Football Field (6 Man).

diamond and preparation of a "skinned" infield, if one is used, do not fit in well with gridiron construction. Drainage for the baseball field should be virtually the same as for the football playing area. Sometimes it is desirable that tile be placed directly under the base lines because they are used most and also because they may be a trifle

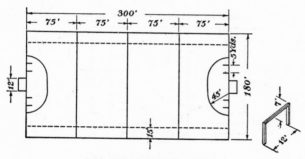

Fig. 12-11. Field Hockey.

lower than the remainder of the infield, especially if it is sodded. If the diamond is laid out so that the direction from home plate to first base is due west, a minimum number of players will have to face the sun. The batter will be facing the sun but he does not have to look at high balls, and only the catcher is called upon to do so when going after high foul balls. There is, however, a difference of opinion in the major leagues as to the general direction scheme for layout of baseball diamonds. Often the field is arranged in major league parks so that spectators, rather than players do not have to face the sun.

Usually home plate should be slightly higher than the surround-

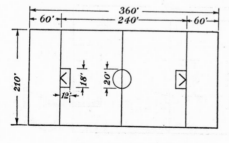

Fig. 12-12. Lacrosse Field.

ing area, sloping to infield level in 6 to 8 feet. The plate itself should be flush with the ground. The pitcher's box may be no more than 15 inches above the base-line levels and must be on a gradual, sloping mound. The pitcher's and batter's boxes, because of their hard usage, should be of clay mixture in order to be firmer than other

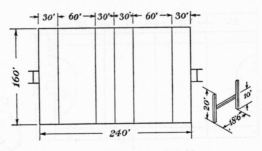

Fig. 12-13. Speedball Field.

parts of the field. Of course they must receive extra protection if it rains because they become sticky sooner than other parts of the infield. If the entire infield is bare, it should be kept absolutely smooth. Roll it every day, raking lightly, if necessary. A large street brush or heavy wire-mesh screen may be used for grading purposes. Such care will "soften" ground-hit balls and make them bound truer. If the infield is covered with grass, it should be watered daily and kept mowed. Grass should be removed from an area of 10-foot radius around home plate. Usually a comparatively small oval or circular area around the pitcher's box is without grass. A path 2½ feet wide between home plate and first base and between home plate

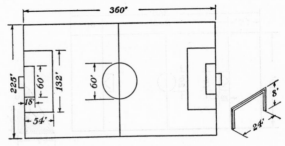

Fig. 12-14. Soccer Field.

and third base should be devoid of grass. As much area as is desired, in addition to the base lines, between first and second base and between second and third base may be "skinned." This includes the area on which the infielders usually play. Minimum distances of 300 feet from home plate to obstructions down the first- and third-base lines are recommended. Figures 12–15 and 12–16 show diagrams and dimensions of a baseball diamond, baseball home plate, batter's box, pitcher's plate, coacher's box, catcher's box, and a softball diamond.

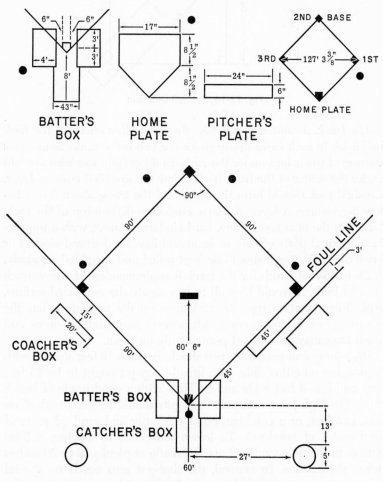

Fig. 12-15. Baseball Diamond (National Federation).

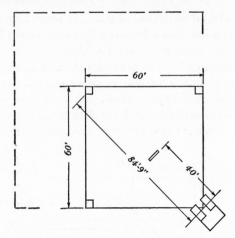

Fig. 12-16. Softball Diamond.

The track. As stated previously, the track often encircles the football field. In such cases drainage for the two is the same. Sometimes a string of tile is laid under the curb. In other instances tiles are laid under the center of the track itself below the so-called cushion layer. Crushed rock should form the bottom of the track, about 2 feet below the surface. A layer of coarse cinders, rolled on top of the rock, furnishes the next layer. Fine, hard cinders are next, with a top surface of equal parts of clay or loam and fine, hard sieved cinders or brick dust. The track should be kept rolled and sprinkled regularly. A 25- to 35-foot width for the track is recommended. If a new track is to be built, it would be well to investigate the new hard-surface, asphalt-combination type of track now on the market. It has the advantage of drying immediately after a rain and all lanes and finish lines may be marked permanently on them.

High-jump and pole-vault pits should be 14 to 16 feet square, with approaches on either side. The broad-jump pit ought to be 25 feet long and 6 to 8 feet wide and be filled with a good grade of beach sand. The high-jump and pole-vault pits should be filled with shavings, sawdust, or a combination of the latter and sand (2 parts of sand and 1 of sawdust). To lessen the shock in landing, a false bottom in the pole-vault pit may be made of planks 18 to 20 inches below the surface. In general, the shot-put area needs no special construction, except that the event should not be conducted on the football playing field. Since the discus and javelin areas are located on the regular gridiron, they need no specific consideration.

A track and field layout separate from the football gridiron was completed a few years ago at Michigan State University, East Lansing. Some special features of the arrangements are listed below, inasmuch as the arrangement is outstanding and, according to former Director Young, "was built according to the best information obtainable." [2]

1. The track is 35 feet wide at all points, permitting eight to twelve individual lanes.

2. Each of the two straightaways is 250 yards long. The oval part of the track is 440 yards.

3. It has "railroad" curves of 104 feet radius. Each curve and straightaway is approximately 110 yards.

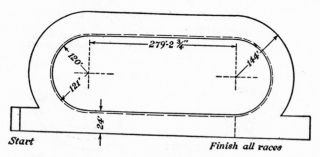

Fig. 12-17. Quarter-Mile Track.

4. Catch basins are staggered on both sides of the track every 35 feet, 3 feet from the curb.

5. All six field events are laid out with permanent runways, pits, rings, and the like, in the infield in such a way as to permit the holding of all field events simultaneously. Warm-up runways, pits, and rings, are located between the two straightaway legs.

6. The broad-jump and pole-vault pits are approached by runways from two directions.

7. The high-jump pit is in the center of an 80-foot circle.

8. The javelin runway is built of cinders and is 75 feet by 25 feet.

[2] General information regarding Michigan State University track furnished by Ralph H. Young, former Director of Athletics.

9. The running track, field-event runways, circles, pits, and landing areas are 3 inches higher than the adjacent level of the field to provide drier conditions in wet weather.

10. The pole-vault landing pit has a false bottom or plank 2 feet below the ground level for extra "give."

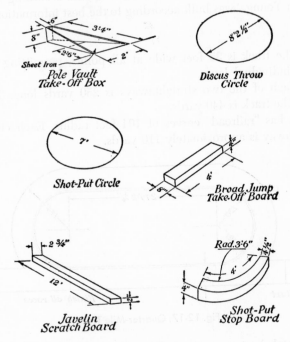

Fig. 12-18. Track and Field Equipment.

11. Portland cement was mixed with the top dressing of cinders and clay for the field-event rings and runways in order to provide for better wear. (Hard-surface, asphalt combination now used.)

12. Portland cement was mixed with the top dressing for the shot-put landing area in order to provide a hard landing area so the competitors may be given the maximum credit for their efforts.

13. There are two separate rings for meet competition in both the discus and shot.

14. The pole lane is used only for the distance events. The dash and hurdle races are held in the lanes farther away from the pole.

15. The top dressing for the running track is a mixture of 2 parts of fine cinders to 1 part of black soil. The soil is a loam containing about 15 per cent organic matter. This type of soil has excellent resilient binding qualities and will not bake like clay.

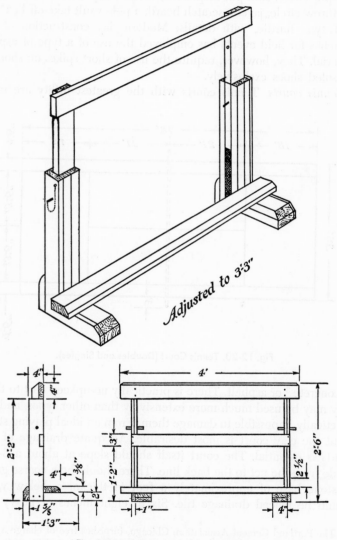

Fig. 12-19. L-Type Hurdle and Details.

16. The stands are placed 25 feet from the track at an angle to the straightaway.

Figures 12–17 to 12–19 show diagrams and dimensions of a track, shot-put circle, shot-put stopboard, broad-jump take-off board, discus-throw circle, javelin scratch board, a pole-vault take-off box, and an L-type hurdle, with details. Modern day construction of approaches for field events has employed the use of a type of asphalt material. They, however, require the use of short spikes on shoes or flat-soled shoes exclusively.

Tennis courts. Tennis courts with the greatest utility are made

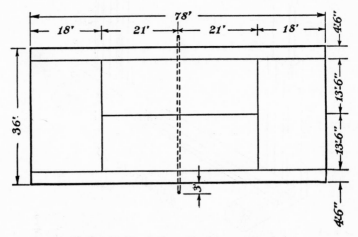

Fig. 12-20. Tennis Court (Doubles and Singles).

of concrete [3] or asphalt. There is practically no upkeep cost to them, they may be used much more extensively than other types, and it is practically impossible to damage them. From an ideal playing standpoint the clay court is most desirable. Adequate drainage of clay courts is essential. The court itself should slope at about a 3-inch grade from the net to the back line. There should be a coarse gravel or stone base of approximately a foot in thickness, below which should be placed drainage tile. Six to eight inches of heavy clay

[3] The Portland Cement Association, Chicago, furnishes free of charge a complete pamphlet and drawings for the construction of concrete tennis courts.

should be rolled on top of the base. If necessary, light sand may be sprinkled on the clay. A calcium chloride preparation improves playing conditions and preserves the clay. Figure 12–20 shows a diagram and dimensions of a tennis court.

Seeding and Maintenance of Athletic Fields

Seeding of athletic fields and their care will depend upon the section of the country in which they are located. Soils also are an important factor in determining the procedure to be followed. It should be realized that more attention must be given to an athletic field than to an ordinary lawn or campus because of the much harder usage it receives. In general, athletic fields must be continually "built up" by the most approved methods. Wherever possible there should be separate practice and playing fields in order that the game field may be saved as much abuse as possible. As a general guide to those in charge of athletic fields, Tables 7 and 8, which give concise directions, are reprinted on pages 364 and 365.

Outdoor Lighted Areas

Despite improved lighting facilities there still is considerable argument for and against outdoor athletic contests being held at night under lights. Many people feel that, generally, football and baseball games or track meets are better events if held in the daytime. In some situations, however, it has seemed necessary to hold these contests at night. An increasing number of schools have become interested in the cost, construction, and possible uses of lighted fields as well as in the opinion of schoolmen whose teams have played under the lights. Some time ago the author conducted a survey of night football in a number of schools in Ohio, Pennsylvania, Kansas, and Michigan. A summary of the information obtained from a half dozen schools in each state is indicated in the following paragraphs.

The common construction practices followed in lighting fields are: (1) from 4 to 8 poles are used on each side of the field, with 5 or 6 being the most common number (towers are used in some instances); (2) poles run from 40 feet to 85 feet high, with 60- to 70-foot poles used most; (3) the most recent practice seems to be that

TABLE 7

Athletic Field Seeding Directions [4]

Sport	Soil	Drainage	Grasses (Never any Clovers)	Reseeding
Football and Soccer	Medium to light	1% surface and underground	Mixture of fescue bluegrass and creeping bent	February, March, or April
Baseball	Medium to heavy	Pitcher's box not over 10 in. above bases provides surface drainage; under ground, drainage usually needed.	Infield good proportion of bent with fescue, bluegrass; outfield possibly without bent, to lower cost	September, October
General Playgrounds	Medium to heavy	½% surface may be sufficient	Mixture of fescue, and bluegrass predominating	September, October, or early spring
Lawn tennis	Medium to light	½% surface and underground	Same as for football	September
Polo	Medium to heavy	½% surface; underground with main line laid just outside playing field on low side of field.	Mostly fescue with bluegrass and bent	September, October
Bowling greens	Medium to light	Facilities for rapid underdrainage; cinders sand in ditches	Creeping bent with fescue and bluegrass	September, February, March
Croquet	Medium to light	Good underground	Fescue and bluegrass with bent	September, February, March

of using single lights in single reflectors, with several reflectors (6 to 12) on each pole; (4) the better lighted fields seem to have from 10–12 to 15–18 foot-candles on the playing field; (5) attention is given to lighting fences, entrances, exits, and spectator stands.

Purposes other than football for which lighted fields were re-

[4] Reprinted from the manual "Campus and Athletic Field," by permission of O. M. Scott & Sons Co., Marysville, Ohio.

TABLE 8

Athletic Field Maintenance Directions [5]

Sport	Rolling	Mowing	Fertilizing	Special Treatment
Football and Soccer	Early spring; possibly light treading or rolling after each game to press roots into ground	Long (1½ in.) except during season	Early spring and possibly light summer applications	Replace loosened turf after each game
Baseball	Early spring	Short during season but let go into winter with 3 or 4 in.	September or early spring	
General playgrounds	Early spring	Long—2 to 3 in.	September or early spring	
Lawn tennis	Early spring, possibly lightly during season	Same as for baseball	September and early spring	If soil packs, spring dressing of powdered charcoal, 150 lbs. to 1000 square feet
Polo	Early spring	Long	September or March	After play replace torn places. Fill bare spaces with topsoil and seed
Bowling greens	Early spring	Same as for baseball	September and early spring	Charcoal as for tennis courts
Croquet	Early spring	Same as for baseball	September and early spring	Charcoal dressing in early spring

[5] "Campus and Athletic Field."

ported in use were: (1) commencements; (2) band concerts, festivals; (3) blossom-week pageants; (4) softball games; (5) annual sports-day programs; (6) baseball games; (7) track meets; (8) winter skating; (9) physical education demonstrations; (10) boxing exhibitions; (11) soccer games; (12) school reviews; (13) church pageants; (14) May Day festivals; (15) Boy Scout pageants; (16) fraternal festivals; (20) county fairs; (21) Halloween celebrations; (22) outdoor motion pictures.

The schools included in this survey were virtually unanimous in indicating that there was no difference in the number or severity of injuries received in night football as compared with the daytime game.

Some interesting comments concerning night games were received from schoolmen who sent in reports. A few of them are listed anonymously.

We are satisfied that night football is not so good as day football, but from a financial standpoint and public relation angle it really is a fine thing. Our town is really strong for it and it presents a fine chance to keep the school before the public.

We are quite enthusiastic about night football here. From a standpoint of spectators it is much superior to the daytime affair since more of the businessmen and more stable people of the community may attend without neglecting their business.

Our student body, faculty, townspeople, and team are very enthusiastic about night football. Lights for night tennis were well received by our people last summer so we followed with night football. In not more than three years the increased profits will pay for the lights.

Generally speaking, I would prefer by all means to play football in the daytime rather than at night. However, I believe we can say that the playing conditions at night are as good, or may even be better, than on a hot September or October afternoon. With the experience of two years of playing football I see no reason why such games, properly administered, can be any more injurious to high school boys than day games. Night football games also generally reduce practice periods to four days per week. This may have advantages as well as disadvantages as far as players are concerned.

Night football, in my estimation, is one of the greatest forward steps made in the past fifteen or twenty years. We used to play our games on Friday afternoon and it meant that our school work on Friday didn't amount to very much. Now we have school the full five days a week. I am very much sold on night football.

I was opposed to night football for many years because I attended several games and was uncomfortable all evening. (I have since bought a suit of long underwear.) I objected to our night trips. That is now past history. Last week about 2,000 of our townspeople accompanied our team to a neighboring town fifty miles distant and I was fearful of the discipline problem. There just wasn't any. At home our crowds are well policed and are easier to handle under the lights than in the afternoon. Night football is much superior to day football as long as the weather is favorable. Then, too, we schoolmen can attend some college games now.

I am not enthusiastic over night football for the following reasons: (1) places scholastic athletics more and more on a commercial basis; (2) students do not receive the benefit of sunshine and fresh air. Usually the weather is cold, damp, and foggy in this locality at night.

I feel that night football should be abolished because the air is harder to breathe. Players are always playing on the ground which is wet and there are more colds among them. It has taken the glamor from the game and commercialized it to such an extent that many problems are arising that otherwise would be eliminated.

. . . Our boys look forward to night games with a little extra enthusiasm. . . . My personal attitude toward night football is that I would prefer to play on Saturday afternoons unless it came to a question of having to make more money in order to continue the sport. Under those conditions I would be perfectly willing to play our home games at night. My preference is slightly in favor of the daytime game.

My impression over three years has been that night football offers a single advantage. It is possible for more adults to attend the games, and consequently the receipts may be somewhat increased. On the other hand, I think several rather serious disadvantages attend night games: (1) adds to an already undesirably large number of night activities; (2) greater difficulty in controlling the student body at night games than at day games; (3) a serious automobile problem is presented. I know of no situation in which I have seen as wild and reckless driving as that following the few night football games I have attended.

From our coach we have the following advantages and disadvantages in relation to night football: Advantages—larger crowds; less interference with school work; boys like to play at night; coaches may see and scout other games. Disadvantages—visiting team may be handicapped by lights; difficult for boys who wear glasses during day to adjust eyes to lights at night; visiting teams travel late at night and if a doctor is needed on return home it is difficult to get one; large high school crowds follow team and crowded cars present a real danger in relation to number of accidents which might occur.

I like the game better in the daytime because of better light but have no serious objections to night games. I haven't noticed any mistakes that could be attributed to poor light. Night games are a novelty to our boys and they get a kick out of them. There may be some objections to having the students following the team at night but we did not have any trouble, although about 150 of our students accompanied our team on a recent out-of-town game. We are very glad to play schools at night if they think it is to their advantage financially to do so.

In 1945, Floyd Rowe, then Directing Supervisor, Bureau of Physical Welfare, Cleveland Board of Education, made a survey of reactions to night football by representative schoolmen he contacted. This survey summarizes the subject under four general headings, from which he makes several significant conclusions.

1. Have you had experience with night football?
   81% Yes—of those replying
2. As an athletic event, what is your reaction to it in terms of:
   a. Size of crowd:
      75% reported larger
      25% reported *much* larger
      One reports 500% increase
   b. Ease of handling crowd:
      55%—no difference
      45%—slightly more difficult
   c. Conduct of pupils following games:
      40% report more difficulties
      40% report same as for day games
      20% report "Noisy but not destructive"
            "We have no complaints"
            "Could be improved upon"

Under Comments on Question 2 are the following:

"Night high school football is a fine community activity"

"The Baltimore Board of Education is building three more (two now in use) lighted athletic fields"

"Would favor night games if receipts were the same as a public relations proposition"

3. Do you think night football is justified educationally?

53%—Yes

47%—No

Comments:

"No difference educationally"

"Financial returns much greater. Can spend increased funds on other school activities"

"Night football provides opportunity to stress importance of sportsmanship and it has worked"

"Night football is accepted as exploitation—which may be justifiable"

"Tends to commercialize and professionalize the contest"

4. If you have not had direct experience with night football, are you contemplating equipping fields for night football?

30%—No

70%—Yes

If so, why?

   a. Desire of schools for financial return?

   50%—Yes

   30%—Partly

   20%—Incidental, but pleasing

   b. There is no evidence that night football is being promoted by the makers of lighting equipment.

   c. There are two educational values mentioned:

   (1) Same as day football, and

   (2) Less interference with classes

Conclusions:

On the whole, the questionnaire results simmer down to:

1. Highly increased receipts

2. More difficult to control actions of spectators, particularly following the game

3. Good community relations promoted, as parents can attend with children

4. Night football has not been promoted by sales pressure of manufacturers

5. Educational values same as for day programs, plus the fact that night games interfere much less with the regular school program

The following is an added thought not brought out directly by any of the replies. The duty of the schools is to educate for living and life. Does our responsibility for educating for proper behavior cease at sundown or any other particular time? If it does not, then night football is just another laboratory for the educator to use in the general educational program.

Most schools have night basketball as an accepted part of the program. Why not night football?

Although the information in this investigation may not be all-inclusive, it does show, among other facts, that increased revenue is a definite outcome of the night game in virtually every instance. If this factor is of sufficient importance to a school to overshadow other possible disadvantages, then games under the lights are justifiable. Apparently, new problems may be added and others eliminated. It is a matter of adjustment. Night contests not only in football but also in baseball, softball, track, tennis, hockey, and skating seem to be here to stay. Many schools have installed their lighting systems in cooperation with city recreation departments and consequently get much greater use of them at a considerable reduction in outlay.

Questions for Study and Discussion

1. What square footage is recommended as the minimum requirement for: (a) softball; (b) volleyball; (c) basketball; (d) football; (e) baseball?

2. Discuss essentials to be considered in layouts for indoor playing facilities.

3. What main considerations should receive attention in building a football field?

4. Discuss the layout and construction of a baseball field. In what direction should the batter face? Why?

5. A track is one of the most difficult athletic facilities to build. List important items to be considered in its construction.

6. List and comment on arguments for and against night athletic contests.

13

Intramural
Athletics

This chapter will concern itself with the place of intramural athletics in our schools, consideration of some of the objectives to be realized from the intramural program, and presentation of the major policies involved in it. Attempts will be made to point out suggestions to be kept in mind in the administration of intramurals in high schools.

Place in the Program

Intramural vs. interschool athletics. The word "intramural" means "within the walls"; therefore, intramural athletics are athletic activities conducted within a school itself as contrasted with athletic contests played between two or more schools. There is no conflict between properly conducted programs of intramural and interscholastic athletics; in fact, they both are a part of the same program. Each group of activities should be complementary to the other. Each has a place in the school program; each may be defended educationally; and each offers opportunities not necessarily possessed by the other.

Intramural activities form the basis of all athletics. All students should have the opportunity to compete regardless of their degree of skill. They have an inherent right to play or to attain self-expression through intramural games. As part of the physical education program of a school, intramurals should receive the major attention of those in charge of the department. They should be the laboratory for the physical education program. Primarily, intramural competition is for the contestants themselves. Of course, this purpose also is the major objective of interschool athletic competition; yet there are school, student spectator, and community interests that must be given consideration as well. The intramural program should be set up so that the boys and girls themselves may play the games in which they are interested individually. They also should have the opportunity to learn new games and, as a result of having learned them, to acquire new skills and new interests.

Interschool athletics by their very nature are more selective than intramurals. This is not an indictment against the former if all the facts are kept in mind. Under no circumstances should a school consider that its interscholastic athletic program is a legitimate substitute for intramural games. As stated previously, each serves different purposes and achieves different ends. Intramural athletics may be likened to the general courses that are taken because, by so doing, students lay the groundwork for other activities and interests. So it is with intramurals.

The intramural athletic program may be viewed in another way. When a student engages in intramurals, which should be under the direction of the physical education department of a school, such participation may be likened to taking part in general activities such as music, debating, public speaking, and dramatics. Out of these general groups the more proficient students are selected to make up the bands, orchestras, and choruses of the school, as well as the debaters, public speakers, and the actors in school plays. They all have been grounded in general fundamentals through the course they have taken. Then, those who show greater skills than others or who possess greater aptitudes or natural abilities are selected for further training and often become their school's representatives if competition in any of these activities is a part of the school program or policy. Ideally, that is the way the athletic program should work. The interscholastic athletic program should represent the training program for those individuals in a school who are most proficient in particular sports. It should be the outgrowth, not the antecedent, of the intramural program, which should have as its objective the teaching of and participation in many games whereby new skills are learned by all the boys and girls in a school. In both instances students will have had the chance to play, which is the most important consideration.

To carry the analogy further, interscholastics very properly may be considered in the light of the elective courses allowed in the school's curriculum. Certain students, very naturally, are more proficient in athletic activities than are other students. They should be allowed to continue their athletics by means of interschool competition. The entire athletic policy, therefore, very easily may be in complete harmony with general objectives of the school program. Intramurals provide the opportunity for play experiences for all. Interscholastics allow for selection and concentration on comparatively few students as far as instruction is concerned, but there are consequent benefits in interests, activities, and sportsmanship opportunities which may be realized by the student body as a whole. The important thing in the school program policy is to be certain that one activity does not crowd out or overshadow the other. Each should have its proper degree of emphasis; the problem is to find and maintain it. In many instances there is no need to de-emphasize interscholastic athletics but rather to build up and give proper emphasis, attention, and recognition to the intramural program. Make intramurals attractive and worth while and they will pay big dividends in interest on the part of the great mass of high school students who merely want a chance to play.

Roy Brammell pointed out some time ago that intramural athletics need not be carried on in conjunction with interscholastic athletics. However, both types of athletic activity can prosper in a school. The purposes of each are distinct, although they both contribute to the larger objective of pupil participation, recreation, and health. Intramural athletics are organized specifically for the purpose of extending the opportunity and pleasure of participation in sports. Intramural athletics, rightly conceived, are directed for the sole benefit of the student body.

This view is logical and defensible because it may give the chief emphasis to the intramural program. That is as it should be if there is any conflict between the two because, when only one program is possible in a school, it should be the one which reaches the greater number of students. In virtually all instances, however, it should be possible for both intramurals and interscholastics to be included in the general program.

World War II showed us conclusively that physical education and intramural programs in our high schools and colleges had failed miserably in teaching a variety of games and skills. True, we found many men who came into the armed forces who knew how to play, and could intelligently watch, football, basketball, and baseball games. However, many more could watch than could play these games. As far as other athletic activities were concerned, even mass games of low organization were generally unknown. During periods of basic or recruit training in the armed forces many opportunities were offered to men and women to engage in athletic competition. Those who had had intercollegiate or interscholastic competition usually did. But this number was small compared to the number who did not play. Why? Because they did not know the games or failed to possess the elementary skills necessary to play them. It was indeed sad to see several hundred men at a training center participating in organized games and then to observe that there were several times this number standing idly around *because they did not know how to play.* In most cases these men and women could have learned something about games and their attendant skills if our school, college, and recreation programs had been organized and administered correctly and had included broad physical education and intramural activities. As a result of intramurals it is possible to make more and better participants as well as better informed spectators.

General Intramural Objectives

As schoolmen came to realize that interscholastics did not achieve all the possible objectives in athletic competition, the development of intramurals began. This phase of the program also has been given great impetus as a result of the attention which it has received comparatively recently in our teacher-training institutions. Men and women graduating from them have been prepared for the handling of intramurals and the establishment of necessary objectives. It is obvious that play for the masses will not be on as high a level of skills in intramurals as in interscholastics. The games and activities to be included should be selected carefully. They should be ones that may be learned easily and be interesting. A minimum amount of equipment should be required and both team and individual sports should be included.

The intramural program must appeal to the student, and the opportunity to play must be the objective most obvious to him. Among other objectives usually advanced for intramurals are the following:

Health. The activity must be healthful in nature. The objective of any activity should be consistent with the first of the cardinal principles of education and contribute to its realization. The same general principles regarding safety and sanitation should obtain for the intramural program as apply to interscholastic athletics. Since there should be many more students participating in intramurals than in interscholastic athletics, the opportunity exists for teaching much more both in immediate and long-range health-education programs. Insist on compliance with common-sense safety and sanitation standards. (See Chapter 11.)

Leisure time and recreation. Physical activity should consume a part of one's leisure time. The opportunity to participate in sports and games in school may open an avenue to a wise selection of use of leisure-time and recreation activities both during school days and afterward.

Development of citizenship. In athletic games, interscholastic and intramural, life situations develop that may aid in helping students adjust themselves to the social order in which they live. The realization of a group spirit which results from team competition is a valuable experience to participants. It teaches responsibility as well as cooperation. Sportsmanship, fair play, truthfulness, and courage are attributes of citizenship that may be realized from intramural competition.

Social contacts. In both large and small schools, friendships are inevitable and invaluable. A broad friendship list is desirable during the adolescent and pre-adult periods. Intramurals offer an additional opportunity for realization of this objective.

There are socializing values derived from participation in intramural athletic sports which are not always recognized by school people. Generally, varsity athletes develop companionships with fellow teammates and perhaps with opponents in rival schools, but the number involved in the socializing experience is comparatively small. Intramural players, however, engage in many sports, participate in various contests, and establish friendships with large numbers of fellow players and opponents in their own schools. In intramural sports the establishment of cordial social relations among opponents, officials, and the few interested spectators is most valuable.

Development of interest and skills. Usually one enjoys doing best those things which he does well. Especially is this true in athletics and recreational activities. The intramural program gives a student the chance to discover and develop his skills. With these discoveries and developments there is bound to be a more permanent interest in many more activities than otherwise could be the case.

Pleasure in playing. The intramural program has little or practically no value if there is not genuine pleasure in the competition it affords. Games and activities should be of varied types so that different interests of students may be served. Make the program afford joyous participation. Special attention should be paid to the inclusion of as many individual sports as possible in the intramural program. This feature is important because it will give the student who is not especially team-minded an opportunity to participate. In this connection, it should be kept in mind that many of us have the time and chance to engage in activities or hobbies only when we are alone or with comparatively few others present. Most highly organized team games offer little chance for participation after high school or college.

Academic standing. There is no definite proof of high correlation between athletic prowess and academic or scholastic standing. In fact, the opposite sometimes is claimed to be more obvious. Neither premise is entirely correct. It is safe to say, however, that wholesome, well-directed athletic activity is a contributing factor to good health. It is also reasonable to presume that an alert body and mind will make for better academic work. Intramurals, therefore, can have a part in this general situation and at the same time be enjoyable experiences for participants.

Integration with the physical education program. Intramurals should be a part of the physical education program. There should be definite correlation between the skills taught in physical education classes and participation in intramural games and contests. It is important, however, that intramural athletics be elective, because the student should want to participate in the activity instead of being forced to do so. The physical educator's problem is to make the intramural program one of such varied and interesting activities that students are attracted to it because they want to play. In reality, the learning may be incidental but the playing should be basic.

Relation with the interschool athletic program. As stated previously, the interschool program should be the outgrowth of the intramural program. When this is realized, each is a contributing factor to the success of the other. Inevitably, varsity players will be discovered through their intramural competition. Thus, varsity competition may be the goal of some who take part in intramural play, but it should not be the dominant one.

Administration of Intramural Athletics

Some of the major problems involved in the administration of an intramural athletic program are discussed briefly below. Naturally, the administrative details will vary according to the size and plan of organization of the school itself. They will be quite different in a school of a hundred students or less from those in a school with several hundred to a few thousand. Further, available facilities and faculty personnel will be most important factors.

Responsibility. Preferably, whoever is in charge of the intramural program should not have the major responsibility of coaching an interscholastic team. In a small school in which this policy may not be feasible, the faculty member in charge should be impressed with the fact that the intramural program is of equal importance with the interscholastic competition. The purpose in recommending that the person in charge of intramurals not be a major interscholastic coach is to ensure that interscholastic interests will not overshadow intramurals. It is advisable to have an intramural athletic council in a school, with a substantial number of its membership composed of students. The principal and the director of intramural athletics should be permanent council members, with one or two additional faculty members who serve for annual or staggered two-year terms. The intramural director should be the executive in active charge of the program. He should be a member of the physical education staff,

if possible, and be aided by faculty and student manager assistants.
Organization. Units of organization will vary with individual schools. Class, homeroom, gymnasium class squads, clubs, color groups, study groups, and the like, are possible units to serve as a basis for competition. Whenever possible, competition should be based on other than class teams, to ensure greater equity in competition. Often it is desirable to select teams using a coefficient involving an age, weight, height, or grade combination, or some one of them. Equal strength of teams is almost essential to the success of intramurals just as it is in other types of competition. As far as possible the intramural program should be a part of the school-day program. Many times an activity period during the day can be utilized for the playing of intramural contests. Noon-hour periods may be used for the less strenuous activities, and in some cases the school day may be lengthened by the addition of an extra class period. Evening, Saturday, and late-afternoon periods usually are not satisfactory.

Program of activities. Following are lists of seasonal activities from which selections may be made:

SENIOR HIGH SCHOOL BOYS

Fall

Archery	Golf	Speedball
Cross-country	Horseshoes	Swimming
Football	Playground ball	Tennis
Football field meet	Soccer	Touch football
		Volleyball

Winter

Badminton	Handball	Skiing
Basketball	Ice hockey	Swimming
Bowling	Ping-pong	Track activities
Boxing	Relay carnivals	Twenty-one
Fowl shooting	Shuffleboard	Water polo
Gymnastics	Skating	Wrestling

Spring

Archery	Horseshoes	Tennis
Baseball	Softball	Track activities
Golf	Swimming	Volleyball

SENIOR HIGH SCHOOL GIRLS

Fall

Archery	Handball	Speedball
Deck tennis	Horseshoes or quoits	Swimming
Fieldball	Newcomb	Tennis
Field hockey	Softball	Volleyball
Golf	Soccer	

Winter

Archery	Fencing	Shuffleboard
Badminton	Fowl shooting	Skating
Basketball	Handball	Skiing
Bowling	Ping-pong	Stunts
Deck tennis	Quoits	Swimming
		Twenty-one

Spring

Archery	Handball	Sixty-yard dash
Deck tennis	Horseshoes or quoits	Soccer
Fieldball	Hurdles, 17 to 24 in.	Speedball
Field hockey	Newcomb	Swimming
Golf	Softball	Tennis
		Volleyball

JUNIOR HIGH SCHOOL BOYS

Fall

Archery	Softball	Swimming
Golf	Soccer	Tennis
Horseshoes	Speedball	Touch football
		Volleyball

Winter

Basketball	Handball	Skating
Boxing	Ice hockey	Swimming
Fowl shooting	Ping-pong	Twenty-one
Gymnastics	Shuffleboard	Wrestling

Spring

Archery	Horseshoes or quoits	Tennis
Fieldball	Newcomb	Track activities
Golf	Softball	Volleyball
Hit-pin ball	Swimming	

JUNIOR HIGH SCHOOL GIRLS

Fall

Archery	Horseshoes or quoits	Paddle tennis
Fieldball	Kickball	Schlagball
Golf	Kick-pin ball	Swimming
Hit-pin ball	Newcomb	Tennis
		Volleyball

Winter

Archery	Ping-pong	Skiing
Basketball	Quoits	Swimming
Fowl shooting	Shuffleboard	Twenty-one
Newcomb	Skating	Volleyball

Spring

Archery	Horseshoes or quoits	Schlagball
Fieldball	Kickball	Swimming
Fifty-yard dash	Kick-pin ball	Tennis
Golf	Newcomb	Volleyball
Hit-pin ball	Paddle tennis	

Eligibility. In general, there should be as few as possible, and preferably no, eligibility regulations in effect for participation in intramural athletic activities. The only exceptions might be those pertaining to violations of discipline rules of the school and the requirement that all contestants must have successfully passed physical examinations. In no sense of the word should rules of scholastic eligibility, as they apply to interschool games, be effective for intramurals. Such a policy would defeat the aim of having as nearly 100 per cent participation as possible. Individuals who are varsity-letter winners in one sport should not be allowed to compete in intramurals in that activity unless their participation does not prevent any other high school student from taking part in that sport. At the same time, intramural competition should be equitable.

Awards. It does not seem necessary or desirable that individual awards be given for intramural competition. In intramurals the competition should be for the pleasure of playing, not for an award, be it of little or considerable intrinsic value. It is suggested that for individual or team competition points be allowed which might lead to the awarding of an individual school letter or a unit trophy, provided that a sufficient number of points are earned. This incentive should result in a wider range of activities on the part of individuals or units.

Intramural competition. Most intramural competition is arranged so that round-robin schedules may be played. These allow for a maximum amount of competition. In such cases, generally, it is desirable to set up leagues of not more than eight teams each, because with more teams than this number, competition is likely to be quite

Table 9

Round Robin Schedule

	3 Teams	4 Teams	5 Teams	6 Teams	7 Teams	8 Teams
First-date games	1 plays 2 3 bye	1 plays 2 3 " 4	1 plays 2 3 " 4 5 bye	1 plays 2 3 " 4 5 " 6	1 plays 2 3 " 4 5 " 6 7 bye	1 plays 2 3 " 4 5 " 6 7 " 8
Second-date games	1 plays 3 2 bye	1 plays 3 2 " 4	1 plays 3 4 " 5 2 bye	1 plays 3 2 " 5 4 " 6	1 plays 3 2 " 5 4 " 7 6 bye	1 plays 3 2 " 4 5 " 7 6 " 8
Third-date games	2 plays 3 1 bye	1 plays 4 2 " 3	1 plays 4 2 " 5 3 bye	1 plays 4 2 " 6 3 " 5	1 plays 4 2 " 6 3 " 7 5 bye	1 plays 4 2 " 3 5 " 8 6 " 7
Fourth-date games			1 plays 5 2 " 3 4 bye	1 plays 5 2 " 4 3 " 6	1 plays 5 2 " 7 3 " 6 4 bye	1 plays 5 2 " 8 3 " 7 4 " 6
Fifth-date games			2 plays 4 3 " 5 1 bye	1 plays 6 2 " 3 4 " 5	1 plays 6 2 " 4 5 " 7 3 bye	1 plays 6 2 " 5 3 " 8 4 " 7
Sixth-date games					1 plays 7 3 " 5 4 " . 6 2 bye	1 plays 7 2 " 6 3 " 5 4 " 8
Seventh-date games					2 plays 3 4 " 5 6 " 7 1 bye	1 plays 8 2 " 7 3 " 6 4 " 5

drawn out with consequent loss of interest. If additional competition is necessary, another round may be played, and so on in order to provide as much competition as is desirable. With a large number of teams it usually works out well to arrange for play-offs between league winners, and often runners-up are included in the post-league competition. Table 9 is a schedule for round-robin competition for teams up to and including eight in number.

Another type of competition is single or straight elimination. In this scheme of play the number of byes must be known before competition starts, in order that all of them may occur in the first round. Entries first should be numbered. The bracket must be arranged for 4, 8, 16, and so on in geometric progression, the byes being arranged to fill out the bracket to the next greater number in the progression. To illustrate, suppose there were 11 entries. The bracket would be for 16 teams, the next greater member in the progression above 11. There will be 5 byes, 2 at the top and 3 at the bottom of the bracket. If the number of byes is even, there is an equal number of them at the top and bottom of the bracket. If not, the extra bye is placed at the bottom. An illustrative 11-team single elimination bracket is shown in Table 10.

A double-elimination or double-"knockout" schedule is seldom used unless the number of teams or individuals is small, usually eight or less. This arrangement provides a maximum amount of tournament play because two defeats are necessary before a team is eliminated. With an eight-team entry the schedule as included in Table 11 is operative. If there are only seven teams there is a bye in game 4, and this bye is carried into game 6 or 8. If there are only six teams, byes obtain in games 1 and 4 and then are carried into games 5, 6, 7, and 8. Teams should be given letters A to H. Draw them from the hat and follow the schedule listed in the table. This procedure will bring the two winners into the finals, all losers having been defeated twice.

In addition to the types of competition discussed here there are the ladder and pyramid tournaments as well as consolation series of eliminations. Ladder and pyramid tournaments work better with individual competition (see Figures 13–1 and 13–2). A player challenges one directly above him on the ladder after drawings have been made. In order to advance, a player must defeat the one above him, in which case their names change places on the ladder. In a

TABLE 10

Single-Elimination Bracket

First round	Second round	Third round	Fourth round	Championship
1. Bye)	A			
2. A)	⎯⎯⎯) A			
3. Bye)	K)	)		
4. K)	⎯⎯⎯	) H		
5. B)	J	)		)
6. J)	⎯⎯⎯) H)		)
7. D)	H)		)
8. H)	⎯⎯⎯		) H
9. E)	C		)
10. C)	⎯⎯⎯) C	)
11. Bye)	F)	)	)
12. F)	⎯⎯⎯	) C)
13. Bye)	I	)	
14. I)	⎯⎯⎯) G)
15. Bye)	G)	
16. G)		

TABLE 11

Double Elimination Schedule (8 Teams)

Game	1–A plays B				Game	2–C plays D
"	3–E " F				"	4–G " H
"	5–Loser	game	1	plays loser	game	2
"	6– "	"	3	" "	"	4
"	7–Winner	"	1	" winner	"	2
"	8– "	"	3	" "	"	4
"	9– "	"	5	" loser	"	7
"	10–Loser	"	8	" winner	"	6
"	11–Winner	"	7	" "	"	8
"	12– "	"	9	" "	"	10
"	13– "	"	11	" "	"	12 (winner is champion; loser is runner-up)
"	14–Loser	game	11	plays loser	game	12 (winner wins 3rd place; loser wins 4th place)

pyramid tournament a player may challenge anyone in the same horizontal row with his name. The successful one in the match may challenge anyone in the row above him. Almost unlimited competition is provided in the ladder and pyramid arrangements—sometimes so much that interest is lost because of inability to conclude. A consolation tournament simply is matching first-round losers in a straight or single-elimination bracket; then a procedure identical with that shown in Table 11 is followed.

Suggested Intramural Policies and Practices

As a check list for the conduct of the intramural athletic program, the following suggested policies and practices are included. It may not be possible to realize them in all schools or under all circumstances, but at least they may provoke thought or provide policy stimulation.

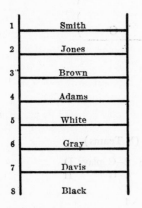

Fig. 13-1. Ladder Tournament.

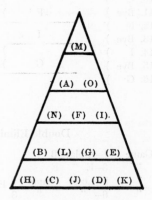

Fig. 13-2. Pyramid Tournament.

1. The intramural program should be an integral part of the physical education program.

2. There should be a director of intramural athletics whose chief interest is the development and administration of these activities.

3. The intramural program should be dignified by its regularity, completeness of schedules, and definiteness of policy.

4. An intramural athletic council should exist in the school.

5. The cost of intramural athletic supplies should be met by the board of education.

6. The local school paper should give an appropriate amount of space to intramural activities.

7. Constant emphasis should be placed on the parity of intramural and interscholastic activities.

8. Keep the school-patron public informed concerning the scope, size, and objectives of the intramural program.

9. No matter how small the school, there is a place for intramural athletic competition in it.

10. Combine the intramural and physical education activities as far as possible but maintain intramurals on an elective or voluntary basis.

11. Use the intramural program as a method of fixing health, safety, and sanitation habits in the lives of participants.

12. Broaden the program to include individual activities as well as team sports.

Extramurals. Relatively recently the term "extramurals" has evolved in connection with the intramural athletic programs in high schools. It usually refers to competition between schools, or between groups from schools, other than that usually found in the regular interscholastic athletic program. Quite often extramurals are the outgrowth or culmination of intramurals in a school. Intramural champions from one school may play similar sports champions from another school. Play days or sports days involving large numbers of participants from two or more schools may be arranged. In extramurals usually no eligibility requirements are in effect other than minimum standards which a local school may establish.

In Michigan the state high school athletic association recognizes and encourages this development as indicated by the following interpretations under its rules governing eligibility and contests between high schools:

For boys there may be participation in a sport by a school within its general or adjacent service area in one interschool athletic contest, tournament, or meet, which is the outgrowth of the intramural programs of the schools concerned, without compliance with State Association Eligibility and Contest Regulations. In such cases, however, no student may compete in such a contest, tournament, or meet who has represented his school during a current school year in an interscholastic athletic contest in that sport.

For girls there may be participation in a sport by a school within its general or adjacent service area in not more than three (3) interschool athletic contests, invitational games, sports days, or meets which are the outgrowth of the intramural programs of the schools concerned, without compliance with State Association Eligibility and Contest Regulations. In such cases, however, no girl may compete in these contests, invitational games, sports days, or meets who has represented her school in that sport other than in this informal type of competition during a current school year.[1]

Questions for Study and Discussion

1. Discuss intramural vs. interscholastic athletics. Are these programs in opposition to each other?

2. How may the interscholastic athletic program be likened to bands, orchestras, school plays? To what can the intramural program be compared?

3. What were some of the disclosures of World War II regarding intramurals?

4. Name and discuss several general intramural objectives.

5. Set up and discuss the administration of an ideal intramural program for a high school of five hundred students.

6. Discuss eligibility requirements and awards policies for intramurals. Should either or both be required? Explain your position fully.

7. List and explain the types of competition common in intramural athletics.

8. What is meant by extramural athletic competition?

[1] Michigan High School Athletic Association, 1961–1962 *Handbook*, pp. 44–45.

14

Athletics
for Girls

Consideration of the subject of girls' athletics is included in this discussion because in many schools it is a part of their general athletic program. There are decided differences of opinion as to the place, if any, which an interscholastic athletic program for girls should have in present-day high schools. The greatest amount of interschool competition for girls remains in the smaller high schools of the country, those pretty largely rural in nature. The objections most frequently heard are leveled against the manner in which the present program is conducted rather than against the policy of athletic competition between girls.

No condemnation of competition for girls is intended here, but definite objection will be taken to some present practices. Views of leaders in the field of physical education and women's athletics will be presented in order to show trends in thought. Suggested substitutes for present objectionable practices also will be presented.

Points of View of Leaders and Organizations

It seems wise to turn to women's organizations themselves for the best thought on the problem of athletic competition for women and girls. This policy has been followed by the author in an attempt to present an unprejudiced viewpoint on this somewhat controversial subject.

An athletic platform. The Women's Division, National Amateur

Athletic Federation of America, was one of the early organizations representing girls and women, many of whom were beyond high school age. Several state high school athletic associations became members of this now defunct organization and endorsed its general objectives which were to promote:

Athletic activities for all girls and women, suited to the individual's age and capacities;

The individual enjoyment of sport and the development of sportsmanship and character rather than competitive athletics which stresses the enjoyment of spectators or the athletic reputation or gate receipts of institutions or communities;

Publicity and awards which emphasize the sport and its values rather than competitors;

The use of medical examinations, "follow-up" and supervision as the basis for participation in athletic activities and the training and employment of women leaders qualified to assume responsibility for the physical education and recreation of girls and women.

The purpose of mentioning and quoting the Women's Division is to present the attitude of this early national organization itself regarding competition in athletics by girls and women. From allusions in the preceding resolution it is apparent that this organization recognized that there had been attendant evils in previous types of girls' athletics. Against these it took its stand. It is interesting to compare these early pronouncements concerning girls' athletics with those of the Division of Girls and Women's Sports of the American Association for Health, Physical Education, and Recreation and note their similarity:

Standards for organization of competitive activities. One of the most comprehensive publications concerning Standards in Athletics for girls has been prepared by the committee on standards of the Division for Girls and Women's Sports of the American Association for Health, Physical Education and Recreation. This committee has prepared a complete pamphlet on Standards in Sports for Girls and Women,[1] and from it an adaptation has been made, entitled "Desira-

---

[1] *Desirable Practices in Sports for Girls and Women,* Division for Girls and Women's Sports, American Association for Health, Physical Education and Recreation, Washington, D. C., 1957.

ble Practices in Sports for Girls and Women." [2] These practices, quoted verbatim below, have been the basis for statements prepared by many state physical education and athletic associations concerning their policies in connection with interscholastic athletics for girls. As will be noted from the recommendations of the Division for Girls and Women's Sports of this organization, suggestions are made concerning standards for desirable practices, leadership, health, publicity, and types of competition.

We believe that, for the welfare of the girls and women who participate in sports, certain practices should be followed. We therefore present the following suggestions for your guidance in conducting athletic programs.

STANDARDS

The program of sports activities for girls and women should:

1. Be based upon the recognition of individual differences in age; body build; interests; ability; experience; health; and the stages of physiological, emotional, and social maturity of the participants.
2. Be organized to provide opportunity for groupings at all skill levels, development from simple to complex skills, development of leadership and group achievement, and evaluation of the suitability of each activity.
3. Encourage the development of skill and sportsmanship by a variety of sound methods and practices.
4. Be scheduled at regular periods of limited length at frequent intervals and at a time of day when energy is at a high level.
5. Provide for the selection of members of all teams so that they play against those of approximately the same ability and maturity.
6. Be taught, coached, and officiated by qualified women *whenever* and *wherever* possible.
7. Be officiated by officials whose decisions are sound, consistent, and impartial.
8. Include the use of official rules authorized by the Division for Girls and Women's Sports of the American Association for Health, Physical Education, and Recreation.
9. Stimulate the participants to play for the enjoyment of playing and not for tangible rewards or because of artificial incentives.
10. Include a variety of sports, both team and individual, and provide

[2] Revision of 1957.

opportunity for all girls wishing to participate to be a member of a team in those sports for which teams are organized.

11. Include informal social events in connection with competition.
12. Require written parental permission for minors engaging in any extramural competition.
13. Include guidance for girls and women concerning appropriate costume for sports.
14. Limit extramural competition to a small geographic area.
15. Furnish safe transportation in bonded carriers.
16. Be financed by the promoting agency and not be dependent on gate receipts for its existence.
17. Include competition for girls independent from that arranged for boys (eliminating such events as double-header games or "curtain raisers") except in those activities in which boys and girls are encouraged to play together on mixed teams.
18. Be limited as to the total length of sports seasons and the maximum number of practice periods and games to be played in a day or a week. Specific recommendations pertaining to the factors mentioned above may be obtained from the specific standards referred to on page 4.

LEADERSHIP

Administrators, teachers or coaches, and players should be primarily concerned with the outcomes of the program.

1. The Administrator is directly responsible for:
   A. Selecting qualified women to direct the program.
   B. Providing facilities, equipment, and finances to carry on the program.
   C. Providing equal use of facilities and equipment for boys and girls.
   D. Providing health safeguards.
   E. Guiding publicity to emphasize the educational and recreational values of the program.
2. The teacher or coach is responsible for:
   A. Having a thorough knowledge of the games and their rules and strategy.
   B. Providing opportunity for all girls to play.
   C. Encouraging skillful play for full enjoyment of the game.
   D. Emphasizing the importance of health examinations.
   E. Developing intelligent leadership and wise followership among the players.
   F. Conducting activities on a sound competitive basis.
   G. Exemplifying those traits which she tries to develop in others.

3. The player is responsible for her own conduct as shown through:
   A. Intelligent health practices.
   B. Courtesy, fair play, and good sportsmanship.
   C. High quality leadership within her own group.
   D. Emotional control in all game situations.
   E. Playing to the best of her ability.

HEALTH

Provision must be made for careful supervision of the health of all players.

1. Participants must have periodic health examinations.
2. After serious illness or injury, written permission from a physician should be required to resume participation.
3. First aid supplies should be available at practices and games.
4. Participation during the menstrual period should be determined on the basis of individual differences.
5. Equipment and facilities should be hygienic and safe.
6. Players should be removed from activity if they are injured or over-fatigued or show evidence of emotional instability.

PUBLICITY

A planned program of publicity should present interesting information on the program, its standards, aims, and outcomes. The publicity should be carefully interpreted to newswriters, parents, community leaders, the players, and their associates. Publicity should stress:

1. The recreational and social values of sports rather than the winning of championships.
2. Achievements of the groups and teams rather than those of individuals.

TYPES OF COMPETITION

The method of organizing competition must be determined in terms of desirable outcomes. The guides to constructive competition are that the program of sports shall offer equal opportunity to all in terms of individual ability, be wide in range, be adapted to the needs and interests of the participants, and be honestly and expertly led.

Intramural. Competition of groups playing one another within their school, industrial group, or organization. Intramural competition should have priority for facilities, time, and leadership because it serves the greatest number of players.

Extramural. Competition involving a group or team from one school, recreational center, industrial group, or organization playing with a group or team from another school, industrial group, or organization. Types of extramural competition are:

1. SPORTS DAYS—An event, frequently including more than one activity, to which several schools, playgrounds, industrial groups, or organizations may bring two or more groups of players. Each group participates as a unit.
2. PLAY DAYS—An informal type of competition in which color teams are selected from the players of the participating schools or clubs.
3. TELEGRAPHIC MEETS—Teams compete with each other by establishing records against time or for score while performing in their own location. Such records are sent to a central committee for comparison. Archery, pistol and rifle, swimming events, bowling, and track and field are adaptable to this plan.
4. INVITATIONAL EVENTS—Such as a symposium, jamboree, game, or match other than a league game.
5. INTERSCHOLASTIC OR INTERCOLLEGIATE GAMES—Games for selected groups trained and coached to play a series of scheduled games and tournaments with similar teams from other schools, playgrounds, cities, or institutions within a limited geographical area. To be offered only as a supplement to adequate intramural and extramural programs.

No one type of competitive organization can be designated as the approved form. The method of organizing competition must be determined by the desirable possibilities it provides, not by the type into which it can be classified.

Psychological considerations. The comment regarding athletics for girls thus far has been general and has included numerous reasons why their athletic activities should be carefully supervised and directed. Mention has been made of physiological differences between boys and girls which must be considered in participation by the latter in an athletic program. There is nothing inherently wrong in competition. The problem is to so arrange the competition that it is beneficial to all concerned. In adopting a competitive program the general physical make-up of participants is an important factor. Boys of certain physical types play football, other distinct physical groups are sprinters or distance men, or they enter weight events. To a greater extent, activities should be adapted to girls because differences in their anatomical and physiological make-ups are more complex than boys. It is thus more difficult for them to choose sports on the basis of superficial or natural selection.

Girl's athletics and the Society of State Directors of Physical and Health Education. As indicated previously, this organization is composed of the men and women who are responsible for administration of state programs of physical and health education in approximately two-thirds of the states. In numerous instances the handling of state recreation and safety programs also comes within their scope of duties. Various resolutions concerning girls' athletic problems, as they have come from practical experience, have been adopted, one of which follows.

WHEREAS, Approximately fifty percent of the public school enrollment is girls; and

WHEREAS, It is generally agreed that athletics are a part of the regular physical education program; therefore,

BE IT RESOLVED, That we, The Society of State Directors of Health and Physical Education, work in close harmony with the Division for Girls and Women's Sports of the American Association for Health, Physical Education, and Recreation to mutually work out a satisfactory program in agreement with the accepted standards of physical education.[3]

Statement of National Federation of State High School Athletic Associations. From a practical and actually existing standpoint, the National Federation has been in a position to summarize the situation concerning girl's interscholastic athletics as it exists in the several states. It has no specific standards or regulations for such programs, and if it had, they would have to be in the form of recommendations because of the nature of its organization. It does, however, present a rather comprehensive picture of the manner in which the problem is handled in general throughout the nation.

Since most State High School Associations are organized to supervise high school activities, boys and girls, the same general operation policies are followed for both. An attempt is made by each State Association and by the National Federation to pool the best thought and experiences of those authorized to work in this field and to crystallize this into a form for practical use. Because there is less intensive competition between schools in girls' athletics, the needs and problems are different and there is a wide variation in procedures in the different states.

[3] Society of State Directors of Health and Physical Education, Twenty-First Annual Meeting, Apr. 19–21, 1947 *Report of Resolutions Committee,* p. 4.

Currently, nine states (Alabama, Colorado, Illinois, Montana, New York, Oregon, Utah, Wisconsin and Wyoming) prohibit athletic contests between schools for girls' teams. Nine additional states prohibit basketball tournaments for girls' teams. Several other states discourage contests between schools for girls' teams. In contrast, about half of the states encourage some interscholastic contests for girls and the states of Arkansas, Saskatchewan, Georgia, South Carolina, North Carolina, Tennessee, Louisiana, Oklahoma, Texas, Iowa, North Dakota and New Brunswick (Canada) have a state championship series in girls' basketball..

No interstate basketball tournament for girls is sanctioned unless it is purely community in character and unless the request is made by both interested state associations and for reasons which seem to make the event in harmony with the policies in effect in such state associations.

State Associations are urged to set up machinery whereby the efforts and viewpoints of all school leaders may be coordinated in a healthy program which will contribute to the development of fitness, enjoyable use of leisure time and those qualities which are associated with wholesome womanhood. Prerequisites to such program are the placing of emphasis on a wide variety of activities, the interesting of great numbers in participation and the availability of adequately trained leaders and coaches.

All groups agree that any adequate athletic program for girls must include a thorough physical checkup at stated intervals; that all participants should be given an opportunity to participate in some type of activity; that the schedule of activity should be based on health safeguards; that the best results are secured when there is adequate supervision and coaching by trained personnel; that competition should be confined to reasonably limited areas; and that provision should be made for friendly social activities in connection with any competitive event.

Several joint meetings of representatives of the National Federation and of the D.G.W.S. have been held. Both groups desire to avoid the excesses which tend to grow up when an extensive program of interscholastic competition is promoted. Attention is directed to the fact that it is possible to build a girls' athletic program on a broad base of intramural contests and social and play activities. State associations and divisions of the D.G.W.S. differ in their beliefs as to whether interscholastic contests for girls make a contribution great enough to balance the difficulties which often arise when such contests are sponsored. These opinions are greatly influenced by conditions in connection with teaching personnel and training facilities. Almost any program, including an interscholastic program, can be made to function efficiently if there are adequate, well trained personnel and proper facilities. In their absence, there are many dangers.[4]

State Association Girls' Athletic Regulations

It is not sound educationally to condemn any of the present undesirable types of athletics for girls without offering something in their place. Complete or partial prohibition of the playing of interscholastic contests between girls' teams may be one way of solving the problem. New York, Wisconsin, Nebraska, and Illinois are among the states which have enacted such regulations. In Nebraska and Illinois, however, substitutes for interschool games have been provided.

As indicated above, some states prohibit only certain types of interschool competition for girls. In New York, however, the provision in its Constitution is specific:

To promote all forms of athletics for high school boys.[5]

Wisconsin indicates the following among the duties of its Board of Control:

It shall prohibit girls from participating in interscholastic athletic competition in baseball, basketball, boxing, football, hockey, soccer, softball, swimming, track, and wrestling.[6]

The regulation in Nebraska is similar to that in Ohio, but in Illinois there are restrictions in some sports and regulatory measures in others:

No school belonging to this Association shall permit girls to participate in interscholastic athletic contests; except that interscholastic contests in golf, archery, and tennis shall be permitted provided they are conducted

[4] National Federation of State High School Athletic Associations, 1960–1961 *Handbook*, p. 59.
[5] New York State Public High School Athletic Association, 1960–1961 *Handbook*, p. 20.
[6] Wisconsin Interscholastic Athletic Association, *Thirty-Seventh Yearbook* (1960), p. 14.

under the rules prescribed by the Illinois League of High School Girls' Athletic Associations.[7]

Other states that prohibit or restrict interscholastic athletic activities for girls have regulations similar to those above. In some states, however, nearly complete programs are maintained. In such cases usually all eligibility regulations which apply to boys' athletics also are in effect for girls' interschool competition, except for specific modifications. In Iowa there is a separate state girls' athletic association that is not affiliated with the Iowa High School Athletic Association. During the 1960–1961 school year several states conducted state basketball championships for girls (see page 59). It is apparent, therefore, that in basketball at least, interschool competition for girls varies from those states which definitely prohibit the activity to those which sponsor state championships in it.

Indiana states that the regulations of its state association apply to girls' athletics except in regard to play days:

Rule 1. Girls' athletics are bound by the rules and regulations of the I. H. S. A. A. except for participation in Girls' Play Day program.

Rule 2. Rules for girls' contests shall be those published for the Division for Girls and Women's Sports of the American Association for Health, Physical Education and Recreation.

Rule 3. Inter-school basketball games and tourneys are not recommended for girls.

Rule 4. It is recommended that women coaches and officials be employed for girls' contests and Play Day programs.

Rule 5. Girls' basketball teams may not play in state or national tourneys.

Rule 6. Play Day program for Girls:

a. A Play Day is a meeting of more than two schools where the program consists of games, sports, folk dancing and social entertainment. Participation is on the basis of color or mixed teams chosen by lot and does not represent specific schools.

b. Parents' and physicians' certificates are required for Play Days.

c. Scholarship, out of season participation, age, and enrollment requirements are the same as for inter-school competition.

d. Play Days shall be approved by the principals of the schools involved and certification given for the girls participating in them.

[7] Illinois High School Association, 1960–1961 *Handbook,* p. 25.

e. Girls who play on color or mixed teams in a Play Day program which may include swimming, archery, tennis, track, volleyball, basketball, softball, etc., do not make themselves ineligible for their own high school teams in these sports in regular inter-school games.[8]

In Pennsylvania the situation is regulated by its general code plus "Additional Rules and Regulations Pertaining to Girls' Athletics" which follow: [9]

[Comment on Girls Interscholastic Athletics by the Women's Committee of the P. I. A. A.

An athletic program for girls should provide opportunities for participation to all girls desiring athletic experience. For this reason a broad intramural program is recommended. Interscholastic competition, when desired, should be an outgrowth of this broad intramural program. Such competition need not be confined to a varsity team alone. Several teams, graded by ability, could participate in this type of program.

Athletics for girls should be recognized on a basis equitable to that given to the program for boys. Therefore, facilities for girls' athletics should provide suitable playing fields, gymnasiums, equipment and the like.

It is understood that, for interscholastic athletic competition all provisions and regulations of the Constitution and By-Laws of the P. I. A. A. shall apply to girls athletics as well as to boys.]

SECTION 1. OFFICIAL RULES FOR SPORTS.

The official rules for the following list of sports are the Official Rules as published for the Division of Girls and Women's Sports of the American Association for Health, Physical Education and Recreation except as they may be modified by the Board of Control of the P. I. A. A.

1.	Archery	8.	Riflery
2.	Badminton	9.	Soccer
3.	Basket Ball	10.	Softball
4.	Bowling	11.	Swimming Aquatics
5.	Golf	12.	Tennis
6.	Hockey	13.	Volley Ball
7.	LaCrosse	14.	Field and Track

[8] Indiana High School Athletic Association, 1960 *Handbook*, p. 38.
[9] Pennsylvania Interscholastic Athletic Association, 1958 *Constitution and By-Laws*, pp. 40–41.

SECTION 2. RULES.

Rule 1. That the total number of games played for interscholastic athletic competition should be limited to one game per week.

Rule 2. That the standard for scheduling games in the following activities should not exceed 8 games in basket ball, 8 games in soccer and 8 games in hockey per season.

Rule 3. That no game be scheduled that would necessitate the team being away over night.

SECTION 3. CONCERNING PERSONS IN CHARGE

Rule 1. A woman professional employee of the district shall be present at all practices and games.

Rule 2. Only women officials who qualify under P. I. A. A. Rules shall officiate girls interscholastic athletic games.

(Note: Rule 2 of Section 3 shall become effective only after qualified women officials are made available by the Board of Control.)

Rule 3. That the director of girls physical education shall be consulted when schedules for girls are being planned.

SECTION 4. CONCERNING PRACTICE IN ATHLETICS.

Rule 1. That a minimum period of three weeks of training precede the playing of the first interschool game. This provision shall apply to each individual player.

SECTION 5. RECOMMENDATIONS.

1. It is recommended that girls athletic teams shall not compete for state championship honors, riflery and golf excepted.

2. That interschool games be played in the afternoon.

In concluding this phase of discussion of athletic programs for girls, Girls' Interscholasic Athletic Regulations in effect in Michigan are included because of differences from the above that they contain:

Note: Regulations relative to girls' interscholastic athletics which have been adopted by the Representative Council appear below. They are effective for all junior and senior high schools sponsoring interscholastic athletics (except skiing) and were recommended to the Representative Council by the Girls' Athletic Committee at its meeting May 2, 1960. It should be understood that all eligibility and contest regulations appearing in Articles I–IV, inclusive, of the State Association Regulations apply alike to boys and girls except as herein modified.

1. Teams in all sports are to be in charge of and under the direct supervision of a woman member of the faculty and shall be coached by women.

2. Each squad shall number at least ten (10) players, preferably fifteen (15) to twenty (20), or more.

3. Practice periods in a sport shall be limited to four (4) hours per week with a maximum of one and one half (1½) hours per period. A maximum practice period of one (1) hour is recommended.

4. Not more than one (1) games per team in any one sport per calendar week shall be played by a school.

5. There shall be a thorough medical examination of each girl on the squad of the sport concerned during the current school year and prior to interscholastic athletic competition in that sport. In any questionable cases the student is to be withheld from competition. After any protracted period of illness of a student there is to be an additional medical examination before she is allowed to compete. It is recommended that when a girl shows continuing symptoms of physical, mental, or emotional disturbance she be referred for professional help and withheld from all athletic participation until approval is given for her return.

6. Girls are not to engage in interscholastic athletic contests when part or all of the membership of one or both of the competing teams is composed of boys.

7. Official girls rules are to be used in all sports as recommended by the Division of Girls and Women's Sports of the American Association for Health, Physical Education, and Recreation.

8. Officials used in all girls interscholastic athletic contests must be registered with the Michigan High School Athletic Association during the current school year. It is recommended that DGWS rated women officials be used in all girls interscholastic athletic contests wherever possible. (Registration fee for women officials is one dollar ($1.00).)

9. High schools having a total enrollment of less than seventy-five (75) in grades nine to twelve, inclusive, may use IN GIRLS SOFTBALL ONLY, students from the eighth grade of that school.

10. For junior and senior high school girls, a broad intramural athletic program is recommended which may be extended by a school to allow participation within its general or adjacent service area in not more than three (3) interschool athletic contests, invitational games, sports days, or meets which are the outgrowth of the intramural programs of the schools concerned, without compliance with State Association Eligibility

and Contest Regulations. In such cases, however, no girl may compete in these contests, invitational games, sports days, or meets, who has represented her school in that sport other than in this informal type of competition during a current school year.

GIRLS BASKETBALL REGULATIONS

1. The girls basket ball schedule of a senior high school is to be limited to a maximum of eight (8) games per team. Junior high schools may have a school schedule of five (5) games, none of which may be intercity.

2. Senior high schools sponsoring more than one girls interscholastic basketball team may not allow a girl to participate in more than one game per week. Participation in any part of a game constitutes a game.[10]

It is apparent that interschool competition for girls should and will continue in many schools for some time to come. In situations in which it is carried on in accordance with the above recommendations, the program may be very satisfactory. Again, the important considerations are the methods of administration and policies upon which the program is founded. It seems as though there is a preponderance of evidence toward the modification of interschool athletic competition for girls, if it is not to be eliminated entirely. A few plans will be discussed that have been substituted for the commonly understood interscholastic athletic program for high school girls.

Invitational contests. Invitational contests generally do not comprise part of a schedule that is drawn up at the start of the season. Rather, the games are usually impromptu and decidedly informal. Often they are the outgrowth of the intramural program in a particular activity, and a few games are played near the end of the season between near-by schools. One school invites another to send over a hockey, volleyball, or basketball team. The affair is social rather than strictly athletic. This type of competition for girls is most applicable where there are several schools in the same city or in metropolitan areas. It furnishes a stimulus for intramurals, allows a limited amount of controlled competition, and results in the games being played for the benefit of the girls themselves. These games usually take place in the afternoon before a restricted student audience.

[10] Michigan School Athletic Association, 1961–1962 *Handbook,* pp. 80–81.

Intramurals. There is not much doubt that intramural athletics have made greater strides in girls' programs than in boys', largely because fewer schools have had interscholastic programs for girls. Whereas a few years ago regular interschool contests were played between girls' teams, intramurals have taken their place in many schools.

In many small schools the point is made that there are not enough girls for both an intramural and an interscholastic program. In such cases the girls' games usually are combined with the boys' game program, which results in various problems and objections. Since most interschool competition for girls still remains in the small schools, these schools should be the first to substitute intramurals or something else. Usually there is an insufficient number of girls to ensure that enough are physically fit to compete at times of scheduled games. Men often do part or all of the coaching. Playing conditions at home or away often are not satisfactory in small schools. It appears much more sensible to attempt to protect high school girls from competing under unfavorable conditions by arranging a local intramural program that may be much more easily controlled.

Play days—Sports days. Mention has been made of a close connection between intramural athletics for girls and athletic play days and sports days. These play and sports days are the outgrowth of intramurals. What is a play day? In it students from several schools engage in competition in which the identity of the individual school is lost. Teams are composed of members of all the schools concerned. Usually, names of colors, animals, or the like are selected for the team. A sports day is one in which the play is between schools whose identities are maintained and they compete as units. In both types varied activities take place and emphasis is placed on social rather than competitive aspects. An occasional sports or play day between two or more schools has a valuable social effect on the girls who participate—it gets them acquainted with other girls; all compete because of the wide range of activities; and such play is for the pleasure of playing, not for the benefit of an audience.

Telegraphic and postal meets culminating in play days sometimes are held. In such cases the competition is arranged so that it is in accordance with established standards. One school competes against the other for high score. This plan is especially effective in competition for achievement standards.

Previous discussion (see page 392) indicates the high value that the Division of Girls and Women's Sports places on play days, sports days, and telegraphic meets for girls' athletic competition. These events have so many definite values that they should be used extensively. They may be carried on with little or no expense, but they do require efficient organization. Among the greatest benefits derived from this type of competition for girls is the broad scope of activities. Incidentally, it may be pointed out that the potentialities of school play day and sports day competition for boys are as yet pretty much unexplored.

Girls' athletic associations. Outstanding among the substitutes for older types of interschool athletics for high school girls has been the successful operation of state girls' athletic associations. At least two states—Illinois and Nebraska—have done considerable work in the development of this project; and in these states the organizations are part of the state athletic or activities associations. As stated previously, Illinois does not allow interscholastic athletic competition for girls' teams except in tennis, golf, and archery. In Illinois a woman is manager of the girls' association; a section of the state activities association bulletin is devoted to girls' activities; and the state association aids in financing the girls' organization.

In general, the procedure followed is the formation of local high school girls' athletic associations which then affiliate with the state organization by payment of a small membership fee. The basis of awards is the earning of points. Local, telegraphic or postal contests and games are held, achievement standards are set up, and usually certain health standards are established whereby girls may earn points in their own schools toward state letter awards. Schools are divided into different groups, dependent in most cases upon the physical education facilities offered by the school; and the points a girl may earn in schools in each group are weighted accordingly. The scope of activities in girls' organizations includes play days and sports in the fall and spring; telegraphic basketball-shooting contests; track and field meets, and the like; skill tests; and a health program. Illinois also has developed the summer camp plan, with numerous camps located throughout the state. Girls receive points for participation in activities that lead toward the receipt of the state association awards.

In some instances, schools in states which do not have girls' athletic associations have local organizations and award school letters for proficiency in many of the activities listed above. This is an excellent plan, but the state award undoubtedly adds some incentive. Often such factors as scholarship, sportsmanship, posture, and adherence to health rules are factors for which points may be received. Women physical education teachers, through local girls' athletic associations, may set up these standards. When everything is considered, it seems that some form of organization for high school girls that gives them an incentive to play and at the same time betters their general health is highly desirable. It appears to have many advantages over the rather traditional types of girls' athletic competition.

Organization of girls' athletic associations. In the two states mentioned above the girls' athletic associations are part of their local state associations. In reality, they are leagues of local high school girls' athletic associations. In all of them, emphasis on interschool competition is reduced to the minimum and in its place programs of local achievement standards, play days and festivals, and telegraphic, telephonic, and postal meets are conducted.

Illinois was the first state to affiliate its League of High School Girls' Athletic Association, with the Illinois High School Association. In 1944 the League became a definite division of the I.H.S.A. The supervision and control of the League rests with the board of directors of the state association but the policy has been followed of calling upon the elected officers of the League for necessary technical advice and assistance. The organization of the Nebraska Girls' Athletic Association is not so elaborate as that in Illinois but its objectives are similar. In that state an advisory committee is appointed by the Board of Control of the Nebraska High School Activities Association to work with the secretary in formulating general policies. As a guide to state associations, as well as local high schools contemplating changes in their girls' athletic programs, the complete provisions in effect in Illinois are presented because this state has been the leader in this field:

THE ILLINOIS LEAGUE OF HIGH SCHOOL GIRLS' ATHLETIC ASSOCIATIONS

Article I—Object

The object of the League shall be to stimulate interest and participation in girls' athletic activities by promoting the organization of Girls' Athletic Associations.

Article II—Membership

Section 1. A local association in any high school that is a member in good standing in the Illinois High School Association is eligible to participate in the program of the League.

Section 2. Such a local association may become a participating member of the League by meeting the following requirements:

(1) Adopting the provisions governing the participation of members of the IHSA in the League program.

(2) Securing the approval of the League Executive Committee upon a local constitution which is drafted in conformity with the outline given in the League Manual.

(3) Making application for participating membership using the League application blank.

(4) Adopting the Point System of the League.

OR

submitting for the approval of the League Executive Committee, a point system which meets the qualifications stated herewith:

(a) Such point systems shall have been established and functioning for at least two years preceding application for participating membership in the Illinois League of High School Girls' Athletic Associations.

(b) The requirements to be fulfilled for all awards shall be comparable to those stated in the League Point System.

(c) Steps shall be taken toward a gradual change to the adoption of the Awards and Point System of the League, which change shall be completed within three years from date of participating membership.

Note of Explanation: This should not be construed to mean that a period of probation is necessary. On the contrary, local associations may be formed at any time.

(5) Paying the annual participation fee to the Treasurer.

Section 3. No local association shall permit girls to participate in interscholastic competition except in golf, tennis and archery. All other competition shall be on an intramural or other intraschool basis. Interscholastic golf, tennis and archery shall be subject to the regulations as stated in Article III of the By-Laws of the League.

Section 4. Any local association failing to comply with any of the requirements of the League shall forfeit its participating membership.

Article III—Meetings

Section 1. Each local association shall be entitled to one voting delegate at all meetings of the League. This delegate shall be a teacher eligible to membership on the Executive Committee as described in Article IV, Section 1, of this Constitution, or the principal of the high school.

Section 2. A meeting may be called by a majority vote of the Executive Committee and shall be called upon petition of twenty participating members acting through their official representatives.

Section 3. Thirty days before any meeting, the Secretary shall notify all members of the exact time and place of meeting.

Section 4. Meetings of the Executive Committee may be called by the President.

Section 5. The official delegates present at a meeting shall constitute a quorum for the transaction of business.

Article IV—Executive Committee

Section 1. The Executive Committee of the League shall consist of eight members as follows:

(a) Five members to be elected, each for a term of three years, as provided in Article V of this Constitution. These members shall be women actively engaged in teaching Girls' Physical Education in high schools that are participating members of the League.

(b) The Assistant Executive Secretary of the Illinois High School Association who conducts the business of the League.

(c) The Executive Secretary and the Treasurer of the Illinois High School Association.

Section 2. A majority of the members of the Executive Committee shall constitute a quorum for the transaction of business.

Article V—Election of Officers

Section 1. For the purpose of electing the members of the Executive Committee and providing equal representation for all parts of the state, the state shall be divided into five districts. (See inside front cover of League handbook.) Each district shall consist of adjacent counties and shall include approximately the same number of participating schools. Beginning in 1948 and each five years thereafter the Executive Committee shall review the districts and if deemed necessary shall redistrict the state.

Section 2. Not later than November 15 each year, the Executive Committee shall cause to be mailed to the principal of each participating school in each district in which an Executive Committee member is to be elected, a letter giving the boundaries of the district and a primary ballot requesting a nomination for a member of the Executive Committee.

One person in each school eligible to serve as a voting delegate as described in Article III, Section 2, of this Constitution, may nominate one person as a candidate. This candidate must be a person eligible to serve as a member of the Executive Committee from the district in which the election is to be held as described in Article IV, Section 1 (a), of this Constitution. These nominations must be in the League Office not later than November 25. A committee of tellers appointed by the Executive Committee shall count the votes. The two persons from each district receiving the highest number of nominating votes shall be declared the nominees and they shall be notified immediately of their nomination by mail. In case of a tie vote in any district, the tellers shall determine the winner or winners of the tie by lot.

Section 3. No member shall succeed herself in office except that a member elected to fill an unexpired term may be elected to succeed herself.

Section 4. Not later than December 1 each year the secretary shall send to the adviser of the Girls' Athletic Association in each participating school in each district in which a member is to be elected a ballot on which are the names of the nominees. The ballot shall be marked by one person eligible to serve as a voting delegate from the school as described in Article III, Section 2, of this Constitution. The ballot shall be returned to the League Office not later than December 10. The ballot shall be counted in the League Office not later than December 15, by a committee of tellers appointed by the Executive Committee. The candidate receiving the highest number of votes in each district shall be declared as elected and shall take office immediately for a term of three years. In case of a tie vote in a district the winner shall be determined by lot.

Section 5. In the event that an Executive Committee member ceases to teach in a participating school in the district from which she was elected, her successor shall be appointed by the Executive Committee.

If an Executive Committee member is removed from her district because of the redistricting of the state but continues to teach in a participating school that was located in the district from which she was elected, she shall continue to represent that district for the balance of her term.

Section 6. Any vacancies occurring on the Executive Committee shall be filled by the Executive Committee. Members appointed to fill such vacancies on the committee shall serve until the next annual election when a permanent member shall be elected to serve the unexpired term.

Section 7. The officers of the Executive Committee shall be President, Vice President, and Secretary. The President and Vice President shall be elected by the Executive Committee from among its members. The Assistant Executive Secretary of the Illinois High School Association who is in charge of the League shall serve as Secretary.

Article VI—Duties of Executive Committee

Section 1. The executive committee shall serve as an advisory committee to the Board of Directors of the Illinois High School Association in all matters pertaining to the League Constitution and By-Laws.

Section 2. All business necessary for organizing and conducting the program of the League, as stated or implied in the Constitution or By-Laws, shall be considered and transacted by the executive committee in accordance with the provisions outlined by the Board of Directors of the Illinois High School Association.

Section 3. Each member of the executive committee shall perform such duties as are expressed or implied in the Constitution and By-Laws for her office as a representative of the League members in her district.

Article VII—Fees

Section 1. The fiscal year of the League shall be from July 1 to June 30.

Section 2. The annual fees for schools that wish to participate in the program of the League shall be based on the fiscal year. Payment for a year must be made on or after March 1 and not later than June 1 of the preeeding year.

Section 3. A penalty of $1.00 will be added to fees paid after June 1.

Section 4. The amount of the annual participation fee shall be based upon the enrollment of the school and shall be as follows:

$1.50—schools whose total enrollment is 99 or less.
$2.50—schools whose total enrollment is 100 through 299.
$5.00—schools whose total enrollment is 300 or more.

Article VIII—Awards and Pins

Section 1. Awards shall be granted students who meet the requirements of the League Point System.

Section 2. There shall be four awards provided for by the point system. Two of these shall be known as Local Awards and two shall be known as State Awards.

Section 3. Each local association shall select and order its own local awards directly from award dealers.

Section 4. State awards shall be purchased from the League office and shall be the same for all schools.

Section 5. All awards shall be paid for by the students earning them unless the local association provides otherwise.

Section 6. No award of any kind having an utilitarian value of more than two dollars, except a school or G.A.A. letter or emblem, shall be given to any member in a participating school.

Section 7. Any member of a local G.A.A. in good standing who has earned at least 24 points according to the League point system is entitled to purchase the State League Pin which is available at the League office.

The Constitution and By-Laws of the League may be amended by the Board of Directors of the Illinois High School Association. It shall be the policy of the Board to seek the advice and assistance of the Executive Committee of the League before making major changes in these provisions.[11]

Article IX—Amendments

As indicated on page 395, the only interscholashtic athletic competition for girls permitted in Illinois is in golf, tennis, and archery, and only then if the contests are conducted under the following League regulations:

REGULATIONS GOVERNING GIRLS' INTERSCHOLASTIC GOLF, TENNIS AND ARCHERY

Section 1. No school that is a member of the Illinois High School Association shall permit its girls to participate in any interscholastic competition except in golf, tennis and archery. All interscholastc contests in golf, tennis and archery in which girls in member schools participate must be conducted in accordance with the rules as stated hereinafter.

Note: This limitation on girls' interscholastic competition does not apply to postal or telegraphic matches, meets or tournaments which are approved by the Board of Directors of the Illinois High School Association.

11 Illinois High School Association, 1960–1961 *Handbook,* pp. 30–33.

Section 2. To represent a school in any interscholastic contest in golf, tennis or archery a student must be eligible under the following rules:

(a) She shall be a bona fide student of the high school which she represents and shall reside in that high school district with her parents or legal guardian.

(b) She shall have an undergraduate standing. That is, she shall not have graduated from any four year high school or its equivalent.

(c) She shall not have reached her twentieth birthday.

(d) She shall not have participated in interscholastic competition more than seven previous semesters.

(e) She shall be an amateur. That is, she must not at any time have used her knowledge or skill for gain as a participant in athletic contests and she must not have played on any team on which there have been one or more paid players.

Note 1: A paid player or one who uses her athletic skill for gain is interpreted as one who receives money or merchandise or other material awards in excess of the amount necessary to cover her actual hotel and travel expense.

Note 2: This rule shall not be interpreted to prohibit acceptance of medals, cups or trophies as symbols of achievement by participants in non-interscholastic contests providing that the award is made by the organization conducting the meet or tournament.

(f) She shall be passing in at least fifteen hours of recognized high school work from the beginning of the semester up to not more than ten days in advance of the day the meet or tournament takes place.

(g) She shall have participated in at least four practices during the current school year in the activity in which the contest is to be held. Such practices must be scheduled as part of the school physical education or athletic program and must be coached by the faculty member in charge of the activity.

(h) She shall file with her high school principal a statement from her parents or guardian approving her participation in interscholastic competition during the current school year.

(i) She shall file with her high school principal a certificate of physical fitness issued by a competent physician during the current school year.

(j) She must not have participated during the current school year in any sport as a member of any team other than that representing her high school without the previous written consent of her principal.

Section 3. A member school shall not:

(a) Participate in any competitive event or activity which involves four or more schools that are members of the Illinois High School Association unless it has been sanctioned by the Board of Directors of the Illinois High School Association.

(b) Participate in any interstate competition involving three or more schools unless it has been sanctioned by the Board of Directors of the Illinois High School Association.

Note: This rule applies to non-competitive events—workshops, clinics, play days, as well as to competitive activities.

Section 4. A member school shall not participate in any interscholastic match, meet or tournament involving students from three or more schools unless all schools are members in good standing in the high school association of their respective states. If there is no recognized high school association or group governing interscholastic competition for girls in a state, members of the IHSA shall compete only with the schools in that state whose standards for competition meet with the approval of the Board of Directors of the Illinois High School Association.

Note 1: This rule shall not be interpreted as applying to high schools conducted by colleges and universities for purposes of education experimentation, research and practice teaching.

Note 2: This rule shall not be interpreted as prohibiting member schools from engaging in invitational meets or tournaments with junior high school teams composed entirely of ninth grade students.

Note 3: In Illinois, "Affiliated Members" shall be interpreted as "members."

Section 5. No contest shall be held with a high school in Illinois that is not a member of the Illinois High School Association except that a dual contest may be held with a school ineligible for membership. Such school must abide by all rules for girls' interscholastic competition in Illinois and must be on the Approved list of the Illinois High School Association.

No contest may be held with any school outside of Illinois unless it is a member in good standing in the high school association in its state. If there is no recognized high school association or group governing interscholastic competition for girls in that state, Illinois High School Association members shall compete only with schools in that state whose standards for girls' competition meet with the approval of the Board of Directors of the Illinois High School Association.

Note: This rule shall not apply to contests between schools both of which are in the same school district and under the same board of education. No member school, however, shall enter into any interscholastic competition with any school no matter where it is located that is under suspension from membership in the Illinois High School Association or is not in good standing in its own local group.

Section 6. The Board of Directors of the Illinois High School Association is definitely instructed not to sanction any meet or tournament conducted or sponsored by any national or interstate organization or by any organization or group wholly or in part outside of the state of Illinois except that they may at their discretion sanction:

(a) Such meets as are directly conducted or sponsored by some department of the United States Government;

(b) such intra- or inter-state or national meets as involve the participants in a negligible amount of travel and which do not require cash deposit or fee from either the school or individual participants, either as direct or indirect membership or entry fees, or in payment for any incidental service or privilege;

(c) purely community or local meets or contests involving areas that would not require extensive travel and expense or undue absence from school even though the community may involve portions of more than one state.

N.B. The North Central Association of Colleges and Secondary Schools in its Criterion 4-F has an identical requirement and the N.C.A. committee in Illinois has named the IHSA Board as the sanctioning committee for Illinois. Therefore, a sanction secured from the Association office satisfies the requirements of both the IHSA and the N.C.A.

Section 7. A member school shall not participate in any interscholastic competition which requires an overnight trip or which involves travel of more than 150 miles for the round trip.

Section 8. No awards of any kind shall be given for participation in interscholastic competition.

Note: This rule shall not apply to awards which a school may wish to present to its own students for participation in interscholastic competition. Such awards shall have an utilitarian value of not more than two dollars except a school letter or emblem.

Section 9. Eligibility lists shall be exchanged so that they will reach the competing schools not less than five days before the date of competition.

Section 10. Only women officials shall be used in interscholastic contests.

Note: If qualified women officials are not available, men officials may be used providing that they are approved by the Principal and the Head of the Girls' Physical Education Department in each of the competing schools.

Section 11. Each school entering one or more contestants in inter-scholastic competition shall send with the contestants a woman faculty member.

Section 12. No admission may be charged spectators and no girls' matches shall constitute part of any program at which admission is charged.

Section 13. The Official Rules of the Division of Girls and Women's Sports of the American Association for Health, Physical Education and Recreation shall be used.

Section 14. A girl shall be permitted to participate in not more than two matches in one week. This participation may be limited to one match a week at the discretion of the instructor or coach.

Section 15. If a contestant or other representative of a competing school shall conduct herself in an unsportsmanlike manner or if her conduct shall reflect unfavorably on herself, her school, or on other representatives or schools, she shall become ineligible for further competition for the remainder of that school year and shall become eligible the next year only upon the consent of the principal and faculty members of the Girls' Physical Education Department of her school.

Section 16. The penalty for a violation of any of the rules governing girls' interscholastic competition in golf, tennis and archery shall be determined by the Board of Directors of the Illinois High School Association.[12]

In concluding the discussion of girls' athletics, it should be understood that emphasis has been placed on changes in method rather than upon their entire elimination. School people are making progress because they are studying all forms of athletic competition— boys' as well as girls'. We should not condemn unless we can suggest something different. Girls' athletics are and should be in the school program. The problem is one of proper administration.

Questions for Study and Discussion

1. Discuss the general thesis of interscholastic athletics for high school girls. Support your position with statements from national authorities.

2. What are the general policies of the Division of Girls and Women's Sports of the American Association for Health, Physical Education and Recreation, concerning competition for women and girls?

[12] *Ibid.,* pp. 33–35.

3. What is the platform of the Society of State Directors of Physical and Health Education on girls' athletics? Discuss.

4. The National Federation of State High School Athletic Associations has presented a general account of girls' athletics throughout the nation. Discuss it briefly.

5. Discuss specific provisions in several states regarding girls' interscholastic athletics.

6. What types of activities for girls are advocated in place of interscholastic competition? Explain each.

7. Explain briefly the Illinois plan for handling girls' athletics.

15   Junior High School Athletics

The junior high school development has had its greatest impetus during the last half century. It came about largely as the result of two things: first, the rapid growth in high school attendance; and second, the realization that a large percentage of those attending high school either would not finish the twelfth grade or, if they did, probably not more than one-third of them would attend college. Thus, the junior high idea was fostered in order that a new type of school could be created in which the great mass of students might be given a broader and more fundamental education than the traditional four-year high school had offered. Seventh, eighth, and ninth graders made up the new organization, so that the later elementary and early high school traditions have contributed to it. The curriculum was enriched, terminal courses were introduced in limited numbers, and sampling or exploratory courses were offered. In fact, much of the philosophy upon which the junior high school has been founded has been based on the idea that it is primarily an exploratory or career-acquainting institution.

Development of athletics in junior high schools. As might be expected, the junior high schools in their early periods of establishment turned to the high school pattern for suggestions much more than to the elementary schools. In many cases the junior high schools became young high schools during the first few years of their existence. This tendency was especially noticeable in their athletic programs. Many junior high schools introduced the accepted athletic activities that had been sponsored for years in high schools and colleges. Junior high school football (Rugby) developed; track and field events, baseball, and basketball became parts of the inter-scholastic program; and junior high school swimming teams were sponsored where facilities permitted. Rules for games and sports activities were modified so they more nearly met the level of competition for students in grades 7, 8, and 9. In other words, our interscholastic program was simply stepped down from the nine-to-twelve grade level to the seven-to-nine grade level.

Continually questions are being raised regarding the advisability of considering the junior high school as a young high school as far as its athletic program is concerned. Similarly, many educators have questioned the extent to which the traditional or senior high school should follow the colleges and universities in its athletic activities. Modifications have been forthcoming all along the line. The feeling of many school people, however, is that the chief athletic interest of the junior high school should be largely intramural in nature, because such a policy is more in keeping with the principles of the junior high school. It enables more students to play more games, to extend and broaden their interests, and to improve their skills. Moreover, usually it is possible to satisfy the desire of students of this age for competition if the intramural program is handled properly.

Interschool and Intramural Athletics for Junior High Schools

There are differences of opinion among physical educators and educators in general regarding the advisability of interschool athletics for junior high school students. Many state high school athletic associations do not recognize that there is such a thing as interscholastic athletic competition by students below the ninth grade or in schools that do not include the upper grades. A number of states, among them Pennsylvania, Indiana, Kansas, and Michigan, have definite regulations for junior high school athletic competition. Such states have felt that it was preferable to set up standards, knowing that certain schools would engage in interschool play.

It must be pointed out that interscholastic athletic programs have been increasing in number in the junior high schools of the country.

Tompkins and Roe [1] found that 85 % of the 2313 junior high schools they surveyed had interscholastic athletics. This development probably parallels the growth of athletics in senior high schools and that for youths of junior high school age conducted by non-school organizations.

In summarizing some of the findings of Tompkins and Roe,[2] it is significant to note that most of the nearly 2,000 junior high schools included in their study have changed their policy by adopting an interscholastic athletic program since 1950. It is indicated that 80 % of them had done so whereas 20 % had not. About 70 % of the schools concerned felt that their intramural programs in junior high schools had been stimulated by the presence of interscholastic athletic competition. It is significant that most of the schools involved were those in large city organizations and quite generally confined competition to schools in their own school systems. There seems to be no general pattern in the financing of junior high school athletics because nearly one-third use combination ticket sales and board of education aid; about the same percentage carry out their programs from board of education budget appropriation only. Sometimes there is a combination of support worked out between both junior and senior high schools in the same system. Practically all of the schools (nearly 95 %) furnished uniforms and equipment for players on their junior high school interscholastic athletic teams.

In the survey it also was indicated that about 40 % of the junior high schools follow regulations established by their state high school athletic associations. In 30 % of such junior high schools they developed their own standards, or as was the case in approximately 25 % of such schools, they conformed to standards established by a local school system. Significant among the findings in this study was the fact that 80 % of the junior high schools do not schedule any interscholastic athletics for girls and nearly 75 % of them do not arrange for play days for girls in athletic activities.

As indicated above there has been a noticeable increase in the development of interscholastic competition for junior high school boys. Particular interest seems to have centered around football. Studies are lacking that definitely prove whether this activity, with

[1] *Interscholastic Athletics in Junior High Schools—A Survey* (Washington, D.C., National Association of Secondary School Principals, 1958), p. 3.
[2] Ibid.

suitable modifications in rules and regulations because of the age of contestants, is desirable. If the purpose solely is to make better senior high school football players, its sponsorship is not justified. Under no circumstances should junior high school football be conducted unless the best possible instruction (coaching) is available; adequate, new (not handed-down) equipment can be furnished; first-class playing facilities are provided (not the school playground); games are limited in number and confined exclusively to junior high schools (weight classifications are recommended if the game is to be played).

Administrative problems. In any school the problem of administering the athletic program is a major one. The junior high school situation is no exception. One of the most difficult considerations is that of equipment. Boards of education, as a rule, do not subsidize the interscholastic athletic program in such schools to any greater extent than they do in senior or four-year high schools. In general, public support is limited because of lack of interest in outcomes of junior high school games; thus contest attendance by adults is comparatively small and provides little revenue with which to conduct the program. The opposition of nearly all physical education authorities to junior high school football (Rugby) adds to the difficulty of securing revenue. It is difficult to arrange schedules so that proper playing time is available. Generally it is recommended that interschool games, if played, not be held in the evening. In case they are, no overnight trips are to be allowed if the usual recommendations are followed. There is difficulty here because of interference with school time if long trips are to be made.

Coaching of teams. The coaching of teams is another problem because available men on the physical education staff usually are busy with intramural activities. Frequently it is difficult to secure the place and time to arrange for "varsity" practice during and after a busy school day. As stated above, there is likely to be interference with the intramural program if there is an extensive interschool athletic setup. If it is possible to make the interscholastic activities the outgrowth of the intramural program and to limit the contests to a few in number, it should be possible to harmonize the two so that neither the services of the coach nor facilities are unreasonably usurped for interscholastics.

Another phase of this entire program, varying in different localities, must be kept in mind. Sometimes the claim is made that junior high school boys are bound to be engaged in some type of competition; hence it is desirable that it be under the direction of school authorities. There is considerable merit in this position. If a school is one of several in a city or metropolitan area and if it has a tradition or feels that interscholastics will fill a need additional to its intramurals, then, perhaps, they have a place in its program. There also are instances where informal "challenge games" are played. Many such schools, however, spend all their energies in developing a well-rounded junior high school intramural program with outstanding success.

Some program principles for junior high school athletics. It is generally recognized that the purposes and accomplishments of the junior high school differ considerably from the traditional high school, as far as most students are concerned. Junior high schools are composed of younger students, for many of whom the school is the terminal in formal education. Since there is a common conception that education is life rather than a preparation for life, it is obvious that the junior high school athletic program has great possibilities of service toward this objective. Boys and girls of the junior high school age are in the period when cooperation, team play, and organization are more prominent in their thinking than when they were in the elementary schools. Junior high schools have made much of these factors, and rightly so. Since they are so important, the opportunity to share in them should be afforded as many students as possible through a broad athletic program that is largely, if not entirely, intramural. In considering objectives of the junior high school in relation to its athletic program, a committee of Michigan junior high school principals formulated the following which still obtain:

RECOMMENDATIONS FOR ADMINISTERING A JUNIOR HIGH SCHOOL ATHLETICS PROGRAM

Proposed by the Michigan Junior High School Athletics Committee

*1—Self-Checking for Quality Programs—*The Michigan Junior High School Athletic Committee believes that the type of the intramural or interscholastic athletic program in a school should, in general, be a matter for local school system determination. It realizes that there are

varying philosophies and basic principles motivating schools to establish aims and objectives to meet the needs of pupils in such schools as
well as the communities which they serve. Before junior high school
children are permitted to participate in interschool athletic contests, play
days, sports days sponsored by local schools, or similar competition sponsored by nonschool groups, the following questions should be answered
to the satisfaction of parents and educators: [3]

1. Are we now meeting the *needs* of all children through *instruction*
in physical education and recreational and intramural activities? What is
the quality of these phases of the program? Must they still be improved
to be reasonably good for all pupils?
2. What kind of leadership will the athletic program have? Are the
leaders professionally qualified? Do they know and understand young
children? Are they interested only in the welfare and happiness of boys
and girls, or do they seek personal advantage-publicity, status, or financial
gain through the exploitation of children?
3. Are the proposed sports and other activities appropriate for the
age, maturity, skill, stage of growth, and physical make-up of the children?
4. Will there be adequate safeguards for health and well-being
through: adequate protective equipment, adjustments in playing time
and other rules, competent coaching and officiating, reasonable schedules
in terms of frequency and time of day of contests, clean drinking water
and other hygienic provisions, limited and safe travel with responsible
adults, and attention to healthful practices of all kinds?
5. Is the program free of undesirable publicity and promotion? Will
the child spectators and participants be permitted to grow up naturally,
to be free of a distorted sense of values, of individual importance and
of other aspects of living? Will they be free of unnecessary and undesirable pressures and over-stimulation?
6. Will the children who participate still have opportunity for a balance in interests and activities or will the demands of athletic competition
restrict their experiences in other worthwhile things, such as home recreation, Boy Scouts, camping trips, hobby groups, music, drama, and arts
and crafts?
II—Planning and Working Together—The Committee firmly believes
that cooperation between school and community leaders is essential in
all phases of education. In planning athletic programs for junior high

[3] Joint Committee Report, DESIRABLE ATHLETIC COMPETITION FOR
CHILDREN; Washington, D.C., American Association for Health, Physical
Education, and Recreation, 1953, pp. 5–6.

school children there must be cooperative working relationships between school people, recreation leaders, representatives of child-serving agencies, civic and service clubs, and other groups. The aid and understanding of parents and other citizens also are necessary to insure desirable community-wide programs for youth.

III—Administrative Suggestions—It is the belief of this Committee that a critical self analysis as suggested above should aid in determining whether a school has the available space, facilities, personnel, equipment, and time allotment to sponsor an interschool athletic program. It also should indicate whether it is providing all the opportunities it can in physical education, intramurals, and recreation *for all the students* before it sponsors interschool athletics. The Committee believes that the following should receive consideration in the administration of the physical education and/or athletic programs:

1. Any program in physical education, intramural or interscholastic athletics, or recreation should be based on the philosophy of the junior high school in which it is sponsored. It should be consistent with, and capable of making a contribution to, the whole school program philosophy.

2. Classes in physical education should be limited in size so that there is opportunity for instruction and participation in small groups.

3. In physical education that part of the program dealing with athletics primarily should be a teaching situation. Intramurals, interscholastics, and recreation activities should parallel or supplement the physical education program.

4. The keynote of athletics is participation by all and junior high schools should maintain comprehensive intramural programs which will provide opportunities for the realization of this objective. When this is accomplished then there may be a place for a limited and well-administered interschool athletic program.

5. It is recommended that community councils be established to consider and evaluate all types of athletic programs and promotions which may be proposed. In many localities such community of inter-agency councils now exist and their full use and cooperation are urged.

6. The gymnasium, playground, and athletic field should be laboratories for testing and improving the activities in the athletic and recreation programs. They should provide opportunities for the individual to discover his or her interests, abilities, and skills in a wide range of activities.

7. Athletics exist to keep alive the fun-spirit of youth; to provide a vigorous type of recreation in which abide pleasure, happiness and joy; to prolong the playtime of youth and preserve the joyous zest of living.

8. Athletics exist to contribute to a healthier type of citizen, the building of sound bodies, the disciplining of character, development of personality and leadership, and the stabilizing of emotional control.[4]

General Recommendations

The junior high school athletic program, like that in any high school, may be both a blessing and a detriment. Its general policies and their administration are the factors which will determine the contributions it will make to the boys and girls concerned. It is essential that policies be well understood and followed within local schools. Since junior high school organization is more common in larger cities, it is imperative that a general school system policy regarding athletics be formulated. If all activities are to be intramural, that policy should be understood. In the event that there are to be both intramural and interschool contests, such procedures should be well defined. It is practically impossible to conceive how there could be only interschool contests with no intramurals in junior high schools. In city systems it seems desirable that the supervisor of physical education be in general charge of the athletic programs of all the junior high schools concerned. The policy-making body, of course, would be the school administration heads, supplemented by the physical education staffs in each school. Physical education men and women should have supervision and direction of the program in their respective schools.

In concluding the discussion of the junior high school athletic program there are listed below several policy-making considerations. Circumstances vary in different schools and in different parts of the country. Density of population, proximity of schools, size of enrollments, and racial or other characteristics of student bodies all are determining factors in the establishment of athletic as well as general educational principles. It is with these variations in mind that these alternatives are offered for consideration.

Intramurals. The first recommendation is that junior high school athletic programs be intramural in character. Both boys and girls may be served equally if this policy is adopted. It will acquaint and expose large numbers of students to new games. The services

---

[4] Michigan High School Athletic Association *Bulletin,* October, 1953, pp. 104–105.

of physical education instructors and school facilities will be available to all.

Intramurals with a few interschool games. This poilcy is a continuation of the intramural program. It may be worked out in cities where there are several junior high schools. Long trips and night games should be avoided. Interschool games, if played at all, probably should come at the end of the season as a possible recognition of intramural prowess.

Point and award systems. Most educators are opposed to an extensive system of awards for athletic competition, and rightly so. They are neither advisable nor necessary. In many instances, however, a point system which is a part of the general physical education and intramural program is beneficial. A school letter award of no intrinsic value will suffice. It is a record of achievement rather than reward for services. Boys and girls of junior high school age are interested in such acknowledgments, and well-organized point systems are excellent substitutes for interscholastic competition.

Play days. Where junior high schools are located favorably there have been very successful play and sports days arranged. Again, these are extensions of the intramural program and have the added advantages inherent in guest-host school relations. With boys it may be more desirable to maintain school identities in team competition, but this feature is not so important in girls' games. Make the occasion one of social and sportsmanship importance and competition *with* the other school rather than *against* it.

It is not to be inferred that the reasons advocated for an intramural program as the basis for junior high school athletics are a condemnation of interschool games. They are different types of competition and serve different ends. Preferably it may be more desirable to postpone intensive interscholastic competition to a later period in the child's life. The point might be raised that interschool competition will not be realized by many junior high school students because they will not attend high school. That is true; but it seems more desirable for such students to have many varied experiences in athletic competition in intramurals than concentration in one or two activities that are interscholastic in nature. The whole point is that concentration should be on intramurals in the junior high school, with interschool games, if played, being incidental.

At a recent national conference [5] on youth and fitness many matters pertaining to athletic and physical education programs in secondary schools were considered. The policy of "athletics for all" was stressed because it was felt that at all levels there should be increased attention paid to physical education, intramurals, extramurals, and interscholastics so that they may be expanded to include every boy in school in order that he might benefit from the experience of competitive sports. This pronouncement applied to junior high school competition as well as to that for senior high schools.

It was the feeling of the conference group, as indicated in its recommendations and in the general statement adopted, that when properly organized, interscholastic athletics in junior high schools can make a significant contribution to youth fitness. There was one exception noted as far as sports were concerned and that was boxing. In general, interscholastic boxing is not allowed by state athletic associations either in junior or senior high schools. The recommendation went on to remind school people that proper procedures should be established which will allow sports to be carried on with consideration for safety, the age and physical development of students which consider weight and height, as well as the amount and frequency of competition and number of games to be played. It also is most important that physical examinations be carefully administered. This is essential for youngsters of junior high school age because of their rapid physical development at this level. It also is important that there be varied programs of athletics for junior high school students as well as for senior high schools. Opportunity should be provided for learning skills in many activities rather than concentration on relatively few.

Questions for Study and Discussion

1. Discuss the development of athletics in junior high schools. In what way was the junior high school originally intended to differ from the senior high school?

[5] *Report of the National Conference on Fitness of Secondary School Youth,* December 7–12, 1958, American Association for Health, Physical Education, and Recreation, Washington, D.C.

2. What are the prevailing opinions of national authorities regarding junior high school interscholastic athletic programs? Cite several in addition to those in the text.

3. Discuss administrative and coaching problems in junior high school athletic programs.

4. What arguments would you present pro and con regarding the establishment of an interschool athletic program in a junior high school with which you were connected?

5. Discuss a junior high school athletic program composed of: (a) intramurals; (b) intramurals with a few interschool games; extramurals; (c) point and award systems; and (d) play and sports days.

16 Trends in High School Athletics

To prophesy developments in any field of endeavor over a long period of years usually is hazardous for the prognosticator. To review the past for quite a length of time and then to point out significant happenings that may be considered trends is not so risky. That is the purpose of this chapter, which is somewhat of a review of those preceding. Conclusions drawn and inferences made are based on developments that actually are taking place, or they are conclusions that have been included in the policies and programs of national authorities. They may be of interest and value to the men and women in high schools who have, or will have, the all-important jobs of directing the athletic activities of millions of American boys and girls.

The war's disclosures. World War II and subsequent required universal military training have taught us many things about the values of physical fitness and athletics. It showed that, at the beginning of the war, our young men of high school and college age were not in good physical condition. Arm, shoulder-girdle, and abdominal muscles were woefully weak. Thirty per cent of the white men coming into the Navy were unable to swim fifty yards. Among Negroes the percentage was half again as high. The leg condition of men was better than anticipated, probably because we are primarily a nation of "leg" games—football, basketball, baseball, track, tennis, and golf. But the discouraging revelation was that there was a very large proportion of men who neither knew nor had

had any experience in any types of games or organized competition. They simply did not know how to play, even games of low organization. Somewhere along the line the schools or recreational agencies had failed to provide this important training which stood out so glaringly when the spotlight of war was thrown upon them. Much of the same criticism still exists today and the renewed emphasis on physical fitness for our youth could pay big dividends. It should be given every possible opportunity to succeed.

It is not contended here that a man necessarily had to have experience in athletics to be a good soldier, sailor, or marine. Thousands of the best we had were deprived of that opportunity before coming into the service. It is believed, however, that a good soldier, sailor, or marine might have been a better one if he had taken part in athletic competition during his school days. Such an experience "did something" for him which manifested itself so clearly during his training period, and in his campaign record as well.

A trust to keep in athletics. We are in the so-called postwar world now, and hundreds of thousands of young men and women have come home and established families. Many other thousands are sleeping in foreign lands or in the oceans. It was they who helped with their all to make it possible for the rest of us to have homes, and it was they who helped to preserve the America we love and rightly think to be the greatest nation in the world. We must prove that America is strong morally, socially, and physically. There is a job to be done, and not the least consideration is the assurance that our athletics are what we claim them to be. Professional athletics have a place in our scheme of things, but they should not be confused with the amateur athletics that have flourished so well in our high schools and colleges, where play should be for "play's sake" and the valuable educational lessons that accrue to the student participants and spectators. We must keep an even keel in our high school athletic programs. Continually there are indications that undesirable promotional schemes are in the offing. Our athletics should be broadened to be more inclusive, both as to numbers competing and varieties of sports. It is just as important to provide opportunities for students to compete in tennis, volleyball, or swimming, as in football, basketball, or baseball. There are no such things as minor sports: each is major to the competitor, or else he is not worthy of being called a competitor. By the same token, there should be more than varsity teams in competition, and the lead taken by some schools in having as many as four teams in league competition is an indication of what can be done. *More students in more sports* should be our goal.

Permanence of athletics. It is a truism that nothing mortal is permanent. But, in the sense that we consider permanence, it seems safe to say that competition will be as nearly permanent in American life and tradition as anything we have. When we take competition out of business, out of our individual achievements, out of our very lives, we will indeed cease to be Americans in the generally accepted sense of the word. In play and recreation we are bound to have competition and in competition we have athletics. They are inseparable. Equality of opportunity and competition are the essence of our educational system. The late Fielding H. Yost once said:

It is, then, in the building of men that competitive sport displays its real significance. I am convinced that because of properly supervised athletics, there are more men in the world than there otherwise would be, who measure up to the standard of true manhood.[1]

The emphasis made by Yost has not changed during the years since these statements were made. They are truer than ever today. It behooves those in charge of athletic programs to see that the right kind of opportunities for competition are provided. For most boys and girls these opportunities will be intramural. For some they will be interschool. Many will be "spectator competitors." They all have their places in the general scheme of things in the athletic as well as in the educational patterns. Regimentation never progressed to any great extent in those countries whose people engage in competitive athletics.

Place of the National Federation of State High School Athletic Associations. The National Federation has performed valuable service since its inception in 1920 and seems destined to increase its scope of influence in the future. It has great possibilities as a coordinating organization in unifying standards for control of high school athletics in the various states. The organization does not seek to usurp local state association powers. It should concern itself

[1] In an address delivered in Bloomington, Ill., before the Illinois Schoolmasters Club.

with the formation of public opinion throughout the United States as to what the educational outcomes of high school athletics ought to be. It has more possibilities in this field than in any other. When one realizes what the combined judgments of schoolmen in forty-nine of the states of this nation might be, one sees that the possibilities of making interschool athletics really educational are unlimited.

Values of state associations. Properly organized and controlled, state athletic and activity associations may be the guarantee that athletics will achieve the educational goals for which they are intended. It seems desirable that such organizations should at least have an affiliated connection with state education departments, or with the physical education divisions of them. There has been a trend toward the development of state activity associations that control other programs as well as athletics, as evidenced by approximately one-half of the states so organized at present. These seem to be performing satisfactory services in those states where such supervision is desired.

Age limits for competition. There is increased interest in fixing both maximum and minimum age limits outside of which a student may not compete. Such regulations protect individual competitors as well as those against whom they compete. Thirty-one of the states now have an upper age limit of nineteen years. Nineteen states have twenty-year age limits. The trend definitely is toward the nineteen-year limit. Several states require that a student must be fourteen years old before he may be a member of an interscholastic athletic team, and in a few the lower age requirement is fifteen years for certain sports.

Number of season contests. Annually more states are limiting the number of regular season contests that schools may play. This policy has been inaugurated because local pressure in some communities has resulted in forcing the scheduling of games not desired by school authorities. The first and last dates during the season on which games may be played are being established in more states each year. Definite stands are being taken regarding postseason, all-star, and out-of-season games, as well as nonschool or nonathletic association-sponsored games with which high school students, recent high school graduates, or school coaching staff personnel are connected.

The local athletic program. Increased attention is being given to the establishment and management of the local athletic program. It is being considered as part of the physical education program, and definite policies determine the manner in which it functions. Added attention is accorded to contest management details, with the result that a more desirable educational experience is provided for both competitors and spectators. It is significant to realize that less emphasis from a commercialized publicity standpoint is being placed on interscholastic athletics than was the case twenty-five years ago. In spite of this fact, however, nearly every high school of any size reports increased interest in athletics and the sponsoring of more sports than formerly.

Safety standards and benefit and protection plans. More attention is being paid to the safety of participants in athletics today than ever before, as is evidenced by the use of better equipment, insistence on health and physical examinations for all participants, improvements in playing rules, better officiating, and the provision for participation in athletic accident benefit and protection plans or with commercial insurance companies in practically all states. Schools, also, are paying more attention to sanitation standards in the conduct of their athletic programs. It is very probable that, in the near future, an accounting will be taken to determine whether high schools are sponsoring athletic activities that do not properly belong in the high school category of sports. One of the most important contributions of athletic accident benefit and protection plans has been the accumulation of valuable data indicating when, where, and how injuries occurred. From this information it has been possible, to some extent, to determine the cause of injuries which may be the result of playing rules or types of equipment worn. In this way it has been, and will continue to be, possible to make modifications in rules and improve playing equipment so that the safety of participants is increased.

Board of education support. Boards of education continually are doing more to aid in the maintenance of the athletic program, both interscholastic as well as intramural. Statutes and court opinions vary in different states regarding the legality of use of public funds for interschool contests. In most of them, however, public funds can be used for general equipment. It is significant that boards of education are aiding in the athletic programs of schools because it puts these activities in their proper educational place.

Intramural athletics. Broad programs of intramural athletics for boys and girls will continue to receive increased emphasis. They are basic both for education generally and for the interschool program which properly may be an extension of intramurals. The two are complementary to each other in most secondary schools, as they should be. Intramurals should be a part of the physical education program; but, as such, they are generally maintained on an elective basis.

Athletics for girls. Old type interschool athletics for girls are being sponsored by fewer high schools annually. In their place comprehensive intramural programs are being substituted. In connection with the intramurals there are interschool play days and sports and local and state girls' athletic associations that have point award systems. Extramurals are a commendable development in girls' athletics. Some state athletic associations have eliminated all interschool athletic competition for girls and made the substitutions mentioned. The general criticism has not been so much against competition for girls as against some undesirable circumstances under which it has been conducted. Several women's divisions of national organizations have formulated policies regarding athletic competition for girls and women. They are most constructive in that they have come from women themselves, and in practically all cases their recommendations have been for a much higher type of competition than practices advocated when men have been in charge of the program. Several state athletic associations have made real beginnings in the encouragement and formation of local school girls' athletic associations that do not advocate the old, traditional types of girls' interscholastic athletic contests.

Community responsibilities of athletic coaches and physical education teachers. The athletic coach and physical education teacher of the future will not consider their work as being confined entirely to school assignments. With enforced increase in the leisure time of many people, the community will look to school athletic and physical education people for the direction of their recreation activities. Those teachers will be doing themselves real favors by being prepared and willing to handle this work. It also is an effective means by which they may make themselves indispensable to the school and community.

In several states it is the practice to continue regular interscholastic athletic schedules by high schools throughout the summer months. This movement seems destined to grow, because students of high school age undoubtedly will not find employment during the summer as they did during the war years. Schools are employing members of their physical education staffs, as well as other teachers, on a full-year basis and they direct these summer programs besides working in recreation programs during this period. Iowa and Minnesota have made beginnings in this program and have sponsored some summer baseball, track, tennis, golf, and swimming activities through their schools.

Classification of schools. There is an increasing tendency on the part of state athletic associations to classify member schools for athletic competition. Over three-fourths of the states now have classification plans in effect for state-wide competition. The result is greater equity in meet or tournament play, and often schools of comparable size form leagues for season schedules.

Meets and tournaments. Because of the influence of the National Federation of State High School Athletic Associations, national meets and tournaments no longer exist. Comparatively few interstate meets are held and then only upon receipt of approval of states concerned and the National Federation. Two tendencies are developing in state tournaments and meets. In a few states, only district or regional competitions are held. In an increasingly large number of states each year, schools are being classified for meet and tournament play. Such classification not only equalizes competition but also de-emphasizes a single class championship. Honors are divided and taken more as matters of course. There are differences of opinion as to the educational value of state championship meets and tournaments in general. In most cases, however, the criticism seems to be against methods of control and the sometimes attendant undesirable situations rather than against the actual competition itself.

Junior high school athletics. Opinions vary as to the advisability of interschool competition for junior high school students. The Legislative Council of the American Association for Health, Physical Education, and Recreation has gone on record as being opposed to such a policy. Better practices seem to obtain in schools with broad intramural programs or variations of them, with possibly a limited amount of carefully supervised interschool play. It is significant, however, that recently there has been increased emphasis on the establishment of more intensive interscholastic athletic competition in junior high schools. Whether or not this agitation is based on sound educational principles, or merely on the desire to develop junior high school students in order that there may be better senior high school teams, remains to be seen. Many factors must be considered carefully before there is widespread acceptance of too much stepping-up of the junior high school interschool athletic program.

Sportsmanship and citizenship in athletics. Rules, regulations, policies, and programs are valueless unless the individuals affected by them are made better by the experiences they have had. We have definite ways of observing whether or not our athletics are paying dividends in good sportsmanship and better citizenship. The values of "carry-over" activities in education may be debatable, but who can question the value of knowing the rules of a game, playing fair, hard, and clean, and being a good sportsman? The potentialities of teaching character and cooperation are unlimited, as is indicated in this concluding analysis of the word "athletics."

The *A* stands for ambition—ambition to be the best possible player in one's position on the team.

The *T* stands for training—the first requisite of any athlete.

The *H* stands for honesty—honesty to oneself and one's teammates.

The *L* stands for loyalty—loyalty to team and to school.

The *E* stands for eligibility—without which an athlete is valueless to his team.

The *T* stands for trustworthiness—a trait all good athletes possess.

The *I* stands for improvement—which is always observable in good athletes.

The *C* stands for courage—courage to do the thing that is right regardless of how the game is going.

The *S* stands for stick-to-it-iveness—the best trait in any athlete.

Questions for Study and Discussion

1. Discuss disclosures of World War II concerning high school athletic programs.
2. What is meant by "permanence in athletics"? Do you believe in it?
3. Discuss the importance and values of the National Federation of State High School Athletic Associations and state high school athletic associations.

4. What are the trends in age limits for competition and in the number of contests per season?

5. Why is the administration of the local athletic program in schools receiving increased attention?

6. Discuss the importance of safety standards in athletics, and the growth and importance of athletic benefit or protection plans.

7. Why should boards of education support, or not support, the interscholastic athletic program?

8. Discuss your position regarding intramurals, and girls' and junior high school interscholastic athletics.

9. Why are athletic coaches and physical education teachers being given more community responsibilities?

10. What is the future of state meets and tournaments? Will the further classification of schools be a factor? Discuss.

11. What is the relationship between sportsmanship and citizenship in athletics? What are the spiritual and moral values of athletics and physical education?

Bibliography

BOOKS AND BULLETINS

Bucher, C. A., *Administration of School Health and Physical Education*. St. Louis: The C. V. Mosby Co., 1958.

Campus and Athletic Field Manual. Marysville, Ohio: O. M. Scott and Sons Co.

Desirable Practices in Sports for Girls and Women. Washington, D.C; Division for Girls and Women's Sports, American Association for Health, Physical Education, and Recreation, 1957.

DeWitt, R. T., *Teaching Individual and Team Sports*. Englewood Cliffs, N.J.: Prentice-Hall, Inc., 1953.

Forsythe, Charles E., *The Athletic Director's Handbook*. Englewood Cliffs, N.J.: Prentice-Hall, Inc., 1956.

Forsythe, Charles E. and Ray O. Duncan, *Administration of Physical Education*. Englewood Cliffs, N.J.: Prentice-Hall, Inc., 1951.

General Information Bulletin, Lansing: Michigan High School Athletic Association Accident Benefit Plan, 1961–62.

Interscholastic Athletics in Junior High Schools–A Survey. Washington, D. C.: National Association of Secondary School Principals, 1958.

Larson, Leonard A., Morey R. Fields, and Milton A. Gabrielsen, *Problems in Health, Physical, and Recreation Education*. Englewood Cliffs, N.J.: Prentice-Hall, Inc., 1953.

Leibee, Howard C., *Liability for Accidents in Physical Education, Athletics and Recreation*. Ann Arbor: Ann Arbor Publishers, 711 N. University Ave., 1952.

Means, Louis E., *The Organization and Administration of Intramural Sports*. St. Louis: The C. V. Mosby Co., 1952.

Mitchell, E. D. (editor), *Sports for Recreation*. New York: A. S. Barnes and Co., 1936.

———, *Intramural Sports*. New York: A. S. Barnes and Co., 1945.

Nash, J. B., Francis J. Moensch, and Jeannette B. Sanborn, *Physical Education: Organization and Administration*. New York: A. S. Barnes and Co., 1951.

National Conference, *Equipment and Supplies for Athletics, Physical Education, and Recreation*. Chicago: The Athletic Institute, Merchandise Mart, or Washington, D. C.: American Association for Health, Physical Education, and Recreation, 1960.

National Facilities Conference, *Planning Facilities for Health, Physical Education and Recreation*. Chicago: The Athletic Institute, Merchandise Mart, 1956.

Naval Aviation Training Manuals, *The Sports Program*. New York: A. S. Barnes and Co., 1946.

Physical Education for High School Students. Washington, D. C. American Association for Health, Physical Education, and Recreation, 1955.
Rates and Schedules Bulletin. Schenectady: New York State High School Athletic Protection Plan, 1961–62.
"Recommendations for Administering a Junior High School Athletic Program." Michigan High School Athletic Association *Bulletin,* Lansing, October 1953.
Rosenfield, H.N., *Liability for School Accidents: A Manual for Educational Administrators and Teachers.* New York: Harper and Brothers, 1940.
Scott, Harry A., *Competitive Sports in Schools and Colleges.* New York: Harper and Brothers, 1951.
Seaton, Don Cash, et al., *Physical Education Handbook.* Englewood Cliffs, N. J.: Prentice-Hall, Inc., 1954.
Shepard, George E. and R. E. Jamerson, *Interscholastic Athletics.* New York: McGraw-Hill Book Co., Inc., 1955.
Successful Financial Plans for School Athletic Departments. Kansas City, Mo.: Lowe and Campbell Athletic Goods Co.,
Van Dalen, Deopold B., Elmer D. Mitchell, and Bruce L. Bennett, *A World History of Physical Education.* Englewood Cliffs, N. J.: Prentice-Hall, Inc., 1953.
Voltmer, E. F. and A. A. Esslinger, *The Organization and Administration of Physical Education.* New York: Appleton-Century-Crofts, Inc., 1958.
Spectator Sportsmanship. Washington, D. C.: American Association for Health, Physical Education, and Recreation, 1961.
Williams, J. F., C. L. Brownell, and E. L. Vernier, *The Administration of Health Education and Physical Education.* Philadelphia: W. B. Saunders Co., 1958.
Youth and Fitness—A Program for Secondary Schools. National Conference Report. Washington, D. C.: American Association for Health, Physical Education, and Recreation, 1959.
Zeigler, Earle F., *Administration of Physical Education and Athletics.* Englewood Cliffs, N. J.: Prentice-Hall, Inc., 1959.

ATHLETIC AND ACTIVITY ASSOCIATION CONSTITUTIONS, HANDBOOKS, AND YEARBOOKS

Alabama High School Athletic Association, 1960–1961 *Handbook.*
California Interscholastic Federation, 1959 *Constitution and By-Laws.*
Chicago Public High Schools Athletic Association, Boys' Division, 1960–1961 *Constitution and By-Laws.*
Colorado High School Activities Association, 1960 *Handbook.*
Detroit Public Secondary School Athletic League, 1960–1961 *Athletic Manual.*
Georgia High School Association, 1960–1961 *Constitution and By-Laws.*
Illinois High School Association, 1960–1961 *Handbook.*
Indiana High School Athletic Association, *Fifty-Seventh Annual Handbook,* 1960.
Iowa High School Athletic Association, *Record Book,* 1960–1961.
Kansas State High School Activities Association, 1960–1961 *Handbook.*
Kentucky High School Athletic Association, 1960–1961 *Constitution and By-Laws.*

Los Angeles City Schools, *Rules and Regulations Governing Interscholastic Athletic Contests*, 1960.

Louisiana High School Athletic Association, 1960–1961 *Handbook*.

Massachusetts Secondary School Principals Association, *Constitution and By-Laws*, 1959.

Michigan High School Athletic Association, 1961–1962 *Handbook*.

Minnesota State High School League, 1960 *Official Handbook*.

Missouri State High School Activities Association, 1960 *Official Handbook*.

Montana High School Athletic Association, *Official Handbook*, 1960–1961.

National Federation of State High School Athletic Associations, 1960–1961 *Handbook*.

Nebraska High School Activities Association, *Twenty-Sixth Annual Yearbook*, 1960.

New Jersey State Interscholastic Athletic Association, 1960–1961 *Constitution and By-Laws*.

New York State Public High School Athletic Association, 1960–1961 *Handbook*.

North Dakota High School League, 1960 *Constitution and By-Laws*.

Ohio High School Athletic Association, 1960–1961 *Constitution and Rules*.

Oklahoma High School Athletic Association, 1960–1961 *Constitution and Rules*.

Oregon High School Athletic Association, 1959 *Constitution*.

Pennsylvania Interscholastic Athletic Association, 1957 *Constitution and By-Laws*.

Philadelphia Board of Education, 1958 *Rules for the Control and Management of Boys' Interschool Athletics*.

South Carolina High School League, 1960–1961 *Constitution*.

South Dakota High School Athletic Association, 1959 *Rules and Regulations*.

Tennessee Secondary School Athletic Association, 1960–1961 *Official Handbook*.

Texas Constitution and Rules of the University Interscholastic League, University of Texas Publication, August 1, 1960.

Utah High School Activities Association, 1960–1961 *Handbook*.

Virginia High School League *Handbook*, University of Virginia Extension, August, 1960.

Washington Interscholastic Activities Association, 1960–1961 *Official Handbook*.

Wisconsin Interscholastic Athletic Association, *Thirty-Seventh Year Book*, 1960.

Index